Frommer's 97

Costa Rica

by Eliot Greenspan

with Karl Samson & Jane Aukshunas

Macmillan • USA

ABOUT THE AUTHOR

Eliot Greenspan is a poet, journalist, and travel writer. He took his backpack and type-writer the length of Mesoamerica before settling in Costa Rica in 1992. Since then he has worked steadily for the *Tico Times* and continued his travels in the region. This is his first guidebook for Frommer's.

ACKNOWLEDGEMENTS

The author would like to thank Anne Becher and Joe Richey, as well as Teresa Rodríguez, who aided throughout the process—on the road and on the phone: "¿ qué más?"

MACMILLAN TRAVEL

A Simon & Schuster Macmillan Company
1633 Broadway
New York, NY 10019

Find us online at **http://www.mgr.com/travel** or
on America Online at **Keyword: Frommer's**.

ISBN 0-02-861140-3
ISSN 1077-890X

Editor: Erica Spaberg
Production Editor: Mike Thomas
Special thanks to Reid Bramblett
Production Editor: Mike Thomas
Design by Michele Laseau
Digital Cartography by Ortelius Design
Page Creation By Linda Quigley, Kathleen Caulfield, Holly Wittenberg, Toi Davis,
Hilary Smith, CJ East, and Bill Levy

SPECIAL SALES

Bulk purchases (10+ copies) of Frommer's travel guides are available to corporations at
special discounts. The Special Sales Department can produce custom editions to be used
as premiums and/or for sales promotion to suit individual needs. Existing editions can be
produced with custom cover imprints such as corporate logos. For more information write
to: Special Sales, Simon & Schuster, 1633 Broadway, New York, NY 10019.

Manufactured in the United States of America

Travel Discount Coupon

This coupon entitles you to special discounts when you book your trip through the

RESERVATION SERVICE

Hotels ◆ Airlines ◆ Car Rentals ◆ Cruises
All Your Travel Needs

Here's what you get: *

A discount of $50 on a booking of $1,000** or more for two or more people!

A discount of $25 on a booking of $500** or more for one person!

Free membership for three years, and 1,000 free miles on enrollment in the unique Miles-to-Go™ frequent-traveler program. Earn one mile for every dollar spent through the program. Earn free hotel stays starting at 5,000 miles. Earn free roundtrip airline tickets starting at 25,000 miles.

Personal help in planning your own, customized trip.

Fast, confirmed reservations at any property recommended in this guide, subject to availability.***

Special discounts on bookings in the U.S. and around the world.

Low-cost visa and passport service.

Reduced-rate cruise packages.

Call us toll-free in the U.S. at 1-888-940-5000, or fax us at 201-567-1832. In Canada, call us toll-free at 1-800-883-9959, or fax us at 416-922-6053.

---

* To qualify for these travel discounts, at least a portion of your trip must include destinations covered in this guide. No more than one coupon discount may be used in any 12-month period, for destinations covered in this guide. Cannot be combined with any other discount or program.
**These are U.S. dollars spent on commissionable bookings.
***A $10 fee, plus fax and/or phone charges, will be added to the cost of bookings at each hotel not linked to the reservation service. Customers must approve these fees in advance.

Valid until December 31, 1997. Terms and conditions of the Miles-to-Go™ program are available on request by calling 201-567-8500, ext 55.

COS123

22 Craneford Way
Twickenham
MIDDX
TW2 7SE

Tel: 081 891 3302

Contents

List of Maps

AN INVITATION TO THE READER

In researching this book, I discovered many wonderful places—hotels, restaurants, shops, and more. I'm sure you'll find others. Please tell us about them, so we can share the information with your fellow travelers in upcoming editions. If you were disappointed with a recommendation, we'd love to know that, too. Please write to:

Eliot Greenspan
Frommer's Costa Rica '97
Macmillan Travel
1633 Broadway
New York, NY 10019

AN ADDITIONAL NOTE

Please be advised that travel information is subject to change at any time—and this is especially true of prices. We therefore suggest that you write or call ahead for confirmation when making your travel plans. The authors, editors, and publisher cannot be held responsible for the experiences of readers while traveling. Your safety is important to us, however, so we encourage you to stay alert and be aware of your surroundings. Keep a close eye on cameras, purses, and wallets, all favorite targets of thieves and pickpockets.

WHAT THE SYMBOLS MEAN

✪ Frommer's Favorites

Hotels, restaurants, attractions, and entertainment you should not miss.

⑤ Super-Special Values

Hotels and restaurants that offer great value for your money.

The following abbreviations are used for credit cards:

AE	American Express	MC	MasterCard
DISC	Discover	V	Visa

The Best of Costa Rica

Formerly the well-kept secret of a few biologists, backpackers, and beachcombers, this small Central American nation has become a major international destination for travelers. The transformation happened somewhat gradually over the last 10 to 15 years, largely due to lower-than-Caribbean prices and a peaceful political situation; now even some American retirees are choosing it over Florida and Arizona for their new home.

Despite this surge in popularity, Costa Rica remains a place rich in natural wonders and biodiversity, but relatively poor in infrastructure and luxurious Caribbean-style beach resorts and hotels. Nature enthusiasts still make up the majority of visitors to Costa Rica, yet those who love the tropics but hate crowds and aren't into gambling may also find Costa Rica to their liking. Here, there are still small lodgings that haven't attracted hordes of tourists, unsullied beaches, jungle rivers for rafting and kayaking, and spectacular cloud and rain forests with ample opportunities for birdwatching and hiking.

Below I've chosen the very best of what this unique country has to offer—the places and the experiences you won't want to miss. Most are covered in greater detail elsewhere in this book; this chapter is merely meant to give you an overview of the highlights so you can start planning your trip.

1 The Best of Natural Costa Rica

- **Rincón de la Vieja National Park** (northeast of Liberia, in Guanacaste): This is an area of rugged beauty and high volcanic activity. The Rincón de la Vieja volcano rises to 6,159 feet, but the thermal activity is spread out along its flanks where numerous geysers, vents, and fumaroles let off its heat and steam. This is a great place to hire a guide and a horse for a day of rugged exploration. There are hot springs, mud baths, and cool jungle swimming holes. You'll pass through pastureland, scrub savannah, and moist secondary forest, and the birdwatching is excellent. See chapter 6.
- **Arenal Volcano/Tabacón Hot Springs** (near La Fortuna, northwest of San José): When the skies are clear and the lava is flowing, Arenal Volcano provides a thrilling light show accompanied by an earthshaking rumble that defies description. All this can be more than a bit exciting, which is why it's nice to have a natural

hot spring to soak in immediately afterward. To really get that one-two punch working, you can sit in the large pool at the **Tabacón Hot Springs Resort** (☎ 506/460-6000) and watch the fireworks at the same time. See chapter 7.

- **The Rio Sarapiquí Region** (north of San José between Guanacaste in the west and the Caribbean coast in the east): This is perhaps the best place for an eco-lodge experience. You'll be able to visit a plethora of life zones and ecosystems as protected tropical forests climb from the Caribbean coastal lowlands up into the Central mountain range. Braulio Carrillo National Park borders several other private reserves here, and there are several eco-lodges in a range of price categories to choose from. See chapter 7.

- **Manuel Antonio** (near Quepos on the Central Pacific Coast): There's a reason this place is so popular and renowned. The road leading into Manuel Antonio provides numerous lookouts that consistently produce postcard-perfect snapshots—even with a throw-away Instamatic. Steep jungle hills meet the sea. Uninhabited islands lie just off the coast. The beaches here are perfect crescents of white sand, and the national park is home to abundant tropical flora and fauna. You'll definitely be sharing it with other visitors, but there's enough beauty here to go around. See chapter 8.

- **Drake Bay** (on the Osa Peninsula): While there are more remote places in Costa Rica, this is my choice for an isolated getaway. No roads lead directly to Drake Bay, and I hope none ever will. Most visitors take a combination plane, bus, and boat journey to get here, although you can charter a sea plane and fly directly to the bay. Once here, you can either stay beside the breathtakingly beautiful bay or find accommodation overlooking the Pacific, with some of Costa Rica's lushest jungle all around you. See chapter 9.

- **Tortuguero Village and Jungle Canals** (on the Caribbean coast, north of Limón): Tortuguero Village is a small collection of rustic wood shacks on a narrow spit of land between the Caribbean Sea and a dense maze of jungle canals. It's been called Costa Rica's Venice, but it actually has more in common with the South American Amazon. You can fly into the small airstrip, but it's better to take one of the slow boats that ply the river and canal route. On the way you'll see a wide variety of herons and other waterbirds, three types of monkeys, three-toed sloths, and huge American crocodiles. If you come between June and October, you may be treated to the awe-inspiring spectacle of a green turtle nesting. The small stretch of Tortuguero beach is the last major remaining nesting site of this endangered animal. See chapter 10.

2 The Best Active Vacations

- **Diving off the Shores of Isla del Coco** (off Guanacaste in the Pacific): Legendary among treasure seekers, pirate buffs, and scuba divers, this small island is considered one of the 10 best dive sites in the world. A protected national park, its surrounding Pacific waters are clear, and its reefs are teeming with life. (Divers regularly encounter schools of hammerhead sharks and docile whale sharks.) Since the island is so remote, the most popular way to visit is on week-long excursions on live-aboard boats. (On a live-aboard boat, guests live, eat, and sleep on board— nights are spent anchored in the harbor, since the park has no overnight facilities for visitors.) **Escenarios Tropicales** (☎ 506/224-2555) regularly runs dive trips to Coco Island. See chapter 4.

- **Hooking a Billfish off the Pacific Coast:** Billfish are plentiful all along Costa Rica's Pacific coast, and boats operate from Playas del Coco to Playa Zancudo.

Costa Rican anglers hold world records for both blue marlin and pacific sailfish. Go to Quepos for the best aprés-fish scene or head down to Drake Bay if you want some isolation. **Americana Fishing Services** (☎ 506/223-4331) can help you find a good charter skipper or specialized fishing lodge. See chapters 4 and 6.

- **Rafting the Upper Reventazon River** (near Turrialba): The class V "Guayabo" section of this popular river is serious white water. Only experienced and gutsy river runners need apply. If you're not quite up to the above, try a two-day Pacuare River trip, which passes through primary and secondary forests and a beautiful steep gorge that, sadly, may be dammed soon. **Aventuras Naturales** (☎ 506/225-3939 or 800/308-3394 in the U.S.) can arrange either of the above tours. See chapter 4.

- **Riding a Horse from Playa Montezuma to a Waterfall** (on the Nicoya Peninsula): This is one of the most popular tours in Montezuma and justifiably so. The 8-kilometer ride to the waterfall is a mixture of beach riding and short sections of jungle trails. Once there you can swim in the perfect swimming hole formed at the meeting place of a 50-foot waterfall and the sea. Leave Montezuma about mid-day, and you should return as the sun is setting. See chapter 6.

- **Surfing & Four-Wheeling Guanacaste Province:** This northwestern province has dozens of respectable beach and point breaks from Witch's Rock at Playa Naranjo near the Nicaraguan border to Playa Nosara over 100 kilometers away. Rent a 4x4 with a roof rack, pile on the boards and explore. See chapter 6.

- **Mountain Biking around Lake Arenal** (near Tilarán and Arenal Volcano): This huge man-made lake, with the majestic Arenal Volcano as a backdrop, has trails all around its shores and into neighboring forests and pasture lands. There are a variety of rides of all difficulty levels. The setting is spectacular, and there are hot springs for sore muscles nearby. Contact **Rio Escondido Mountain Bikes** (☎ 800/678-2252 in the U.S.) or **Rock River Lodge** (☎ 506/695-5644). See chapter 7.

- **Windsurfing Lake Arenal:** With steady gale-force winds and stunning scenery, the northern end of Arenal Lake has become a major international windsurfing hot spot. See chapter 7.

- **Hiking Mount Chirripó** (near San Isidro de El General on the Central Pacific Coast): The highest mountain in Costa Rica, Mount Chirripó is one of the few places in the world where (on a clear day) you can see both the Atlantic and the Pacific oceans at the same time. Hiking to Chirripó's 12,412- foot summit will take you through a number of distinct bioregions, ranging from lowland pastures and a cloud forest to a high-altitude páramo, a tundra-like landscape with stunted trees and morning frosts. See chapter 8.

- **Kayaking Around the Golfo Dulce:** Slipping through the waters of the Golfo Dulce by kayak gets you intimately in touch with the raw beauty of this underdeveloped region. Spend several days poking around in mangrove swamps, fishing in estuaries, and watching dolphins frolic in the bay. **Escondido Trex** (☎ 506/735-5210) provides multi-day custom kayaking trips out of Puerto Jiménez on the Osa Peninsula. See chapter 9.

- **Surfing Pavones** (on the Caribbean coast): Just 8 miles from the Panamanian border at the southern reaches of Costa Rica's Pacific coast, Pavones is reputed to have one of the longest rideable waves in the world. When this left-point break is working, surfers enjoy rides of over a kilometer in length. Much more can be said about this experience, but if you're a surfer, you've heard it all before. **Tour Tech International** (☎ 800/882-2636) specializes in surf tours to Costa Rica and will give current wave reports. See chapter 9.

3 The Best Beaches

With over 750 combined miles of shoreline on its Pacific and Caribbean coasts, Costa Rica offers beachgoers an embarrassment of riches. Whether you want a broad stretch of sand all your own, a lively beach town with all-night discos, or just a quiet place to leisurely hunt for shells, there's a beach here just for you.

- **Playa Conchal:** A short section of beach made entirely of small polished and crushed shells, Playa Conchal isn't great for swimming, but it's a beachcomber's delight. You should have no problem filling your pockets—and a few additional plastic bags—with a wide range of colorful shells and fragments. Better bathing beaches are just a short walk away in either direction. The expected opening of a 300-plus room resort in summer 1996 will certainly change the feel of this once isolated beach, but there are plenty of shells to go around for quite some time. See chapter 6.

- **Playa Montezuma:** This tiny beach town at the tip of the Nicoya Peninsula has weathered fame and infamy, and yet still retains a funky sense of individuality. European backpackers, vegetarian yoga enthusiasts, and UFO seekers choose Montezuma's beach over any other in Costa Rica. The waterfalls are what set it apart from the competition, but the beach stretches for miles, with plenty of isolated spots to plop down your towel or mat. See chapter 6.

- **Playa Tamarindo:** While not overdeveloped, Tamarindo provides ample lodgings to suit every budget and excellent restaurants at almost every turn. The beach here is long and broad, with sections calm enough for swimmers and others just right for surfers. Located about midway along the stretch beaches of Guanacaste province, Tamarindo makes a good base for exploring other nearby stretches of sand. There are plenty of surfers here, and one of the most lively nightlife scenes on this coast. See chapter 6.

- **Santa Rosa National Park:** If you want to really get away from it all, the beaches here are a good bet. Located in the northwest corner of Costa Rica, you will either have to four-wheel drive or hike 13 kilometers from the central ranger station to reach the beach. Once there, you will find only the most basic of camping facilities—outhouse latrines and cold-water showers. But you will probably have the place almost to yourself. In fact, the only time it gets crowded is in October, when thousands of olive Ridley sea turtles nest in one of their yearly *arribadas* (arrivals). See chapter 6.

- **Manuel Antonio:** The first beach destination to become popular in Costa Rica, it still retains its charms—despite burgeoning crowds and mushrooming hotels. The beaches inside the park are idyllic, and the views from the hills approaching the park are enchanting. This is one of the few remaining habitats for the endangered squirrel monkey. Rooms with views tend to be a bit expensive, but many a satisfied guest will tell you they're worth it. See chapter 8.

- **Punta Uvita:** Part of the Ballena Maritime National Park, this is a wide beach with calm water and plenty of trees for shade. At low tide a sandbar connects the mainland to a small offshore island. Most people visit for the day and stay in nearby Dominical. See chapter 8.

- **Punta Uva:** Below Puerto Viejo, the beaches of Costa Rica's Atlantic coast take on true Caribbean splendor, with turquoise waters, coral reefs, and palm-lined stretches of nearly deserted white-sand beach. By far the most beautiful is Punta Uva, just a few kilometers by gravel road from Puerto Viejo. Tall coconut palms line the shore, providing shady respite for those who like to spend a full day on the sand. See chapter 10.

4 The Best Day Hikes & Nature Walks

- **Lankester Botanical Garden:** If you want a really pleasant, but not overly challenging day hike, consider a walk among the hundreds of distinct species of flora on display here. **Lankester Garden** (☎ 506/551-9877 or 506/552-3247) is just 17 miles from San José and makes a wonderful day's expedition. The trails meander from areas of open well-tended garden to shady natural forest. See chapter 5.

- **Monteverde Biological Cloud Forest Preserve:** In the morning rush of high season, when groups and tours line up to enter the preserve, you'd think the sign says "crowd forest." Still, the guides here are some of the most professional and knowledgeable in the country. Take a tour in the morning to familiarize yourself with the forest, then spend the late morning or afternoon (your entrance ticket is good for the whole day) exploring the preserve. Once you get off the main thoroughfares, Monteverde reveals its rich mysteries with stunning regularity. Walk among the grey mist and look up at the dense tangle of epiphytes and vines. The only noises you'll hear are the rustlings of birds or monkeys and the occasional distant rumble of Arenal Volcano. The trails are well-marked and regularly tended. See chapter 7.

- **La Fortuna to the Río Fortuna Waterfall:** The hike that leads to this waterfall, about 3¹/₂ miles outside La Fortuna, is one of my favorites —but it's not for everyone. In fact it's as much of a scramble as a hike. Follow the signs out of town along dirt roads and pasture land. Once you reach the waterfall lookout, you've got another 20 minutes navigating down a very slippery and muddy path to the base of the falls. The roar of the crashing water is almost deafening. If you want to swim, go just slightly downstream. It's a refreshing rinse, but prepare to get muddy again as you scramble and haul yourself up roots and vines on the way back. See chapter 7.

- **Corcovado National Park:** This large swath of dense lowland rain forest is home to Costa Rica's second largest population of scarlet macaws. The park has a well-designed network of trails, ranger stations, and camping facilities. Most of the lodges in Drake Bay and Puerto Jiménez have day hikes through the park, but if you really want to experience it, you should hike in and stay at one or more of the campgrounds. This is strenuous hiking, and you will have to pack in some gear and food, but the reward is some of Costa Rica's most spectacular and unspoiled scenery. Because strict limits are placed on the number of visitors allowed into the park, you will always feel far from the madding crowds. See chapter 9.

5 The Best Birdwatching

- **Observing Oropendula and Blue-crowned Motmot at Parque del Este:** A boon for city birdwatchers, this San José park rambles through a collection of lawns, planted gardens, and harvested forest, but also includes second-growth scrub and dense woodland. Oropendula and blue-crowned motmot are common species here. Take the San Ramón/Parque del Este bus from Avenida 2 between calles 9 and 11. See chapter 5.

- **Spotting Hundreds of Marsh and Stream Birds along the Rio Tempisque Basin:** Hike in to the Palo Verde Biological Station, or take a boat trip down the Bebedero River with **Guanacaste Tours** (☎ 506/666-0306) or **Safaris Corobici** (☎ 506/669-1091). This area is an important breeding ground for gallinules, jacanas, and limpkins, as well as a common habitat for numerous heron and kingfisher species. See chapter 6.

- **Looking for Over 300 Species of Birds in La Selva Biological Station:** With an excellent trail system through a variety of habitats, from dense primary rain forest to open pasture lands and cacao plantations, this is one of the finest places for birdwatching in Costa Rica. With such a variety of habitats, the number of spotted species top well over 300. See chapter 7.
- **Catching a Scarlet Macaw in Flight over Carara Biological Reserve:** Home to Costa Rica's largest population of scarlet macaws, Carara Biological Reserve is a special place for devoted birdwatchers and recent converts. Macaws are noisy and colorful birds that spend their days in the park, but choose to roost in the evenings near the coast. They arrive like clockwork every morning and then head for the coastal mangroves around dusk. These daily migrations give birders a great chance to see these magnificent birds in flight. See chapter 8.
- **Looking for a Resplendent Quetzal in the Cerro de la Muerte:** The ancient Aztec and Maya revered this spectacular bird. Serious birdwatchers won't want to leave Costa Rica without crossing this bird off their life lists, and neophytes may be hooked for life after seeing one of these iridescent green wonders fly overhead, flashing its brilliant red breast and trailing 2-foot-long tailfeathers. **Albergue de Montaña Tapantí** (☎ /fax 506/232-0436) can almost guarantee a sighting. See chapter 8.
- **Taking Advantage of the Caribbean's Best Birding at Aviarios del Caribe** (☎ 506/382-1335): In just a few short years, Aviarios del Caribe has established itself as the prime birdwatching resort on the Caribbean. If it flies along this coast, chances are good you'll spot it here; over 300 species of birds have been spotted so far. See chapter 10.

6 The Best Family Vacation Experiences

- **San José:** If your family is like mine, you'll want to spend your nights in San José far away from the traffic and street chaos of downtown. The best place for all of you to experience Costa Rica's capital city (and still get a decent night's sleep) is the **Cariari Hotel & Country Club** (☎ 506/239-0022). With facilities that include several large pools, an 18-hole golf course, 11 tennis courts, and a game room (not to mention babysitting service), there's something here for everyone. Located just 15 minutes from downtown, it is well situated for exploring all of the city's sights and attractions. See chapter 5.
- **Hotel Hacienda La Pacifica** (north of Cañas; ☎ 506/669-0266): This hotel is set on expansive grounds with marked trails. There's a neighboring zoo, and a variety of tours and activities are close at hand. The gentle Corobici river is a good river float for all ages, and there are bicycles for rent, birdwatching guides, and educational tours to a nearby historic ranch. See chapter 6.
- **Monteverde:** Not only does this area host the country's most famous cloud forest, but it also sports a wide variety of related attractions and activities. After hiking through the preserve, you should be able to keep most kids happy and occupied riding horses, squirming at the local serpentarium, or visiting the butterfly farm and hummingbird gallery. See chapter 7.
- **Playa de Jacó:** This is Costa Rica's liveliest and most developed beach town. The streets are lined with souvenir shops, ice cream stands, and inexpensive eateries; there is even a miniature golf course. This is a good place for a family to rent a few mopeds for an afternoon cruise. Older children can rent a boogie board, though everyone should be careful with the rough surf here. **Hotel Club del Mar** (☎ 506/643-3194) is situated at the calm southern end of the beach. The hotel has a small

pool and some shady grounds, and is accommodating to families traveling with small children. See chapter 8.

7 The Best Offbeat Travel Experiences

- **Studying Spanish and/or Taking Latin Dance Classes while Staying with a Costa Rican Family:** If you really want to dive in and get a feel for the culture, this is the way to go. Numerous language institutes in San José combine intensive classroom work with a pre-arranged homestay. The **Costa Rican Language Academy** (☎ 506/233-2070 or 506/223-8938) combines Spanish lessons with classes in Latin dance and Tico cooking. See chapter 3.

- **Ballooning above Naranjo:** Ballooning is new to Costa Rica. But a quiet wind-borne ride in a hot air balloon is a wonderful way to get a different perspective of the Costa Rican countryside. Fly over coffee plantations and small mountain villages in the cool morning air and soft post-dawn light (trips are all scheduled early, before the heavier afternoon winds pick up). Contact **Serendipity Adventures** (☎ 506/450-0328 or in the U.S. 800/635-2325) to arrange a hot air balloon ride during your vacation. See chapter 4.

- **Seeing Costa Rica from Coast to Coast by Horse, Raft, Bike, and Foot:** **Coast To Coast Adventures** (Apdo. 2135-1002, San José, Costa Rica; ☎ 506/225-6055) offers a two-week trip spanning the country that combines horses, rafts, mountain bikes, and hiking, but doesn't include travel by motor vehicle. You'll see just about all the natural beauty the country has to offer, burn plenty of calories, and conserve fossil fuels in the process. See chapter 4.

- **Waiting for the Olive Ridley Arribada at Playa Nancite:** This isolated beach in Santa Rosa National Park is the site each October of the massive nesting of olive Ridley turtles. Tens of thousands of these marine reptiles come ashore en masse to lay eggs over a period of several days. The exact dates remain up to the turtles' discretion, but the beach and month are amazingly consistent. This is a national park, so bring a tent and some supplies, and you might just get lucky. See chapter 6.

- **Volunteering at a National Park:** The Costa Rican National Parks Service accepts volunteers to work at various parks around the country. A minimum commitment of two months is required. Room and board are provided, and in return you will be expected to work at ranger stations, maintain trails, and provide upkeep to the facilities. You may not have much choice in your park assignment. For more information, contact the **National Parks Office** (☎ 506/257-0922).

8 The Best Views

- **The Summit of Volcano Irazú** (near San José): From this vantage point, you can see (albeit on a very clear day) both the Pacific Ocean and the Caribbean Sea. Even if this experience eludes you, you will have a view of the volcano's spectacular landscape, the Meseta Central, and the Orosi Valley. See chapter 5.

- **Arenal Observatory Lodge** (near Arenal Volcano; ☎ 506/257-9489 or 506/257-3273): It seems so close, you'll think you can reach out and touch the volcano. Unlike the view mentioned directly above, when the volcano rumbles and spews you may have the urge to bolt out of bed and head for cover. Make sure you ask for a room with a view. See chapter 7.

- **La Mariposa** (Quepos; ☎ 506/777-0355): Couples who choose to dine here arguably have the best view in Manuel Antonio, and that's saying a lot. Come for breakfast or a sunset drink, because unfortunately I've had bad luck with dinner here. See chapter 8.

- **The Outdoor Restaurant at Villa Caletas** (Playa Hermosa de Jacó; ☎ 506/257-3653): You'll have a view over the Golfo de Nicoya and the Pacific Ocean beyond. Sunsets here are garnering legend, but it's beautiful during the day as well. See chapter 8.
- **La Paloma Lodge** (Drake Bay; ☎ 506/239-0954): Look out your window through flowering hibiscus and swaying palm fronds to the Pacific Ocean and Caño Island just beyond. You may never want to get out of bed. See chapter 9.

9 The Best Drives

Driving in Costa Rica can be unpleasant, to say the least. Routes are rarely marked, roads resemble bombing ranges, and the famously peaceful Ticos become downright homicidal once they climb behind the wheel of a car. Nevertheless, renting a car provides freedom and independence, and there are some drives that are noteworthy for their scenery.

- **Irazú Volcano and the Orosi Valley:** This makes an excellent day tour and drive. Start out early to reach the peak of the volcano while the skies are clearest, then spend the afternoon touring the Orosi Valley, with scenic lookouts at both Orosi and Ujarrás. See chapter 5.
- **Braulio Carrillo National Park:** A trip to the Caribbean coast will take you through this vast national park of mountainous cloud and rain forests. Giant elephant-ear plants line the steep jungle roadside. Broad vistas open up to reveal a number of waterfalls cascading out of the forested mountains. A bridge crosses over the juncture of the clear General River and the sulfuric yellow Río Sucio (Dirty River). Be careful about stopping, and don't leave your car parked here for long: Robberies have been reported along this stretch of highway. See chapter 7.
- **La Fortuna–Tilarán–Monteverde:** This route connects two of the country's prime tourist destinations—Arenal Volcano and Monteverde Cloud Forest. Along the way you can marvel at the beauty of Lake Arenal and stop at the wonderful Arenal Botanical Gardens. A four-wheel-drive vehicle is highly recommended for this route, as the section between Tilarán and Monteverde is, to put it mildly, rugged. See chapter 7.
- **The Rocky Coast South of Dominical:** This has often been compared to Big Sur, California. For years this stretch of road was the definition of rugged, but recent improvements have now made this an enjoyable ride. All along the way there are informal lookouts where you can pull over and watch the waves crash on the rocks below. On the inland side of the road are dense lowland rain forests with side roads that lead to hiking trails and mountain waterfalls. See chapter 8.

10 The Most Scenic Towns & Villages

Earthquakes and isolation have deprived Costa Rica of the architectural splendor found in neighboring nations. San José is an unremarkable city, rapidly becoming a textbook example of what a hectic pace of poorly planned urban development can do to a Second or Third World city. Most of the towns and villages in the country are very simple farming communities, with few attractions for traditional tourists. Still, there are towns and villages both on and off the beaten track that are worth the trip.

- **Cartago:** Located 15 miles southeast of San José, Cartago was the country's first capital. The city contains the most traces of the country's Spanish Catholic colonial past. Churches—some still standing, others in ruins—dominate this small city. **The Basilica de Nuestra Señora de los Angeles** is the most striking example of an active church and is the site of a massive annual pilgrimage. A public park now occupies what was once the site of a large unfinished church, destroyed in the wake of the 1910 earthquake. Just outside the city are the ruins of the Ujarrás church. Built in 1693, it is the country's oldest church. Cartago makes an easy and interesting day trip out of San José. See chapter 5.

- **Guayabo:** Costa Rica's oldest known city, Guayabo is nestled amid the lush forests of the mountainous Turrialba region about 45 miles east of San José. Today, it has the distinction of being the country's only major archeological site.

  While it lacks the ornate majesty of such Mayan cities as Tikal, Chichén Itza, and Cópan, it has a wonderful, homey, lived-in feel. It is believed its residents were Olmecs fleeing Aztec persecution more than 1,000 years before Christ. Excavations have revealed that the ancient city had a well-designed water system, clearly defined living areas, and a stone-paved "highway" running through the city center. Today, visitors can experience this Indian past by walking among building foundations, marveling at the still-working aqueducts, viewing carved petroglyphs, and touring burial sites. Guayabo National Monument is best visited as a day trip from San José. See chapter 5.

- **Liberia:** The capital and commercial hub of the northern province of Guanacaste, Liberia still retains much of its classic Spanish colonial architecture. Walk around town and admire the plentiful adobe buildings with ornate wooden doors, heavy beams, central courtyards, and faded, sagging red-tile roofs. Liberia is the only major city in Costa Rica not situated in the temperate Central Valley. Instead, Liberia is located on a hot and dry lowland savannah, surrounded by cattle land and distant foothills. There are plenty of lodging options, and Liberia makes a great base for exploring the beaches and national parks of Guanacaste. See chapter 6.

- **Golfito:** The hub of Costa Rica's southern Pacific zone, Golfito is 210 miles south of San José. Steep jungle hills meet the water, and you'll find the town spread out along one main road that hugs the winding coastline of the Golfo Dulce (Sweet Gulf). Golfito was once the largest base for United Fruit Company's banana operations. United Fruit pulled out, but they left behind their company housing. Many of these old wooden homes with gingerbread trim and manicured lawns have been turned into comfortable budget lodgings. You won't want to stay in Golfito too long (unless you are an avid sportsfisherman or botanical garden fan), but if you'll be exploring the Osa Peninsula or the Golfo Dulce, it makes a good base. See chapter 9.

11   The Best Places to Shop

Shopping can be difficult in Costa Rica. The best buy and most representative product to bring home is coffee. Costa Rica does not have a strong handcraft and artisan tradition. Most of the crafts and colorful textiles you will see for sale come from Guatemala, Panama, and Ecuador. While these may seem cheap by northern standards, they are obviously more expensive than you'd find them in their countries of origin.

- **Boutique Annemarie** (San José; ☎ 506/221-6063): This bilevel store is actually part of the Hotel Don Carlos in San José; it sells a broad selection of crafts and clothing. This is a good place to choose a clay or silver reproduction of some pre-Colombian figure. Most items are similar to those you'll see on the streets or in other stores, but they're under one roof here, and the atmosphere is friendlier and more relaxed. See chapter 5.

- **Central Market** (San José): No trip to the city is complete without a tour of this indoor labyrinth of shops, stalls, and restaurants. Everything from crafts and clothing to fresh butchered meats is sold here. The surrounding streets host a daily farmer's market. This is the best place to buy fresh roasted whole bean coffee. See chapter 5.

- **Sarchí** (Central Valley): This small city outside of San José has long served as the headquarters for Costa Rica's modest craft industry. Woodwork is the most developed and available craft, with traditional painted oxcarts coming in a wide range of styles and sizes. See chapter 5.

12 The Most Luxurious Hotels & Resorts

Luxury is a relative term in Costa Rica. To date, no hotel I've found hits truly high standards across the board. Magnificent settings abound, but service and food can sometimes fall short. The pickiest of travelers will usually find something to fault. Still, there are a few places that are doing their best.

- **Hotel L'Ambiance** (San José; ☎ 506/222-6702): You'll find more frills and facilities at other larger and more expensive hotels in San José, but you won't find more charm or elegance. The restored stucco building contains a spacious central courtyard, representative of Spanish colonial architecture. Hardwood floors and antique furniture abound. You'll find a helpful staff and even a concierge. You won't find a tour agency, health spa, business center or casino, but then again, perhaps you won't mind. See chapter 5.

- **Hotel El Jardín del Eden** (Playa Tamarindo; ☎ 506/653-0111): This hotel provides the best meals, service, and setting along this stretch of the Guanacaste coast. Spacious rooms come with either large patios or ocean-view balconies. The French owner has brought a sense of European sophistication and some of his native cuisine to the hotel. The grounds are lushly planted and perennially flowering. You'll be 150 meters from the beach, but there are two swimming pools and a whirlpool right here. See chapter 6.

- **Villas Caletas** (north of Jacó; ☎ 506/257-3653): Spread out over a steep hillside, high above the Pacific Ocean, these individual villas have a Mediterranean feel. The Greek Doric amphitheater follows the same motif. Carved into the steep hillside, the theater frequently features evening concerts of jazz or classical music. The "infinity pool" here was one of the first in Costa Rica and is still the most interesting. Sitting in a lounge chair at the pool's edge, you'll swear it joins the sea beyond. See chapter 8.

13 The Best Moderately Priced Hotels

- **Hotel Grano de Oro** (San José; ☎ 506/255-3322): San José boasts dozens of old homes that have been converted into hotels, but few offer the luxurious accommodations or professional service that can be found at the Grano de Oro. Throughout all the guest rooms, you'll find attractive hardwood furniture, including old-fashioned wardrobes in some rooms. When it comes time to relax, you can soak in a hot tub or have a drink in the rooftop lounge, with a commanding view of San José. See chapter 5.

- **Hotel Santo Tomas** (San José; ☎ 506/255-0448): If you want to stay in downtown San José, this restored old mansion offers a sense of luxury at a very moderate price. There are hardwood floors and hardwood furniture throughout. Friendly service, clean and comfortable rooms, and a great location make this one of the best bets in town. See chapter 5.

- **Amor de Mar** (Playa Montezuma; ☎ 506/642-0262): This hotel has brightly varnished woodwork, immaculate rooms, hammocks strung under shady mango trees, a wide grass lawn overlooking the Pacific Ocean, and a swimming pool–sized tide pool carved into the adjoining rocky shore. They could charge much more. See chapter 6.

- **El Velero Hotel** (Playa Hermosa, Guanacaste; ☎ 506/670-0330): This delightful hotel is located right on the beach, has comfortable, light and cool rooms, its own swimming pool, and a namesake sailboat ("velero" means sailboat in Spanish) for sunset cruises and day charters. See chapter 6.

- **Sapo Dorado** (Monteverde; ☎ 506/645-5010): Here, spacious wooden cabins with fireplaces and private porches are spread across an open hillside planted with fruit trees and tropical flowers. The hotel has an excellent restaurant and some of the best sunsets in Monteverde. See chapter 7.

- **Hotel Casitas Eclipse** (Manuel Antonio; ☎ 506/777-0408): First, a caveat: Only one or two of the rooms here have a view. However, you might not care once you're settled into a villa-styled room, watching squirrel monkeys from your private patio or lounging around one of the three pools. See chapter 8.

14 The Best Eco-Lodges & Wilderness Resorts

The term eco-tourism is fast becoming ubiquitous within the travel industry; unfortunately, it is often trumpeted by tourism operators and hotel owners who do very little in their day-to-day professional lives to combat environmental damage. (Some even contribute to it.)

Eco-lodge options in Costa Rica range from tent camps with no electricity, cold water showers and communal buffet-style meals to some of the most luxurious accommodations in the country.

Generally, outstanding eco-lodges and wilderness resorts are set apart by an ongoing commitment (financial or otherwise) to minimizing their effect on surrounding ecosystems and to supporting residents of local communities. They should also be able to provide naturalist guides and plentiful information. All of the following do.

- **Selva Verde Lodge** (Sarapiquí; ☎ 506/766-6077): One of the early, exemplary eco-lodges in Costa Rica, it is also among the most luxurious. The setting, on the banks of the Sarapiquí River, is spectacular. The rooms all have a balcony or verandah with views of the rain forest, and the birdwatching is excellent. There are resident naturalists, a library of reference books, and plenty of guided tours and activities to keep you busy. See chapter 7.

- **Rara Avis** (near Las Horquetas; ☎ 506/764-4187): A pioneer in eco-tourism, this eco-resort still provides a premier natural experience in the heart of Costa Rica's Central Mountain rain forest. Getting to Rara Avis is no longer the kidney-splitting 4-hour ordeal it once was, but you'll still spend plenty of time in a tractor-pulled covered wagon before reaching the isolated yet comfortable Waterfall Lodge. If you're looking for a more rustic nature experience, stay at their El Plastico Lodge, a former penal colony. See chapter 7.

- **La Paloma Lodge** (Drake Bay; ☎ 506/239-0954): If your idea of the perfect nature lodge is one where your front porch provides some prime-time viewing of flora and fauna, this place is for you. If you do decide to leave the comfort of your porch, the Osa Peninsula's lowland rain forests are just outside your door. See chapter 9.

- **Lapa Rios** (Osa Peninsula; ☎ 506/735-5130): Situated at the southern tip of the Osa Peninsula, this is the most luxurious eco-lodge in Costa Rica. The 14 bungalow rooms all have spectacular views and are set into a lush forest. A lot of care went into the design and construction of this hotel. There are a host of tours available for guests, and the guides are usually local residents who are intimately familiar with the environment. See chapter 9.

- **Aviarios del Caribe** (Cahuita; ☎ 506/382-1335): Avid birdwatchers cannot help but cross off a large portion of their life lists here. Walk the grounds, sit on the porch, take a boat ride through the mangroves, and check off species after species as your stay unfolds. The accommodations are modern and clean, and the rooms are always well stocked with fresh flowers. See chapter 10.

- **Cabinas Chimuri** (Puerto Viejo; ☎ 506/798-4244): These Bribri style A-frame cabins are built out of local materials and are owned and managed by Mauricio Salazar, a local Bribri Indian. The tours, setting, and surroundings make this the perfect way to really get to know the people, customs, and ecology of the Talamanca region. Mauricio will take you to visit the nearby reservation and show you some of the secrets of jungle herbology and bush medicine. The accommodations are basic, but you'll have a mosquito net and a porch to sit on, and you can watch the Caribbean birds pass by. See chapter 10.

15   The Best Bed-and-Breakfasts & Small Inns

- **Finca Rosa Blanca Country Inn** (Santa Bárbara de Heredia; ☎ 506/269-9392): If the cookie-cutter rooms of international resorts leave you cold, then perhaps the unique rooms of this unusual inn will be more your style. Square corners seem to have been prohibited here in favor of turrets and curving walls of glass, arched windows, and a semicircular built-in couch. Set into the lush hillsides just 20 minutes from San José. See chapter 5.

- **Almost Paradise** (Playa Nosara; ☎/fax 506/685-5004): The name is appropriate. Sure, you could be right on the beach instead of 200 meters away, and sure, things could be fancier and more private. But at these prices, this *is* almost paradise. See chapter 6.

- **Sueño del Mar** (Playa Tamarindo; ☎/fax 506/653-0284): You may think you're dreaming here. The rooms feature African dolls on the window sills, Kokopeli candle holders and open-air showers with sculpted angelfish, hand-painted tiles, and lush tropical plants. The fabrics are from Bali and Guatemala. Somehow, all this works well together, along with the requisite hammocks under shade trees right on the beach. The breakfasts here are earning local renown; yours comes with the price of a room. See chapter 6.

- **Casa Verde** (Puerto Viejo; ☎ 506/798-4244): This is my favorite budget lodging along the Caribbean coast. The rooms are clean and airy and have comfortable beds with mosquito nets. The owner is friendly and is always doing some work in the gardens or around the grounds. See chapter 10.

- **Magellan Inn** (Cahuita; ☎/fax 506/755-0035): This small inn is situated at the far end of Playa Negra (about 2 kilometers north of Cahuita), and is the most luxurious hotel in the area. There's a sense of elegance here that borders on tropical decadence. The pool is set into a crevice in an ancient coral reef that has been exposed with the passing of time. The birdwatching is phenomenal. See chapter 10.

16   The Best Restaurants

- **Bijahua** (San José; ☎ 506/225-0613): This restaurant has led the way toward the creation of a nouvelle Costa Rican cuisine under the careful hand of chef Isabel Campabadal. Traditional ingredients are taken to new heights in such dishes as tiquizque soup, gnocchi ñampi, and shrimp in tamarind butter. See chapter 5.
- **La Cocina de Leña** (San José; ☎ 506/255-1360 or 506/223-3704): Located in the El Pueblo shopping, dining, and entertainment center, La Cocina de Leña (The Wood Stove) has a rustic feel to it and, slightly overpriced, takes on traditional Costa Rican cooking. The more adventurous dishes include oxtail stew served with yuca and platáno, or *chilasuilas,* tortillas filled with fried meat. See chapter 5.
- **La Masia de Triquel** (San José, ☎ 506/296-3528): For years this elegant restaurant has been serving gourmet Spanish cuisine, with a level of refinement rare in Costa Rica. The paella is wonderful, of course, but so are the lamb, the rabbit, and the langostinas, a large local crawfish. See chapter 5.
- **Machu Pichu** (San José; ☎ 506/222-7384): The ceviche and mixed seafood platter are enough to earn this listing. The *pisco* sours, potato appetizers and lively atmosphere just bolster the claim. Some of the fish plates come in heavy cream sauces, so ask first if you are watching your weight. See chapter 5.
- **La Piraña** (Jacó; ☎ 506/643-3725): For some reason, this beach town has been blessed with one of the most innovative and exotic restaurants in the country. The menu is an international potpourri, and the atmosphere is lively, with bright primary colors, simple furniture, and gentle cross-breezes aided by plenty of slow-turning ceiling fans. See chapter 8.
- **The Garden** (Puerto Viejo; no phone): For years, travelers to the Caribbean coast have dubbed this their favorite restaurant in Costa Rica, and the reasons are as numerous as the exotic dishes on the menu. Wonderfully spiced Thai curry, local rundown (a spicy stew made with whatever ingredients the cook can "run down" that day), and Jamaican Jerk chicken all coexist effortlessly and are served garnished with fresh flowers and grilled pineapple. See chapter 10.

17   The Best Places to Go After Dark

- **El Cuartel de la Boca del Monte** (Avenida 1 between calles 21 and 23, San José; ☎ 506/221-0327): This is where San José's young, restless, and beautiful congregate. From Wednesday through Saturday the place is jam-packed. Originally a gay and bohemian hangout, it is now decidedly yuppie. See chapter 5.
- **La Esmeralda** (Avenida 2 between calles 5 and 7, San José; ☎ 506/221-0530): This restaurant serves as a meeting place and central dispatch center for scores of local mariachi bands, some of whom even print the restaurant's pay phone number on their business cards. It's open 24 hours a day. Hire your own combo for a song or two, or just enjoy the cacophony as the bands battle it out through the night. See chapter 5.
- **Salsa 54** (Calle 3 between avenidas 1 and 3, San José; ☎ 506/221-3220): This is one of the more serious dance halls in San José. Couples dancing is an art form here. Salsa 54 is large, with several separate dance floors and plenty of tables with good views for those who just like to watch. They even have a raised stage for those with the fanciest footwork. See chapter 5.
- **San Pedro** (San José): This is San José's University district, and at night its streets are filled with students strolling among a variety of bars and cafés. If you'd like to

join them, keep in mind that **La Villa** (☎ 506/225-9612), **La Maga** (100 meters east of the Church in San Pedro, ☎ 506/283-5040), and **Ventanas** (no phone) cater to artists and bohemians, **El Pulpo** (no phone) is popular with young Tico rockers, and **Pizza Caccio** (☎ 506/283-2809) seems to attract a good share of the U.S. students studying here. All of the spots listed above (except La Maga) are located in a three-block stretch that begins 200 meters east of the Church in San Pedro and heads north. See chapter 5.

- **Teatro Nacional** (San José; ☎ 506/221-1329): This 100-year-old classical opera house has recently been restored and sits like a gem in the center of San José. Catch a show here, admire the classical ceiling mural, and then wander next door for a nightcap at the Gran Hotel's outdoor café. Most of the theater and popular concerts are in Spanish, but there are plenty of classical music concerts, dance performances, and other events that cross language barriers. See chapter 5.

Getting to Know Costa Rica   2

Costa Rica—in Spanish, the name means "Rich Coast," and when the Spanish named this region, they felt Costa Rica had great promise. In those days, gold and Indian souls, to convert and enslave, were the goal of the Spanish, and when Costa Rica yielded up little of either, the name became somewhat of a misnomer, at least as far as the Spanish were concerned. It took nearly 500 years for the Rich Coast to finally yield its true bounty—the green gold of its natural tropical beauty. The same dense forests, volcanic peaks, and rugged coastlines that created only impediments to Spanish settlement in Costa Rica are today attracting hundreds of thousands of visitors each year. They come to see some of Central America's most unspoiled forests and beaches, to learn about rain forests and cloud forests, to go birdwatching and white-water rafting, horseback riding and diving, or just to sit on the verandah of one of the country's many hotels, eco-lodges, or *cabinas* with a tall, cool drink in hand and contemplate chucking it all to join the more than 30,000 Americans who already call Costa Rica home.

Costa Rica is, and has been for many years, a relative sea of tranquillity in a region that has been troubled by turmoil for centuries. When former Costa Rican president Oscar Arias Sánchez was awarded the Nobel Peace Prize for negotiating a peace settlement in Central America in 1987, Costa Rica was able to claim credit for exporting a bit of its own political stability to the rest of Central America. For more than 100 years, Costa Rica has enjoyed a stable democracy and a relatively high standard of living for Latin America. The literacy rate is high, as are medical standards and facilities. Perhaps most significant, at least for proud Costa Ricans, this country does not have an army.

Costa Rica has become acutely aware of the riches it has to offer tourists, and as a result, the country is undergoing phenomenal tourist-related growth. This rapid growth is putting great strains on Costa Rica's natural resources and natural beauty. Though the nation has one of the world's best records in conservation, its forests are still being deforested at an alarming rate, and stretches of its coastline are being developed into massive mega-resorts with little regard for the impact such developments will have on the local environment or adjacent towns and villages. However, Costa Rica should remain for many years one of the more fascinating natural destinations in the Americas, largely due to the efforts being made by American and Costa Rican–based ecological organizations to keep it that way for as long as possible.

1 The Natural Environment

Costa Rica occupies a central spot in the land bridge that joins North and South America. For millennia this land bridge served as a migratory thoroughfare and mating ground for species native to the once separate continents. It was also the meeting place of Mesoamerican and Andean pre-Colombian indigenous cultures.

The country comprises only 0.01% of the earth's land mass, yet it is home to 5% of the planet's biodiversity. There are over 10,000 identified species of plants, 850 species of birds, 800 species of butterflies, and 500 species of mammals, reptiles, and amphibians combined here.

The key to this biological richness lies in the many distinct life-zones and ecosystems that can be found in Costa Rica. It may all seem like one big mass of green to the untrained eye, but the differences are profound.

In any one spot in Costa Rica, temperatures remain relatively constant year-round. However, they vary dramatically according to altitude, from uncomfortably hot and steamy along the coasts to below freezing at the highest elevations.

Costa Rica's lowland rain forests are true tropical jungles. Rainfall in them can be well over 200 inches per year, and their climate is hot and humid. Trees grow tall and fast, fighting for sunlight in the upper reaches. In fact, life and foliage on the forest floor is surprisingly sparse. The action is typically 100 feet above in the canopy, where long vines stream down, lianas climb up, and bromeliads grow on the branches and trunks of towering hardwood trees. You can find these lowland rain forests along the southern Pacific coast and Osa Peninsula, as well as along the Caribbean coast.

At higher altitudes you'll find Costa Rica's famed cloud forests. Here the steady flow of moist air meets the mountains and creates a nearly constant mist. Epiphytes, plants which live cooperatively on the branches and trunks of other trees, are both abundant and resourceful in cloud forests, where they must literally extract their moisture and nutrients from the air. Since cloud forests are found in generally steep, mountainous terrain, the canopy here is lower and less uniform than in lowland rain forests, providing better chances for viewing elusive fauna. Costa Rica's most spectacular cloud forest is in Guanacaste province: Monteverde Biological Cloud Forest Preserve.

At the highest reaches, the cloud forests give way to elfin forests and páramo. More commonly associated with the South American Andes, a páramo is characterized by a variety of tundra-like shrubs and grasses, with a scattering of twisted, windblown trees. Reptiles, rodents, and raptors are the most common residents here.

In a few protected areas of Guanacaste, you will still find examples of the otherwise vanishing tropical dry forest. During the long and pronounced dry season (it lasts half the year, from November to March), no rain relieves the unabating heat. In an effort to conserve much-needed water, the trees drop their leaves but bloom in a riot of color: purple jacaranda, scarlet poró, and brilliant orange flame-of-the-forest are just a few examples. Then, during the rainy season, this deciduous forest is transformed into a lush and verdant landscape. Because the foliage is not so dense, the dry forests are also excellent places to view a variety of species of wildlife.

Along the coasts, primarily where river mouths meet the ocean, you will find extensive mangrove forests and swamps. Around these seemingly monotonous tangles of roots exists one of the most diverse and rich ecosystems in the country. All sorts of fish and crustaceans live in the brackish tidal waters. Caiman and crocodiles cruise

Air Plants

Long before Michael Jordan ever won a slam dunk contest, epiphytes were dazzling biologists and rain forest trekkers with their acrobatic flights of fancy, far above the forest floor. For this reason, epiphytes, which set no roots in solid ground, have been dubbed *air plants*. Unlike parasites, epiphytes coexist with—but do not kill—their hosts. Epiphytes grow on trees in temperate northern rain forests, such as the Olympic peninsula in Washington state, and tropical rain forests, such as Monteverde, Corcovado, and Braulio Carrillo National Park in Costa Rica. They reach their greatest heights in lowland tropical rain forests and middle-elevation cloud forests, where up to one quarter of all plant species in any given area may be epiphytes. Just look up, you can't miss them.

The diversity of epiphytic plants is immense. There are mosses, ferns, lichen, cacti, orchids, and grand bromeliads with sharp, radiant leaves. Since their roots cannot burrow into the earth in search of water and nutrients, epiphytes have developed a series of complex processes to meet their needs. Some, by trapping particles of organic matter in the rich canopy environment, create their own miniature patches of soil or mats on tree branches. Others, like bromeliads, have leaf structures that fan out to collect and store water in natural cisterns. Many of these cisterns are used by other forest species as homes, drinking sources, and nesting sites.

the maze of rivers and unmarked canals, and hundreds of herons and marsh birds nest and feed along the silty banks. Mangrove swamps are often havens for waterbirds—cormorants, frigate birds, pelicans, and herons. The larger birds tend to nest up high in the canopy, while the smaller ones nestle in the underbrush. The gulf of Nicoya is a particularly popular among frigate birds, whose nests sometimes rise as high as 10 feet over the mudflats.

Over the last few years, Costa Rica has taken great strides toward protecting its rich biodiversity. Whereas 30 years ago it was difficult to find a protected area anywhere, now over 11% of the country is protected within the national park system. Another 10–15% of the land enjoys effective preservation as part of private and public reserves, Indian reserves, and wildlife refuges and corridors. Still, Costa Rica's precious tropical hardwoods continue to be harvested at an alarming rate—often illegally—while other primary forests are clear-cut for short-term agricultural gain. Many experts predict that Costa Rica's unprotected forests will be gone by the early part of the 21st century.

This is also a land of high volcanic and seismic activity. There are three major volcanic mountain ranges in Costa Rica, and many of the volcanoes are still active, allowing visitors to experience the awe-inspiring sight of steaming fumaroles and intense lava flows during their stay. Two volcanoes near the capital—Poas and Irazu—are currently active, although relatively quiet. The best places to see volcanic activity are farther north in Rincón de la Vieja National Park and at Arenal Volcano.

Costa Rica's last major earthquake shook the city of Límon on April 22, 1991. Tremors and aftershocks were felt as far away as San José. It's unlikely you will experience a major quake during your visit, but small tremors are relatively common. The first rule of thumb in an earthquake is not to panic. The best place to stand is underneath a doorway—if you can get there in time. (Most tremors will have already come and gone by the time you can get yourself into position.)

Costa Rica

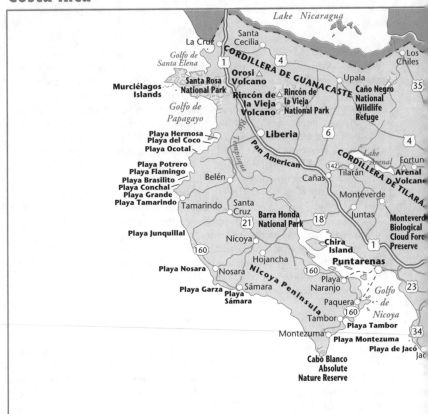

Lake Nicaragua

La Cruz
Santa Cecilia
Golfo de Santa Elena
CORDILLERA DE GUANACASTE
Orosi Volcano
Upala
Los Chiles
35
Murciélagos Islands
Santa Rosa National Park
Rincón de la Vieja Volcano
Rincón de la Vieja National Park
Caño Negro National Wildlife Refuge
Golfo de Papagayo
Playa Hermosa
Playa del Coco
Playa Ocotal
Liberia
6
CORDILLERA DE TILARÁN
Lake Arenal
Fortun
4
Playa Potrero
Playa Flamingo
Playa Brasilito
Playa Conchal
Playa Grande
Playa Tamarindo
Belén
Pan American
142
Tilarán
Arenal Volcano
Cañas
Monteverde
Tamarindo
Santa Cruz
Juntas
Monteverde Biological Cloud Fore Preserve
Barra Honda National Park
21
18
1
Playa Junquillal
Nicoya
Chira Island
160
Puntarenas
Hojancha
160
Playa Naranjo
23
Playa Nosara
Nosara
Golfo de Nicoya
Playa Garza
Sámara
Paquera
Playa Sámara
Nicoya Peninsula
160
Tambor
Playa Tambor
34
Montezuma
Playa Montezuma
Playa de Jacó
Cabo Blanco Absolute Nature Reserve
Jac

Pacific

Coco Island

Ocean

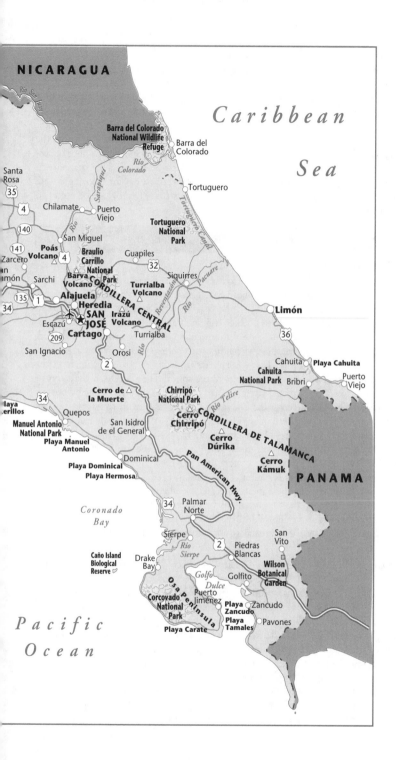

NICARAGUA

Caribbean

Sea

Santa
Rosa
(35)

Barra del Colorado
National Wildlife
Refuge

Barra del
Colorado

Río
Colorado

Tortuguero

(4) Chilamate

Puerto
Viejo

Tortuguero
National
Park

(140)

San Miguel

(141) Poás
Volcano

Braulio
Carrillo

Guapiles

Zarcero

Barva
Volcano

National
Park

(32)

an
món

Sarchi

Siquirres

(135) (1)

Alajuela

Turrialba
Volcano

(34)

HEREDIA

Irazú
Volcano

Limón

Escazú

SAN
JOSÉ

(209)

Cartago

Turrialba

(36)

San Ignacio

Orosi

Cahuita

Playa Cahuita

(2)

Cahuita
National Park

Bribri

Puerto
Viejo

Cerro de
la Muerte

Chirripó
National Park

laya
erillos

(34)

Quepos

Cerro
Chirripó

CORDILLERA DE TALAMANCA

Manuel Antonio
National Park

San Isidro
de el General

Cerro
Dúrika

Playa Manuel
Antonio

Cerro
Kámuk

PANAMA

Dominical

Playa Dominical

Pan American Hwy.

Playa Hermosa

Coronado
Bay

(34)

Palmar
Norte

Caño Island
Biological
Reserve

Sierpe

Río
Sierpe

Drake
Bay

(2)

Piedras
Blancas

San
Vito

Wilson
Botanical
Garden

Golfo
Dulce

Golfito

Corcovado
National
Park

Osa Peninsula

Puerto
Jiménez

Playa
Zancudo

Zancudo

Playa
Tamales

Pavones

Playa Carate

Pacific

Ocean

19

ENJOYING COSTA RICA'S BIOLOGICAL DIVERSITY

It's hard not to enjoy Costa Rica's varied natural landscape, but keeping a few pointers in mind can make your visit even more pleasurable.

Remember, animals in the forests are predominantly nocturnal. When they are active in the daytime, they are usually elusive and on the watch for predators. Although the idea of visiting a rain forest may seem like the ultimate tropical fantasy, in reality rain forests are so dense and dark that it's extremely hard for the casual visitor to pick anything out. Birds are much easier to spot in clearings or secondary forests than they are in primary forests. Unless you have lots of experience in the tropics, a trained and knowledgeable guide is your best bet for enjoying a walk through the jungle, and a good pair of rubber boots (usually provided on a guided tour) is essential.

2 The Land & Its People

REGIONS IN BRIEF

Costa Rica rightfully should be called Costas Ricas since it has two coasts, one on the Pacific Ocean and one on the Caribbean Sea. These two coasts are as different from one another as are the Atlantic and Pacific coasts of North America. The Pacific coast, which can be divided into three distinct regions (Guanacaste and the Nicoya Peninsula, the Central coast, and the Southern coast), is characterized by a rugged, though mostly accessible, coastline where mountains often meet the sea to create spectacular stretches of coastline. This coast varies from the dry, sunny climate of the northwest to the hot, humid rain forests of the south. The Caribbean coast can be divided into two roughly equal stretches, half of which is only accessible by boat or small plane. This remote coastline is a vast flat plane laced with rivers and covered with rain forest. Farther south, along the stretch of coast accessible by car, there are uncrowded beaches and even a bit of coral reef.

Bordered by Nicaragua in the north and Panama in the southeast, Costa Rica (19,530 square miles) is only slightly larger than Vermont and New Hampshire combined. Much of the country is mountainous, with three major ranges running northwest to southeast. Among these mountains are several volcanic peaks, some of which are still active. Between the mountain ranges are fertile valleys, the largest and most populated of which is the Central Valley. With the exception of the dry Guanacaste region, much of Costa Rica's coastal area is hot and humid and covered with dense rain forests.

The Central Valley   The Central Valley is characterized by rolling green hills between 3,000 and 4,000 feet above sea level, where the climate is mild and springlike year-round. It is Costa Rica's primary agricultural region, with coffee farms making up the majority of landholdings. The rich volcanic soil of this region makes it ideal for growing almost anything. The country's earliest settlements were in this area, and today the Central Valley is a densely populated area laced with good roads and dotted with small towns. Surrounding the Central Valley are high mountains, among which are four volcanic peaks. Two of these, Poás and Irazú, are still active and have caused extensive damage during cycles of activity in the past two centuries. Many of the mountainous regions to the north and to the south of the capital of San José have been declared national parks to protect their virgin rain forests from logging. Here you can enjoy the unusual experience of exploring a high-altitude cloud forest, usually shrouded in mist.

❓ Did You Know?

- Costa Rica has the oldest democracy in Central America.
- San José, the capital, is farther south than Caracas, Venezuela.
- Costa Rica has no army, navy, air force, or marine corps.
- Costa Rica has 10% of the butterflies in the world and more than the entire African continent, as well as more than 1,200 varieties of orchids and more than 850 species of birds.
- Isla del Coco, the largest uninhabited island in the world, is part of Costa Rica.
- On a clear day, you can see both the Caribbean Sea and the Pacific Ocean from the top of Costa Rica's Mount Chirripó.
- During an arribada more than 15,000 sea turtles may nest on the same beach over a period of only a few nights.
- In the rain forests of the Osa Peninsula it sometimes rains as much as 200 inches per year.

Guanacaste and the Nicoya Peninsula   With about 65 inches of rain a year, this region is by far the driest in the country and has been likened to west Texas. Guanacaste province sits at the border of Nicaragua and the Pacific Ocean and is named after the shady trees that still shelter the herds of cattle that roam the dusty savannah here. In addition to cattle ranches, Guanacaste boasts semiactive volcanos, several lakes, and one of the last remnants of tropical dry forest left in Central America (dry forest once stretched all the way from Costa Rica to the Mexican state of Chiapas).

This area is the site of many of Costa Rica's sunniest and most popular beaches. Because many Americans have chosen to build beach houses and retirement homes here, Guanacaste in particular is experiencing quite a bit of new development. While Cancun-style high-rise hotels are far from the norm, condos, luxury resorts, and golf courses are springing up with alacrity.

The Northern Zone   This region lies to the north of San José and includes rain forests, cloud forests, the country's two most active volcanos (Arenal and Rincón de la Vieja), Braulio Carrillo National Park, and numerous remote lodges. Because this is one of the few regions of Costa Rica without any beaches, it primarily attracts people interested in nature and active sports. Arenal Lake boasts some of the best windsurfing in the world, and several good mountain biking trails thread along its shores.

The Central Pacific Coast   The central Pacific coast is the most easily accessible coastline in Costa Rica and consequently boasts the greatest number of beach resorts and hotels. Playa de Jacó is primarily a charter company destination attracting Canadian and German tourists, while Manuel Antonio caters to people seeking a bit more tranquillity and beauty. This region is also the site of the highest peak in Costa Rica—Mount Chirripó—where frost is common.

The Caribbean Coast   Most of the Caribbean coast is a wide, steamy lowland laced with rivers and blanketed with rain forests and banana plantations. The culture here is predominantly black, with many residents speaking English or Caribbean patois. The northern section of this coast is accessible only by boat or small plane and is the site of Tortuguero National Park, which is known for its nesting sea turtles and river-boat trips. The southern half of the Caribbean coast has several beautiful beaches and, as yet, has few large hotels.

The South Pacific Coast   This is one of Costa Rica's most remote and undeveloped regions. Much of the area is protected in Corcovado and La Amistad national parks. This is a hot, humid region characterized by dense rain forests and rugged coastlines.

THE COSTA RICAN PEOPLE

Costa Rica has a population of just under three million, over half of whom live in the Central Valley and are classified as urban. The people are ethnically the most homogeneous of Central America: nearly 96% of the population is of European or Spanish descent, and it is not at all surprising to see blond Costa Ricans. This is largely because the indigenous population in place when the first Spaniards arrived was small, and therefore soon reduced by wars and disease until they became a minority. There are still some remnant indigenous populations, primarily on reservations around the country, however. In addition, on the Caribbean coast there is a substantial population of English-speaking black Créoles who came over from the Antilles to work on the railroad and in the banana plantations.

In general Costa Ricans (who call themselves *Ticos,* a practice that stems from their tendency to add a diminutive, either "tico" or "ito," to the ends of words to connote familiarity or affection) are a friendly and outgoing people. They believe their country to be a classless society where anyone, through hard work and intelligence, can improve his or her lot in life, and while the average family is wealthy by Latin American standards, the median household income is only $3000 U.S. per year. Nonetheless, with high levels of literacy (93%) and education, it is not uncommon to find Costa Ricans who speak English.

In conversation and interaction with tourists, they are very open and helpful. In fact, one of my pet peeves is that Ticos try so hard to be accommodating that they frequently will make promises they can't keep or tell you what they think you want to hear—whether or not it is true—just to please you.

In a region plagued by internal strife and civil wars, Costa Ricans are proud of their peaceful history, political stability, and relatively high level of development. This however can also translate into arrogance and prejudice towards immigrants from neighboring countries, who make up a large percentage of the workforce on the banana and coffee plantations.

Roman Catholicism is the official religion of Costa Rica, although freedom to practice any religion is guaranteed by the country's constitution. Over 90% of the population defines itself as being Roman Catholic, yet there are small, but visible, evangelical Christian, Protestant, and Jewish communities. By and large, Ticos are relatively religious. While many city dwellers lead quite secular lives, those in small villages and towns attend mass regularly. Most Ticos have a fatalistic streak that causes them not to question the accepted order of things. This is best expressed by their saying "si Dios quiere," which translates as "if God wills." Time also has relative meaning to Ticos. While most tour companies and other establishments operate efficiently, don't expect punctuality.

3 Costa Rica Today

Modern Costa Rica is a nation of contrasts. On the one hand, it is the most technologically advanced and economically stable nation in Central America. Even the smallest towns have electricity, the water is safe to drink, and the phone system is

Impressions

We, the people of Costa Rica, believe that peace is much more than the absence of hostility among men and nations . . . To us peace is the only ideal that, once achieved, will give us the right to call ourselves . . . human beings.
    —Oscar Arias, Former Costa Rican President and Nobel Peace Prize Laureate

excellent; there isn't a huge gulf between rich and poor; and politically, the nation possesses the most stable democracy in Central America. Since Costa Rica received independence from Spain in 1821, only a handful of its presidents have come from the military (which was disbanded completely in 1948), and it has had even fewer leaders who could be called dictators. (The country's most recent elections in 1990 were so peaceful that crowd control at some polling places was handled by school-children.)

On the other hand, Costa Rica finds itself mired in economic crisis. The country's per-capita debt ranks among the world's worst. Four years ago, inflation reached a high point of 25%. In an attempt to come to terms with decades of trade deficits and pay back its debt, a more austere economic course has been taken, causing the country's vast network of social services, as well as its health care system and its educational institutions, to be overburdened and underfunded. Goaded by the World Bank and the International Monetary Fund, recent administrations have begun the process of privatizing state institutions in order to raise funds and reduce bureaucracy. This, however, has led to increased unemployment, lower wages, and more expensive goods and services.

Tourism has surpassed cattle ranching and coffee and banana exports to the point of becoming the nation's top source of income. Now Ticos whose fathers and grandfathers were farmers find themselves hotel owners, tour guides, and waiters. While most have adapted gracefully and regard the industry favorably as a source for new jobs and opportunities for economic advancement, restaurant and hotel staff can seem gruff or disinterested at times, especially in rural areas. And, unfortunately, with greater numbers of tourists have also come increases in crime, prostitution, and drug trafficking.

Common sense and street savvy are required in San José and Limón, and it never hurts to be cautious and alert wherever you travel in the country, but only if you're reckless are you likely to have trouble.

4 A Look at the Past

EARLY HISTORY

Little is known of Costa Rica's history prior to its colonization by Spanish settlers. The pre-Columbian Indians who made their home in this region of Central America never developed the large cities or advanced culture that flowered farther north in what would become Guatemala, Belize, and Mexico. However, from scattered excavations around the country, primarily in the northwest, ancient artifacts have been unearthed that indicate a strong sense of aesthetics. Beautiful gold and jade jewelry, intricately carved grinding stones, and artistically painted terra-cotta

Dateline

- **13,000 B.C.** Earliest record of human inhabitants in Costa Rica.
- **1,000 B.C.** Olmec people from Mexico arrive in Costa Rica searching for rare blue jade.
- **1,000 B.C.–A.D. 1400** City of Guayabo is inhabited by as many as 10,000 people.

continues

- **1502** Columbus discovers Costa Rica in September, landing at what is now Limón.
- **1519–1561** Spanish explore and colonize Costa Rica.
- **1563** City of Cartago is founded in Central Valley.
- **1737** San José is founded.
- **Late 1700s** Coffee is introduced as a cash crop.
- **1821** On September 15, Costa Rica, with the rest of Central America, gains independence from Spain.
- San José is named the capital.
- **1848** Costa Rica is proclaimed an independent republic.
- **1856** Battle of Santa Rosa: Costa Ricans defeat the United States, who backed proslavery advocate William Walker.
- **1870s** First banana plantations are formed.
- **1889** First election is won by an opposition party, establishing democratic process in Costa Rica.
- **1899** The United Fruit Company is founded by railroad builder Minor Keith.
- **1948** After aborted revolution, Costa Rican army is abolished.
- **1987** President Oscar Arias Sánchez is awarded the Nobel Peace Prize for orchestrating the Central American Peace Plan.
- **1994** President Rafael Angel Calderón hands over the reigns of government to José María Figueres, in a peaceful replay of their fathers' less amenable and democratic transfer of power in 1948.

ware point toward a highly skilled, if not large, population. The most enigmatic of these ancient relics are carved stone balls, some measuring several yards across and weighing many tons, that have been found along the southern Pacific coast. The purpose of these stone spheres remains a mystery: Some archeologists say that they may have been boundary markers; others think that they were celestial references. Still other scientists now claim that they are not manmade at all, but rather natural geological formations.

In 1502, on his fourth and last voyage to the New World, Christopher Columbus anchored just offshore from present-day Limón. Whether it was he who gave the country its name is open to discussion, but it was not long before the inappropriate name took hold. The earliest Spanish settlers found that, unlike the Indians farther north, the native population of Costa Rica was unwilling to submit to slavery. Despite their small numbers, scattered villages, and tribal differences, they fought back against the Spanish. However, the superior Spanish firepower and the European diseases that had helped to subjugate the populations farther north conquered the natives. But when the fighting was finished, the settlers in Costa Rica found that there were very few Indians left to force into servitude. The settlers were forced to till their own lands, an exercise unheard of in other parts of Central America. Few pioneers headed this way because they could settle in Guatemala, where there was a large native work force. Costa Rica was nearly forgotten, as the Spanish crown looked elsewhere for riches to plunder and souls to convert.

It didn't take long for Costa Rica's few Spanish settlers to head for the hills, where they found rich volcanic soil and a climate that was less oppressive than in the lowlands. Cartago, the colony's first capital, was founded in 1563, but it would not be until the 1700s that more cities were founded in this agriculturally rich region. In the late 18th century, the first coffee plants were introduced, and because these plants thrived in the highlands, Costa Rica began to develop its first cash crop. Unfortunately, it was a long and difficult journey transporting the coffee to the Caribbean coast and then to Europe, where the demand for coffee was growing.

FROM INDEPENDENCE TO THE PRESENT

In 1821, Spain granted independence to its colonies in Central America. Costa Rica joined with its neighbors to form the Central American Federation, but in 1838 it withdrew to form a new nation and pursue its own interests, which differed considerably from those of the other Central American nations. By the mid-1800s, coffee was the country's main export. Land was given free to anyone willing to plant coffee on it, and plantation owners soon grew wealthy and powerful, creating Costa Rica's first elite class. Coffee plantation owners were powerful enough to elect their own representatives to the presidency.

This was a stormy period in Costa Rican history, and in 1856 the country was invaded by William Walker, a soldier of fortune from Tennessee who had grandiose dreams of presiding over a slavery state in Central America. Prior to his invasion of Costa Rica, he had invaded Baja, California and Nicaragua. The people of Central America were outraged by the actions of this man, who had backing from U.S. president James Buchanan. The people of Costa Rica, led by their own president, Juan Rafael Mora, marched against Walker and chased him back to Nicaragua. Walker eventually surrendered to a U.S. warship in 1857, but in 1860 he attacked Honduras, claiming to be the president of that country. The Hondurans, who had had enough of Walker's shenanigans, promptly executed him.

Until 1890, coffee growers had to transport their coffee either by ox cart to the Pacific port of Puntarenas, or by boat down the Río Sarapiquí to the Caribbean. In the 1870s, a progressive president proposed a railway from San José to the Caribbean coast to facilitate the transport of coffee to European markets. It took nearly 20 years for this plan to reach fruition, and more than 4,000 workers lost their lives constructing the railway, which passed through dense jungles and rugged mountains on its journey from the Central Valley to the coast. Partway through the project, as funds were dwindling, the second chief engineer, Minor Keith, proposed an idea that not only enhanced his fortunes, but changed the course of Central American history. Banana plantations would be developed along the railway right-of-way (land on either side of the tracks). The export of this crop would help to finance the railway, and in exchange Keith would get a 99-year lease on 800,000 acres of land with a 20-year tax deferment. The Costa Rican government gave its consent, and in 1878 the first bananas were shipped from the country. In 1899 Keith and a partner formed the United Fruit Company, a business that would eventually become the largest landholder in Central America and cause political disputes and wars throughout the region.

In 1889 Costa Rica held what is considered the first free election in Central American history. The opposition candidate won the election, and the control of the government passed from the hands of one political party to those of another without bloodshed or hostilities. Thus Costa Rica established itself as the region's only true democracy. In 1948 this democratic process was challenged by a former president (from 1940 to 1944), Rafael Angel Calderón, who lost a bid at a second term in office by a narrow margin. Calderón, who had the backing of Communist labor unions and the Catholic church, refused to yield the country's leadership to the rightfully elected president, Otillio Ulate, and a revolution ensued. Calderón was eventually defeated by José "Pepe" Figueres. In the wake of this crisis, a new constitution was drafted; among other changes, it abolished Costa Rica's army so that such a revolution could never happen again.

Peace and democracy have become of tantamount importance to Costa Ricans since the revolution of 1948. When Oscar Arias Sánchez was elected president in 1986, his main goal was to seek a solution to the ongoing war in Nicaragua, and one of his first actions was to close down Contra bases inside Costa Rica and enforce Costa Rica's position of neutrality. In 1987 Sánchez won the Nobel Peace Prize for initiating a Central American peace plan aimed at settling the war in Nicaragua.

In 1994, history seemed to repeat itself—peacefully this time—when José Maria Figueres took the reigns of government from another son of a former president, Rafael Angel Calderón.

Costa Rica's 100 years of nearly uninterrupted democracy have helped make it the most stable economy in Central America. This stability and adherence to the democratic process are a source of great pride to Costa Ricans. They like to think of their country as the "Switzerland of Central America," not only because of its herds of dairy cows but also because of its staunch position of neutrality in a region that has been torn by nearly constant civil wars and revolutions for more than 200 years.

5 Gallo Pinto, Ceviche & Frescos: Costa Rican Food & Drink

Very similar to other Central American cuisines, Costa Rican food is not especially memorable. Perhaps that's why there's so much international food available throughout the country. However, if you really want to save money, you'll find that Costa Rican food is always the cheapest food available. It is primarily served in *sodas*, Costa Rica's equivalent of diners.

MEALS & DINING CUSTOMS

Rice and beans are the basis of Costa Rican meals. Mixed together and generally served at breakfast, they're called *gallo pinto* and come with everything from eggs to steak to seafood. At lunch or dinner, rice and beans are an integral part of a *casado* (which also means "married"). A casado usually comes with cabbage-and-tomato salad, fried plantains (a type of banana), and a meat dish of some sort.

Dining hours in Costa Rica are flexible: Some downtown restaurants in San José are open 24 hours, a sign that Ticos are willing to eat at any time of the night or day. However, expensive restaurants tend to open for lunch between 11am and 2pm and for dinner between 6 and 11pm.

Appetizers   *Bocas* are served with drinks in most bars. Often the bocas are free, but even if they aren't, they're very inexpensive. Popular bocas include gallos (stuffed tortillas), ceviche (a marinated seafood salad), and tamales.

Soups   Black-bean soup, *sopa negra*, is a watery soup served with a poached or boiled egg on top. It's one of Costa Rica's most popular soups and is showing up on many menus. *Olla de carne* is a delicious soup made with large chunks of beef and several local vegetables, including chayote, ayote, yuca, and plantains, all of which have textures and flavors similar to various winter squashes. *Sopa de mondongo* is made with tripe, the stomach of a cow, which some love and others find disgusting. *Picadillos* are vegetable purées made of potato, chayote, or plantains with a little bit of meat. They are often served as a side dish with a casado, or as bocas.

Sandwiches & Snacks   Ticos love to snack, and there are a large variety of tasty little sandwiches and snacks available on the street, at snack bars, and in sodas. *Arreglados* are little meat-filled sandwiches, as are *tortas*, which are served on little rolls with a bit of salad tucked into them. *Gallos* are tortillas piled with meat, beans, or cheese. Tacos, tamales, and empanadas also are quite common.

Meat   Costa Rica is beef country, one of the tropical nations that has converted much of its rain-forest land to pastures for raising beef cattle. Consequently, beef is cheap and plentiful, although it may be a bit tougher than you are used to. Spit-roasted chicken is also very popular here, and is surprisingly tender.

Seafood   Costa Rica has two coasts, and as you would expect, there is plenty of seafood available everywhere in the country. Corvina (sea bass) is the most commonly served fish, and it is prepared innumerable ways, including as ceviche, a sort of

A Glossary of Spanish & Costa Rican Terms

An ability to speak Spanish is by no means a prerequisite for visiting Costa Rica—many folks get by just fine without it, especially if they stick to the well-worn tourist path, where there's almost always someone who understands and speaks English. Nevertheless, even the most basic stabs at Spanish will be greatly appreciated by Costa Ricans and will open doors for you. Perhaps your two most important phrases will be *por favor* and *gracias*—please and thank you. Beyond that, a few more essential phrases appear below.

¿ Donde esta _____?	Where is _____?
¿ Qué hora es?	What time is it?
Por favor, ponga la maria.	Please turn on the (taxi) meter.
¿ Me puede traer un vaso de agua?	Would you bring me a glass of water?
¿ Cuanto cuesta este chunche?	How much is this knicknack?

In addition to the above phrases, there are a few particular words and expressions that are typically Costa Rican, such as *gallo pinto* (a mixture of rice and beans, usually served at breakfast with eggs or meat). A partial list follows.

bocas	Appetizers
casado	Lunch or dinner meal consisting of rice, beans, a main dish, salad, and fried plantains
ceviche	Marinated seafood salad
chunche	Knicknack; thing; as in "whatchamacallit"
con mucho gusto	"With pleasure." You'll hear this from waiters, hotel staff, taxi drivers, and strangers on the street
corvina	Sea bass
frescos	Water- or milk-based drinks made in a blender with fresh fruit
horchata	Fresco made with rice flour and cinnamon
mae	Translates a lot like "man"; used by teenagers as constant verbal punctuation
plátanos	Plantains; similar to bananas
pura vida	Literally "pure life," a Tico phrase for "everything's great"
rancho/ranchito	An open-air structure, usually round, with a high, thatched roof; houses a restaurant or bar at many Pacific coast hotels and inns
si Dios quiere . . .	"God willing." You'll hear Ticos say this at nearly every opportunity, a reflection of their Catholic roots
tortas	Small sandwiches
tuanis	Means the same as *pura vida* above, but used by a younger crowd

marinated salad. Be careful: In many cheaper restaurants, particularly in San José, shark meat is often sold as corvina. Surprisingly, although Costa Rica is a major exporter of shrimp and lobster, both are very expensive here. In fact, shrimp is often more expensive than lobster. The reason is that most of the shrimp and lobster are exported, causing them to be very expensive at home.

Vegetables   On the whole, you will find vegetables surprisingly lacking in the meals you are served in Costa Rica. The standard vegetable with any meal is a little pile of shredded cabbage topped with a slice or two of tomato. For a much more satisfying and filling salad, order *palmito* (hearts of palm salad). Hearts of palm are considered a delicacy in most places, because an entire palm tree (albeit a small one) must be cut down to extract the heart. The heart is a bit like the inner part of an artichoke—many leaves layered around one another. These leaves are chopped into large pieces and served with other fresh vegetables, and a salad dressing on top. Even here, where the palms are plentiful, palmito is relatively expensive. If you want something more than this, you'll have to order a side dish such as *picadillo*, a stew or purée of vegetables with a bit of meat in it. Most people have a hard time thinking of *plátanos* (plantains) as vegetables, but these giant relatives of bananas require cooking before they can be eaten. Green plantains have a very starchy flavor and consistency, but become as sweet as candy as they ripen. Fried plátanos are one of my favorite dishes. *Yuca* (manioc root) is another starchy staple vegetable of Costa Rica.

One more vegetable worth mentioning is the *pejibaye*, a form of palm fruit that looks like a miniature orange coconut. Boiled pejibayes are frequently sold from carts on the streets of San José. When cut in half, a pejibaye reveals a large seed surrounded by soft, creamy flesh and looks a bit like an avocado. You can eat it like an avocado, too, by just scooping the flesh out.

Fruits   Costa Rica has a wealth of delicious tropical fruits. The most common are mangoes (the season begins in May), papayas, pineapples, and bananas. Other less well-known fruits include the *marañon*, which is the fruit of the cashew tree and has orange or yellow glossy skin; the *granadilla* or *granada* (passion fruit); the *mamón chino,* which Asian travelers will immediately recognize as the rambutan; and the *carambola* (star fruit). When ordering *ensalada de fruita* (fruit salad) in a restaurant, make sure that it is made with fresh fruit and does not come with ice cream and Jell-O (unless that is what you want). What a shock I had when I first received a bowl of canned fruit covered with Jell-O cubes and three scoops of ice cream!

Desserts   *Queque seco*, which literally translates as "dry cake," is the same as pound cake. *Tres leches* cake on the other hand is so moist you almost need to eat it with a spoon. *Flan de coco* is a sweet coconut flan. There are many other sweets available, many of which are made with condensed milk and raw sugar (rich and sweet).

BEVERAGES

Frescos, a bit like milkshakes, are my favorite drinks in Costa Rica. They are usually made with fresh fruit and milk or water. Among the more common fruits used are mangoes, papayas, blackberries (*moras*), and pineapples. You will also come across *maracuya* (a type of passion fruit) and *carambola* (star fruit). Some of the more unusual frescos are *horchata* (made with rice flour and a lot of cinnamon) and *chan* (made with the seed of a plant found mostly in Guanacaste—definitely an acquired taste). The former is wonderful; the latter requires an open mind (it's reputed to be good for the digestive system). Order *un fresco de leche sin hielo* if you are trying to avoid untreated water.

Water & Soft Drinks   Although water in most of Costa Rica is said to be safe to drink, visitors often become ill shortly after arriving in Costa Rica. Play it safe, and stick to bottled water, which is readily available. *Aqua mineral,* or simply *soda,* is sparkling water in Costa Rica. It's inexpensive and refreshing. Most major brands of soft drinks are also available.

Beer, Wine & Liquor   The German presence in Costa Rica over the years has produced several fine beers, which are fairly inexpensive. Licensed local versions of Heineken and Rock Ice are also available. Costa Rica distills a wide variety of liquors, and you'll save money by ordering these rather than imported brands. Imported wines are available at reasonable prices in the better restaurants throughout the country. You can save money by ordering a South American wine rather than a Californian or European one. Café Rica and Salicsa are two coffee liqueurs made in Costa Rica; the former is very similar to Kahlua, and the latter is a cream coffee liqueur. Both are delicious.

6 Recommended Books

Some of the books mentioned below may be difficult to track down in U.S. bookstores, but you'll find them all in abundance in Costa Rica's bookstores. Buy them during your trip to deepen your Costa Rica experience, or bring them home with you to illuminate your memories.

GENERAL   *The Costa Ricans* (Prentice Hall Press, 1987), by Richard, Karen, and Mavis Biesanz, is a well-written account of the politics and culture of Costa Rica.

To learn more about the life and culture of Costa Rica's Talamanca Coast, an area populated by Afro-Caribbean people whose forebears immigrated from Caribbean islands in the early 19th century, pick up a copy of *What Happen: A Folk-History of Costa Rica's Talamanca Coast* (Publications in English, 1993) by Paula Palmer. Or, for a look at the perspective of the indigenous people of the Talamanca region, read Palmer, Sanchez, and Mayorga's *Taking Care of Sibö's Gifts: An Environmental Treatise from Costa Rica's KéköLdi Indigenous Reserve* (Editorama, 1991).

The Costa Rica Reader (Grove Press, 1989), edited by Marc Edelman and Joanne Kenen, is a collection of essays on Costa Rican topics. For insight into Costa Rican politics, economics, and culture, this weighty book is invaluable. *Costa Rica: A Traveler's Literary Companion* (Whereabouts Press, 1994), edited by Barbara Ras and with a forward by Oscar Arias Sánchez, is a collection of short stories by Costa Rican writers, organized by region of the country.

NATURAL HISTORY   *Costa Rica National Parks* (Editorial Heliconia, Fundacion Neotropica, 1988), by Mario A. Boza, is published in Madrid and is available in both hardbound and softcover editions. It is a beautiful picture book of Costa Rica's national parks. Each of the country's national parks is represented by several color photos and a short description of the park in Spanish and English. *Costa Rica's National Parks and Preserves* (The Mountaineers, 1993), by Joseph Franke, is similar but with fewer photos. *The Illustrated Geography of Costa Rica* (Trejos Hermanos, 1991) is also a hardcover book full of wonderful photos and makes a good memento of your trip.

Dr. Donald Perry's fascinating *Life Above the Jungle Floor* (Simon & Schuster, 1986) is an account of Perry's research into the life of the tropical rain-forest canopy. Perry is well known for the cable-car network he built through the rain-forest treetops at Rara Avis, as well as the new commercial Aerial Tram.

Lessons of the Rainforest (Sierra, 1990), edited by Suzanne Head and Robert Heinzman, is a collection of essays by leading authorities in the fields of biology, ecology, history, law, and economics who look at the issues surrounding tropical deforestation. *A Guide to the Birds of Costa Rica* (Cornell University Press, 1989), by F. Gary Stiles and Alexander Skutch, is an invaluable guide to identifying the many birds you'll see during your stay. It is often available for examination at nature lodges.

Other interesting natural-history books that will give you a look at the plants and animals of Costa Rica include *Sarapiquí Chronicle* (Smithsonian Institution Press, 1991) by Allen Young; *Costa Rica Natural History* (University of Chicago Press, 1983) by Daniel Janzen; *Butterflies of Costa Rica* (Princeton University Press, 1987) by Philip DeVries; *A Neotropical Companion* (Princeton University Press, 1989) by John C. Kricher; and *Tropical Nature* (Scribner's & Sons, 1984) by Adrian Forsyth and Ken Miyata.

3

Planning a Trip to Costa Rica

Costa Rica is one of the fastest-growing tourist destinations in the Americas, and as the number of people visiting Costa Rica increases, so does the need for pretrip planning. When is the best time to go to Costa Rica? The cheapest time? Should I rent a car and what will it cost? Where should I go in Costa Rica? What are the hotels like? How much should I budget for my trip? These are just a few of the important questions that this chapter will answer for you so you can be prepared when you arrive in Costa Rica.

1 Visitor Information and Entry Requirements

VISITOR INFORMATION

In the United States, you can get information on Costa Rica by contacting the **Costa Rica Brochure Service** (☎ 800/327-7033), a representative of the **Costa Rican Tourist Board (ICT, or Instituto Costarricense de Turismo)** in the United States.

If you have a computer and access to the World Wide Web, you will be able to find a wealth of information on Costa Rica just by sitting at your terminal. You can run a specific search, or try one of these Web sites: **Costa Rica Homepage** (http://www.cr); **Costa Rica's TravelWeb** (http://www.magi.com/crica); **Costa Rica's TravelNet** (http://www.catalog.com/calypso); or **Tico Net** (http://www.ticonet.co.cr).

ENTRY REQUIREMENTS

DOCUMENTS   Citizens of the United States, Canada, Great Britain, and most European nations may visit Costa Rica for a maximum of 90 days. No visa is necessary, but you must have a valid passport. Citizens of Australia and New Zealand can enter the country without a visa and stay for 30 days. Citizens of the Republic of Ireland need a visa, valid passport, and a round-trip ticket in order to enter.

If you overstay your visa or entry stamp, you will have to pay $45 for an exit visa and a nominal fee for each extra month you've stayed. If you need to get an exit visa, talk to a travel agent in San José. They can usually get the exit visa for you for a small fee and save you the hassle of dealing with Immigration yourself. If you want to stay longer than the validity of your entry stamp or visa, the easiest thing to do is cross the border into Panama or Nicaragua for 72 hours and then re-enter Costa Rica on a new entry stamp or visa. However, be careful. In late 1995 the Costa Rican government began cracking down on "perpetual tourists," and if they notice a continued pattern of exits and entries, they may deny you re-entry.

If you need a visa or have other questions about Costa Rica, you can contact any of the following Costa Rican embassies: in the **United States,** 2112 S. St. NW, Washington, DC 20008 (☎ 202/234-2945); in **Canada,** 135 York St., Suite 208, Ottowa, Ontario K1N 5T4 (☎ 613/562-2855); in **Great Britain,** 14 Lancaster Gate, London, England W2 3LH (☎ 71-706-8844). In the United States, Costa Rica also maintains consulates in Atlanta, New Orleans, Chicago, Denver, and Miami.

LOST DOCUMENTS   If you lose your passport or need special assistance once inside Costa Rica, contact your embassy, listed in "Fast Facts: Costa Rica," below.

Most embassies can replace your passport and help you get an exit visa in about 24 hours. If your embassy won't get your exit visa for you, see a local travel agent or **OTEC Viajes,** Edificio Ferencz, 2nd floor, Calle 3 between avenidas 1 and 3,275 meters north of the National Theater (☎ 506/256-0633). If you try to deal with Immigration yourself, you will face long lines, long waits, and endless frustration. Local travel agents and agencies regularly deal with Immigration and will charge you about $5 to $10 for the service (free if you ticket with them).

2 Money

CASH & CURRENCY

The unit of currency in Costa Rica is the colón (¢). In early 1996, there were approximately 198 colónes to the American dollar, but because the colón has been in a constant state of devaluation, expect this rate to have changed somewhat by the time you arrive. Because of this devaluation and accompanying inflation, this book lists prices in U.S. dollars only.

The colón is divided into 100 centimos. There are coins of 10, 25, and 50 centimos and 1, 2, 5, 10, and 20 colónes; however, because of their evaporating value, you will rarely see or have to handle centimos. There are paper notes in denominations of 50, 100, 500, 1,000, and 5,000 colónes. You might also encounter a special issue 5-colón bill that is a popular gift and tourist souvenir. It is valid currency, although it sells for much more than its face value. You may hear people refer to a *roja* or *toucan*, which are slang terms for the 1,000 and 5,000 colón bills respectively. One hundred colón denominations are called *tejas*, so *cinco tejas* would be 500 colónes.

In recent years forged bills have become increasingly common. When receiving change in colónes it is a good idea to check the larger denomination bills, which should have protective bands or hidden images that appear when held up to the light.

EXCHANGING MONEY

You can exchange money at state-owned banks and most hotels; however, the service at these banks is so slow and cumbersome that this simple transaction can take over an hour and cause unnecessary confusion and anxiety. I don't recommend it. Most hotels and some private banks provide faster service, but shave a few colónes off the exchange rate. Costa Rica recently passed a law opening up the state's banking system. Accordingly, by late 1996, private banks will be able to perform many of the functions previously reserved for state institutions, including exchanging money and cashing traveler's checks. It's expected that the level of service offered by all banks will improve dramatically as a result.

The Colón, the U.S. Dollar & the British Pound

In early 1996, there were approximately 198 colónes to the American dollar, or 299 colónes to the British pound. However, because the colón has been in a constant state of devaluation, expect this rate to have changed somewhat by the time you arrive. Because of this devaluation and the accompanying inflation, this book lists prices in U.S. dollars only.

Colónes	U.S.$	U.K.£
5	.025	0.017
10	.05	0.033
25	.126	0.084
50	.253	0.167
75	.379	0.25
100	.505	0.33
200	1.01	0.66
300	1.52	1.00
400	2.02	1.34
500	2.53	1.67
750	3.79	2.51
1,000	5.05	3.34
5,000	25.25	16.72
10,000	50.51	33.44
25,000	126.26	83.61
50,000	252.53	167.22
75,000	378.79	250.84
100,000	505.05	334.45
200,000	1,010.10	668.90
300,000	1,515.15	1,003.34
500,000	2,525.25	1,672.24
1,000,000	5,050.50	3,344.48

Be very careful about exchanging money on the streets; it is extremely risky. In addition to forged bills and short counts, street money changers frequently work in teams that can leave you holding neither colónes, nor dollars.

TRAVELER'S CHECKS

Traveler's checks can be readily cashed at hotels and banks. The exchange rate at banks is sometimes higher than at hotels, but it can take a very long time to cash a traveler's check or exchange money at a bank. If time is an issue, cash your traveler's checks at your hotel. Just be advised that the exchange rate you receive may not be as favorable.

CREDIT CARDS & ATMS

Major international credit cards accepted readily at hotels throughout Costa Rica include American Express, MasterCard, and Visa. The less expensive hotels tend to

What Things Cost in San José	U.S. $
Taxi from the airport to the city center	12.50
Local telephone call	.05
Double at Hotel Parque del Lago (expensive)	95.00
Double at Hotel Grano de Oro (moderate)	70.00
Double at Hotel Bienvenido (inexpensive)	19.00
Lunch for one at Café de Teatro Nacional (moderate)	9.50
Lunch for one at Soda La Central (inexpensive)	2.50
Dinner for one, without wine, at Bijahua (expensive)	17.50
Dinner for one, without wine, at La Cocina de Leña (moderate)	10.00
Dinner for one, without wine, at Restaurante Campesino (inexpensive)	5.20
Bottle of beer	.85
Coca-Cola	.85
Cup of coffee	.50
Roll of ASA 100 Kodacolor film, 24 exposures	6.85
Admission to the Jade Museum	Free
Admission to the Gold Museum	5.00
Movie ticket	2.50
Ticket at Teatro Melico Salazar	3.50–15.00

take cash only. Many restaurants and stores also accept credit cards. Before paying for a hotel with your credit card, check to see if the policy is to charge extra (from 5% to 10%) for credit card use.

I've heard it's possible to get cash from local ATM machines, but so far I've been unable to verify this rumor, so it's best to be prepared and come to Costa Rica with enough cash and traveler's checks. Banks can give you cash advances on your credit card, but expect to be assessed a service charge and spend a lot of time dealing with bureaucracy.

WIRING FUNDS

If you need cash in a hurry, **Western Union** (☎ 506/283-6336) is on Calle 9 between avenidas 2 and 4 in San José. Money can be electronically wired from any Western Union office in the United States to the central office listed above. The receiver can then call the central office and arrange to pick up the cash at any one of 30 Western Union offices in Costa Rica. The process doesn't come cheap, though. A $100 wire will cost $22, and a $1,000 wire will cost $99.

3 When to Go

Costa Rica's high season for tourism runs from late November to late April, which coincides almost perfectly with the northern winters and major holiday travel periods. It also coincides perfectly with the Costa Rican dry season. If you want some unadulterated time on a tropical beach and a little less rain during your rain forest experience, this is the time to come. During this period you will find tourism in full tilt—prices are higher, attractions are more crowded, and you will need to make reservations in advance.

In recent years local tourism operators have begun calling the tropical rainy season (from May through November) the "green season." The adjective is appropriate. At this time of year, even brown and barren Guanacaste province becomes lush and verdant. I love traveling around Costa Rica during the rainy season. It's easy to find and bargain for reduced rates, there are far fewer fellow tourists, and the rain is often limited to a few hours each afternoon.

CLIMATE

Costa Rica is a tropical country and has distinct wet and dry seasons. However, some regions are rainy all year and others are very dry and sunny for most of the year. Temperatures vary primarily with elevation, not with season. On the coasts it is hot all year, while up in the mountains, it can be cool at night any time of year. In the highest elevations (10,000 to 12,000 feet), frost is common.

Average Monthly Temperatures and Rainfall in San José

	Jan	Feb	Mar	Apr	May	June	July	Aug	Sept	Oct	Nov	Dec
Temp (°F)	66	66	69	71	71	71	70	70	71	69	68	67
Temp (°C)	19	19	20.5	21.5	21.5	21.5	21	21	21.5	20.5	20	19.5
Days of Rain	1	0	1	4	17	20	18	19	20	22	14	4

Generally speaking, the rainy season (or "green season") is from May to mid-November. Costa Ricans call this wet time of year their winter. The dry season, considered summer by Costa Ricans, is from mid-November through April. In Guanacaste, the dry northwestern province, the dry season lasts several weeks longer than in other places. Even in the rainy season, days often start sunny, with rain falling in the afternoon and evening. On the Caribbean coast, especially south of Limón, you can count on rain all year round, although this area gets less rain in September and October than the rest of the country. The best time of year to visit is in December and January, when everything is still green from the rains, but the sky is clear. However, advantages to traveling to Costa Rica in the rainy season are that prices are lower, the country is greener, and there are fewer tourists. Rain doesn't usually fall all day long, and when it does, it's a good opportunity to climb into a hammock and catch up on your reading.

HOLIDAYS

Because Costa Rica is a Roman Catholic country, most of its holidays and celebrations are church-related. The major celebrations of the year are Christmas, New Year, and Easter, which are all celebrated for several days. Keep in mind that Holy Week (Easter Week) is the biggest holiday time in Costa Rica and many families head for the beach (this is the last holiday before school starts). Also there is no public transportation on Holy Thursday or Good Friday. Government offices and banks are closed on official holidays, transportation services are reduced, and stores and markets may also close.

Official holidays in Costa Rica include: **January 1** (New Year's Day), **March 19** (St. Joseph's Day), **Thursday** and **Friday** of **Holy Week**, **April 11** (Juan Santamaría's Day), **May 1** (Labor Day), **June 29** (Saints Peter and Paul's Day), **July 25** (annexation of the province of Guanacaste), **August 2** (Virgin of Los Angeles's Day), **August 15** (Mother's Day), **September 15** (Independence Day), **October 12** (Discovery of America/Día de la Raza), **December 8** (Immaculate Conception of the Virgin Mary), **December 24** and **25** (Christmas), **December 31** (New Year's Eve).

COSTA RICA CALENDAR OF EVENTS

January

- **Fiesta of Santa Cruz,** Santa Cruz, Guanacaste. A religious celebration honoring the Black Christ of Esquipulas (a famous Guatemalan statue) that features folk dancing, marimba music, and bullfights. Mid-January.

February

- ✪ **Fiesta of the Diablitos,** Rey Curré village near San Isidro de El General. Boruca Indians wearing wooden devil and bull masks perform dances representative of the Spanish conquest of Central America; there are fireworks displays and an Indian handcrafts market. Date varies; call the Costa Rican Tourist Board (☎ 800/327-7033) for current dates.

March

- **Día del Boyero** (Ox Cart Drivers' Day), San Antonio de Escazú. Colorfully painted ox carts parade through this suburb of San José and local priests bless the oxen. Second Sunday.

April

- **Holy Week** (week before Easter). Religious processions are held in cities and towns throughout the country. Dates vary from year to year (between late March and early April).
- **Juan Santamaría Day,** Alajuela. Costa Rica's national hero is honored with parades, concerts, and dances. April 11.

May

- **Carrera de San Juan.** The country's biggest marathon runs through the mountains, from the outskirts of Cartago to the outskirts of San José. May 17.

July

- ✪ **Fiesta of the Virgin of the Sea,** Puntarenas. A regatta of colorfully decorated boats carrying a statue of Puntarenas's patron saint marks this festival. A similar event is held at Playa de Coco. Saturday closest to July 16.
- **Annexation of Guanacaste Day,** Liberia. Tico-style bullfights, folk dancing, horseback parades, rodeos, concerts, and other events celebrate the day when this region became part of Costa Rica. July 24.

August

- **Día de San Ramon,** San Ramon. More than two dozen statues of saints from various towns are brought to San Ramon where they are paraded through the streets. August 31.
- ✪ **Fiesta of the Virgin of Los Angeles,** Cartago. This is the annual pilgrimage day of the patron saint of Costa Rica. Many people walk from San José to the basilica in Cartago. August 2.

September

- **Costa Rica's Independence Day.** Celebrated all over the country. Most distinctive are the nighttime parades of children. September 15.

October

- **Fiesta del Maiz,** Upala. A celebration of corn with local beauty queens wearing outfits made from corn plants. October 12.
- ✪ **Limón Carnival/Día de la Raza,** Limón. A smaller version of Mardi Gras complete with floats and dancing in the streets. Commemorates Columbus's discovery of Costa Rica. Week of October 12.

December

❌ **Festejos Populares,** San José. Bullfights, a horseback parade (El Tope), a carnival with street dancing and floats, and an amusement park all take place at the fairgrounds in Zapote. On the night of December 31, there is a dance in the Parque Central. Last week of December.

- **Día de la Polvora,** San Antonio de Belen and Jesus Maria de San Mateo. Fireworks displays to honor Our Lady of the Immaculate Conception. December 8.
- **Fiesta de la Yeguita,** Nicoya. A statue of the Virgin of Guadalupe is paraded through the streets accompanied by traditional music and dancing. December 12.
- **Fiesta de los Negritos,** Boruca. Boruca Indians celebrate the feast day of their patron saint, the Virgin of the Immaculate Conception, with costumed dances and traditional music. December 8.
- **Las Posadas.** A country-wide celebration during which children and carolers go door-to-door seeking lodging in a re-enactment of Joseph and Mary's search for a place to stay. Begins December 15.

4 Spanish-Language Courses & Latin Dance Classes

Costa Rica offers numerous Spanish-language programs and Latin dancing schools. If you've already got some background in either of these areas, a week or two of classes will put some polish on your skills. It's a good idea to reserve your place in a Spanish class or program before you depart for Costa Rica, whereas dance classes can be arranged upon arrival. If you want to be fluent in Spanish and you've never studied the language, it's best to choose a month-long course with a homestay. Most schools are located in San José, but others have begun to pop up in more scenic spots.

SPANISH LANGUAGE PROGRAMS   As more and more people travel to Costa Rica with the intention of learning Spanish, the number of options increase. Courses are of varying lengths and intensiveness, and often include cultural activities and day excursions. Most Spanish schools can also arrange for homestays with a middle-class Tico family for a total immersion experience. Classes are intensive and often one-on-one. Listed below are some of the larger and more established Spanish-language schools, with approximate costs. Contact the schools for the most current price information.

   Central American Institute for International Affairs (ICAI), Apdo. 10302, San José, Costa Rica (☎ 506/233-8571; fax 506/221-5238), offers a four-week Spanish-language immersion program, along with a homestay, for $962. They also offer courses in Central American studies and other topics. In the United States, contact the Language Studies Enrollment Center, P.O. Box 5095, Anaheim, CA 92814 (☎ 714/527-2918; fax 714/826-8752).

   Centro Cultural Costarricense Norteamericano, Apdo. 14489-1000, San José, Costa Rica (☎ 506/225-9433; fax 506/224-1480), is an extension of the U.S. embassy and government programs in Costa Rica. Its facilities are the most extensive of any language school in the country. Classes cost $245 for a week (20 hours of instruction). Homestays are also available.

   Centro Lingüístico Conversa, Apdo. 17-1007, Centro Colón, San José, Costa Rica (☎ 800/354-5036, fax 506/233-2418 from the U.S.; 506/221-7649 in Costa Rica), provides an attractive environment for studying Spanish at its El Pedregal farm 10 miles west of San José. A four-week course here, including room and board with a Costa Rican family, costs $1,650 for one person.

   Costa Rica Spanish Institute (COSI), Apdo. 1366-2050, San Pedro, Costa Rica (☎/fax 506/253-2117), offers small classes in the San Pedro neighborhood of San

José, as well as a program at the Pacific beach of Playa Ballena. The cost is $390 per week with a homestay in San José, $450 at the beach.

Costa Rican Language Academy and More, Avenida Central across from Calle 25B and the Nicaraguan Embassy (Apdo. 233-2070), San José (☎ 506/233-2070 or 506/223-8938; fax 506/233-8670), offers 3, 4, or 5 hours of daily Spanish instruction in one- to four-week packages. Four hours per day for four weeks costs $900, including a homestay. The school also offers classes in Latin dance and Costa Rican cooking.

Forester Instituto Internacional, Apdo. 6945-1000, San José, Costa Rica (☎ 506/225-3155, 506/225-0135 or 506/225-1649; fax 506/225-9236), is located 75 meters south of the Automercado in the Los Yoses district of San José. The cost of a four-week language course with a homestay and excursions is approximately $1,300.

Instituto Interamericano de Idiomas (Intensa), Calle 33 between avenidas 5 and 7 (Apdo. 8110-1000), San José (☎ 506/224-6353; fax 506/253-4337), offers two- to four-week programs. A four-week, 4 hour per day program with a homestay costs $975.

La Escuela Idiomas D'Amore, Apdo. 67, Quepos (☎ 213/912-0600, fax 414/781-3151 from the U.S.; ☎ 506/777-1143, fax 506/777-0543 in Costa Rica) is situated in the lush surroundings of Manuel Antonio National Park. Four weeks of classes (4 hours per day) costs $1,040; with a homestay, the cost rises to $1,290. Part of your tuition is donated to the World Wildlife Fund.

Pura Vida Instituto, Avenida 3 between calles 8 and 10 (Apdo. 890-3000), Heredia (☎ 506/237-0387 or 506/260-6269). For $280, you receive five days of classroom instruction, and seven days lodging (room and board) with a Costa Rican family.

LATIN DANCE CLASSES   If you are interested in learning or polishing up your salsa, merengue, or mambo skills, San José is a good place to do it. It may take years to get all the moves and spins down, but even an introductory class or two can give the most terminal wallflowers the confidence to get out on the dance floor. When you feel confident enough, you can try out what you've learned at some of the area nightclubs. The schools listed below all have ongoing classes. Most allow casual drop-in attendance, but some like to start beginning classes at specific times, so call in advance to see when an appropriate class is being offered. Prices range from around $5 for a single hour class to $50 per month for biweekly crash courses. Dance schools in the San José area include the following.

Costa Rican Language Academy and More, Avenida Central across from Calle 25B and the Nicaraguan Embassy (☎ 506/233-2070 or 506/223-8938; **Malecon,** Calle 17 between avenidas 2 and 4 (☎ 506/222-3214); **Merecumbe** (☎ 506/224-3531), with locations in San José, San Pedro, Sabanilla, and Tibas; and **Danza Viva,** 75 meters south of the Higueron, in San Pedro (☎ 506/253-3110).

5 Health & Insurance

STAYING HEALTHY

Staying healthy on a trip to Costa Rica is predominantly a matter of being a little cautious about what you eat and drink, and using common sense. Know your physical limits and don't overexert yourself in the ocean, on hikes, or in athletic activities. Respect and protect yourself from the tropical sun. Try not to eat in seedy dives where cockroaches outnumber fellow diners. I recommend buying and drinking bottled water or soft drinks, but the water in San José and in most of the heavily traveled tourist spots is safe to drink. The sections below will deal with some specific health concerns you should be aware of.

VACCINATIONS   No vaccinations are required for a visit to Costa Rica, unless you are coming from an area where yellow fever exists. However, because sanitation is generally not as good as it is in developed countries, you may be exposed to diseases for which you may wish to get vaccinations: typhoid, polio, tetanus, and infectious hepatitis (gamma globulin). If you are planning to stay in major cities, you stand little risk of encountering any of these diseases, but if you venture out into remote regions of the country, you stand a higher risk.

TROPICAL DISEASES   Your chances of contracting any serious tropical disease in Costa Rica are slim, especially if you stick to the beaches or traditional tourist spots. However, malaria, dengue fever, and leptospirosis all exist in Costa Rica, so it's a good idea to have an idea of what they are.

Malaria is found in the lowlands on both coasts and in the northern zone. Although it is rarely found in urban areas, it is still a problem in remote wooded regions, and along the Atlantic coast. Malaria prophylaxes are available, but several have side effects and others are of questionable effectiveness. Consult your doctor as to what is currently considered the best preventative treatment for malaria. Be sure to ask whether a recommended drug will cause you to be hypersensitive to the sun. It would be a shame to come down here for the beaches and then never be able to go out in the sun. Because malaria-carrying mosquitoes come out only at night, you should do as much as possible to avoid being bitten by mosquitoes after dark. If you are in a malarial area, wear long pants and long sleeves, use insect repellent, and sleep under a mosquito net or burn mosquito coils (similar to incense, but with a pesticide).

Of greater concern may be dengue fever, which has had periodic outbreaks in Latin America since 1993. Dengue fever is similar to malaria, and is spread by an aggressive daytime mosquito. This mosquito seems to be most common in lowland urban areas, and Liberia and Limón have been the worst hit cities in Costa Rica. Dengue is also known as "bone break fever," because it is usually accompanied by severe body aches. The first infection with dengue fever will make you very sick, but should cause no serious damage. However, a second infection with a different strain of the dengue virus can lead to internal hemorrhaging and may be life threatening.

Many people are convinced that taking B-complex vitamins daily will help prevent mosquitoes from biting you.

One final tropical fever you should know about is leptospirosis. There are over 200 strains of leptospiri, which are animal-borne bacteria transmitted to humans via contact with drinking, swimming, or bathing water. This bacterial infection is easily treated with antibiotics; however, it can quickly cause very high fever and chills, and should be treated promptly.

If you should develop a high fever accompanied by severe body aches, nausea, diarrhea, or vomiting during or shortly after a visit to Costa Rica, it is a good idea to consult a physician as soon as possible.

Costa Rica has been relatively free from the cholera epidemic that has spread through much of Latin America in recent years. This is largely due to an extensive public awareness campaign that has promoted good hygiene and increased sanitation. Your chances of contracting cholera while you're here are very slight. However, it is still advisable to avoid *ceviche*, a raw seafood salad, if it has any shellfish in it. Shellfish are known carriers of cholera.

RIPTIDES   Many of Costa Rica's beaches have riptides, strong currents that can drag swimmers out to sea. A riptide occurs when water that has been dumped on the shore by strong waves forms a channel back out to open water. These channels have strong currents. If you get caught in a riptide, you can't escape the current by swimming toward shore; that is the equivalent of swimming upstream in a river. To break free of the current, swim parallel to shore, and use the energy of the waves to help you get back to the beach.

BEES & SNAKES   Although Costa Rica has Africanized bees and several species of venomous snakes, your chances of being bitten are minimal, especially if you refrain from sticking your hands under rocks in the forest and into hives. If you know that you are allergic to bee stings, consult your doctor before traveling. Your best bet for seeing a fer-de-lance or eyelash viper is a visit to San José's Serpentarium (see chapter 5).

INSURANCE
HEALTH/ACCIDENT/LOSS
Before leaving on your trip, contact your health-insurance provider and find out whether your insurance will cover you while you are away. If not, contact a travel agent and ask about travel health-insurance policies. A travel agent can also tell you about trip insurance to cover cancellations or loss of baggage. If you have homeowner's or renter's insurance, you may be covered against theft and loss even while you are on vacation. Be sure to check this before taking out additional insurance. Some credit cards provide trip insurance when you charge an airline ticket, but be sure to check with your credit-card company before assuming you have it. If you decide that your current insurance is inadequate, you can contact your travel agent for information on various types of travel insurance, including insurance against cancellation of a prepaid tour should this become necessary.

The following companies offer various types of travel insurance: **Teletrip** (Mutual of Omaha), P.O. Box 31685, Omaha, NE 68131 (☎ 800/228-9792); **Wallach and Co., Inc.,** P.O. Box 480, Middleburg, VA 22117-0480 (☎ 800/237-6615); and **Access America, Inc.,** P.O. Box 90315, Richmond, VA 23286-4991 (☎ 800/424-3391 or 800/284-8300).

6 Tips For Special Travelers
FOR SENIORS
Many airlines now offer senior-citizen discounts, so be sure to ask about these when making reservations. Due to its temperate climate, stable government, low cost of living, and friendly pensionado program, Costa Rica is popular with retirees from North America. There are excellent medical facilities in San José, and plenty of community organizations to help retirees feel at home. If you would like to learn more about retiring in Costa Rica and applying for residency, contact the **Association of Residents of Costa Rica** in San José (☎ 506/233-8068 or 506/221-2053).

Elderhostel, 75 Federal St., Boston, MA 02110 (☎ 617/426-7788), offers very popular study tours to Costa Rica. To participate in an Elderhostel program, either you or your spouse must be at least 60 years old. Great birdwatching excursions and lectures on Costa Rican culture and history are some of the more interesting aspects of these trips.

FOR SINGLES
You'll pay the same penalty here that you would elsewhere: Rooms are more expensive if you aren't traveling in a pair. If you are looking for someone to travel with,

Travel Companions Exchange, P.O. Box 833, Amityville, NY 11701-0833 (☎ 516/454-0880), provides listings of possible travel companions categorized under such headings as special interests, age, education, and location. It costs a minimum of $99 for an 8-month membership and subscription to the service. It is also possible to subscribe to the organization's bimonthly newsletter without becoming a member. The newsletter costs $24 for a 6-month subscription.

FOR FAMILIES

Hotels in Costa Rica occasionally give discounts for children under 12 years old, and usually children under 3 or 4 years old are allowed to stay for free. However, don't expect the same type of discounts you'll find in the United States.

FOR GAY & LESBIAN TRAVELERS

Costa Rica is a conservative, *macho* country and public displays of same-sex affection are considered rare and shocking. However, gay and lesbian travelers are generally treated with respect and should not experience any harassment.

The **International Gay and Lesbian Association** (☎ 506/234-2411) can provide helpful information and tips. **Casa Yemaya,** located in the nearby suburb of Moravia (☎ 506/223-3652 or 506/257-8529), is a feminist center and guest lodge that organizes classes, activities, and tours exclusively for women.

FOR STUDENTS

Costa Rica is the only country in Central America with a network of hostels that are affiliated with the International Youth Hostel Federation. Ask at the **Toruma Youth Hostel,** Avenida Central between calles 29 and 31, San José (☎ 506/224-4085) for information on hostels at Rara Avis, La Fortuna, Lake Arenal, San Isidro, Jacó Beach, Liberia, and Rincón de la Vieja National Park. In San José, there is also a student travel agency: **OTEC,** Edificio Ferencz, 2nd floor, Calle 3 between avenidas 1 and 3, 275 meters north of the National Theater (☎ 506/256-0633). If you already have an **international student identity card,** you can use your card to get discounts on airfares, hostels, national and international tours and excursions, car rentals, and store purchases. If you don't have one, stop by the OTEC office with a passport or other identification that shows you are under 35 years old, proof of student status, and two passport photos; for about $10, they'll prepare an ID card for you.

Students interested in a working vacation in Costa Rica should contact the **Council on International Educational Exchange (CIEE),** 205 E. 42nd St., New York, NY 10017 (☎ 212/661-1414 or 212/661-1450). This organization also issues official student identity cards and has offices all over the United States. They also recently published *Smart Vacations: The Traveler's Guide to Learning Adventures Abroad* (St. Martin's Press, 1993), a directory of companies, organizations, and schools offering educational travel programs.

FOR TRAVELERS WITH DISABILITIES

Although facilities are beginning to be adapted for those with disabilities, in general, there are few handicapped-accessible buildings in Costa Rica. In San José, sidewalks are crowded and uneven. Few hotels offer handicapped-accessible accommodations, and there are neither public buses nor private vans for transporting disabled individuals. It is difficult for a person with disabilities to get around in Costa Rica.

Kosta Roda, P.O. Box 1312-1100, San Juan de Tibás (☎ 506/236-5185) is a Costa Rican organization dedicated to bringing about successful travel experiences for persons with disabilities. They can provide you with a list of hotels, museums, tours, and attractions that are wheelchair accessible.

Mobility International USA, P.O. Box 10767, Eugene, OR 97440 (☎ 541/343-1284), is a membership organization that promotes international educational exchanges for all ages of people with disabilities. In the past they have had trips to Costa Rica and may again in the future. For a $25 membership fee, you'll receive their quarterly newsletter and access to their referral service.

7 Getting There

BY PLANE

It takes between 3 and 7 hours to fly to Costa Rica from most U.S. cities, and as Costa Rica becomes more and more popular with North American travelers, more flights are made into San José's Juan Santamaría International Airport. There are several car rental agencies at the airport. Driving in Costa Rica is not for everyone, however. See "Getting Around" in this chapter and "Getting There" in chapter 5 for further information.

THE MAJOR AIRLINES   The following airlines currently serve Costa Rica from the United States, using the gateway cities listed. **American Airlines** (☎ 800/433-7300) has daily flights from Miami and Dallas/Fort Worth. **Aviateca** (Guatemalan, ☎ 800/327-9832) flies daily from Los Angeles and Miami, and three times weekly from Houston. **Continental** (☎ 800/231-0856) offers flights daily from Houston. **Lacsa** (Costa Rican, ☎ 800/225-2272) has service from New York, Miami, Orlando, New Orleans, Los Angeles, and San Francisco. **Mexicana** (☎ 800/531-7921) has flights from New York, Denver, Miami, Dallas/Fort Worth, San Antonio, San Jose (California), and San Francisco, although with these flights it is necessary to transfer and spend a night in Mexico City. If you travel from Chicago or Los Angeles on Mexicana, you can get to San José in one day. **Taca** (El Salvadoran, ☎ 800/535-8780) offers flights from Los Angeles, San Francisco, Houston, New Orleans, Miami, and Washington. **United Airlines** (☎ 800/241-6522) has daily flights from Los Angeles and Washington, with one stop either in Mexico or El Salvador. **Aero Costa Rica** (☎ 800/237-6274) has flights from Atlanta, Orlando, and Miami. From Europe, you can take any major carrier to a hub city such as Miami or New York and then make connections to Costa Rica. Alternately, **Iberia** (☎ 800/772-4642) from Spain and **LTU International Airways** (☎ 800/888-0200) from Germany have established routes to San José, stopping in Miami.

REGULAR AIRFARES   In recent years airfares have been very unstable and price wars have flared up unexpectedly. Fares also vary seasonally. Such instability makes it very difficult to quote an airline ticket price. APEX (advance-purchase excursion) fares are often similar from airline to airline, but the cost of a first-class ticket can vary greatly. At press time, an APEX or a coach ticket from New York to San José was running between $649 and $789; from Los Angeles, between $590 and $802. First class from New York starts at about $1,850; from Los Angeles, $2,400. On rare occasions, special fares may be offered at rock-bottom prices, but don't count on it. Regardless of how much the cheapest ticket costs when you decide to fly, you can bet it will have some restrictions. It will almost certainly be non-refundable, and you may have to pay for it within 24 hours of making a reservation. You'll likely have to buy the ticket in advance (anywhere from one week to 30 days). You will also likely have to stay over a weekend and limit your stay to 30 days or less.

TICKET BROKERS/CONSOLIDATORS   You can shave a little bit off the price you pay by purchasing an airline ticket from what is known as a ticket broker or consolidator. These ticketing agencies sell discounted airfares on major airlines; although the tickets have as many, and sometimes more, restrictions than an APEX ticket, they can help you save money. You'll find ticket brokers' listings—usually just a column of destinations with prices beside them—in the Sunday travel sections of major city newspapers. You'll almost never get the ticket for the advertised price, but you will probably get it for less than the airline would sell it to you. If you'd like to shop around, try **Cheap Tickets, Inc.** (☎ 800/377-1000) or **World Travel Consultants** ☎ 800/318-8802.

BY BUS

Bus service runs regularly from both Panama City, Panama, and Managua, Nicaragua. From Panama City it is a 20-hour, 900-kilometer trip; buses leave Panama City daily at 12pm. The one-way fare is $20. Call the **Tica Bus Company** (☎ 506/221-8954) for further information. From Managua, it is 11 hours and 450 kilometers to San José. Buses leave Managua daily at 6am; the one-way fare is $10–$15. For more information, call the Tica Bus Company or **Sirca Company** (☎ 506/222-5541 or 506/223-1464).

Neither of these bus companies will reserve a seat by telephone, so buy your ticket in advance—several days in advance if you plan to travel on weekends or holidays.

BY CAR

It is possible to travel to Costa Rica by car, but it can be difficult, especially for U.S. citizens. The Interamerican Highway (also known as the Panamerican Highway) passes through Guatemala, El Salvador, Honduras, and Nicaragua after leaving Mexico and before reaching Costa Rica. All of these countries can be problematic for travelers for a variety of reasons, including internal violence, crime, and visa formalities. If you do decide to undertake this adventure, take the Gulf coast route from the border crossing at Brownsville, Texas, as it involves traveling the least number of miles through Mexico. A good resource for those planning this journey is *Drive the Pan-Am Highway to Mexico and Central America* by Audrey and Raymond Pritchard, available by contacting P.O. Box 526770, Miami, FL 33152.

CAR DOCUMENTS   You will need a current driver's license, as well as your vehicle's registration and a copy of its title in order to enter the country.

CENTRAL AMERICAN AUTO INSURANCE   Contact **Sanborn's Insurance Company,** 2009 S. 10th St., McAllen, TX 78505 (☎ 210/686-0711 or 800/222-0158), located about 1 1/2 hours from Brownsville, Texas. They can supply you with trip insurance for Mexico and Central America—insurance is not available after you have left the United States—and an itinerary. Sanborn's also has branches at other U.S./Mexico border crossings.

SAFETY   Along the way, it is advisable not to drive at night because of the danger of being robbed by bandits, and be sure to drink only bottled drinks.

BY CRUISE SHIP

More than 200 cruise ships stop each year in Costa Rica, calling at Limón on the Caribbean coast and at Puerto Caldera on the Pacific coast. Cruise lines that offer stops in Costa Rica include **Cunard, Royal Caribbean, Holland American, Princess, Regency,** and **Royal Cruise Line.** Contact these companies directly or visit a travel agent to find out more information about cruising to Costa Rica. Most cruise travel is wholesaled and the best bargains can usually be obtained from such wholesalers and consolidators as **Cruise World** (☎ 800/588-7447); **Cruises, Inc.** (☎ 800/596-5529); and **Forever Cruising** (☎ 800/338-8005).

PACKAGE TOURS

It is sometimes cheaper to purchase an airfare-and-hotel package, rather than just an airline ticket. This is especially true if airfares happen to be high and you plan to travel with a companion. There are a multitude of both tour operators and packagers, with various specialties, so it's best to work with a travel agent to select the tour or package that's right for you.

Some companies that specialize in travel to Costa Rica include **Costa Rica Experts**, 3166 N. Lincoln Ave., Chicago, IL 60657 (☎ 312/935-1009 or 800/827-9046); **Tourtech International**, 17780 Fitch St., Suite 110, Irvine, CA 92714 (☎ 800/882-2636); and **Holbrook Travel**, 3540 NW 13th St., Gainsville, FL 32609 (☎ 904/377-7111 or 800/451-7111). One Canadian company specializing in tours to Costa Rica is **Mony Tours**, 5540 Cote des Neiges, Montreal, H3T 1V9 (☎ 514/733-8277).

In addition, quite a few U.S.- and Costa Rican-based tour operators offer natural-history and "soft adventure" tours and packages that can include stays at remote nature lodges; you'll find a comprehensive listing of these organizations in chapter 4.

8 Getting Around

BY PLANE

Flying is one of the best ways to get around Costa Rica. Because the country is quite small, flights are short and not too expensive. The domestic airlines of Costa Rica are **Sansa,** Calle 24 between Avenida Central and Avenida 1 (☎ 506/233-0397, 506/233-3258, or 506/233-5330), which offers a free shuttle bus from their downtown office to the airport, and **Travelair** (☎ 506/232-7883 or 506/220-3054), which charges more for flights to the same destinations, but is popular because it is more reliable. Flights last between 20 and 50 minutes. Travelair operates from Pavas Airport, 4 miles from San José, and Sansa operates from San José's Juan Santamaría International Airport.

In the high season (December to May), be sure to book reservations well in advance. If you plan to return to San José, buy a round-trip ticket, as they tend to be less expensive than two one-way tickets.

BY BUS

This is by far the best way to visit most of Costa Rica. Buses are inexpensive, relatively well maintained, and they go nearly everywhere. There are three types of buses. Local buses are the cheapest and slowest; they stop frequently and are generally a bit dilapidated. Express buses run between San José and most beach towns and major cities; they sometimes only operate on weekends and holidays. A few luxury buses and minibuses drive to destinations frequented by foreign tourists. For details on how to get to various destinations from San José, see the "Getting There" sections of the regional chapters that follow.

BY CAR

Car Rentals   Renting a car in Costa Rica is not something to be entered into lightly. The roads are in terrible shape, most rural intersections are unmarked, and for some reason, sitting behind the wheel of a car seems to turn peaceful Ticos into homicidal maniacs. In addition, since all rental cars in Costa Rica bear special license plates, they are readily identifiable to thieves. Nothing is ever safe in a car in Costa Rica, although parking in guarded parking lots helps. The tourist plates also signal police that they can extort money from unwary tourist motorists. Never pay money directly to a police officer who stops you for any traffic violation. Before driving off with a rental car, be sure that you inspect the exterior and point out to the rental company representative every tiny scratch, dent, tear, or any other damage. It is a common practice with many Costa Rican car-rental companies to claim that you owe payment for damages the company finds when you return the car.

On the other hand, renting a car allows you much greater freedom to explore remote areas of the country. Several people have written to me to say that they feel visitors should always rent four-wheel-drive vehicles. I have always rented a regular car during the dry season, and though there are roads I can't drive down, I have always managed to get around just fine (including to Monteverde). During the rainy season and on the Nicoya Peninsula, four-wheel-drive vehicles are recommended. If, after weighing the alternatives, you decide you want to rent a car, read on.

Avis, Budget, Hertz, National, and **Thrifty** all have offices in Costa Rica. You will save somewhere between $35 and $75 per week on a car rental if you make a reservation in your home country at least one week before you need the car. For example, at press time, the least expensive Avis car rents for $276 per week, plus insurance (for a total of $374) in San José, but if you book this same car in advance from the United States, you can get it for $198 per week, plus insurance (for a total of $296). To rent a car in Costa Rica, you must be at least 21 years old and have a valid driver's license and a major credit card in your name. See the "Getting Around" section of chapter 5 for details on renting a car in San José. Cars can also be rented in Quepos, Jacó, Liberia, and Limón.

GASOLINE   Regular leaded gasoline is what is most readily available in Costa Rica, and most rental cars take regular. However, some of the newer models run on unleaded, which is sold as "super." Ask your rental agent what type of gas your car takes. When going off to remote places, try to leave with a full tank of gas since gas stations can be very hard to find. If you need to gas up in a small town, you can sometimes get gasoline from enterprising families who sell it by the liter from their houses. Look for hand-lettered signs that say "gasolina."

ROAD CONDITIONS   Road conditions in San José and throughout the country became a political issue in 1995, after years of corruption and neglect in the Transportation Ministry had caused the roads to deteriorate to the point that local newspapers were running contests to find the largest potholes. There was no lack of contenders. Despite the uproar and indignation, little relief or repair work is in sight. If possible, before you rent a vehicle, find out about the road conditions to see if it is necessary to have a four-wheel-drive vehicle to get to your destination. Some paved roads are still badly potholed, so stay alert. Road conditions get especially tricky during the rainy season, when heavy rains and runoff can destroy a stretch of pavement in the blink of an eye. Route numbers are rarely used on road signs in Costa Rica, though there are frequent signs listing the number of kilometers to various towns or cities.

MAPS   Car-rental agencies and the ICT information centers (see "Information & Entry Requirements" at the beginning of this chapter) at the airport and in downtown San José have adequate road maps. Other sources in San José are Chispas Books, Calle 7 between avenidas Central and 1 (☎ 506/256-8251); Libreria Lehmann, Avenida Central between calles 1 and 3 (☎ 506/223-1212); and Jimenez & Tanzi, Calle 3 between avenidas 1 and 3 (☎ 506/233-8033).

DRIVING RULES   A foreign driver's license is valid for the first 3 months you are in Costa Rica. Seat belts are required for the driver and front-seat passengers.

Motorcyclists must wear a helmet. Highway police use radar, so keep to the speed limit if you don't want to get pulled over. Speeding tickets can be charged to your credit card for up to a year after you leave the country if they are not paid before departure.

BREAKDOWNS   If your car breaks down and you are unable to get off the road, check to see if there are reflecting triangles in the trunk. If there are, place them as a warning for approaching traffic gently extending out from the shoulder, in a line starting about 100 feet before your car. If not, try to create a similar warning marker using a pile of leaves or branches.

BY FERRY

There are four different ferries operating across the Gulf of Nicoya. Three are car ferries: one across the Rio Tempisque, one from Puntarenas to Playa Naranjo, and one from Puntarenas to Paquera; and one is a passenger ferry which runs from Puntarenas to Paquera. For more detailed information, see chapters 6 and 7.

HITCHHIKING

Although buses go to most places in Costa Rica, they can be infrequent in the remote regions, and consequently, local people often hitchhike to get to their destination sooner. If you are driving a car, people will frequently ask you for a ride. In rural areas, a hitchhiker carrying a machete is not necessarily a great danger, but use your judgement. Hitchhiking is not recommended on major roadways or in urban areas. In rural areas it is usually pretty safe. However, women should be extremely cautious about hitchhiking anywhere in Costa Rica. If you choose to hitchhike, keep in mind that if a bus doesn't go to your destination, there probably aren't too many cars going there either. Good luck.

LOCATING ADDRESSES

While there are some street addresses in Costa Rica, they are almost never used. Addresses are usually given as a set of coordinates, such as "Calle 3 between Avenida Central and Avenida 1." Many addresses include additional information such as the number of meters or *varas* (an old Spanish measurement roughly equal to a yard) from a specified intersection or some other well-known landmark. Often the additional information is confusing to visitors, but essential for taxi drivers. In San José, many addresses use distances from the Coca-Cola bottling plant that once stood near the market. The bottling plant is long gone, but the address descriptions remain. In outlying neighborhoods, addresses can become long directions such as "50 meters south of the old church, then 100 meters east, then 20 meters south." Luckily for the visitor, these directions are often precise.

SUGGESTED ITINERARIES

Planning Your Itinerary

The following are the main tourist destinations in Costa Rica: San José; Manuel Antonio National Park; Jacó Beach; the beaches of Guanacaste and the Nicoya Peninsula; Monteverde Cloud Forest Reserve (or another cloud-forest region); Tortuguero National Park; Irazú Volcano; Poás Volcano; Arenal Volcano and Arenal Lake; The Osa Peninsula; jungle lodges throughout the country; Cahuita/Puerto Viejo; and Dominical.

If You Have 1 Week

Day 1   Visit the museums and the National Theater in San José.
Day 2   Make an excursion to the Orosi Valley, Lankester Gardens, and Irazú Volcano.
Days 3 and 4   Travel to Monteverde (or another cloud-forest region) and spend a day exploring the cloud forest.
Days 5 and 6   Head to one of the many Pacific coast beaches.
Day 7   Return to San José.

If You Have 2 Weeks

Day 1   Visit the museums and the National Theater in San José.
Days 2 and 3   Make an excursion to the Orosi Valley, Lankester Gardens, and Irazú Volcano one day and go river rafting on the other day.
Days 4 and 5   Travel to Lake Arenal to see the edruptions of Arenal Volcano, soak in some hot springs, and maybe go to Caño Negro National Wildlife Refuge.
Days 6 and 7   Travel to Monteverde (or another cloud-forest region) and explore the cloud forest.
Day 8   Explore Rincon de la Vieja or Santa Rosa National Park.
Days 9, 10, 11, and 12   Spend these days relaxing on a beach or perhaps exploring the Corcovado Peninsula.
Days 13 and 14   Fly to Tortuguero National Park and spend a day there, returning the next day by boat and bus.

If You Have 3 Weeks

If you have three weeks, you can spend more time on the beach, perhaps several different beaches. With this much time, you can easily visit both coasts. You could also do trips to two or three different remote lodges in different parts of the country. You might even consider doing a week-long cruise along the Pacific coast.

Themed Choices

The most common choice for a themed vacation in Costa Rica is to make it a naturalist tour by visiting as many of the national parks and private nature reserves as you can in the amount of time available. Another possible theme would be to sample as many of the different beaches as you can, or do a surf tour of the Pacific coast.

9   Tips on Accommodations

When the tourist boom hit Costa Rica in the late 1980s, hotels began popping up like mushrooms after a few days of rain. The past few years have seen the opening of the first megaresorts, and several more are under construction and near completion. There is a hotel glut, and the next few years should be a weeding out period for the hotel industry; this is good news for tourists and bargain hunters. There are still few hotels or resorts offering the sort of luxurious accommodations you'll find in Hawaii or the Caribbean. Yes, there are hotels of international standards, but Costa Rica is not yet a luxury resort destination.

The country's strong point is its moderately priced hotels. In the $60 to $90 price range, you'll find comfortable accommodations almost anywhere in the country. However, within this price range, room size and quality vary quite a bit. Don't expect the uniformity you find in the United States in this price range. Moreover, there are also quite a few good deals for less than $60 per double room.

Bed-and-breakfast inns have also been proliferating. Though the majority of these are in the San José area, you will now find B&Bs (often gringo owned and operated) throughout the country. Another welcome hotel trend in the San José area is the renovation and conversion of old homes into small hotels. Most of these hotels are in the Barrio Amon district of downtown San José, and though there is a problem with noise and exhaust fumes in this neighborhood, they have more character than any other hotels in the country. You'll find similar hotels in the Paseo Colón and Los Yoses districts.

Costa Rica has been riding the eco-tourism wave, and there are now small nature-oriented eco-lodges throughout the country. These lodges offer opportunities to see wildlife (including sloths, monkeys, and hundreds of species of birds) and learn about tropical forests. They range from spartan facilities catering primarily to scientific researchers to luxury accommodations that are among the finest in the country. Keep in mind that though the nightly room rates at these lodges are often quite moderate, the price of a visit starts to climb when you throw in transportation (often on chartered planes), guided excursions, and meals. Also, just because your travel agent can book a reservation at most of these lodges does not mean they're not remote. Make sure to find out how you will be getting to and from your eco-lodge and just what tours and services are included in your stay. Then think long and hard about whether you really want to put up with hot, humid weather (cool and wet in the cloud forests), biting insects, rugged transportation, and strenuous hikes to see wildlife.

A couple of uniquely Costa Rican accommodation types you may encounter are the *apartotel* and the *cabina*. An apartotel is just what it sounds like, an apartment hotel, where you'll get a full kitchen and one or two bedrooms. Cabinas are Costa Rica's version of cheap vacation lodging. They are very basic, very inexpensive, and are often cinder-block buildings divided into small rooms. Occasionally you'll find a cabina where the units are actually cabins, but these are a rarity. Cabinas often have clothes-washing sinks or *pilas*, and kitchenettes, since they cater primarily to Tico families on vacation.

Please note that room rates listed in this book do not include the 18.5% room taxes. These taxes will add considerably to the cost of your room. I have separated hotel listings throughout this book into several broad categories. These categories are: **Very Expensive,** $125 and up; **Expensive,** $80–$125; **Moderate,** $40–$80; and **Inexpensive,** under $40 double.

10   Tips on Dining

Simply put, Costa Rican cuisine is unmemorable. San José remains the unquestioned gastronomic capital of the country, and here you can find the cuisines of the world served with formal service at moderate prices. There are several excellent French and Italian restaurants around the San José area, as well as Peruvian, Japanese, Swiss, and Spanish establishments. One recent development is worth noting, and it may soon make my opening caveat untrue. With the increase in international tourism and the need to please a more sophisticated palate, local chefs have begun to create a "nouvelle Costa Rican cuisine," updating time-worn recipes and using traditional ingredients in creative ways. Costa Rica is a major producer and exporter of beef, and consequently, San José also has plenty of good steakhouses. At the most expensive restaurant in San José, you'll have to drink a lot of wine to spend more than $40 on dinner.

Outside of the capital, your options get very limited, very fast. In fact, many beach resorts are so remote that you have no choice but to eat in the hotel's dining room, and on other beaches, the only choices aside from the hotel dining rooms are cheap local places or overpriced tourist traps serving indifferent meals. At remote jungle lodges, the food is usually served buffet- or family-style and can range from bland to inspired. However, meals at these lodges hinge almost entirely on who is doing the cooking at the moment, and turnover is high. I hesitate to recommend food in such lodges because the cook I had when I visited may be long gone by the time you arrive.

If you're looking for cheap eats, you'll find them in little restaurants known as *sodas,* which are the equivalent of diners in the United States. At a soda you'll have lots of choices: rice and beans with steak, rice and beans with fish, rice and beans with chicken, or—for vegetarians—rice and beans. You get the picture. The Tico standards of rice and beans are the norm and are served at three meals a day. Also, though there is plenty of seafood available throughout the country, at sodas it all-too-often is served fried.

Costa Ricans love to eat, and they love to have a view when they eat. Almost anywhere you go in the country, if there is a view, there will be a restaurant taking advantage of it. These restaurants are often called *mirador.* If you are driving around the country, don't miss an opportunity to dine with a view at some little roadside restaurant. The food may not be fantastic, but the view will be.

I have separated restaurant listings throughout this book into three price categories based on the average cost of a meal, including tax and service charge, but not including beer or wine. The categories are as follows: **Expensive,** more than $15; **Moderate,** $8 to $15; and **Inexpensive,** less than $8. Whenever you eat out, keep in mind that there is an additional 15% sales tax. Moreover, most restaurants also tack on a 10% service charge. Ticos rarely tip, but that doesn't mean you shouldn't. If the service was particularly good and attentive, you should probably leave a little extra.

11 Tips on Shopping

Buy coffee. If you're a coffee drinker or if you know some coffee drinkers (I guess that's all of us), then be sure to stock up on fresh-roasted coffee beans before you head home. **Café Britt** is the coffee you'll see sold in hotels and souvenir shops all over the country. Sure, it's good coffee, but it's also overpriced. If you go into the central market in downtown San José or a grocery store anywhere in the country, you'll find coffee at much lower prices. Just be sure you're buying whole beans. Costa Rican grinds are much finer than U.S. grinds and often have sugar mixed right in with the coffee. Costa Rica also produces its own coffee liqueur (**Café Rica**), and a creme liqueur (**Salicsa**), both of which are quite inexpensive. These are best purchased in a liquor store or a grocery store. In duty-free shops at the airport, you'll pay more for either of these local liqueurs. **Salsa Lizano,** a flavorful green sauce used the same way we use steak sauce in the U.S., is another comestible worth bringing home with you.

Costa Rica is not known for its handcrafts, though it does have a town—**Sarchí**—that is filled with handcraft shops. So scant are the country's handcraft offerings that most tourist shops sell Guatemalan clothing, Panamanian appliquéd textiles, El Salvadoran painted wood souvenirs, and Nicaraguan rocking chairs. There is quite a bit of wood carving being done in the country but it is, for the most part, either tourist-souvenir wooden bowls, napkin holders, and the like, or elegant and expensive art pieces. Sarchí is best known as the home of the colorfully painted Costa Rican ox cart, reproductions of which are manufactured in various scaled-down sizes. These make excellent gifts. If you want a larger ox cart, they can be easily disassembled and shipped to your home. There is also a lot of furniture made in Sarchí.

A few other items worth keeping an eye out for include reproductions of pre-Columbian gold jewelry and carved-stone figurines. The former is available either in solid gold, silver, or gold plated. The latter, though interesting, is extremely heavy.

On the streets of San José you'll see a lot of hammocks for sale. I personally find the Costa Rican hammocks a little crude and unstable. The same vendors usually have single-person hanging chairs, which are strung similarly to the full-sized hammocks and are a better bet.

FAST FACTS: Costa Rica

American Express   American Express (☎ 506/257-1792) has a counter in San José at the Banco de San José on Calle Central between avenidas 3 and 5. It's open Monday through Friday from 8am to 7pm, and Saturday from 9am to 1pm. To report a lost or stolen card from inside Costa Rica, call toll-free 001-800-528-2121.

Business Hours   Banks are usually open Monday through Friday from 9am to 3pm, though many have begun to offer extended hours. Offices are open Monday through Friday from 8am to 5pm (closed for 2 hours at lunch). Stores are generally open Monday through Saturday from 9am to 7pm (many close for an hour at lunch). Bars are open until 1 or 2am.

Cameras/Film   Most types of film are available, as are developing services. However, prices are higher than in the United States.

Climate   See "When to Go," earlier in this chapter.

Crime   See "Safety," below.

Currency   See "Money," earlier in this chapter.

Customs   You can bring in half a kilo of tobacco products, 3 liters of liquor, and two cameras duty-free. You can also bring in personal electronic equipment such as laptop computers and tape recorders.

Documents Required   See "Information & Entry Requirements," earlier in this chapter.

Driving Rules   See "Getting Around," earlier in this chapter.

Drug Laws   Drug laws in Costa Rica are strict, so stay away from marijuana and cocaine. Many prescription drugs are sold over the counter here, but often the names are different than in the United States and Europe. It is always best to have a prescription from a doctor.

Drugstores   A drugstore in Costa Rica is a *farmacia*. You'll find at least one in nearly every town.

Electricity   The standard in Costa Rica is the same as in the United States: 110 volts. However, three-pronged outlets can be scarce, so it's helpful to bring along an adaptor.

Embassies/Consulates   The following embassies and consulates are located in San José: **United States Embassy**, in front of Centro Commercial, on the road to Pavas (☎ 506/220-3939); **Canadian Consulate**, Calle 3 and Avenida 1 (☎ 506/255-3522); **British Embassy**, Paseo Colón between calles 38 and 40 (☎ 506/221-5566).

Emergencies   In case of an emergency, dial 911; for an **ambulance** call 128; to report a **fire** call 118; to contact the **police** call 506/221-1365 or 506/221-5337.

Etiquette   Ticos tend to dress conservatively and treat everyone very respectfully. Both sexes shake hands, though men and women often kiss lightly on one cheek on parting.

Hitchhiking   This is permitted and is fairly common in rural areas. Women, however, should exercise caution in hitchhiking. Buses, which are quite inexpensive, go almost everywhere in the country.

Holidays   See "When to Go," earlier in this chapter.

Information   See "Visitor Information & Entry Requirements," earlier in this chapter. Also see individual city sections for local information offices.

Language   Spanish is the official language of Costa Rica. *Berlitz Latin-American Spanish Phrasebook and Dictionary* (Berlitz Guides, 1992) is probably the best phrasebook to bring with you.

Laundry   Laundromats are few and far between in Costa Rica—more common are expensive hotel laundry services. For listings of laundromats, see individual city and town sections.

Liquor Laws   Alcoholic beverages are sold every day of the week throughout the year, with the exception of the two days before Easter and the two days before and after a presidential election.

Lost or Stolen Credit & Charge Cards   If you lose your credit or charge card, it's best to call the Costa Rican office of the company that issued the card immediately. **American Express,** ☎ 001-800-528-2121; **Master Card,** ☎ 506/223-8855; **Visa,** ☎ 506/252-2155.

Mail   Mail to the United States usually takes a little over one week to reach its destination. Postage for a postcard is 25¢; for a letter, 35¢. A post office is called a *correo* in Spanish. You can get stamps at the post office, and at gift shops in large hotels. If you are sending mail to Costa Rica, it can take as much as a month to get to the more remote corners of the country. Plan ahead. Also, many hotels and eco-lodges have mailing addresses in the United States. Always use these addresses when writing from North America or Europe. Never send cash, checks, or valuables through the Costa Rican mail system.

Maps   The Costa Rican Tourist Board (ICT), (see "Visitor Information & Entry Requirements" in this chapter), can usually provide you with good maps of both Costa Rica and San José. Other sources for maps in San José are **Chispas Books,** Calle 7 between avenidas Central and 1 (☎ 506/256-8251); **Libreria Lehmann,** Avenida Central between calles 1 and 3 (☎ 506/223-1212); and **Jimenez & Tanzi,** Calle 3 between avenidas 1 and 3 (☎ 506/233-8033).

Newspapers/Magazines   There are three Spanish-language dailies in Costa Rica and one English-language weekly, the *Tico Times.* There is also a bilingual tourist weekly, *Costa Rica Today.* In addition, you can get *Time, Newsweek,* and several U.S. newspapers at hotel gift shops and a few of the bookstores in San José.

Passports   See "Visitor Information & Entry Requirements," earlier in this chapter.

Pets   If you want to bring your cat or dog, be sure it has been vaccinated against rabies and distemper in the last year and you have the documentation to prove it.

In addition, it's best to check with where you plan to stay before assuming your furry companion is welcome.

Police The numbers for the **Judicial Police** are 506/221-1365 or 221-5337. The numbers for the **Traffic Police** or Policia de Transito are 222-9330 or 222-9245.

Radio/TV There are about 10 local TV channels; cable and satellite TV from the United States is also common. There are more than 100 radio stations on the AM and FM dials.

Restrooms These are known as *sanitarios* or *servicios sanitarios*. They are marked *damas* (women) and *hombres* or *caballeros* (men).

Safety Though most of Costa Rica is safe, crime has become much more common in recent years. San José is known for its pickpockets—never carry a wallet in your back pocket. In fact, never carry anything of value in your pants pockets or in a daypack on your back. A woman should keep a tight grip on her purse (keep it tucked under your arm). Be sure not to leave valuables in your hotel room. Don't park a car on the street in Costa Rica, especially in San José; there are plenty of public parking lots around the city.

Because all rental cars have special plates, they are easily spotted by thieves who know that such cars are likely to be full of expensive camera equipment, money, and other valuables. Don't ever leave anything of value in a car parked on the street, not even for a moment. Public intercity buses are also frequent targets of stealthy thieves. Never check your bags into the hold of a bus if you can avoid it. If this cannot be avoided, keep your eye on what leaves the hold any time the bus stops. If you put your bags in an overhead rack, be sure you can see the bags at all times. Try not to fall asleep.

For safety tips while swimming, see "Riptides" under "Health & Insurance," above.

Taxes All hotels charge 18.45% tax. Restaurants charge 15% tax and also add on a 10% service charge, for a total of 25% more on your bill. There is an airport departure tax of $16.50.

Taxis Taxis are common and inexpensive in San José, but harder to find and more expensive in rural areas. In San José taxis are supposed to charge metered fares. Outside of the city and on longer rides, be sure to agree upon a price beforehand.

Telegrams & Wiring Money **Western Union** (☎ 506/283-6336) is on Calle 9 between avenidas 2 and 4 in San José. Along with a telegram service, it offers a money wiring service. **Radiográfica** (☎ 506/287-0087) at Calle 1 and Avenida 5 in San José has telegram service.

Telephones & Faxes Costa Rica has an excellent phone system, with a dial tone similar to that heard in the United States. All phone numbers in Costa Rica have seven digits. For **information**, dial 113. A pay phone costs 10 colónes (5¢) and most phones take 5-, 10-, or 20-colón coins, though some take 5- or 10-colón coins only.

For making calling-card and collect calls, you can reach an **AT&T** operator by dialing 0-800-011-4114, **MCI** by dialing 0-800-012-2222, **Sprint** by dialing 0-800-013-0123, **Canada Bell** by dialing 0-800-015-1162, and a **Costa Rican international operator** by dialing 116 (pay phones may sometimes require a coin deposit). The Costa Rican telephone system allows direct international dialing, but it is expensive. To get an international line, dial 00 followed by the country code and number.

To call Costa Rica from the United States, dial 011 followed by the country code 506, then the local number.

You can make international phone calls, as well as send faxes, from the **ICE** office, Avenida 2 between calles 1 and 3, in San José. The office is open daily from 7am to 10pm. Faxes cost between $4 to $5 per page. (Many hotels will also offer the same service for a fee.) **Radiográfica** (☎ 506/287-0087) at Calle 1 and Avenida 5 in San José has fax service.

Time   Costa Rica is on Central Standard Time, 6 hours behind Greenwich mean time.

Tipping   Tipping is not necessary in restaurants, where a 10% service charge is always added to your bill (along with a 15% tax). If service was particularly good, you can leave a little at your own discretion, but it is not mandatory. Porters and bellhops get around 75¢ per bag. You don't need to tip a taxi driver unless the service has been superior—a tip is not usually expected.

Tourist Offices   See "Visitor Information & Entry Requirements," earlier in this chapter. See also specific cities.

Visas   See "Visitor Information & Entry Requirements," earlier in this chapter.

Water   Though the water in San José is said to be safe to drink, outside of the city, water quality varies. Because many tourists do get sick within a few days of arriving in Costa Rica, I recommend playing it safe and sticking to bottled drinks as much as possible and avoiding ice.

4 Birdwatching, River Rafting & Other Active Vacations

Although it's possible to come to Costa Rica and stay clean and dry, most visitors want to spend some time getting their hair wet, their feet muddy, and their bodies bitten by bugs. To many, tropical rain and cloud forests are the stuff of myth and legend. Those who are lucky enough to explore them come back speaking about what they've experienced with awe and admiration. Partly because evolution is a slow process, and partly because much of the country's natural landscape is protected in national parks and bioreserves, Costa Rica's primary forests are still in pretty much the same state as early explorers such as Columbus found them, and are open to adventurous travelers. Along the coasts and just offshore, there are an equal number of options for the active traveler.

As awareness of the value of tropical forests and interest in visiting them has grown, dozens of lodges and tour companies have sprung up to cater to travelers interested in enjoying the natural beauties of Costa Rica. These lodges are usually situated in out-of-the-way locations, sometimes deep in the heart of a forest and sometimes on a farm with only a tiny bit of natural forest. However, they all have one thing in common: they cater to environmentally aware people with an interest in nature. Birdwatching, rafting, kayaking, horseback riding, and hiking are among the most popular activities offered at these lodges. For detailed listings of these lodges, many of which offer special packages, see the "Where to Stay & Dine" sections of the regional chapters that follow (chapters 6–10).

There are myriad approaches to planning an active vacation in Costa Rica. This chapter lays out your options, from tour operators who run multi-activity package tours that often include stays at eco-lodges; to the best places in Costa Rica to practice particular activities (with listings of tour operators, guides, and outfitters that specialize in each); to an overview of the country's national parks and bioreserves. Because so many of Costa Rica's adventure travel offerings take place in these protected areas, this latter section includes suggestions for how to combine a visit to one or two of these places during your stay. After a few tips on health and safety in the wilderness, the chapter closes with a list of educational and volunteer travel options for those with a little more time on their hands and a desire to actively assist Costa Rica in the maintenance and preservation of its natural wonders.

1 Organized Adventure Travel Package Tours

Since many travelers have limited time and resources, organized eco-tourism or adventure travel packages, run by tour operators in the United States or Costa Rica, are a popular way of combining several activities. Birdwatching, horseback riding, rafting, and hiking can be teamed with, say, visits to Monteverde Biological Cloud Forest Preserve and Manuel Antonio National Park.

Traveling with a group has several advantages over traveling independently: Your accommodations and transportation are arranged and most (if not all) of your meals are included in the cost of a package. You'll proceed to each of your destinations quickly without the snags and long delays that those traveling on their own can face. You'll also have the opportunity to meet like-minded souls who are interested in nature and active sports.

Fortunately, most of the tours are run by companies with a genuine concern for preserving the fragile ecosystems through which you'll be traveling. Group size is usually kept small (no more than 10–20 people), and tours are almost always escorted by knowledgeable guides who are naturalists or animal biologists. Be sure to ask about difficulty levels when you are choosing a tour. While most companies offer "soft adventure" packages that those in moderately good, but not phenomenal, shape can handle, others focus on more hard-core activities that only seasoned athletes or adventure travelers should take on.

U.S.-BASED ADVENTURE TOUR OPERATORS

These agencies and operators specialize in well-organized and coordinated tours, set up for your entire stay. Many travelers prefer to have everything arranged and confirmed before arriving in Costa Rica, and this is a good idea in the high season.

International Expeditions Inc., One Environs Park, Helena, AL 35080 (☎ 205/428-1700 or 800/633-4734), specializes in independent programs and 10-day natural history group tours.

Journeys International, Inc., 4011 Jackson Rd., Ann Arbor, MI 48103 (☎ 313/665-4407 or 800/255-8735), offers small group (no more than 4–12 people) natural history tours guided by Costa Rican naturalists. Horseback riding is included. 8-day, 10-day, and three-week itineraries are available.

Mountain Travel•Sobek, 6420 Fairmount Ave., El Cerrito, CA 94530 (☎ 510/527-8100 or 800/227-2384), offers natural history tours with naturalist guides. 10-day itineraries can include visits to Corcovado and Tortuguero National Parks, Monteverde, and Arenal Volcano; activities include jungle walks, boat rides, snorkeling, and swimming. All accommodations are in lodges, with the exception of the first and last nights of each itinerary—these are spent in hotels in San José.

Wilderness Travel, 801 Allston Way, Berkeley, CA 94710 (☎ 510/548-0420 or 800/368-2794), specializes in natural history and birdwatching 14-day group tours. Tier-priced, depending upon the number of people who sign up (cost increases with a smaller group). Tours include visits to Corcovado and Tortuguero National Parks, Monteverde, Arenal Volcano, and Caño Negro National Wildlife Refuge, among other destinations.

Overseas Adventure Travel, 625 Mount Auburn, Cambridge, MA 02138 (☎ 617/876-0533 or 800/221-0814), offers natural history and "soft adventure" 10- and 12-day itineraries, with optional three-day add-on excursions. Tours are limited to no more than 16 people and are guided by naturalists. All accommodations are in small hotels, lodges, or tent camps. Itineraries include visits to most major national parks and private nature reserves.

Costa Rica Connections, 75 Oso St., San Luis Obispo, CA 93401 (☎ 805/543-8823 or 800/345-7422), specializes in natural history tours of major national parks. There is a complete range of independent packages and scheduled group departures for birdwatching, fishing, eco-tourism, kayaking/rafting, and dive trips, plus the Costa Rica National Orchid show.

In addition to the above-mentioned companies, many environmental organizations, including **The Sierra Club** (☎ 415/977-5522, between 8:30am and 5pm PST), **The Nature Conservancy** (☎ 800/727-9041), and **The National Audubon Society** (☎ 800/274-4201), regularly offer organized trips to Costa Rica.

COSTA RICAN TOUR AGENCIES

Since many U.S.-based companies subcontract portions of their tours to established Costa Rican companies in the field, some travelers like to set up their tours directly with these companies, therefore cutting out the middleman.

There are literally scores of agencies in San José that offer a plethora of adventure options. These agencies can generally arrange everything from white-water rafting, to sightseeing at one of the nearby volcanoes, to a visit to a butterfly farm. Because these tours are sometimes held only when there are enough interested people or on set dates, it pays to contact a few of the companies before you leave the U.S. and find out what they might be doing when you plan to be in Costa Rica.

Adventure Land/Tam Tours, P.O. Box 1864-1000, San José, Costa Rica (☎ 506/222-3866 or 506/222-2642, fax 506/222-3724), offers a full gamut of San José-based day tours to such destinations as Arenal Volcano and Tabacón Hot Springs, Carara Biological Reserve, and local national parks. All tours include transportation, entry fees, lunch, and a guide.

Costa Rica Expeditions, Dept. 235, P.O. Box 025216, Miami, FL 33102 (☎ 506/257-0766 or 506/222-0333, fax 506/257-1665), offers three-day/two-night and two-day/one-night tours of Monteverde Biological Cloud Forest Preserve, Tortuguero National Park, and Corcovado National Park, as well as one- to two-day white-water rafting trips and other excursions. All excursions include transportation, meals, and lodging.

Costa Rica Sun Tours, Apdo. 1195-1250, Escazú (☎ 506/255-3418, fax 506/255-3529), specializes in multi-day tours that include stays at small country lodges for nature-oriented travelers. Destinations visited include Arenal Volcano (with stays at the Arenal Observatory Lodge); Monteverde Cloud Forest with stops in Poàs and Sarchí; and Corcovado and Manuel Antonio National Parks (with overnight stays at Tiskita Jungle Lodge, Corcovado Tent Camp, Lapa Rios, and Drake Bay Wilderness Lodge, among other accommodations).

Ecole Travel, Calle 7, between Avenidas Central and 1, San José, Costa Rica (☎ 506/223-2240, fax 506/223-4128), offers tours and day trips around the country.

Fantasy Tours, Apdo. 962-1000, San José, Costa Rica (☎ 506/220-2126 or 506/220-0042, fax 506/220-2393), offers a comprehensive list of full-day tours to destinations that include: Arenal Volcano and Tabacón Hot Springs; Poás and Irazu volcanos; Manuel Antonio National Park; Carara Biological Reserve; and Bosque de Paz, a private biological reserve. White-water rafting expeditions, fishing trips, island cruises, and multi-day tours are also available.

Geotur, Apdo. 469 Y-1011, San José (☎/fax 506/227-4029), specializes in one-day visits to Carara Biological Reserve. It also offers three-day horseback riding trips through the Guanacaste dry forest, a full-day "Resplendent Quetzal" tour, plus a wide range of one-day and longer excursions and tours of the major national parks.

OTEC Viajes, Apdo. 323-1002, San José, Costa Rica (☎ 506/256-0633, fax 506/233-2321), offers a wide range of tour options. Specializes in student and discount travel.

Pura Natura, Apdo. 10923-1000 (Avenida 1, between calles 1 and 3, Edificio Cristal), San José (☎ 506/233-9469 or 506/233-9709, fax 506/223-9200), offers one- to five-day hiking, mountain-biking, and horseback-riding trips that are among the most adventurous of any available in Costa Rica. You can hike through Corcovado National Park or up to the peak of Mount Chirripó, among other trips.

2 Special-Interest Adventure Travel & Active Sports

This section is an A–Z compendium of the many activities and active sports available in Costa Rica. Each listing describes the best places to practice a particular sport or activity and lists tour operators and outfitters that you can contact. If you only want to focus on one active sport during your Costa Rican stay, these companies are your best bets for quality equipment and knowledgeable service.

BIKING

Although there are several major regional and international touring races in Costa Rica each year, in general, the major roads are dangerous and inhospitable for cyclists. The roads are narrow, there's usually no shoulder, and most drivers show little care or consideration for those on two wheels.

The options are much more appealing for mountain bikers and off-track riders, however. Fat-tire explorations are relatively new to Costa Rica, but growing fast. If you plan to do a lot of biking and are very attached to your rig, bring your own. However, several companies in San José and elsewhere rent bikes, and the quality of the equipment is improving all the time. See the regional chapters for listings of places that rent bicycles.

The best place for mountain biking in Costa Rica is all around **Lake Arenal and Arenal Volcano.** The scenery's great, with primary forests, waterfalls, and plenty of trails. And nearby **Tabacón Hot Springs** is a perfect place for those with aching muscles to unwind at the end of the day. (See chapter 7.)

TOUR OPERATORS & OUTFITTERS

Coast To Coast Adventures, Apdo. 2135-1002, San José, Costa Rica (☎ 506/225-6055), specializes in two-week trips spanning the country that combine horses, rafts, mountain bikes, and hiking, but no motor vehicles. Other trips are available.

EcoTreks Adventure Company, Dept. 262, P.O. Box 025216, Miami, FL 33102 (☎ 506/289-8192 or 800/328-2288 in the U.S., fax 506/289-8191), specializes in mountain biking trips, among other sports.

Experience Plus/Specialty Tours, Inc., 1925 Wallenburg Drive, Ft. Collins, CO 80526 (☎ 800/685-4565), offers self-guided and assisted bike tours across the country.

Rio Escondido Mountain Bikes, c/o Rock River Lodge, Apdo. 95, Tilarán, Costa Rica (☎ 506/695-5644 or in the U.S. 800/678-2252), offers rentals and tours around the Lake Arenal area.

Serendipity Adventures, Apdo. 64200, Naranjo, Costa Rica (☎/fax 506/450-0328 or 800/635-2325 in the U.S.), offers mountain biking trips, among other expeditions.

Where to See the Resplendent Quetzal

Revered by pre-Columbian cultures throughout Central America, the resplendent quetzal has been called the most beautiful bird on earth. Ancient Aztec and Maya Indians believed the quetzal protected them in battle, and even the bird's brilliant breast plumage has an Indian legend to explain it: When Spanish conquistador Pedro de Alvarado defeated Maya chieftain Tecun Uman in 1524 near what is today the town of Quezaltenango, Guatemala, the Maya chief was mortally wounded in the chest. Tecun Uman's protector quetzal covered the dying chieftain's body, and when, upon Tecun Uman's death, the quetzal arose, the once white-breasted bird had a blood-red breast. So integral a part of Guatemalan culture is the quetzal that its name is given to that country's currency.

About the size of a robin, the males of this species have brilliant red breasts; iridescent emerald green heads, backs, and wings; and white tail feathers complemented by a pair of iridescent green tail feathers that are nearly two feet long. These birds live only in the dense cloud forests that cloak the higher slopes of Central America's mountains. Throughout their range, quetzals are endangered, and though many areas of cloud forest have been preserved as habitat for these beautiful birds, researchers have recently discovered that the birds do not spend their entire lives within the cloud forest. After nesting, between March and July, quetzals migrate down to lower slopes in search of food. These lower slopes have not been preserved in most cases, and now conservationists are trying to salvage enough lower elevation forests to help the quetzals survive. Hopefully, enough land will soon be set aside to assure the perpetuation of this magnificent species of bird.

Though for many years Monteverde Biological Cloud Forest Preserve was the place to see quetzals, throngs of people crowding the preserve's trails now make it difficult to see any wildlife. Other places where you are more likely to see quetzals are in the Los Angeles Cloud Forest Reserve near San Ramón, on the Cerro de la Muerte between San José and San Isidro de El General, in Tapantí National Wildlife Refuge, and in Chirripó National Park.

BIRDWATCHING

As one of the world's foremost eco-travel destinations, Costa Rica is visited by thousands of avid birdwatchers each year. Lodges with the best birdwatching include: **Albergue de Montaña Savegre** and **Albergue de Montaña Tapantí,** both on the road to San Isidro de El General (they can almost guarantee sightings of resplendent quetzals); **La Paloma Lodge** in Drake Bay (where you can sit on the porch of your cabin as the avian parade goes by); **Villa Blanca** in San Ramón (on the edge of a cloud forest reserve where quetzals are often seen); **Selva Verde Lodge,** Chilamate (the rooms overlook some woods, and the rain forest is just across the river); **Aviarios del Caribe** just north of Cahuita; **Lapa Rios** on the Osa Peninsula (where I spotted two species of toucan parakeets and hummingbirds before I ever made it in from the parking area); and **D'Galah Hotel** in San José (the University of Costa Rica, an oasis of greenery in the city, is directly across the street).

Some of the best parks and preserves to visit include **Monteverde Biological Cloud Forest Preserve** (resplendent quetzals and hummingbirds); **Corcovado National Park** (scarlet macaws); **Caño Negro Wildlife Refuge** (wading birds, including jabiru storks); **Guayabo, Negritos, and Pájaros islands biological reserves** in the Gulf of Nicoya (magnificent frigate birds and brown boobies); **Palo Verde**

National Park (ibises, jacanas, storks, roseate spoonbills); **Tortuguero National Park** (great green macaws); and **Rincón de la Vieja National Park** (parakeets, curassows). Some good excursions to consider if birdwatching is your passion are rafting float trips down the Corobicí near Liberia, boat trips to or at Tortuguero National Park, and hikes in any cloud forest.

U.S. TOUR OPERATORS

Costa Rica Connections, 958 Higuera St., San Luis Obispo, CA 93401 (☎ 305/279-3252 or 800/882-4665), generally offers three birdwatching trips a year, including a 12-day "Tropical Birding" tour.

Geostar Travel, 6050 Commerce Blvd., Suite 110, Rohnert Park, CA 94928 (☎ 707/584-9552 or 800/633-6633), has 7-day and 10-day tours ($1,090 7 day, $1,460 10 day).

Osprey Tours, P.O. Box 030211, Fort Lauderdale, FL 33302 (☎ 305/767-4823), specializes in customized group birdwatching tours.

COSTA RICAN TOUR AGENCIES

San José Travel, Apdo. 889, San José 1007 (☎ 506/221-0593, fax 506/221-5148); and **Geotur,** Apdo. 469Y, San José 1011 (☎ 506/234-1867, fax 506/253-6338), both offer one-day quetzal tours. **Jungle Trails,** Apdo. 2413, San José 1000 (☎ 506/255-3486, fax 506/255-2782), sponsors one-day birding excursions to Braulio Carrillo and Poàs national parks as well as an extensive 15-day tour.

BUNGEE JUMPING & BALLOONING

Both of these sports are new to Costa Rica, so as yet, there's only one operator to work with. The price you'll pay is generally cheaper than in the U.S. and the scenery is certainly more lush, so if you've never done either activity, this is a great place to give it a try. **Tropical Bungee** (☎ 506/233-6455) will let you jump off a 265-foot bridge for $45; if you want to do it twice, they'll charge you $70. **Serendipity Adventures** (☎ 506/450-0328 or 800/635-2325 in the U.S.) will take you up and away in one of their hot air balloons on a variety of single- or multi-day tours, beginning around $195 per person.

CAMPING

Heavy rains, difficult access, and limited facilities make camping a real challenge in Costa Rica. Nevertheless, a backpack and tent will get you far from the crowds and into some of the most pristine and undeveloped nooks and crannies of Costa Rica. Those who relish sleeping out on a beach, but wouldn't mind a bit more luxury (beds, someone to prepare meals for you, and running water), might want to consider staying in one of the tent camps on the Osa Peninsula (Drake Bay Wilderness Camp, Corcovado Adventure Tent Camp, or Corcovado Lodge Tent Camp). See chapter 9 for details. Camping isn't allowed in all national parks, so read through the write-ups for each park carefully before you pack a tent.

If you'd like to participate in an organized camping trip, contact **Serendipity Adventures,** Apdo. 64200, Naranjo, Costa Rica (☎/fax 506/450-0328 or 800/635-2325 in the U.S.). In addition to their other expeditions, they offer climbing and camping trips.

In my opinion, the best place to pop up a tent on the beach is in Santa Rosa National Park, or at the Puerto Vargas campsite in Cahuita National Park. The best camping trek is, without a doubt, a hike through Corcovado National Park, or a climb up Mt. Chirripó.

CANOPY TOURS

Canopy tours are taking off in Costa Rica, largely because they are such a unique way to experience tropical rain forests. It is estimated that some two-thirds of a typical rain forest's species live in the canopy, or the uppermost branching layer. From the relative luxury of the Aerial Tram's high-tech funicular to the rope and climbing gear rigs of more basic operations, a trip into the canopy will give you a bird's-eye view of a neotropical forest. There are now canopy tour facilities in Drake Bay, Corcovado National Park, Monteverde, and Rincón de la Vieja National Park, as well as on Tortuga Island. With the exception of the Aerial Tram, most involve strapping yourself into a climbing harness and being winched up to a platform some 100 feet above the forest floor.

CANOPY TOUR OPERATORS

Aerial Tram, Apdo. 592-2100, San José, Costa Rica (☎ 506/257-5961, fax 506/257-6053), is located 50 minutes from San José. This modern tram takes you on a 2-hour trip through the rain forest canopy. Cost $47.50, transportation extra.

   Canopy Tours, Apdo. 751-2350, San José, Costa Rica (☎/ fax 506/257-5149 or 506/256-7626), is a loose grouping of more adventurous canopy tour operations around the country.

CRUISING

Cruising options in Costa Rica range from motorized floating resorts to converted fishing boats taking a few guests out for a sunset cruise. Perhaps the most popular of the former is a day trip to **Isla Tortuga** in the Nicoya Gulf from San José (see "Recreational Day Trips" in chapter 5, under the section "Easy Excursions from San José"). Alternatively, you can book a cruise to Tortuga from **Playa Montezuma** at the tip of the Nicoya Peninsula. From here, the cost is much cheaper (around $25 per person), but the excursion does not include the gourmet lunch that is usually a feature on cruises leaving from San José (see chapter 6 for details).

   Another interesting option is to take a cruise on the *Temptress.* This small cruise ship plies the waters off Costa Rica's Pacific coast from Santa Rosa National Park in the north to Corcovado National Park in the south. The ship usually anchors in remote, isolated, and very beautiful spots. Each day you have an option of a natural-history tour or a recreational and cultural tour. For information, contact ***Temptress* Cruises,** 1606 NW LeJeune, Suite 301, Miami, FL 33126 (☎ 305/871-2663 or 506/220-1679 in Costa Rica, or 800/336-8423).

   If diesel fumes and engine noise bother you, the best places to charter a sailboat are **Playa del Coco** and **Playa Hermosa,** in Guanacaste province (see chapter 6); **Quepos,** along the Central Pacific Coast (see chapter 8); and **Golfito,** along the Southern Pacific Coast (see chapter 9). Ask at any one of the larger lodgings in these areas, and you should be able to find a captain who will take you out. My favorite place to charter a sailboat is **Golfito.** From here, it's a pleasant, peaceful day's sail around the Golfo Dulce. (See chapter 9.) Alternatively, you could charter a sailboat through **Veleros del Sur Sail Boat Chartering** (Apdo. 13-5400, Puntarenas; ☎ 506/661-1320 or 506/661-3880) and explore the Gulf of Nicoya.

DIVING

Off Costa Rica's coastline lie many islands, reefs, caves, and rocks that are more than adequate for underwater exploration. Visibility varies with season and location. Generally heavy rainfall tends to swell the rivers and muddy the waters, even well offshore. Banana plantations and their runoff have destroyed most of the Caribbean reefs, although there's still good diving at **Isla Uvita,** just off the coast of Limón. Most divers choose Pacific dive spots like **Caño Island, Bat Island,** and the **Catalina Islands,** where you're likely to spot manta rays, moray eels, white-tipped sharks, and plenty of smaller fish and coral species. But the ultimate in Costa Rican dive experiences is a week spent on a chartered boat, diving off the coast of **Coco Island**.

SCUBA DIVING OUTFITTERS & OPERATORS

In addition to the companies listed below, check the listings at specific beach and port destinations in the regional chapters.

Buzos del Tropico, Apdo. 366-3100, Sto. Domingo de Heredia, Costa Rica (☎/fax 506/222-5481), offers equipment rental, certification classes, and trips. **Escenarios Tropicales,** Apdo. 2047-1000, San José (☎ 506/224-2555, fax 506/234-1554), specializes in live-aboard trips to Caño and Cocos islands. **Mundo Aquatico,** P.O. Box 7875-1000, San José, Costa Rica (☎ 506/224-9729, fax 506/234-2982), offers equipment rental, certification classes and tours. **EcoTreks Adventure Company,** Dept. 262, P.O. Box 025216, Miami, FL 33102 (☎ 506/289-8191 or 800/328-2288 in the U.S., fax 506/289-8191), sponsors diving excursions, in addition to mountain biking and surfing trips.

FISHING

Anglers in Costa Rican waters have landed more than 65 world-record catches, including blue marlin, Pacific sailfish, dolphin, wahoo, yellowfin tuna, guapote, and snook. Whether you want to head offshore looking for a big sail, wrestle a tarpon near a Caribbean river mouth, or choose a quiet spot on Arenal Lake to cast for guapote, you'll find it here. The best place to land a marlin is anywhere up or down the Pacific coast.

FISHING LODGES & TOUR OPERATORS

The lodges and operators listed below cater specifically to anglers. Many of the Pacific port and beach towns—Quepos, Puntarenas, Playas del Coco, Tamarindo, Flamingo, Golfito, Drake Bay, Zancudo—support large charter fleets; see chapters 4, 8, and 9 for recommended boats and captains.

Isla de Pesca Lodge, P.O. Box 7-1880-1000, San José, Costa Rica. ☎ 506/239-1025 or 305/858-7478 in the U.S. Fax 506/239-2405.

Rio Colorado Lodge, 2121 West Juneau Avenue, Tampa, FL 33604. ☎ 506/232-4063 or 800/243-9777 in the U.S. Fax 813/933-3280.

Silver King Lodge, Rainforest Excursions, 1107 East Lemon St., Tarpon Springs, FL 34689. ☎/fax 506/288-0849.

Americana Fishing Services, Apdo. 6241-1000, San José, Costa Rica. Ask for Richard Krug. ☎ 506/223-4331. Fax 506/221-0096.

Costa Rican Dreams, P.O. Box 79, Belén, Heredia, Costa Rica. ☎ 506/239-3387 or 506/777-0593. Fax 506/239-3383.

Fresh Water Fishing Adventures, Via Alta, Bello Horizonte, Escazú, Costa Rica. ☎ 506/228-4812 or 800/434-6867 in the U.S.

J.P. Tours, P.O. Box 66-1100, Tibás, Costa Rica. ☎ 506/284-7592 or in the U.S. 800/308-3394. Fax 506/244-0552.

HORSEBACK RIDING

As Costa Rica moves away from a primarily agricultural economy, it continues to retain its rural roots. This is perhaps most evident in the continued use of horses for real work and transportation throughout the country. What this means for travelers is that horses are easily available for riding, whether you want to take a sunset trot along the beach, a ride through the cloud forest, or a multi-day trek through the northern zone. Almost anywhere outside San José is fine for climbing into a saddle.

OUTFITTERS & TOUR OPERATORS

Rancho Savegre Horseback Tours, Rancho Savegre, c/o Hotel Sirena, P.O. Box 02592, Miami, FL 33102 (☎/fax 506/777-0528 or in the U.S. ☎ 800/355-2389 in the U.S.). Offers one- and multi-day horseback tours, based out of Rancho Savegre, near Quepos.

    Coast To Coast Adventures, Apdo. 2135-1002, San José, Costa Rica (☎ 225-6055), specializes in two-week trips spanning the country that combine horses, rafts, mountain bikes, and hiking, but no motor vehicles. Other trips are available.

SURFING

When *Endless Summer II,* the sequel to the all-time surf classic, was filmed, the production crew brought its boards and cameras to Costa Rica. Up and down Costa Rica's immense coastline are point and beach breaks that work almost all year-round. **Playas Hermosa and Tamarindo** are becoming surf mini-Meccas. Salsa Brava in **Puerto Viejo** has a habit of breaking boards, but the daredevils keep coming back for more. You'll almost never find a crowd, but the less sociable and more adventurous keep finding secret spots all around the Osa and Nicoya Peninsulas and along the northern Guanacaste coast. The most memorable rides are to be had at Playa Pavones, which is reputed to have one of the longest waves in the world.

WATCHING SEA TURTLES NESTING

Few places in the world have as many sea turtle nesting sites as Costa Rica. Along both coasts, five species of these huge marine reptiles come ashore at specific times of the year to dig nests in the sand and lay their eggs. Sea turtles are endangered throughout the world due to overhunting, accidental deaths in fishing nets, development on beaches formerly used as nesting areas, and the collection and sale (often illegally) of their eggs. International trade in sea turtle products is already prohibited by most countries (including the United States), but sea turtle numbers continue to dwindle.

    Among the species of sea turtles that nest on Costa Rica's beaches are olive Ridley (known for their mass egg-laying migrations known as *arribadas*), leatherback, hawksbill, green, and Pacific green turtles. Excursions to see nesting turtles have become common, and though these tours are fascinating, please make sure that you and your guide do not disturb the turtles. Any light source (other than red-tinted flashlights) can confuse female turtles and cause them to return to the sea without laying their eggs. In fact, as more and more development takes place on the Costa Rican coast, the lights created by hotels may cause the number of nesting turtles to drop. Luckily, many of the nesting beaches have been protected as national parks. The following are the main places to see nesting sea turtles: **Santa Rosa National Park** (near Liberia), **Las Baulas National Marine Park** (near Tamarindo), **Ostional National Wildlife Refuge** (near Playa Nosara), and **Tortuguero National Park** (on the northern Caribbean coast).

    See the regional chapters for listings of local tour operators and companies through which you can arrange to see sea turtles nesting.

WINDSURFING

Windsurfing is still not very popular on the high seas here, where winds are fickle, and rental options are limited—even at beach hotels. However, Lake Arenal is considered one of the top spots in the world for high-wind board sailing. During the winter months many of the regulars from Washington's Columbia River Gorge take up residence around the town of Tilarán. Small boards, water starts, and fancy gibes are the norm. The best time for windsurfing on Lake Arenal is between December and March. See chapter 7 for more information.

WHITE-WATER RAFTING & KAYAKING

Whether you are a first-time rafter or a world-class kayaker, Costa Rica's got some white water suited to your abilities. Rivers rise and fall with the rainfall, but you can get wet and wild here even in the dry season. If you're just experimenting with river rafting, stick to class II and III rivers, like the **Reventazon, Sarapiquí,** and **Savegre.** If you already know which end of the paddle goes in the water, there are plenty of class IV and V sections to run. The best river ride is still the scenic Pacuare river, which, unfortunately, may be dammed soon.

WHITE-WATER RAFTING & KAYAKING OUTFITTERS

Aventuras Naturales, P.O. Box 107360-1000, San José, Costa Rica. ☎ 506/ 225-3939 or 800/308-3394 in the U.S. Fax 506/253-6934; **Costa Rica White Water,** Dept. 235, P.O. Box 025216, Miami, FL 33102. ☎ 506/257-0766 or 506/ 222-0333. Fax 506/257-1665; **Costa Sol Rafting,** P.O. Box 8-4390-1000, San José, Costa Rica. ☎ 506/293-2151 or 800/245-8420 in the U.S. Fax 506/293-2155 or 305/858-7478 in the U.S.; **Escondido Trex,** Apdo. 9, Puerto Jiménez, Osa Penin- sula, Costa Rica. ☎/fax 506/735-5210; **Iguana Tours,** Apdo. 207, Quepos, Costa Rica. ☎/fax 506/777-1262 or 506/777-0574. **Rancho Leona Kayak Tours,** Rancho Leona, La Virgen de Sarapiquí, Heredia, Costa Rica. ☎ 506/761-1019; **Rios Tropicales,** Apdo. 472-1200, Pavas, Costa Rica. ☎ 506/233-6455. Fax 506/ 255-4354; and **Serendipity Adventures,** Apdo. 64200, Naranjo, Costa Rica. ☎/fax 506/ 450-0328 or 800/635-2325 in the U.S. In addition to their ballooning, mountain biking, climbing, and camping trips, they offer river-rafting expeditions.

3 Costa Rica's National Parks & Bioreserves

Costa Rica has 31 national parks protecting over 11% of the country. The parks range in size from the 530-acre Guayabo National Monument to the 474,240-acre La Amistad National Park. Many of these national parks are undeveloped tropical for- ests, with few services or facilities available for tourists. Others, however, offer a wealth of natural wonders for visitors to explore and enjoy.

ADMISSION FEES

In 1995, the government of Costa Rica drastically raised admission fees to its national parks, with a two-tiered fee system for residents and foreign visitors. Guess who got to pay more? Following an initial backlash, the government backed down slightly and instituted a confusing system of varied park fees, combined with advanced purchase discounts. Tourists, tour operators, and hotel owners all complained about the lunacy of the situation. Apparently, the government and park system were befuddled as well. In April 1996, the government instituted its fourth national park pricing scheme in two years, settling on a flat $6 per person per day fee for any foreigner visiting any national park. No advance purchases are necessary. Costa Ricans and for- eign residents continue to pay just $1. At parks where camping is allowed, there is an additional charge of $1.50 per person per day.

The section that follows is not a complete listing of all of Costa Rica's national parks and protected areas, but rather a selective list of just those parks that are of greatest interest and accessibility. They're popular, but they're also among the best. For more information on the national parks, call the national parks office at 506/ 257-0922 from the U.S., or by dialing 192 from Costa Rica. Or you can stop by the **National Parks Foundation** office (☎ 506/257-2239) in San José, which is located between Calle 23 and Avenida 15. It's open 9am to 5pm daily.

THE MOST POPULAR PARKS & BIORESERVES—FROM A TO Z

Below are brief descriptions of the more accessible and frequently visited national parks and bioreserves. You will find detailed information about food and lodging options near some of the individual parks in the regional chapters that follow. As you'll see from the descriptions, Costa Rica's national parks vary greatly in terms of attractions, facilities, and accessibility. If you're looking for a camping adventure or an extended stay in one of the national parks, I would recommend **Santa Rosa, Rincón de la Vieja, Chirripó,** or **Corcovado.** Any of the others are better suited for day trips or in combination with your travels around the country. Since the entrance fees are rather steep, it makes sense to plan ahead and try to pick a park (or parks) that fits your needs and interests.

ARENAL NATIONAL PARK

A new park, created to protect the ecosystem that surrounds Arenal Volcano, it has few services or attractions. Basically, the government has set up a toll booth on the access road one must drive to get close to the volcano's lava flows. Most tourists and tour operators choose to forgo this park and watch the volcano from spots along the dirt road leading to the Arenal Observatory Lodge. From there, you are only approximately 1 kilometer away, and still plenty close to the volcano. Location: 80 miles northwest of San José. See chapter 7.

BARRA HONDA NATIONAL PARK

Costa Rica's only underground national park, Barra Honda features a series of limestone caves that were once part of a coral reef, some 60 million years ago. Today the caves are home to millions of bats and impressive stalactite and stalagmite formations. There is a camping area, restrooms, and an information center here. Location: 208 miles northwest of San José. See chapter 6.

BRAULIO CARRILLO NATIONAL PARK

This park occupies a large area of the nation's Central mountain range. This is the park you pass through on your way between San José and the Caribbean coast. A deep rain forest, Braulio Carrillo receives an average of 177 inches of rain per year. There are beautiful rivers, majestic waterfalls, and over 6,500 species of plants and animals. The park has an information center, picnic tables, restrooms, and hiking trails. Camping is allowed. Be careful here. Make sure you park your car and base your explorations from the park's main entrance and not just from anywhere along the highway. There have been several robberies and attacks against tourists reported at trails leading into the park from the highway. This park also seems to have the highest incidence of lost hikers. Location: 14 miles north of San José. See chapter 7.

CAHUITA NATIONAL PARK

A combination land and marine park, Cahuita National Park protects one of the few remaining living coral reefs in the country. The topography here is lush lowland tropical rain forest. Monkeys and numerous bird species are common. Camping is permitted and there are basic facilities at the Puerto Vargas entrance to the park. If you only want to visit for the day, however, enter from Cahuita village, because as of press time, the local community had taken over the entrance and was only asking for a voluntary donation. Location: On the Caribbean coast, 26 miles south of Limón. See chapter 10.

CAÑO NEGRO NATIONAL WILDLIFE REFUGE

A lowland swamp and drainage basin for several northern rivers, Caño Negro is excellent for birdwatching. This wildlife refuge makes a good day trip from the La Fortuna/Arenal area. Location: 12.5 miles south of Los Chiles, near the Nicaraguan border. Entry fee $6. See chapter 9.

CHIRRIPÓ NATIONAL PARK

Home to Costa Rica's tallest peak, 12,536 foot Mount Chirripó, Chirripó National Park is quite a hike, but on a clear day, you can see both the Pacific Ocean and Caribbean Sea from its summit. There is camping and a number of interesting climbing trails. Location: 94 miles southeast of San José. See chapter 8.

COCO ISLAND NATIONAL PARK

A large uninhabited island located 360 miles off Costa Rica's Pacific coast, Coco Island National Park is beautiful, with many endemic species of flora and fauna. The diving here is also world-renowned. See "Diving," under "Special-Interest Adventure Travel and Active Sports," for a recommendation of an operator that runs dive trips out here.

CORCOVADO NATIONAL PARK

The largest single block of virgin lowland rain forest in Central America, Corcovado National Park receives over 200 inches of rain per year. One of Costa Rica's increasingly popular national parks, it is still largely a remote area (it has no roads, and only dirt tracks lead into it). Scarlet macaws live here, as do countless other neotropical species, including two of the country's largest cats, the endangered puma and jaguar. There are camping facilities and trails throughout the park. Location: 208 miles south of San José, on the Osa Peninsula. See chapter 9.

GUAYABO NATIONAL MONUMENT

The country's only significant pre-Colombian archeological site, it is believed that Guayabo supported a population of about 10,000 people, some 1,000 years before Christ. Location: 12 miles northeast of Turrialba. See chapter 5.

IRAZÚ VOLCANO NATIONAL PARK

Irazú Volcano is one of Costa Rica's four active volcanoes and a popular day trip from San José. At 11,260 feet, it is the country's highest volcano. A paved road leads right up to the crater, and the lookout also allegedly allows you a view of both oceans on a clear day. The volcano last erupted in 1963—the same day President John F. Kennedy visited the country. There is an information center, picnic tables, restrooms, and a parking area here. Location: 34 miles east of San José. See chapter 5.

MANUEL ANTONIO NATIONAL PARK

The grand dame of Costa Rican national parks, Manuel Antonio supports the largest number of hotels and resorts of any national park at its edge. This lowland rain forest is home to a healthy monkey population, including the endangered squirrel monkey. The park is best known for its splendid beaches. However, with such a steep entrance fee, you may want to think about finding another place to sunbathe and beachcomb. Location: 80 miles south of San José. See chapter 8.

Costa Rica's National Parks & Bioreserves

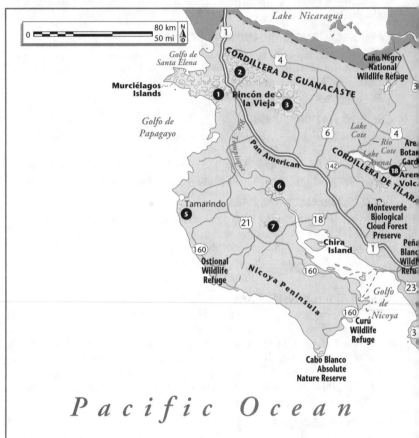

Lake Nicaragua

Golfo de Santa Elena

CORDILLERA DE GUANACASTE

Caño Negro National Wildlife Refuge

Murciélagos Islands

Rincón de la Vieja

Golfo de Papagayo

Río Tempisque

Pan American

Lake Cote

Río Cote

Lake Arenal

CORDILLERA DE TILARA

Aren Botan Gard

Aren Volc

Tamarindo

Monteverde Biological Cloud Forest Preserve

Peña Blanc Wildl Refu

Chira Island

Ostional Wildlife Refuge

Nicoya Peninsula

Golfo de Nicoya

Curú Wildlife Refuge

Cabo Blanco Absolute Nature Reserve

Pacific Ocean

Coco Island

LEGEND

✈ Airport

Arenal National Park **18**
Ballena Marine National Park **12**
Barra Honda National Park **7**
Braulio Carrillo National Park **9**
Cahuita National Park **15**
Carara Biological Reserve **21**
Chirripó National Park **13**
Coco Island National Park **20**
Corcovado National Park **16**
Guanacaste National Park **2**
Guayabo National Monument **22**

Irazú Volcano National Park **10**
Juan Castro Blanco National Park **17**
La Amistad National Park **14**
Las Baulas Marine National Park **5**
Manuel Antonio National Park **11**
Palo Verde National Park **6**
Poás Volcano National Park **8**
Rincón de la Vieja National Park **3**
Santa Rosa National Park **1**
Tapantí National Wildlife Refuge **19**
Tortuguero National Park **4**

2360

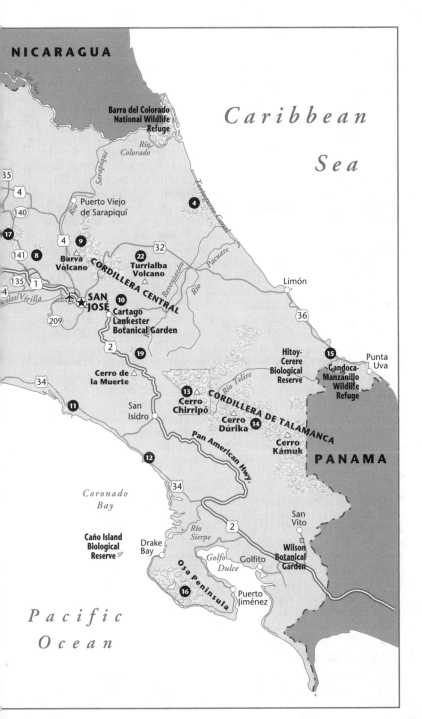

NICARAGUA

Barra del Colorado
National Wildlife
Refuge

*Río
Colorado*

Caribbean

Sea

35

4

140

Puerto Viejo
de Sarapiquí

4

17

141

8

4 9

135

1

4

coles/Vir-illa

209

SAN
JOSÉ

Barva
Volcano

CORDILLERA CENTRAL

22

Turrialba
Volcano

32

10

Cartago
Lankester
Botanical Garden

2

19

Cerro de
la Muerte

11

San
Isidro

13

Cerro
Chirripó

CORDILLERA DE TALAMANCA

Cerro
Dúrika

14

Cerro
Kámuk

Hitoy-
Cerere
Biological
Reserve

15

Gandoca-
Manzanillo
Wildlife
Refuge

Punta
Uva

Limón

36

PANAMA

12

Pan American Hwy.

34

*Coronado
Bay*

Caño Island
Biological
Reserve

Drake
Bay

*Río
Sierpe*

2

*Golfo
Dulce*

Golfito

San
Vito

Wilson
Botanical
Garden

Osa Peninsula

16

Puerto
Jiménez

Pacific

Ocean

67

Monkey Business

No trip to Costa Rica would be complete without at least one monkey sighting. Home to four distinct species of primates, which inhabit the forests along both coasts as well as those in between, Costa Rica offers the opportunity for one of the world's most gratifying wildlife-watching experiences. You'll need a good guide to see your first few families, but in no time you'll be spotting them on your own. The deep guttural call of a howler or the rustling of leaves overhead on a jungle trail, are your cues.

Costa Rica's most commonly spotted monkey is the white-faced or capuchin monkey (*mono cara blanca* in Spanish). You may recognize this monkey as the infamous culprit from the film *Outbreak.* Contrary to the film's plot, however, these monkeys are endemic to the New World tropics, and do not exist in Africa. Capuchins are agile, medium-sized monkeys that make good use of their long prehensile tails. They inhabit a diverse collection of habitats, ranging from the high-altitude cloud forests of the central region to the lowland mangroves of the Osa Peninsula. It's almost impossible not to spot capuchins at Manuel Antonio (see chapter 8), where the resident white-faced monkeys have become a little too dependent on fruit and junk-food feedings by tourists. Please do not feed wild monkeys, and boycott establishments that try to attract both monkeys and tourists with daily feedings.

Howler monkeys (*mono congo* in Spanish) are named for their distinct and eerie call. Large, and mostly black, these monkeys can seem ferocious because of their physical appearance and deep, resonant howls that can carry for over a mile—even in dense rain forest. (To make these guttural noises, the throat sacs of male howlers vibrate. When a male howler howls, biologists believe he is marking the boundaries of his territory.) Among humans, however, howlers are in fact a little timid, and tend to stay higher up in the canopy than their white-faced cousins. Howlers are fairly common and easy to spot in the dry tropical forests of coastal Guanacaste and the Nicoya Peninsula (see chapter 6).

Even more elusive are spider monkeys (*mono araña* in Spanish). These long, slender monkeys are dark brown to black, and prefer the high canopies of primary rain forests. Spiders are very adept with their prehensile tails, but actually travel through the canopy with a hand-over-hand motion frequently imitated by their less graceful human cousins on playground "monkey bars" around the world. I've had my best luck spotting spiders along the edges of Tortuguero's jungle canals (see chapter 10), where howlers are also quite common.

The rarest and most endangered of Costa Rica's monkeys is the tiny squirrel monkey (*mono titi* in Spanish). These small brown monkeys have dark eyes surrounded by large white rings, white ears, white chests, and very long tails. In Costa Rica, squirrel monkeys can only be found in Manuel Antonio (see chapter 8) and the Osa Peninsula (see chapter 9). These seemingly hyperactive monkeys are predominantly fruit eaters, and often feed on bananas and other fruit trees near hotels in both of the above-mentioned regions. Despite being endangered, squirrels usually travel in large bands, so if you do see them, you'll likely see quite a few.

PALO VERDE NATIONAL PARK

A must for nature lovers and birdwatchers, Palo Verde National Park is one of Costa Rica's best-kept secrets. This part of the Tempisque River lowlands supports a population of over 50,000 waterfowl and forest bird species. Various ecosystems here include mangroves, savannah brush lands, and evergreen forests. There are camping facilities, an information center, and a scientific research station here. Location: 125 miles northwest of San José. See chapter 6.

POÁS VOLCANO NATIONAL PARK

Poás is the other active volcano close to San José. The main crater is over 1 mile wide, and it is constantly active with fumaroles and hot geysers. The area around the volcano is lush, but much of the growth is stunted due to the gasses and acid rain. The park sometimes closes when the gasses get too feisty. There are nature trails, picnic tables, rest rooms, and an information center. Location: 23 miles northwest of San José. See chapter 5.

RINCÓN DE LA VIEJA NATIONAL PARK

Rincón de la Vieja National Park is a large tract of park land of high volcanic activity. There are numerous fumaroles and geysers, as well as hot springs, cold pools, and mud pots. You should hire a guide for any hot spring or mud bath expeditions, because inexperienced visitors have been burned. Camping is permitted, and there is an information center, picnic area, and restrooms. Location: 165 miles northwest of San José. See chapter 6.

SANTA ROSA NATIONAL PARK

Occupying a large section of Costa Rica's northwestern Guanacaste province, Santa Rosa National Park contains the country's largest area of tropical dry forest, as well as important turtle nesting sites and the historically significant La Casona monument. There are also caves for exploring, and the beaches here are pristine and have basic camping facilities. An information center, picnic area, and restrooms are located at the main campsite and entrance. Location: 160 miles northwest of San José. See chapter 6.

TORTUGUERO NATIONAL PARK

Tortuguero National Park has been called the Venice of Costa Rica, because of its maze of jungle canals that meander through a dense lowland rain forest. Small boats, launches, and canoes carry visitors through these waterways, where Caiman, manatee, and numerous bird and mammal species are common. The extremely endangered great green macaw lives here. On the beaches, green sea turtles nest here every year between June and October. Still, many visitors to Tortuguero only pass through the park on their way to and from the village, since nearby canals outside of the park (hence free from entrance fees) offer many of the same sights and thrills. Nevertheless, the park does have a helpful information stand and some well-marked trails. Location: 160 miles from San José. See chapter 9.

4 Tips on Health, Safety & Etiquette in the Wilderness

Much of what is discussed below is common sense. For more detailed information, see "Health & Insurance" in chapter 3.

HEALTH & SAFETY

While most tours and activities are extremely safe, there are risks involved in any adventure activity. Know and respect your own physical limits before undertaking any strenuous activity. Be prepared for extremes in weather—ventures into the Costa Rican wilderness will probably expose you to extremes in temperature and rainfall.

Be prepared for wide fluctuations in weather. A sunny morning hike can quickly become a cold and wet ordeal. It's usually a good idea to carry along some form of rain gear when hiking in the rain forest, or to have a dry change of clothing waiting at the end of the trail. Make sure to bring along plenty of sunscreen when you're not going to be covered by the forest canopy.

If you do any backcountry packing or camping, remember, it really is a jungle out there. Don't go poking under rocks or fallen branches: Snake bites are very rare, but don't do anything to increase the odds. If you do encounter a snake, stay calm, don't make any sudden movements, and *do not* try to handle it. Also, avoid swimming in major rivers unless a guide or local operator can vouch for its safety. Though mountainous and white water sections are generally pretty safe, most mangrove canals and river mouths in Costa Rica support healthy crocodile and caiman populations.

Bugs and bug bites will probably be your greatest health concern in the Costa Rican wilderness. Mostly, bugs are an inconvenience, although mosquitoes can carry malaria or dengue (see chapter 3 for more information). A strong repellent and proper clothing will minimize both the danger and inconvenience. On the beaches you will probably be bitten by sand fleas, or *pirujas*. These nearly invisible insects leave an irritating welt. Try not to scratch, as this can lead to open sores and infections. Pirujas are most active at sunrise and sunset, so you might want to cover up or avoid the beaches at these times.

ETIQUETTE

Here's where common sense and some consideration come in handy. Whenever you enter and enjoy nature you should tread lightly and try not to disturb the natural environment. If you must take home a souvenir, take photos. Do not cut or uproot plants or flowers. Pack out everything you pack in, and **please** do not litter.

5 Ecologically Oriented Volunteer & Study Programs

Below are some institutions and organizations that are working on ecology and sustainable-development projects. Contact them if you are interested in studying or volunteering with them. Many of these projects are ongoing and ask that volunteers devote more than a week of their time.

Global Volunteers, 375 Little Canada Rd., St. Paul, MN 55117 (☎ 800/487-1074 or 612/482-0295), is a unique U.S.-based organization which offers travelers who've always wanted to have a "Peace Corps-like" experience but felt they couldn't make a 2-year commitment the opportunity of a lifetime. For two to three weeks, you can join one of their working vacations in Costa Rica. A certain set of skills, such as engineering or agricultural knowledge, is helpful, but by no means necessary. Each trip is undertaken at a particular community's request, to complete a project that has been requested by them.

Institute for Central American Development Studies (ICADS), Apdo. 3-2070 Sabanilla, San José (☎ 506/225-0508, fax 506/234-1337), offers internship and research opportunities in the areas of environment, agriculture, human rights, and women's studies. They also offer an intensive Spanish-language program. Their United States address is Dept. 826, P.O. Box 025216, Miami, FL 33102-5216.

Organization for Tropical Studies, Apdo. 676, San José (☎ 506/240-6696), represents several Costa Rican and U.S. universities. This organization's mission is to promote research, education, and the wise use of natural resources in the tropics. Research facilities include La Selva Biological Station near Braulio Carrillo National Park and the Wilson Botanical Gardens near San Vito.

At first blush, San José may seem little more than a chaotic jumble of cars, buses, buildings, and people. The central downtown section of San José is an urban planner's nightmare. The once quiet streets are now overburdened by traffic and in a near constant state of gridlock. Leaded fuels and a lack of emission controls have given San José a brown cloud. The city bustles, but is not particularly hospitable to tourists. Sidewalks are poorly maintained and claustrophobic, and street crime is on the rise. Most visitors quickly seek the sanctuary of their hotel room and the first chance to escape the city.

Still, San José is the most cosmopolitan city in Central America. Costa Rica's stable government and the Central Valley's climate have, over the years, attracted people from all over the world. There is a large diplomatic and international business presence here. One result has been the amazing variety of cuisines available in the city's restaurants. Another more recent result has been the proliferation of small hotels in renovated historic buildings. Together these restaurants and hotels provide visitors with a greater variety of options than are to be found anywhere between Mexico City and Bogotá.

San José is a city built on coffee. This is not to say that the city runs on bottomless pots of java. No, San José was built on the profits of the coffee export business. Between the airport and downtown you pass by coffee farms, and glancing up from almost any street in the city you can see, on the volcanic mountains that surround San José, a patchwork quilt of farm fields, most of which are planted with the *grano de oro* (golden bean), as it is known here. San José was a forgotten backwater of the Spanish empire until the first shipments of the local beans made their way to sleepy souls in Europe late in the 19th century. Soon, San José was riding high on this vegetable gold. Coffee planters, newly rich and craving culture, imposed a tax on themselves in order to build the Teatro Nacional, San José's most beautiful building. Coffee profits also built the city a university. Today, you can smell the coffee roasting as you wander the streets near the central market, and in any cafe or restaurant you can get a hot cup of sweet, milky café con leche to remind you of the bean that built San José.

Why does coffee grow so well around San José? It's the climate. The Central Valley, in which the city sits, has a perfect climate. At 3,750 feet above sea level, San José enjoys springlike temperatures year-round. It is this pleasant climate and the beautiful views of lush green mountainsides that make San José a memorable city to visit. All you have to do is glance up at those mountains to know that this is one of the most beautiful capital cities in Central America. And if a glance isn't enough for you, you'll find that it's extremely easy to get out into the countryside from San José. Within an hour or two, you can climb a volcano, go white-water rafting, hike through a cloud forest, and stroll through a butterfly garden, among many other activities.

1 Orientation

ARRIVING

BY PLANE   Juan Santamaría International Airport (☎ 506/443-2942 for 24-hour airport information) is located near the city of Alajuela, about 20 minutes from downtown San José. A taxi into town will cost around $12.50, and a bus only 45¢. The Alajuela–San José buses run frequently and drop you on Avenida 2 between Calle 12 and Calle 14. At the airport you'll find the bus stop about 100 meters directly in front of the main terminal. Make sure to ask if the bus is going to San José, or you'll end up in Alejuela. If you have much luggage you should probably take a cab. There are several car-rental agencies located at the airport, although if you are planning on spending a few days in San José, a car is a liability. If you are heading off to the beach immediately, it is much easier to pick up your car here than at a downtown office. You'll find the taxi stands up the stairs and after you clear Customs. The car rental agencies are located on a little island in front of the main terminal.

You have several options for exchanging money when you arrive at the airport. There is an official state bank inside the main terminal. It's open Monday through Friday from 9am to 4pm. When the bank is closed (and even when it's open), there are usually official money changers (with badges) working both inside and outside the terminal. Outside the terminal, you may be approached by unofficial money changers. Though black-market money changing is illegal, it is quite common and the airport is one of the safer places to try it.

Even though the distance is negligible, and you are certainly welcome to do it yourself, it is common to have a porter carry your bags to a taxi or rental car agency. Most of these porters wear a uniform identifying them as such, but sometimes "improvised" porters will try to earn a few dollars here. Either way, make sure you keep an eye on your bags. You should tip the porters about 50¢ per bag.

BY BUS   If you arrived in Costa Rica over land and are coming to San José for the first time by bus, where you disembark depends on where you are coming from. Bus companies have their offices all over downtown San José. Ask your specific bus company where you'll be let off, when you buy your ticket. In general, buses arriving from Nicaragua first enter the city on the west end of town on Paseo Colón. If you are staying here you can ask to be let off before the final stop. Buses entering from Panama pass first through Cartago and San Pedro before letting passengers off in downtown San José.

VISITOR INFORMATION

There is an **ICT (Instituto Costarricense de Turismo)** office at Juan Santamaría International Airport, open daily from 8am to 5pm, where you can pick up maps and brochures before you head into San José. You'll find the office just to the left after you exit the terminal, having cleared customs. The main tourist information center is at the Plaza de la Cultura, on Calle 5 between Avenida Central and Avenida 2 (☎ 506/222-1090), beside the entrance to the underground Gold Museum. The

---

"I know there's got to be a number here somewhere . . . ": The Arcane Art of Finding An Address in San José

This is one of the most confusing aspects of visiting San José in particular and Costa Rica in general. Though there are often street addresses and building numbers for locations in downtown San José, they are almost never used. Addresses are given as a set of coordinates such as "Calle 3 between Avenida Central and Avenida 1." It is then up to you to locate the building within that block, keeping in mind that the building could be on either side of the street. Many addresses include additional information, such as the number of meters or *varas* (an old Spanish measurement roughly equal to a yard) from a specified intersection or some other well-known landmark. These landmarks are what become truly confusing for visitors to the city because they are often simply restaurants, bars, and shops that would only be familiar to locals. Things get even more confusing when the landmark in question no longer exists. The classic example of this is the Coca-Cola plant, one of the most common landmarks used in addresses in the blocks surrounding San José's main market. It refers to a Coca-Cola bottling plant that once stood in this area. Unfortunately, the edifice is long gone, but the address descriptions remain. You may also try to find someplace near the *antiguo higuerón* ("old fig tree") in San Pedro. This tree was felled years ago. In outlying neighborhoods, addresses can become long directions such as "50 meters south of the old church, then 100 meters east, then 20 meters south." Luckily for the visitor, most downtown addresses are straightforward. Oh, if you're wondering how mail deliverers manage, you'll be reassured to know that nearly everyone in San José uses a post office box. This is called the *apartado* system, and is abbreviated Apdo. or A.P. on mailing addresses.

---

people here are very helpful. This office is open Monday through Friday from 9am to 5pm and Saturday from 9am to 1pm.

CITY LAYOUT

MAIN ARTERIES & STREETS   Downtown San José is laid out on a grid. *Avenidas* (avenues) run east and west, while *calles* (streets) run north and south. The center of the city is at **Avenida Central** and **Calle Central.** To the north of Avenida Central, the avenidas have odd numbers beginning with Avenida 1; to the south, they have even numbers beginning with Avenida 2. Likewise, calles to the east of Calle Central have odd numbers, and those to the west have even numbers. The main downtown artery is **Avenida 2,** which merges with Avenida Central on either side of the downtown area. West of downtown, Avenida Central becomes **Paseo Colón,** which ends at Sabana Park and feeds into the highway to Alajuela, the airport, and the Pacific coast. East of downtown, Avenida Central leads to San Pedro and then to Cartago and the Interamerican Highway heading south. Calle 3 will take you out of town to the north and put you on the road to the Caribbean coast.

NEIGHBORHOODS IN BRIEF

San José is sprawling. Today it is divided into dozens of neighborhoods known as *barrios.* Most of the listings in this chapter fall within the main downtown area, but there are a few outlying neighborhoods you will need to know about.

Downtown   This is San José's busiest area and is where you'll find most of the city's museums. There are also many tour companies, restaurants, and hotels downtown.

San Jose

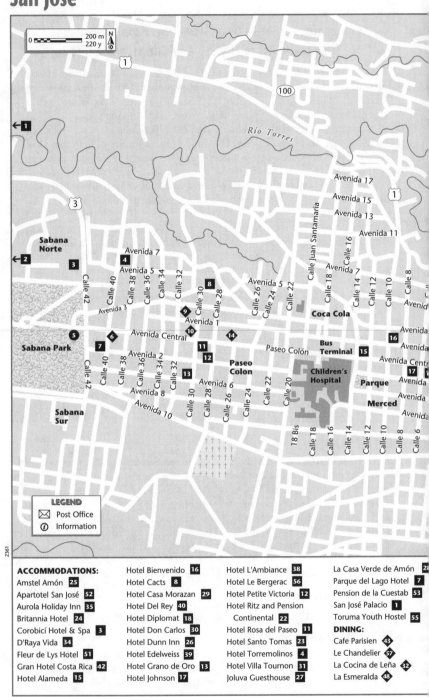

ACCOMMODATIONS:

Amstel Amón 25
Apartotel San José 52
Aurola Holiday Inn 35
Britannia Hotel 24
Corobicí Hotel & Spa 3
D'Raya Vida 34
Fleur de Lys Hotel 51
Gran Hotel Costa Rica 42
Hotel Alameda 15

Hotel Bienvenido 16
Hotel Cacts 8
Hotel Casa Morazan 29
Hotel Del Rey 40
Hotel Diplomat 18
Hotel Don Carlos 30
Hotel Dunn Inn 26
Hotel Edelweiss 39
Hotel Grano de Oro 13
Hotel Johnson 17

Hotel L'Ambiance 38
Hotel Le Bergerac 56
Hotel Petite Victoria 12
Hotel Ritz and Pension
  Continental 22
Hotel Rosa del Paseo 11
Hotel Santo Tomas 23
Hotel Torremolinos 4
Hotel Villa Tournon 31
Joluva Guesthouse 27

La Casa Verde de Amón 2
Parque del Lago Hotel 7
Pension de la Cuestab 53
San José Palacio 1
Toruma Youth Hostel 55

DINING:

Cafe Parisien 43
Le Chandelier 57
La Cocina de Leña 32
La Esmeralda 48

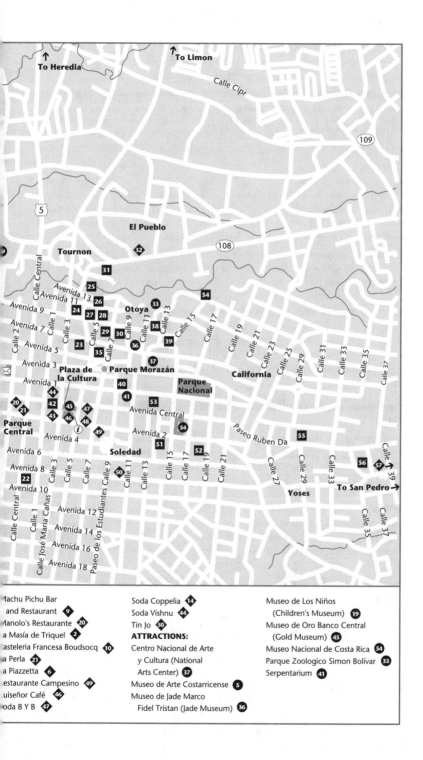

↑ To Heredia
↑ To Limon

Calle Cipr

(109)

(5)

El Pueblo

Tournon

(108)

32

31

25

Avenida 13
Avenida 11
26

34

Avenida 9

24

Otoya

33

27 28

Calle 9

Calle 11

Calle 13

Calle 15

Calle 17

Avenida 7

29

30

38

Calle 19

Calle 21

Calle 23

Calle 25

Calle 29

Calle 31

Calle 33

Calle 35

Calle 37

Avenida 5

23

35

36

39

Avenida 3

Plaza de
la Cultura

Parque Morazán

37

California

Avenida 1

40

44

41

Parque
Nacional

42

45

47

53

20

46

i

48

Avenida Central

Paseo Ruben Da

55

21

43

49

Parque
Central

Avenida 4

Avenida 2

54

51

Avenida 6

Soledad

52

56

57

Avenida 8

Calle 3

Calle 5

Calle 7

Calle 9

Calle 11

Calle 13

Calle 15

Calle 17

Calle 19

Calle 21

Calle 27

Calle 29

Calle 33

22

Yoses

To San Pedro →

Avenida 10

Calle Central

Calle 1

Calle José María Cañas

Avenida 12

Paseo de los Estudiantes

50

Calle 35

Calle 37

Avenida 14

Avenida 16

Avenida 18

Machu Pichu Bar
and Restaurant **9**

Manolo's Restaurante **20**

a Masía de Triquel **2**

astelería Francesa Boudsocq **10**

a Perla **21**

a Piazzetta **6**

estaurante Campesino **49**

uiseñor Café **46**

oda B Y B **47**

Soda Coppelia **14**

Soda Vishnu **44**

Tin Jo **50**

ATTRACTIONS:

Centro Nacional de Arte
y Cultura (National
Arts Center) **37**

Museo de Arte Costarricense **5**

Museo de Jade Marco
Fidel Tristan (Jade Museum) **36**

Museo de Los Niños
(Children's Museum) **19**

Museo de Oro Banco Central
(Gold Museum) **45**

Museo Nacional de Costa Rica **54**

Parque Zoologico Simon Bolívar **33**

Serpentarium **41**

Unfortunately, traffic noise and exhaust fumes make this one of the least pleasant parts of the city. Streets and avenues are usually bustling and crowded with pedestrians and vehicular traffic, and street crime is most rampant here.

Barrio Amon/Barrio Otoya   These two neighborhoods, just north and east of the downtown, are the site of the greatest concentration of historic buildings in San José, and in the past few years, enterprising entrepreneurs have been renovating the old buildings and turning them into hotels. If you're looking for character and don't mind the noise and exhaust fumes, this neighborhood makes a good base for exploring the city.

La Sabana/Paseo Colón   Paseo Colón, a wide boulevard west of downtown, is an extension of Avenida Central and ends at La Sabana Park. It has several good, small hotels and numerous excellent restaurants. This is also where many of the city's rental-car agencies have their offices. Because this area is really part of downtown, I have not treated it as a separate area in the hotel and restaurant listings.

San Pedro/Los Yoses   Located east of downtown San José, Los Yoses is an upper-middle class neighborhood that is home to many diplomatic missions and embassies. San Pedro is a little further east and is the site of the University of Costa Rica. There are numerous college-type bars and restaurants all around the edge of the campus, and several good restaurants and small hotels in both neighborhoods.

Escazú/Santa Ana   Located in the hills west of San José, Escazú and Santa Ana are suburbs with a small-town feel. Although the area is only 15 minutes from San José by taxi, it feels much farther away because of its relaxed atmosphere. This area has a large expatriate community. Many bed-and-breakfast establishments are located here.

2 Getting Around

BY BUS

Bus transportation around San José is cheap—the fare is usually somewhere around 15¢. The most important buses are those running east and west along Avenida 2 and Avenida 3. The Sabana/Cementerio bus runs from Sabana Park to downtown and is one of the most convenient buses to use. You'll find a bus stop for the outbound Sabana/Cementerio bus across the street from Costa Rica Expeditions on Avenida 3 near the corner of Calle Central. San Pedro buses leave from the Social Security building on Avenida 2, and will take you out of downtown heading east. Buses are always boarded from the front, and the bus drivers can make change, although they don't like to receive larger bills. Be especially mindful of your wallet, purse, or other valuables since pickpockets often work the crowded buses. The Alajuela–San José buses that run in from the airport cost 45¢.

BY TAXI

Although taxis in San José have meters *(marías)*, the drivers sometimes refuse to use them, so occasionally you'll have to negotiate the price. However, always try to get them to use the meter first. The official rate at press time is around 65¢ for the first kilometer and around 25¢ for each additional kilometer. If you have a rough idea of how far it is to your destination, you can estimate how much it should cost from these figures. After 10pm taxis are legally allowed to charge a 20% surcharge. Some of the meters are programmed to automatically include the extra charge. Be careful, some drivers will use the evening setting during the daytime, or try to charge an extra 20% on top of the higher meter setting. Tipping taxi drivers is not expected. You'll find taxis in front of the Teatro Nacional (high prices) and around the Parque Central at

Avenida Central and Calle Central. Taxis in front of hotels and the El Pueblo tourist complex usually charge more than others, although this is technically illegal. You can also get a cab by calling 506/235-9966, 506/224-6969, or 506/226-1366.

ON FOOT

Downtown San José is very compact. Nearly every place you might want to go is within a 15-by-4 block area. Because of the traffic congestion, you'll often find it faster to walk than to take a bus or taxi. Be careful when walking the streets by day or night. Flashy jewelry, loosely held handbags or backpacks, and expensive camera equipment tend to attract thieves. You should also watch your step. Between the earthquakes, wear and tear, and negligence, the sidewalks in San José have become veritable obstacle courses, and the cause of more than one sprained ankle. Avenida Central is a pedestrians-only street for several blocks around Calle Central towards the Cultural Plaza. At press time they were repaving this section of the avenue to create a pedestrian mall.

BY MOTORCYCLE

Motorcycles rent for about the same amount as cars, $35 a day or $210 a week. Due to poor road conditions and the difficulty of driving in Costa Rica, they are not recommended unless you are an experienced rider. This is even truer in the city. If you really want to rent a motorcycle in the San José area, try **Heat Rent A Moto,** Avenida 2 between calles 11 and 13 (☎ 506/221-6671).

BY CAR

It will cost you around $40 per day to rent a car in Costa Rica, unless you make a reservation before you leave home. If you do decide to rent a car, and pick it up in downtown San José, be prepared for some very congested streets. The following international companies have desks at Juan Santamaría International Airport, as well as offices downtown: **Avis Rent A Car** (☎ 800/331-1212 in the U.S., 506/442-1321 at airport, 506/232-9922 in downtown San José); **Budget Rent A Car** (☎ 800/527-0700, 506/441-4444 at airport, 506/223-3284 in downtown San José); **Hertz Rent A Car** (☎ 800/654-3131, 506/221-1818 at airport, 506/223-5959 in downtown San José); and **National Car Rental** (☎ 800/328-4567, 506/441-6533 at airport, 506/233-4044 in downtown San José). **Thrifty Car Rental** has an office in downtown San José (☎ 506/255-4141 or toll-free 800/367-2277).

You will save somewhere between $35 and $75 per week on a car rental if you make a reservation in your home country at least one week before you need the car. For example, the least-expensive Avis car available rents for about $276 per week, plus insurance (total of around $374) in San José, but if you book this same car in advance from the United States, you can get it for $198 per week, plus insurance (total of around $296). Though it is possible at some rental-car agencies to waive the insurance charges, you will have to pay all damages before leaving the country if you are in an accident. Even if you do take the insurance, you will have a deductible between $500 and $1,250. At some agencies you can buy additional insurance to lower the deductible.

There are dozens of other rental-car agencies in San José, and most of them will arrange for airport or hotel pickup or delivery. Some of the more dependable agencies include: **Ada Rent a Car,** 50 meters north of Pizza Hut on Paseo Colón (☎ 506/233-7733 or in the U.S. 800/232-7368); **Adobe Rent a Car,** Calle 7 between avenidas 8 and 10 (☎ 506/221-5425); **American Rent a Car,** 425 meters north of the Toyota dealership on Paseo Colón (☎ 506/221-5353); **Hola! Renta Car,** west of Hotel Irazú, La Uruca, San José (☎ 506/231-5666); **Elegante Rent A Car,** Calle 10 between avenidas 13 and 15 and Paseo Colón at Calle 34 (☎ 506/221-0066 or in the U.S. 800/582-7432); and **Tico Rent A Car,** Paseo Colón between calles 24 and 26 (☎ 506/222-8920 or 506/223-9642).

To rent a car in Costa Rica, you must be at least 21 years old and have a valid driver's license and a major credit card in your name.

FAST FACTS: San José

American Express   **American Express** (☎ 506/257-1792) has a counter in San José at the Banco de San José on Calle Central between avenidas 3 and 5. It's open Monday through Friday from 8am to 7pm, and Saturday 9am to 1pm. To report a lost or stolen card from inside Costa Rica call toll free 001-800-528-2121.

Airport   See "Arriving," earlier in this chapter.

Babysitters   Your only chance for a babysitter in San José is to check with the front desk of your hotel.

Bookstores   **Chispas Books,** Calle 7 between avenidas 1 and Central (☎ 506/256-8251) has a wide range of new and used books in English, with an excellent selection of tropical biology, bird, and flora books; it's open daily from 9am to 7pm. For used books in English, stop by **Book Traders** (☎ 506/255-0508), open Monday through Saturday from 9am to 6pm and Sunday from 10am to 5pm, it's located on Avenida 1 between calles 5 and 7.

Camera Repair   **Equipos Fotograficos Canon,** Avenida 3 between calles 3 and 5 (☎ 506/233-0176), specializes in Canon, but may be able to repair other brands.

Car Rentals   See "Getting Around," earlier in this chapter.

Climate   See "When to Go," in chapter 3.

Country Code   The country code for Costa Rica is 506; there are no city or area codes.

Crime   See "Safety," below.

Currency Exchange   The best thing to do is to exchange money at your hotel. If they can't do this for you, they can direct you to a private bank where you won't have to stand in line for hours. Avoid exchanging money on the street.

Dentist   If you need a dentist while in San José, your best bet is to call your embassy, which will have a list of recommended dentists. Many bilingual dentists also advertise in the *Tico Times.* Because treatments are so inexpensive in Costa Rica, dental tourism has become a popular option for people needing extensive work.

Doctor   Contact your embassy for information on doctors in San José.

Drugstores   There are countless pharmacies and drugstores in San José. Many of them will deliver at little or no extra cost. **Farmacia Fischel,** Avenida 3 and Calle 2, is across from the main post office (☎ 506/257-7979). It's open Monday through Saturday from 8am to 7pm.

Embassies/Consulates   See "Fast Facts: Costa Rica," in chapter 3.

Emergencies   In case of fire dial 118; for the police dial 117; for an ambulance dial 128; and for general emergencies dial 911.

Express Mail Services   Many international courier and express mail services have offices in San José, including: **DHL,** on Paseo Colón, between calles 30 and 32

(☎ 506/290-3020); **EMS Courier,** with desks at the principal metropolitan post offices (☎ 506/233-2762); and **United Parcel Service,** Avenida 3 between calles 30 and 32 (☎ 506/257-7447). *Beware:* despite what you may be told, packages sent overnight to U.S. addresses tend to take 3–4 days to reach their destination.

Eyeglasses Look for the word *optica*. **Optica Jiménez** (☎ 506/257-4658 or 506/233-4475) and **Optica Vision** (☎ 506/255-2266) are two dependable chains, with stores around San José. They can do everything from eye exams to repairs.

Holidays See "When to Go," in chapter 3.

Hospitals **Clinica Biblica,** Avenida 14 between Calle Central and Calle 1 (☎ 506/257-5252 or, for emergencies, 506/257-0466), is conveniently located close to downtown and has several English-speaking doctors.

Information See "Visitor Information," earlier in this chapter.

Laundry/Dry Cleaning **Sixaola,** Avenida 2 between calles 7 and 9 (☎ 506/221-2111), open Monday through Friday from 7am to 6pm and Saturday from 8am to 1pm, is a dependable place downtown to get clothes cleaned. Unfortunately, their prices are quite high. Ask at your hotel—most offer a laundry service, though these too are usually expensive.

Libraries **The Centro Cultural Norteamericano-Costarricense,** Calle 35 in Los Yoses (☎ 506/225-9433) has the most extensive English-language library in town. Tourists can get a temporary library card here for about $20, plus a $25 refundable deposit. The National Library is at the corner of Avenida 3 and Calle 15.

Lost Property If you lose something in San José, consider it gone.

Luggage Storage/Lockers Most hotels will store luggage for you while you are traveling around the country. Sometimes there is a charge for this service.

Maps The Costa Rican Tourist Board (ICT), (see "Visitor Information " in this chapter), can usually provide you with good maps of both Costa Rica and San José. Other sources in San José are **Chispas Books,** Calle 7 between avenidas Central and 1 (☎ 506/256-8251); **Libreria Lehmann,** Avenida Central between calles 1 and 3 (☎ 506/223-1212); and Jimenez & Tanzi, Calle 3 between avenidas 1 and 3 (☎ 506/233-8033).

Newspapers/Magazines The *Tico Times* is Costa Rica's principal English-language weekly paper and serves both the expatriate community and tourists. You will also see *Costa Rica Today*, a bilingual weekly geared towards tourists, which has almost no news. You can also get the *International Herald Tribune, Miami Herald, New York Times, USA Today, Time,* and *Newsweek* as well as other English-language publications. You'll find these publications in hotel gift shops and in bookstores selling English-language books.

Photographic Needs Film is expensive in Costa Rica, so bring as much as you will need. In a pinch can buy film and other photographic equipment at several places around town. I recommend that you wait to have your film processed at home, but if you must develop your prints down here try **Fuji Foto,** Avenida Central between Calle 1 and Calle Central (☎ 506/222-2222).

Police Dial 117 for the police.

Post Office The main post office (*correo*) is on Calle 2 between avenidas 1 and 3. It's open Monday through Friday from 7am to 10pm, and Saturday from 8am to noon for purchasing stamps from vending machines. For mailing packages and buying stamps from a person, hours are Monday through Friday from 8am to 5pm.

Radio/TV   There are about 10 TV channels, plus local cable and satellite TV from the United States. There are dozens of AM and FM radio stations in San José.

Religious Services   The *Tico Times* has a listing of churches in San José. You can also ask at the tourist office for a list of the city's churches, or ask at your hotel. The following are a number of suggestions for English-language services. Call for locations. **Episcopal:** Church of the Good Shepherd (☎ 506/222-1560); **Reform Judiasm:** B'nai Israel (☎ 506/257-1785); **Roman Catholic:** the International Chapel of St. Mary at the Hotel Herradura complex (☎ 506/239-1780); **Nondenominational Christian:** Christian Fellowship (☎ 506/228-0594); **Baptist:** International Baptist Church (☎ 506/253-7911); **Quaker:** Call 506/233-6168 for information.

Restrooms   These are known as *sanitarios* or *servicios sanitarios*. They are marked *damas* (women) and *hombres* or *caballeros* (men).

Safety   Never carry anything you value in your pockets or purse. Pickpockets and purse slashers are rife in San José, especially on public buses, in the markets, or near a hospital. Leave your passport, money, and other valuables in your hotel safe, and only carry as much as you really need when you go out. It's a good idea to make a photocopy of your passport's opening pages and carry that with you. If you do carry anything valuable with you, keep it in a moneybelt or special passport bag around your neck. Day packs are a prime target of brazen pickpockets throughout the city. Stay away from the red-light district northwest of the Central Market. Also, be advised that the Parque Nacional is not a safe place for a late-night stroll.

Other precautions include walking around corner vendors, not between the vendor and the building. The tight space between the vendor and the building is a favorite spot for pickpockets. Never park a car on the street, and never leave anything of value in a car, even if it's in a guarded parking lot. Don't even leave your car by the curb in front of a hotel while you dash in to check on your reservation. With these precautions in mind you should have a safe visit to San José. Also see "Safety" in "Fast Facts: Costa Rica," in chapter 3.

Shoe Repair   Ask at your hotel for the repair shop nearest you.

Taxes   All hotels charge 18.45% tax. Restaurants charge 15% tax and also add on a 10% service charge, for a total of 25% more on your bill. There is an airport departure tax of $16.50.

Taxis   See "Getting Around," earlier in this chapter.

Telegrams/Telexes   You can send telegrams and telexes from the **ICE office** on Avenida 2 between calles 1 and 3 (open daily from 7am to 10pm) or from the Western Union office (☎ 506/283-6336), Calle 9 between avenidas 2 and 4.

Telephones   Pay phones are not as common in San José as they are in North American cities. When you do find one, whether on the street, in a restaurant, or hotel lobby, it may take coins of various denominations, or it may take only 5- or 10-colón coins. A call within the city will cost 10 colónes. Pay phones are notoriously unreliable, so it may be better to make calls from your hotel, though you will likely be charged around 100 colónes per call.

For making calling card and collect calls, you can reach an **AT&T operator** by dialing 0-800-011-4114; **MCI** by dialing 0-800-012-2222; **Sprint** by dialing 0-800-013-0123; **Canada Bell** by dialing 0-800-015-1162; and a **Costa Rican international operator** by dialing 116 (pay phones may sometimes require a coin deposit). The Costa Rican telephone system allows direct international dialing but it is expensive. To get an international line, dial 00 followed by the country code and number.

Time Zone   San José is on Central Standard Time, 6 hours behind Greenwich mean time.

Useful Telephone Numbers   For directory assistance, call 113; for international directory assistance, call 124; for the exact time, call 112.

Water   The water in San José is said to be perfectly fine to drink. Residents of the city will swear to this. However, tourists nonetheless sometimes experience stomach discomfort during their first few days of drinking local water. If you want to be cautious, drink bottled water and *frescos* made with milk instead of water. *Sin hielo* means "no ice."

Weather   The weather in San José (including the Central Valley) is usually temperate, never getting extremely hot or cold. May to November is the rainy season, though the rain usually falls in the afternoon and evening.

3 Accommodations

Whereas once hotels were popping up all over downtown San José, in the last few years the hotel boom seems to have stopped. Nonetheless, there are some new arrivals on the scene worth noting. They include the **Hotel Europa Zurqui,** near downtown, the **Hampton Inn,** at the airport, and the **Camino Real Hotel,** in Santa Ana. While the flurry of construction may have hit a pause, there is nevertheless, a glut of hotels in San José. A healthy degree of competition exists among them, so it pays to shop around and ask if any are offering promotions or special packages when you plan to visit.

Of the many hotels in San José, your choices range from luxury resorts to budget pensions charging only a few dollars a night. However, these two extremes are the exceptions, not the norm. The vast number of accommodations, and the best deals, are to be found in the $30-to-$90 price range. Within this moderately priced bracket you'll find restored homes that have been turned into small hotels and bed-and-breakfasts. You will also find modern hotels with swimming pools and exercise rooms, and older downtown business hotels. When considering where to stay in San José, you should take into consideration how long you plan to stay, what you expect to do while you're here, and whether or not you want to be in the heart of the city or out in the suburbs.

Downtown hotels, many of which are in beautifully restored homes, are convenient to museums, restaurants, and shopping, but are often very noisy. Many people are also bothered by the exhaust fumes that permeate downtown streets. If you want clean air and a peaceful night's sleep, consider staying out in the suburbs. **Escazú** is quiet and has great views, while **Los Yoses** is fairly close in yet still quiet. If you have rented a car, I do not recommend staying at a downtown hotel because parking is often expensive and the traffic congestion is trying, to say the least. If you plan to take some day tours, you can just as easily arrange these from a hotel situated outside downtown San José.

In the past few years, dozens of bed-and-breakfast inns have opened up around the San José area. Most are in residential neighborhoods that are quieter—though less convenient—than downtown locations. You can find out about many bed-and-breakfasts by contacting the **Costa Rica Bed & Breakfast Group** (☎ 506/223-4168 or 506/228-9200) or looking for the sections titled "Bed-and-Breakfasts and Small Inns . . . ," below.

If you plan to be in town for a while or are traveling with family or several friends, you may want to consider staying in an apartotel. As the name implies, these are a cross between an apartment and a hotel. You can rent by the day, week, or month, and you get a furnished apartment with a full kitchen, and housekeeping and laundry service.

A word about laundry service at hotels: Laundry is often charged by the piece and prices can be ludicrous. At one hotel, my wife and I did a quick tally of our dirty clothes and came up with something like $75 for a load of laundry. Rinse out your own clothes if possible, or take them to a laundromat.

The price categories used below are defined as follows (for a double room): **Very Expensive,** $125 and up; **Expensive,** $80 to $125; **Moderate,** $40 to $80; **Inexpensive,** $40 and under. However, please keep in mind that the $18.45% hotel-room tax, which adds quite a bit to the price of a room, is not included in rates listed below. If you have set $90 as your total daily room budget, you will want to look for a hotel charging between $65 and $75 per night before tax.

HOTELS IN DOWNTOWN SAN JOSÉ
VERY EXPENSIVE

Aurola Holiday Inn. Avenida 5 and Calle 5 (Apdo. 7802-1000), San José. ☎ **506/223-7233.** Fax 506/255-1036. 188 rms, 16 suites. A/C TV TEL. $138–$158 double; $180–$462 suite. AE, DC, MC V. Free parking.

This is San José's only high-rise deluxe hotel and is situated directly across the street from the attractive Parque Morazán. If familiarity in a foreign country is a comfort to you, this is the place to stay. Unfortunately, you may have to put up with less than gracious service from a staff that seems to be overworked. The hotel has been around for quite a few years, but a recent renovation added new carpets, new elevators, and key-card locks. Try to get one of the upper-floor rooms on the north side for one of the best views in the city.

Dining/Entertainment: The Mirador, up on the 17th floor, is the Aurola's top restaurant and serves good continental and international fare. The view is the best in San José. There is also a casino on this same floor. Just off the lobby is the more casual Tropicana, which serves an impressive, though pricey, breakfast buffet. Bar La Palma overlooks the lobby and Parque Morazan. There is also a snack bar adjacent to the pool.

Services: Room service, laundry service, car-rental desk, travel agency, tour desk.
Facilities: Indoor pool, hot tub, saunas, exercise room, gift shop, executive center.

Corobicí Hotel & Spa. Autopista General Canas, Sabana Norte (Apdo. 2443-1000), San José. ☎ **506/232-8122** or 800/227-4227 in the U.S. Fax 506/231-5834. 177 rms, 26 suites. A/C TV TEL. $120–$140 double; $155–$425 suite. All rates include breakfast. AE, DC, MC, V. Free parking.

Located just past the end of Paseo Colón and on the edge of Parque La Sabana, the Corobicí is more convenient for downtown explorations than the resorts out by the airport, but is rather sterile and austere both inside and out. The lobby is a vast expanse of marble floor faced by blank walls, though the modern art deco furnishings lend a bit of character. Guest rooms are quite modern and comfortable, with good beds and walls of glass through which, on most floors, you get good views of the valley and surrounding mountains. Joggers will find that the proximity of Parque La Sabana makes this a good choice.

Dining/Entertainment: Perhaps the hotel's greatest attributes are its restaurants. Fuji serves authentic Japanese meals amid equally authentic surroundings. La

Gondola serves good Italian food. These two restaurants are open for lunch and dinner only. At El Tucan Coffee Shop, you can get an inexpensive meal throughout the day. The Guacamaya is a quiet lobby bar, while the Pub Bar is a bit more lively and features karaoke music. There is also a casino.

Services: 24-hour room service, valet/laundry service, downtown shuttle, tour desk, car-rental desk.

Facilities: The Corobicí claims to have the largest health spa in Central America; you'll find a well-equipped exercise room, sauna, hot tub, and aerobics classes. The hotel's outdoor pool is rather small and uninviting. Other facilities include a beauty parlor and a gift shop.

EXPENSIVE

Amstel Amón. Avenida 11 and Calle 3 bis (Apdo. 4192-1000), San José. ☎ **506/257-0191** or 800/575-1253 in the U.S. Fax 506/257-0284. 60 rms, 30 suites. TV TEL. $105 double; $123–$252 suite. All rates include continental breakfast. AE, MC, V. Free parking.

This hotel is the newest addition to the local Amstel chain and is located on the north edge of the Barrio Amón historic neighborhood. The building stands out in size and luxury from most of the smaller hotels in this zone. In terms of service, location, and price this hotel gets the nod over the nearby Holiday Inn. The rooms are spacious and up to international standards. The Danube restaurant is the hotel's most formal dining option, but there is also a 24-hour snack bar and the Tamesis Bar. The hotel also features a sizeable casino, tour desk, and gift shop.

✪ Hotel L'ambiance. 949 Calle 13 (Apdo. 1040-2050), San José (mailing address in the U.S.: C/O INTERLINK, 179, P.O. Box 526770, Miami, FL 33152). ☎ **506/222-6702.** Fax 506/223-0481. 6 rms, 1 suite. TV TEL. $90 double; $140 suite. No credit cards. Parking nearby.

L'Ambiance is a beautifully restored stucco building with a central courtyard patio reminiscent of old Spain, and is the closest you'll come to colonial luxury in Costa Rica. The building is on a quiet street only a few blocks from the heart of downtown San José, so you get both the convenience of the city and the quiet of a suburban location. Tile floors in the halls and on the verandah surrounding the courtyard provide a touch of old Costa Rica, while European and North American antiques add a bit of international flavor. Guest rooms have high ceilings and either hardwood floors or carpeting. There is a mix of antique and modern furnishings, and though there is no air-conditioning, overhead fans manage to keep the rooms cool. Rooms vary in size.

Dining/Entertainment: The hotel's dining room/bar is a surprising contrast to the rest of the hotel. Potted plants and white lattice walls give it a greenhouse feel. The menu, which changes regularly, offers a limited selection of well-prepared continental dishes. Prices are quite reasonable.

Services: Concierge service, laundry service.

Parque Del Lago Hotel. Avenida 2 between calles 40 and 42 (Apdo. 624-1007), San José (mailing address in the U.S.: P.O. Box 025216-1634, Miami, FL 33102-5216). ☎ **506/257-8787.** Fax 506/223-1617. 30 rms, 10 suites. A/C TV TEL. $95 double; $130–$210 suite. All rates include continental breakfast, VIP business service available at additional charge. AE, MC, V. Free parking.

Located just one block from Parque La Sabana, this new luxury hotel is set up with business travelers in mind. Beautifully designed, the hotel incorporates Italian marble, antique Costa Rican tile floor, and ornate colonial-styled number plaques beside each guest-room door. Room sizes and styles vary, but in the standard rooms you'll find such amenities as minibars, coffeemakers, and clock radios. There are also marble-topped desks and cafe tables. Light sleepers will appreciate the double glass on all the windows. Suites offer the same luxurious styling as well as considerably more room. The third floor, which has the best views, is the VIP floor.

Dining/Entertainment: There is no restaurant in the hotel, but there are several nearby.

Services: Airport shuttle, secretarial services, concierge service, sports-equipment rentals.

Facilities: Business center and gift shop.

MODERATE

✪ **Britannia Hotel.** Calle 3 and Avenida 11 (Apdo. 3742-1000), San José. ☎ **506/223-6667** or 800/263-2618 in the U.S. Fax 506/223-6411. 24 rms. TV TEL. $85–108 double. Rates include breakfast. AE, DC, MC, V. Parking nearby.

Of the many hotels that have been created from restored old houses in downtown San José, this is the most luxurious. The big, pink building, with its wraparound verandah, is unmistakable and is certainly one of the most attractive old houses in the neighborhood. In the lobby, tile floors, stained-glass clerestory windows, a brass chandelier, and reproduction Victorian decor all help set a tone of tropical luxury. Along with restoring the old home, the owners have built a four-story addition, which is separated from the original building by a narrow atrium. Rooms in the original home have hardwood floors and furniture; high ceilings and fans help keep these rooms cool. In the deluxe rooms, you'll find a hair dryer and basket of toiletries in the bathroom. Though the streetside rooms have double glass, light sleepers will still want to avoid these rooms. The quietest rooms are those toward the back of the addition. In what was once the wine cellar, you'll find a casual restaurant. The buffet breakfast is served in the adjacent skylit room. Afternoon tea and happy hour drinks are also served. There is room service, and the hotel has an airport shuttle.

Hotel Casa Morazan. Calle 7 and Avenida 9 (Apdo. 10063-1000), San José. ☎ **506/257-4187.** Fax 506/257-4175. 11 rms. A/C TV TEL. Nov 15–Apr 14, $75 double; Apr 15–Nov 14, $65 double. All rates include breakfast. MC, V. Parking nearby.

The Barrio Amon district of downtown San José has seen a rapid proliferation of hotels in the past few years, and this is another of the better ones. The interior styling is very modern, with art deco accents throughout. Guest rooms are carpeted and many have king-size beds. The bathrooms are of average size but have modern fixtures. Unfortunately, most of the rooms get quite a bit of traffic noise. The hotel has a small restaurant, serving continental meals at reasonable prices. The staff here is very helpful and can help with tour and rental-car arrangements, as well as laundry and luggage storage.

Fleur de Lys Hotel. Calle 13 between avenidas 2 and 6, 50 meters south of the Plaza de la Democracia (Apdo. 10736-1000), San José. ☎ **506/222-4391** or 506/257-2621. Fax 506/ 257-3637. 18 rms, 1 suite. TV TEL. $78 double; $85–$105 suite. Rates include breakfast. AE, DC, MC, V. Parking nearby.

Located close to the National Museum and Plaza de la Democracia, the Fleur de Lys is a restored mansion that has been painted an eye-catching pink. Inside, the historic mansion is less ostentatious. The lobby and hallways feature polished hardwoods and old tiles, while in the guest rooms, each of which is different, there are modern furnishings. The standard rooms tend to be a bit small, so if you need space, you may want to opt for a suite. All the rooms are decorated with unusual original artworks that give this hotel a character unique in San José. Carpeting and modern tiled bathrooms with contemporary fixtures assure you of the creature comforts. The most

👪 Family-Friendly Hotels

Cariari Hotel & Country Club *(p. 93)*   Not only is there a big pool and recreation area that the kids will love, but there's a babysitting service that allows Mom and Dad some time to themselves.

Hotel Herradura *(p. 94)*   The large grounds and three swimming pools give the kids plenty of places to burn off excess energy, and babysitting services are also available.

Apartotel San José *(p. 86)*   This place provides apartment-style accommodations complete with kitchens, which are a definite plus if you want to save a little money or have fussy kids to feed.

unusual room is the master suite, which has black lacquer furnishings, a cordless phone, halogen lamps, a black-tile bathroom, and a tiny sunroom off the bedroom. This room is definitely worth the extra expense. There is an elegant little restaurant off the lobby serving modern interpretations of traditional Costa Rican cuisine, and a bar in a front room with a streetside terrace.

Gran Hotel Costa Rica. Avenida 2 between calles 1 and 3, San José. ☎ **506/221-0796** or 506/221-4000. Fax 506/221-3501. 105 rms, 8 suites. TV TEL. $62 double; $70 triple; $77–$180 suite. Rates include breakfast. AE, MC, V. Free parking.

Though the Gran Hotel Costa Rica can claim the best location of any downtown hotel, it does not, unfortunately, offer rooms to match the prestigious location or name. Though most of the guest rooms here are fairly large, they have not been well maintained over the decades, giving them an adequate, but run-down feel, especially in the bathrooms.

The Café Parisien is the hotel's greatest attribute, and it is memorable not so much for its food as for its atmosphere. The restaurant is an open-air patio that overlooks the National Theater, street musicians, and all the activity of the Plaza de la Cultura. On the opposite side of the lobby, there is a small and very casual casino. The hotel also maintains a tour desk and gift shop, and it offers 24-hour room service and laundry service.

Hotel del Rey. Avenida 1 and Calle 9 (Apdo. 6241-1000), San José. ☎ **506/221-7272** or 506/257-3130. Fax 506/221-0096. 104 rms, 3 suites. TV TEL. $68–$75 double; $75–$85 triple; $125 suite. AE, MC, V. Parking nearby.

This is one of the newest larger hotels to open in downtown San José and it offers the amenities and services of other downtown choices of this size. The difference is that most of the Del Rey's competitors haven't been upgraded in the past 20 or 30 years. You can't miss the Del Rey; it's a massive pink corner building with vaguely colonial styling. The lobby continues the facade's theme with pink-tile floors and stone columns. Inside there are carved hardwood doors for every guest room. Behind these impressive doors, you'll find wall-to-wall carpeting and hardwood furniture. The rooms vary in size and comfort: There are quiet interior rooms that have no windows, and larger rooms with windows (but also street noises). Try for a sixth floor room with a balcony. The hotel has its own casino, as well as a casual dining room serving well-prepared continental meals and American standards. The hotel has a full-service tour desk and serves as the unofficial urban hub for the country's sport fishing community. The small bar is very popular with sports fans and prostitutes.

✪ **Hotel Grano de Oro.** Calle 30 no. 251, between avenidas 2 and 4, 150 meters south of Paseo Colón (Apdo. 1157-1007, Centro Colón), San José (in the U.S.: SJO 36, P.O. Box 025216, Miami, FL 33102-5216). ☎ **506/255-3322.** Fax 506/221-2782. 35 rms, 3 suites. TV TEL. $70–$92 double; $120–$140 suite. AE, MC, V (add 6% surcharge). Free parking.

San José boasts dozens of old homes that have been converted into hotels, but few offer the luxurious accommodations or professional service that can be found at the Grano de Oro. Located on a quiet side street off of Paseo Colón, this small hotel offers a variety of room types to fit most budgets and tastes. Personally, I like the patio rooms, which have French doors opening onto private patios. However, if you want a room with plenty of space, ask for one of the deluxe rooms, which have large, modern, tiled baths with big tubs. Throughout all the guest rooms, you'll find attractive hardwood furniture, including old-fashioned wardrobes in some rooms. For additional luxuries, you can stay in one of the suites, which have whirlpool tubs. The hotel's patio garden restaurant serves excellent international meals and some of the best desserts in the city, and when it comes time to relax you can soak in a hot tub or have a drink in the rooftop lounge, which has a commanding view of San José.

Hotel Rosa del Paseo. 2862 Paseo Colón (Apdo. 287-1007), San José. ☎ **506/257-3213** or 506/257-3258. Fax 506/223-2776. 18 rms, 1 suite. TV TEL MINIBAR. Nov 15–Apr 30, $70–$90 double; $85–$100 triple; $115 suite; May–Nov 14, $65–$75 double; $75–$85 triple; $95 suite. All rates include continental breakfast. AE, DC, MC, V. Parking nearby.

This hotel is housed in one of San José's most beautiful old stucco homes, but unfortunately it is right on busy Paseo Colón. If you should be so unfortunate as to get one of the front guest rooms, I don't think you would be able to sleep at all. However, if you get a room in back, you should be well insulated from the noise. Built more than 110 years ago, this old home underwent a complete renovation and modernization a few years ago and is now richly appointed and surprisingly evocative of 19th-century Costa Rica. There are beautiful details—transoms, ornate stucco door frames, polished hardwood floors—throughout the hotel. Reproduction antique and wicker furnishings evoke both the tropics and the past century.

There is no restaurant on the premises, but snacks and cold meals are available and there are a wealth of restaurants nearby. You'll also find 24-hour bar/beverage service, laundry service, airport transportation, a craft shop, and an art gallery.

Hotel Villa Tournon. Calle 3, 200 meters north of Avenida 13 (Apdo. 6606-1000), San José. ☎ **506/233-6622.** Fax 506/222-5211. 80 rms. TV TEL. $69–$79 double. AE, MC, V. Free parking.

Formerly the Hotel Bougainvillea, this was one of San José's earlier luxury hotels. Today the styling and furnishings are a bit dated, but the prices are still pretty reasonable for a well-maintained hotel with a pool. Some of the rooms here have parquet floors while others (more expensive) have carpeting. The less expensive rooms have two twin beds, while for a bit extra you can get a room with two doubles. The front of the hotel receives a fair amount of traffic noise, so ask for a room on the south side. There's a large restaurant serving international dishes, plus a small bar. Hotel amenities include room service and a car-rental desk. El Pueblo (a restaurant, entertainment, and shopping complex) is only a block away, and downtown is also walkable (in daylight hours).

INEXPENSIVE

Apartotel San José. Avenida 2 between calles 17 and 19 (P.O. Box 4192-1000), San José, ☎ **506/265-2191** or 800/575-1253 in the U.S. Fax 506/221-6684. 12 apts. TV TEL. $53–$60 double; $58–$65 triple. MC, V. Free parking.

Operated by the same company that runs the Amstel hotels, this apartotel is located across the street from the National Museum. The furnishings here are a bit dated, but there is plenty of space. The building is on a side street off of Avenida 2. Though it is fairly quiet, try to get a room as far from the avenue as possible. There are other apartotel options around town, but this one is the most centrally located and convenient. Maid, laundry, and valet service are all available.

⑤ Hotel Alameda. Avenida Central between calles 12 and 14 (Apdo. 680) San José. ☎ **506/223-6333.** Fax 506/222-9673. 52 rms. TV TEL. $31.80 double; $36.70 triple; $41.35 quad. Rates include breakfast. AE, DC, MC, V. Parking nearby.

This is another of San José's large old hotels, but a remodeled lobby and steady upkeep give it a modern feel. The rooms here are of medium size, with carpeting, older furniture, small tiled baths, and plenty of closet space. There are large windows so the rooms are bright, but the windows also let in the street noises. There's a large restaurant on the second floor; the menu features international and Costa Rican dishes at prices ranging from about $2.50 to $15. There is also room service and a laundry and dry-cleaning service.

Hotel Cacts. 2845 Avenida 3 between calles 28 and 30 (Apdo. 379-1005), San José. ☎ **506/221-2928** or 221-6546. Fax 506/221-8616. 25 rms (21 with private bath). $35–$50 double; $45–$55 triple. Rates include breakfast. No credit cards. Parking nearby.

This is one of the most interesting and unusual budget hotels I've ever seen, housed in an attractive tropical contemporary home on a business and residential street. The original building is a maze of rooms and hallways on several levels (the house is built on a slope). The newer rooms all come with telephones and televisions. My favorite room is the huge bilevel family room with its high beamed ceiling. There's a third-floor open terrace that serves as the breakfast area. The hotel has it's own tour desk and gift shop. The staff here is very helpful and the hotel will receive mail and faxes, change money, and store baggage for guests.

Hotel Diplomat. Calle 6 between Avenida Central and Avenida 2 (Apdo. 6606-1000), San José. ☎ **506/221-8133** or 221-8744. Fax 506/233-7474. 29 rms (all with bath). TEL. $23.50–$25.25 double. AE, MC, V. Parking nearby.

It's easy to miss the entrance to this hotel. Watch for it on the east side of the street. The lobby is narrow, and the front door is fairly nondescript. The carpeted rooms are rather small but comfortable nonetheless, and some rooms on the upper floors have nice views of the mountains. The tiled baths are clean, and the water is hot. If you get too claustrophobic in your room, there is a sitting area on each floor. For some reason, the Diplomat seems to be popular with North American retirees and businesspeople. The hotel's restaurant is a very attractive dark room with pink tablecloths, flowers on every table, and pastel walls. For those seeking an intimate place for dinner, try one of the tiny booths for two. Prices range from $2.25 for a sandwich to $15 for a lobster dinner.

⑤ Hotel Torremolinos. Calle 40 and Avenida 5 bis (Apdo. 114-1017), San José. ☎ **506/222-9129.** Fax 506/222-5266. 71 rms, 14 suites. TV TEL. $60 double; $70 triple; $80–$90 suite. AE, MC, V. Free parking.

If you want to be close to downtown, have a pool, sauna, jacuzzi, and exercise room, and not spend a fortune, this is your best choice. Located at the west end of Paseo Colón, the Torremolinos is on a fairly quiet street and is built around a colorful and well-tended garden that makes the hotel's pool a wonderful place to while away an afternoon. The rooms are simply furnished and have plenty of space. Most also, for some strange reason, feature Egyptian artwork on the walls. There's a moderately priced restaurant serving international dishes, a lobby bar, conference room, tour desk, downtown shuttle bus, and room service.

⑤ Hotel Bienvenido. Calle 10 between avenidas 1 and 3 (Apdo. 389-2200), San José. ☎ **506/221-1872.** Fax 506/233-2161. 48 rms (44 with bath). $19 double; $23 triple. No credit cards. Parking nearby.

This very basic hotel is one of the most popular in the city with travelers on a tight budget. The rooms are clean, though a bit dark, and there is always ample hot water. There are a few very inexpensive rooms with collective baths, for groups of four or more. The hotel was created from an old movie theater, and there are still a few architectural details remaining from the building's former incarnation. This place fills up by early afternoon in the high season, so call ahead for a reservation and ask for a quiet room in the back.

Hotel Johnson. Calle 8 between Avenida Central and Avenida 2, (Apdo. 6638-1000), San José. ☎ **506/223-7633** or 506/223-7827. Fax 506/222-3683. 57 rms, 3 suites (all with bath). TEL. $15.10 double; $18.80 triple; $16.50–$22.80 suite. AE, DC, MC, V. Parking nearby.

The lobby of this large, centrally located hotel is on the second floor. You'll find the hotel patronized primarily by Costa Rican businesspeople and families, but it is a good choice for any budget traveler. In the lobby there is a TV and several lounge chairs, and on each of the residence floors above there is a sitting area. The rooms have tile floors and open onto a narrow air shaft that lets in a bit of light and noise from other rooms. Bathrooms are relatively clean and roomy. Most rooms come with twin beds (you might want to test a few beds if you're picky about mattresses). Depending on availablility, you can pay a little extra for a color TV. There's a bar and a dining room where you can get inexpensive meals; the special of the day goes for $2.25, while à la carte meals run from $3 to $5.50.

Hotel Ritz and Pension Continental. Calle Central between avenidas 8 and 10 (Apdo. 6783-1000), San José. ☎ **506/222-4103.** Fax 506/222-8849. 25 rms (5 with bath). $12.25–$19.60 double without bath, $23.70 double with bath; $15.50 triple without bath, $27 triple with bath; $18.80 quad without bath, $31 quad with bath. AE, MC, V. Parking nearby.

These two side-by-side budget hotels are under the same management and together have rooms to fit most budget travelers' needs. There is even a travel agency and tour company on the first floor, so you can arrange all of your travels around Costa Rica without leaving the hotel. Rooms vary greatly in size and comfort levels, but tend to be dark and a bit musty. Bathrooms are a bit old and those showers that do have hot water use showerhead heaters that just barely work. If the first room you see isn't to your liking, just ask to see another in a different price category. The current owners are Swiss, so you'll probably meet quite a few Swiss travelers if you stay here.

Joluva Guesthouse. 936 Calle 3B between avenidas 9 and 11, San José. ☎ **506/223-7961** or 800/298-2418 in the U.S. Fax 506/257-7668 or 619/294-2418 in the U.S. 8 rms (6 with private bath). TV. $30 double without bath, $40 double with bath. Rates include continental breakfast. MC, V. Parking nearby.

Though you can find a less expensive hotel, there are few in this price range that offer the old-fashioned architectural detail of the Joluva. There are old tile and hardwood floors throughout, and high ceilings (in one room, beautiful plasterwork on the ceiling). However, the rooms are small and a bit dark, with windows that open into a covered courtyard. The breakfast room has skylights, which help brighten it a bit. This hotel caters to a gay clientele, but guests of all stripes are welcome.

⑤ Toruma Youth Hostel. Avenida Central between calles 29 and 31, San José. ☎ **506/224-4085.** 105 beds (all with shared bath), $6.50 per person per night with an IYHF card; $8.15 with student ID; $9.80 general public. MC, V. Free parking.

This attractive old building, with its long verandah, is the largest hostel in Costa Rica's system of official youth hostels. Although it is possible to find other accommodations around town in this price range, any such room would not likely be as clean. The atmosphere here is convivial and will be familiar to anyone who has hosteled in Europe. The large lounge in the center of the building has a high ceiling and a great deal of light. The dorms have four to six beds per room. The staff here can help you arrange stays at other hostels and trips around the country, and you can store luggage here for 25¢ per day.

BED-AND-BREAKFASTS & SMALL INNS IN DOWNTOWN SAN JOSÉ

MODERATE

La Casa Verde de Amón. Calle 7 and Avenida 9 no. 910, San José (mailing address in the U.S.: Dept. 1701, P.O. Box 025216, Miami, FL 33102-5216). ☎ /fax **506/223-0969.** 5 rms, 3 suites. TV TEL. Dec 1–Apr 30, $72–$96 double; $96–$126 suite; May 1–Nov 30, $55–$72 double; $72–$116 suite. All rates include continental breakfast. AE, MC, V. Parking nearby.

This tropical Victorian house was built around 1910 and was completely renovated between 1989 and 1992. There are beautiful old tile and polished hardwood floors throughout the building, which give the house a patrician air. Off the lobby, there is a small patio and open-air breakfast room. Up on the second floor, there is a large central seating area with a 110-year-old baby grand piano and stained-glass clerestory windows at the top of the high ceiling. These windows bathe this room in a beautiful blue light. Rooms are all different, but most are furnished with antiques. Some have their original porcelain fixtures and brass faucets, which means you may find a bathtub or only a shower in your bathroom. The Don Carlos suite is huge, with a high ceiling, king beds, and a separate seating area. All the rooms have clock radios, but unfortunately, it is likely that traffic noises will wake you in the morning if you have a room on the streetside of the hotel. The hotel offers round-trip airport transfers.

D'raya Vida. Apdo. 493-1000, San José (in the U.S.: P.O. Box 025216-1638, Miami, FL 33102-5216). ☎ **506/223-4168.** Fax 506/223-4157. 5 rms (2 with private bath). Nov–Apr, $85 double; May–Oct, $65 double. Rates include full breakfast. AE, MC, V. Free parking.

This little bed-and-breakfast is so secluded that it seems to be in a world all its own, yet it is in downtown San José. To find the inn, go east on Avenida 9, then turn left on Calle 17. In 100 meters, turn left on Avenida 11. Follow this road to the dead end at the inn's front gate. Behind the gate, in a shady old garden, is a miniature villa. The restored old stucco home is furnished with the owners' eclectic collection of crafts from around the world, and in the living room, you'll find a grand piano and fireplace. (Sounds like a B&B up north, doesn't it?) Guest rooms are all different. One of the upstairs rooms has its own private balcony, while the other has an unusual four-poster bed. My favorite rooms, however, are the two downstairs, which have private bathrooms. One is decorated with masks from around the world, and the other has Indian art and a fountain just outside. Be forewarned, however, that there is an active railroad track right next to the house, although trains only run during the day. D'Raya Vida offers free airport pick-up.

Hotel Dunn Inn. Calle 5 and Avenida 11 (Apdo. 6241-1000), San José. ☎ **506/222-3232** or 222-3426. Fax 506/221-4596. 27 rms, 1 suite. TV TEL. $45–$55 double; $88.50 suite. Rates include continental breakfast. AE, V. Free parking.

Located in the Barrio Amon historic neighborhood, the Dunn Inn is among the better small hotels in the area. Part of the hotel is housed in a century-old mansion, while other rooms are in a new wing. This inn offers quiet sophistication at reasonable rates.

The courtyard of the old mansion has been partially covered and turned into the dining room and bar, which, if you have a room directly above, can be a bit noisy at night. Orchids and bromeliads hang from the brick walls, and a fountain bubbles away beside a huge philodendron vine. The new wing has some very nice rooms with exposed brick walls. Although it is quite a bit more expensive than the normal rooms, the one suite is quite luxurious with a whirlpool bath, minibar, hardwood and carpeted floors, potted bromeliads, dual sinks, a lot of sunshine in the bathroom, and paneled walls.

Hotel Edelweiss. Avenida 9 between calles 13 and 15, 100 meters east of the Condovac offices, San José. ☎ **506/221-9702.** Fax 506/222-1241. 16 rms. TEL. $65 double. Rates include continental breakfast. MC, V. Parking nearby.

Up at the top of the hill on Avenida 9, you'll find another renovated and converted old home that is now a pleasant, small hotel. There's lots of polished hardwood throughout the hotel, including floors and furniture in many of the the guest rooms. Rooms vary in size, and those in front are very noisy. In the center of the building is an unusual little bar under a translucent roof.

ⓢ **Hotel Petite Victoria.** Paseo Colón, Frente a la Sala Garbo, San José. ☎ **506/233-1812** or 506/233-1813. Fax 506/233-1812. 15 rms (all with bath) TV. $44.80 double; $53 triple. AE, MC, V. Free parking.

One of the oldest houses in San José, this tropical Victorian home was once the election campaign headquarters for Oscar Arias Sánchez, Costa Rica's former president who won a Nobel Peace Prize. Today, after extensive remodeling and restoration, it is an interesting little hotel that offers a historic setting at inexpensive rates. The big covered patio is perfect for sitting and taking in the warm sun, and doubles as the hotel's restaurant. Guest rooms have high ceilings and fans to keep the air cool and medium-to-large tiled bathrooms. Inside, walls are made of wood, so noise can be a bit of a problem, but this is a small price to pay for such old-fashioned elegance. Tour arrangements and laundry service are also offered.

✪ **Hotel Don Carlos.** 779 Calle 9 between avenidas 7 and 9 (in the U.S.: Dept. 1686, P.O. Box 025216, Miami, FL 33102-5216). ☎ **506/221-6707.** Fax 506/255-0828. 36 rms. $50–$60 double. Rates include continental breakfast. AE, MC, V. Parking nearby.

If you are looking for a small hotel that is unmistakenly tropical and hints at the days of the planters and coffee barons, this is the place for you. Located in an old residential neighborhood only blocks from the business district, the Don Carlos is popular with both vacationers and businesspeople. A large pre-Columbian reproduction of a carved-stone human figure stands outside the front door of this gray inn, which was a former president's mansion. Inside you'll find many more pre-Columbian stone reproductions, as well as orchids, ferns, palms, and parrots. The wicker furniture in the lounge and the small courtyard leading to a sunny deck with a bubbling fountain tempt guests to relax in the tropical breezes after a day of exploring the capital. Most of the rooms are quite large, and each is a little different from the others. In case you're interested, the paintings throughout the hotel are for sale. The gift shop here is one of the largest in the country and there's a helpful in-house tour company. The complimentary breakfast and moderately priced meals are served in the Pre-Columbian Lounge. Unfortunately, many people can't tolerate the traffic noises here.

✪ **Hotel Santo Tomas.** Avenida 7 between calles 3 and 5, San José. ☎ **506/255-0448.** Fax 506/222-3950. 20 rms. TV TEL.$55–$85 double; $85–$95 triple (5% discount on entire stay after three consecutive days). Rates include continental breakfast. Credit cards accepted for room reservation guarantee only. Parking nearby.

Even though it is on an otherwise nondescript street, this converted mansion is a real jewel inside. Built around 100 years ago by a coffee baron, the house was once slated to be bulldozed in order to expand the Aurola Holiday Inn's parking lot. Under the direction of American Thomas Douglas, the old mansion has been restored to its former grandeur. The first thing that you see when you walk through the front door is the beautiful carved-wood desk that serves as the reception area. Throughout the guest rooms you'll find similar pieces of exquisitely crafted antique reproductions made here in Costa Rica from rare hardwoods. The hardwood floors throughout most of the hotel are original and were made from a type of tree that has long since become almost impossible to find. The rooms vary in size, but most are fairly large and have a small table and chairs. Skylights in some bathrooms will brighten your morning, and queen-size beds will provide a good night's sleep. Maps of Costa Rica hang on the walls of all the guest rooms so you can get acquainted with the country. There are a couple of patio areas, as well as a TV lounge and combination breakfast room and outdoor bar. Laundry service and a baggage storage room are available. The staff and management are extremely helpful with tour arrangements and any other needs or requests. The Santo Tomas recently acquired the adjacent property, and there's talk of expansion and even a possible swimming pool.

INEXPENSIVE

🄢 **Pension De La Cuesta.** 1332 Cuesta de Nuñez, Avenida 1 between calles 11 and 15. ☎/fax **506/255-2896**. 9 rms (none with private bath). $26 double; $34 triple. Rates include breakfast. MC, V. Parking nearby.

If you don't mind a clean collective bathroom down the hall from your room, this little bed-and-breakfast is definitely worth considering. It was once the home of Otto Apuy, a well-known Costa Rican artist, and original artwork abounds. The building itself is a classic example of a tropical wood-frame home and has been painted an eye-catching pink with blue-and-white trim. The rooms can be a bit dark and are very simply furnished, but there is a very sunny and cheery sunken lounge-court area in the center of the house. You'll find this hotel on the hill leading up to the Parque Nacional.

SMALL HOTELS IN SAN PEDRO/LOS YOSES
MODERATE

🄒 **Hotel Le Bergerac.** 50 S. Calle 35 (Apdo. 1107-1002), San José. ☎ **506/234-7850**. Fax 506/225-9103. 18 rms TV TEL. $68–$78 double; Corporate rates available. Rates include continental breakfast. AE, DC, MC, V. Free parking.

With all the sophistication and charm of a small French inn, the Hotel Le Bergerac has ingratiated itself with business travelers and members of various diplomatic missions. What these visitors have found (and what you too will find should you stay here) is a tranquil environment in a quiet suburban neighborhood, spacious and comfortable accommodations, personal service, and gourmet meals. The owners have a total of 29 years of hotel experience, which accounts for the professionalism with which Le Bergerac is operated. The hotel is comprised of three houses with courtyard gardens in between. Almost all of the rooms are quite large, and each is a little different. My favorite rooms are those with private patio gardens. Some rooms have king beds, and in the old master bedroom, you'll find a little balcony. In the evenings candlelight and classical music set a relaxing and romantic mood. The innovative chef of Paprika Restaurant has recently set up shop here and now gourmet French and continental dinners are available for guests and by reservation. The hotel also has a helpful tour desk.

INEXPENSIVE

D'galah Hotel. Calle Masis, 100 meters past Calle La Cruz (Apdo. 208-2350), San José. ☎/fax **506/234-1743.** 30 rms. TV TEL. $33.50–$43.25 double. AE, MC, V. Free parking.

If you want to be close to downtown, but away from the smog and traffic, this budget hotel is a good choice. Directly across the street from the hotel is the University of Costa Rica, which is an oasis of greenery that attracts many species of birds, especially among the bamboo groves. Rooms are a bit old-fashioned and dark, but for the most part are quite spacious and acceptable if you aren't too demanding. The largest rooms are those with kitchenettes and sleeping lofts. The newest rooms have carpets and private little patios. Amenities include a small swimming pool, a sauna, and a breakfast room.

SMALL HOTELS & BED-AND-BREAKFASTS IN ESCAZÚ

This affluent suburb about 15 minutes west of San José is popular with North American retirees and expatriates. Quite a few little bed-and-breakfasts have sprung up to cater to the needs of visiting friends. If you're interested in staying here you might contact the **Costa Rica Bed & Breakfast Group** (☎ 506/223-4168 or 506/228-9200).

VERY EXPENSIVE

Tara Resort Hotel & Spa. Apdo. 1459-1250, Escazú. ☎ **506/228-6992.** Fax 506/228-9651. 30 suites and bungalows. TV TEL. $125–$190 suite; $200 bungalow. AE, MC, V. Free parking.

Located 1 kilometer south of the village of San Antonio de Escazú (follow the signs), Tara is perched high on a mountainside overlooking the entire Central Valley and surrounding volcanic peaks. The view is breathtaking and so is the setting. The owner here has a fixation on *Gone With the Wind* and everything at this spa/resort follows the theme, from the O'Hara Dining Hall down to one of Rhett's Vitality Baths. Antebellum southern grandeur has been re-created here in Costa Rica much to the delight of anyone with the finances to spend a night or two. Room rates are high, but every room is a suite or bungalow. The suites are all part of the main house and each has its own balcony (try to get one overlooking the valley). Rooms vary in size, but in the larger rooms you might find a seating area, a big bathroom with two sinks, a tub, a heat lamp, and perhaps even two balconies. Furnishings are traditional American styles that fit right in with the architecture.

Dining/Entertainment: The Atlanta Dining Gallery is an elegant setting for fine meals; unfortunately, the windows do not do justice to the view. In the evenings there is live jazz and piano music. Meals are often served on the large back patio, which has an unobstructed view of the valley.

Services: Full assortment of spa treatments, including massage, facials, and aromatherapy.

Facilities: Outdoor swimming pool, hot tub, sauna, small gym, various lawn and indoor games, conference facilities, and a tour desk.

MODERATE

Costa Verde Inn. Apdo. 89, Escazú (in the U.S.: SJO 1313, Box 025216, Miami, FL 33102). ☎ **506/228-4080** or 506/289-9509. Fax 506/289-8591. 8 rms (6 with private bath). Nov 15–Apr 15, $50 double without bath, $60 double with bath, $70 triple with bath; Apr 16–Nov 14, lower rates apply. All rates include continental breakfast. MC, V (add 8% surcharge). Free parking.

If you're a tennis player or someone who values peace and quiet, the Costa Verde Inn is an excellent choice. This sprawling, modern home incorporates flagstone and stone walls throughout and has a vaguely colonial feel. A large and lush garden, complete with lighted tennis court, surrounds the inn. My favorite rooms are the two by the tennis courts, one of which has a sunken stone-floored shower. Other rooms have hardwood floors, and in all the rooms you'll find king-size beds. Common areas include a large living room with fireplace and a wide tiled patio that overlooks the garden. Throughout the inn, you'll see old black-and-white photos that have been hand colored; ask the innkeeper about the photographer who took these pictures. You can also find out here about various excursions around the country, and the inn offers airport pickups.

INEXPENSIVE

Hotel Mirador Pico Blanco. Apdo. 900 Escazú. ☎ **506/289-6197.** Fax 506/289-5189. 23 rms. $40 double; $45 triple. AE, MC, V. Free parking.

If you'd like a room with a view but can't afford the prices charged at most mountainside inns around the area, check out this cozy and casual hotel. There's nothing fancy about the rooms here, but there are absolutely fabulous views from most rooms, and from the dining room and terrace. Some rooms have high ceilings that give the rooms the appearance of spaciousness, and almost all of them have balconies (albeit small ones). A small pool with an inviting terrace has recently been added. The restaurant is a popular and inexpensive spot, probably the cheapest view restaurant in the valley. A taxi up here from the airport will cost you about $15.

HOTELS IN THE HEREDIA/ALAJUELA/AIRPORT AREA
VERY EXPENSIVE

Cariari Hotel & Country Club. Autopista General Cañas, Ciudad Cariari (Apdo. 737-1007 Centro Colón), San José. ☎ **506/239-0022** or 800/227-4274 in the U.S. Fax 506/239-2803 or 506/239-0285. 220 rms, 24 suites. A/C TV TEL. $132–$165 double; $215–$435 suite. AE, MC, V. Free parking.

Located about halfway into San José from the airport, the Cariari is the only resort hotel in the Central Valley with its own golf course (the only regulation 18-hole course in the country so far), and as such is a must for golfers vacationing in Costa Rica. The Cariari, with its use of stone walls, an open-air lobby, and lush garden plantings, also has more of a tropical feel than the city's other luxury hotels. However, the landscaping is not as impeccably manicured as that at the Herradura (see below), nor is the hotel itself as elegant. Though, many of the guest rooms were recently remodeled, and all have plenty of space. The basic rooms have king beds and small baths. Poolside rooms are quite a bit more expensive, and though they have minibars, hair dryers, and safes, they seem a bit overpriced. All in all, the rooms lack the sort of quality furnishings and styling that you would expect in this price range. Try to get an upper-floor room; those on the lower floor tend to be a bit dark.

Dining/Entertainment: Los Vitrales is the hotel's most formal restaurant and serves well-prepared French and continental fare. For more casual meals, there is Las Tejas, where there's a breakfast buffet. For seafood and cocktails there is the tropical, open-air atmosphere of Los Mariscos, which also has live Latin and jazz music in the evenings. More entertainment is provided by the hotel's casino, which is open nightly until 2am.

Services: 24-hour room service, complimentary city shuttle, tour desk, car-rental desk, golf lessons and club rentals, babysitting, massage.

Facilities: The large pool is surrounded by plenty of patio space and lots of lounge chairs, and has a swim-up bar. In addition to the 18-hole golf course, there are 11 tennis courts, a pro shop, and a health club with saunas, whirlpool tubs, an exercise room, a game room, and an Olympic-sized swimming pool. Other facilities include a gift shop, beauty parlor, and barber shop.

Hotel Herradura, Autopista General Cañas. Ciudad Cariari (Apdo. 7-1880), San José. ☎ **506/239-0033** or 800/245-8420 in the U.S. Fax 506/239-2292 or 305/858-7478 in the U.S. 202 rms, 32 suites. A/C TV TEL. $130–$190 double; $210–$795 suite. AE, DC, MC, V. Free parking.

Big and sprawling, the Herradura is the most impeccably designed and maintained of San José's resort hotels. It is also the city's largest conference center, and as such is often bustling with businesspeople and assorted convention traffic. However, despite the crowds, service here never seems to falter. The superior rooms (there are no standard rooms) are all in the midst of a hotel-wide remodel and upgrade, which should spruce them all up a bit. Still, bathrooms in these rooms are small, and most have no view to speak of. The deluxe rooms, on the other hand, are very attractive and luxurious. The walls of glass let in plenty of light and usually a good view ($30 extra for pool-view rooms). There are balconies and marble-topped cafe tables, and in the bathrooms, there are green-marble counters, phones, and hair dryers.

Dining/Entertainment: For quiet dining, there is Sakura, a Japanese restaurant with an indoor garden setting, sushi bar and table-side teppanyaki preparations. For a formal Spanish dinner, there's the Sancho Panza Restaurant. Casual meals, including buffets, are available at the 24-hour Tiffinay's Restaurant coffee shop. Bambolleo is a lounge that offers nightly piano music and light snacks. Gamblers can spend their time at the elegant Casino Krystal.

Services: 24-hour room service, city shuttle, car-rental desk, tour desk, babysitting.

Facilities: The Herradura's main swimming pool (there are three) is one of the largest and most attractive in San José, with a beachlike patio, a swim-up bar, tiled cafe tables in the water, and attractive landscaping around the edges of the pool. The resort's 18-hole golf course, 11 tennis courts, pro shop, and health club are the same ones that are used by the nearby Cariari Hotel (see above). Other facilities include extensive conference and banquet facilites, gift shop, beauty salon, chapel, and a small exercise room.

San José Palacio. Autopista General Cañas (Apdo. 458-1150), San José. ☎ **506/220-2034** or 506/220-2035. Fax 506/220-2036. 254 rms, 25 suites. A/C TV TEL MINIBAR. $135–$155 double; $195–$430 suite. AE, DC, MC, V. Free parking.

Owned by the Barcelo company, the developer of the controversial Tambor project on the Nicoya Peninsula, the Palacio tries very hard to live up to its name. This is as luxurious a hotel as you will find in Costa Rica. The Palacio is not as far out of town as the Cariari or Herradura, and so it is more convenient for exploring downtown San José. The hilltop location assures good views from nearly every room. Business travelers, visiting celebrities, and conferences seem to be the bulk of the business here.

Rooms are very modern and all have angled walls of glass to take in the superb views. Furnishings are of the highest quality, and in some rooms there are even leather chairs. If you choose to stay in one of the executive rooms, you'll receive a continental breakfast and afternoon coffee.

Dining/Entertainment: Ambar is the hotel's premier dining room, and the creative continental cuisine is reasonably priced and among the best in town. Anfora is a larger and more casual dining room that does an impressive, though expensive, lunch buffet. El Bosque is the hotel's main lounge and is adjacent to the small casino.

Services: Room service, massage, car-rental desk, travel agency, babysitting.

Facilities: Free-form pool with adjacent grill and piano bar, exercise room, sauna, jacuzzi, two tennis courts, three racquetball/squash courts, business center, conference center, shopping arcade, barber shop, beauty parlor.

Hampton Airport Inn. Autopista General Cañas, by the Airport (Apdo. 962-1000), San José. ☎ **506/443-0043** or in the U.S. 800/426-7866. Fax 506/442-9539. 100 rms. TV TEL. $60–$65 double to quad. Rates include continental breakfast. AE, MC, V. Free parking.

If familiarity, basic comfort, and proximity to the airport are important to you, then the Hampton Airport Inn is your best bet. The rooms are what you'd expect from a budget chain, and since the hotel is new, they don't show much wear and tear. The hotel has an outdoor swimming pool, free parking, airport shuttle, and allows free local phone calls. This is a good choice if your plane arrives very late or leaves very early, and you don't plan on spending any time in San José.

BED-AND-BREAKFASTS & SMALL INNS IN THE HEREDIA/ ALAJUELA/AIRPORT AREA
VERY EXPENSIVE

✪ **Finca Rosa Blanca Country Inn.** Santa Bárbara de Heredia (in the U.S.: SJO 1201, P.O. Box 025216, Miami, FL 33102-5216). ☎ **506/269-9392.** Fax 506/269-9555. 6 suites, 2 villas. $125–$208 double; $25 each additional person. Rates include breakfast. AE, MC, V. Free parking.

This is another Central Valley inn that is difficult to find but well worth searching out. If the cookie-cutter rooms of international resorts leave you cold, then perhaps the fascinatingly unique rooms of this unusual inn will be more your style. Finca Rosa Blanca is an architectural confection set amid the lush green hillsides of a coffee plantation. Square corners seem to have been prohibited in the design of this beautiful home. There are turrets and curving walls of glass, arched windows, and a semi-circular built-in couch. Everywhere the glow of polished hardwood blends with blindingly white stucco walls and brightly painted murals. The best way I can describe the architecture of this inn is as 21st-century pueblo.

Inside is original artwork everywhere. Each room is decidely different and unique. There's the black-and-white room with a patio and bed made from coffee-tree wood. Another room has a bed built into a corner and a handmade tub with windows on two sides. The view is fabulous. If breathtaking bathrooms are your idea of the ultimate luxury, then consider splurging on the master suite, which has a stone waterfall that cascades into a tub in front of a huge picture window. This suite also has a spiral staircase that leads to the top of the turret. Two new villas have been added with the same sense of eclectic luxury, as well as a free form swimming pool.

Dining/Entertainment: For $25 per person you can arrange to have a five-course gourmet dinner served in the small dining room. Be sure to reserve early because the dinning room has limited seating. In a tiny space off of the living room, there is an honor bar tucked into a reproduction of a typical Costa Rican ox cart.

Services: Car rentals and guide services can be arranged through the hotel, as well as transportation to and from the airport.

MODERATE

✪ **Hotel Bougainvillea.** Apdo. 69-2120, San José. ☎ **506/240-1414.** Fax 506/240-1313. 44 rms. TV TEL. $80 double. AE, MC, V. Free parking.

The Hotel Bougainvillea is an excellent choice if you are looking for a reasonably priced hotel in a quiet residential neighborhood not far from downtown. The hotel offers most of the amenities of the more expensive resort hotels around the valley, but charges considerably less. The views across the valley from this hillside location are beautiful, and the gardens of the hotel are beautifully designed and well tended. Guest rooms, though they lack any Costa Rican style, are as predictable as those in any international hotel. Rooms are carpeted and have small triangular balconies oriented to the views. Though there is no air-conditioning, there are fans, and temperatures are rarely too hot here. The hotel's dining room features continental dishes, with flambéed Delmonico steak being one of the specialities. Prices here are quite reasonable. There is also a quiet bar just off the lobby and room service. A complimentary downtown shuttle bus will take you in and out of town. The hotel's swimming pool is in its own private, walled garden and is quite attractive. There are also tennis courts and a jogging trail.

4 Dining

For decades, Costa Rican cuisine has been dismissed and disparaged. Rice and beans are served at nearly every meal, the selection is minimal, and Ticos generally don't go for spicy food, or so the criticism goes. In recent years, though, some contemporary and creative chefs have been trying educate and enlighten the Costa Rican palate, particularly in San José, and the early results are promising. Still, most visitors to the capital city quickly tire of Tico fare, even in its more chi-chi incarnation, and start seeking out the many local restaurants serving international cuisines. They are richly rewarded.

San José has a rather amazing variety of restaurants serving cuisines from all over the world and you'll never pay much even at the best restaurants. In fact, you really have to work at it to spend more than $40 per person for an extravagant six- or seven-course meal (not including liquor). Most restaurants fall into the moderately priced range. However, service can be indifferent at many restaurants, since the gratuity is already tacked on to the check, and tipping is not common among locals.

For a true deal, head to a *soda,* the equivalent of a diner in the United States, where you can get good, cheap, and filling Tico food. Rice and beans are the staples here and show up at breakfast, lunch, and dinner. When mixed together, they're called *gallo pinto,* and are usually served for breakfast, garnished with everything from fried eggs to steak. At lunch and dinner, rice and beans are the main components of a *casado* (which means "married")—the Costa Rican equivalent of a "blue plate special." Casado generally is served with a salad of cabbage and tomatoes, fried bananas, and steak, chicken, or fish. A plate of gallo pinto might cost $2, and a casado might cost $2.75–$3.

While in Costa Rica, be sure to taste a few *frescos.* A fresco is a bit like a fresh fruit milkshake without the ice cream, and when made with mangos, papayas, bananas, or any of the other delicious tropical fruits of Costa Rica, it is pure ambrosia. These frescos are also made with water (*con agua*), and preferences vary. Certain fruits like carambola (star fruit), maracuya (a type of passion fruit), and cas (you'll just have to try it), are only made with water. But remember, while the water in Costa Rica is generally very safe to drink, those with tender stomachs and intestinal tracts should stick to frescos made with milk.

For the following listings I considered a restaurant expensive if a meal without wine or beer costs more than $15 for one person. Moderate restaurants serve complete dinners for between $8 and $15, and inexpensive places are those where you can get a complete meal for less than $8. You should note that in the price ranges for the following restaurants, the highest prices are almost always for shrimp or lobster dishes. Other fish and meat dishes are considerably less expensive. If you want to save money on a meal, skip wine, which is almost always imported and expensive. Beer is more affordable as long as you don't order enormous quantities.

IN DOWNTOWN SAN JOSÉ
EXPENSIVE

✪ **La Masía De Triquel.** Sabana Norte, 175 meters north and 175 meters west of the Datsun Agency. ☎ **506/296-3528** or 506/232-3584. Reservations recommended on weekends. Main courses $6.50–$20.50. AE, DC, MC, V. Mon–Sat 11:30am–2pm and 6:30–11pm. SPANISH.

Despite the death of founding chef Francisco Triquell, relocation, and a healthy field of competitors, La Masía de Triquel is still San José's finest Spanish restaurant. Francisco Triquell Jr. has seen to that. Service is extremely formal and the regular clientele includes most of the city's upper crust. Although Costa Rica is known for its beef, here you'll also find wonderfully prepared lamb, quail, and rabbit. Seafood dishes include the usual shrimp and lobster, but also squid and octopus. However, there is really no decision to be made when perusing the menu: Start with a big bowl of gazpacho and then spend the rest of the evening enjoying all the succulent surprises you'll find in a big dish of *paella*.

La Piazzetta. Paseo Colón near Calle 40 (opposite Banco de Costa Rica). ☎ **506/222-7896** or 506/221-8451. Reservations recommended. Main courses $4.10–$25.50. AE, MC, V. Lunch Mon–Sat noon–2:30pm; dinner Mon–Sat 6:30–11pm. ITALIAN.

With an amazingly long menu and service by waiters in suits and bow ties, this restaurant hearkens back to the Italian restaurants of old in the United States, when southern Italian cooking was still an exotic ethnic cuisine.

The menu includes quite a few *risotto* (rice) dishes, which is a surprise, since most Italian restaurants in Costa Rica stick to spaghetti. There also are some other unexpected dishes that make appearances here, including smoked salmon, lobster, and truffles. Salads are colorful and artistically arranged. Try *baugna cauda,* anchovies and peppers in an olive oil–based broth, if you're in no fear of a coronary. For dessert, sample a classic chocolate mousse, or tiramisu.

MODERATE

Café Parisien. Gran Hotel Costa Rica, Avenida 2 between calles 1 and 3. ☎ **506/221-4011.** Sandwiches $2–$3.50; main courses $3–$19.20. AE, MC, V. Daily 24 hours. INTERNATIONAL.

The Gran Hotel Costa Rica is hardly the best hotel in San José, but it does have a picturesque patio cafe right on the Plaza de la Cultura. A wrought-iron railing, white columns, and arches create an Old World atmosphere, and on the plaza in front of the cafe a marimba band performs and vendors sell handcrafts. It's open 24 hours a day and is one of the best spots in town to people watch. Stop by for the breakfast buffet ($6.50) and fill up as the plaza vendors set up their booths; peruse the *Tico Times* over coffee while you have your shoes polished; or simply bask in the tropical sunshine while you sip a beer. Lunch and dinner buffets are also offered for $7.50.

La Cocina De Leña. El Pueblo. ☎ **506/255-1360** or 506/223-3704. Main courses $5–$19.50. AE, DC, MC, V. Daily 11am–11pm. COSTA RICAN.

Located in the unusual El Pueblo shopping, dining, and entertainment center, La Cocina de Leña (The Wood Stove) has a rustic feel to it. There are stacks of firewood on shelves above the booths, long stalks of bananas hanging from pillars, tables suspended by heavy ropes from the ceiling, and most unusual of all—menus printed on paper bags. In many ways this is simply a glorified soda, but if you're adventurous you could try some of the more unusual dishes. Perhaps oxtail stew served with yuca and plátano might appeal to you; if not, there are plenty of steaks and seafood dishes on the menu. *Chilasuilas* are delicious tortillas filled with fried meat. Black-bean soup with egg is a Costa Rican standard and is well done here, and the corn soup with pork is equally satisfying. For dessert there is très leches cake as well as the more unusual sweetened *chiverre*, which is a type of squash that looks remarkably like a watermelon.

Machu Pichu Bar and Restaurant. Calle 32 between avenidas 1 and 3, 150 meters north of the Kentucky Fried Chicken on Paseo Colón. ☎ **506/222-7384.** Main courses $3.50–$11. No credit cards. Daily 11am–3pm and 6–10pm. PERUVIAN/CONTINENTAL.

Located just off Paseo Colón near the Kentucky Fried Chicken, Machu Pichu is an unpretentious little restaurant that has become one of the most popular places in San José. The menu is primarily seafood (especially sea bass), and consequently most dishes tend toward the upper end of the menu's price range. Also, many of these fish dishes come in thick cream sauces. You're better off sticking with the two-person seafood sampler, combined with different appetizers. One of my favorite entrees is the *Causa Limeña*, lemon-flavored mashed potatoes stuffed with shrimp. The ceviche here is excellent, as is the *aji de gallina*, a dish of chopped chicken in a fragrant cream sauce, and octopus with garlic butter. Be sure to ask for a *pisco sour*, a Peruvian specialty drink.

✪ **Tin Jo.** Calle 11 between avenidas 6 and 8. ☎ **506/221-7605.** Main courses $3.75–$10.15. AE, MC, V. Mon–Sat 11:30am–3pm and 5:30–10:30pm; Sun 11:30am–10pm. CHINESE/THAI.

San José has hundreds of Chinese restaurants, but most simply serve up tired takes on chop suey, chow mein, and fried rice. In contrast, Tin Jo has a wide and varied menu, with an assortment of Cantonese and Szechuan staples, as well as a few Thai dishes. The *mu shu* is so good here, you may even forgive the fact that the pancakes are actually thin flour tortillas. Some of the dishes are served in edible rice noodle bowls, and the *pineapple shrimp in cocunut milk curry* is served in the hollowed out half of a fresh pineapple. The bow-tied-and-vested waiters here are helpful, and you'll have real tablecloths and cloth napkins. There's one table set in a small courtyard garden that adds a touch of romance to the meal.

INEXPENSIVE

✪ **Ruiseñor Café.** Teatro Nacional, Avenida 2 between calles 3 and 5. ☎ **506/233-4488.** Sandwiches and soups $3.45–$4.50; main courses $4.40–$8. MC, V. Mon–Sat 10:30am–6pm. CONTINENTAL.

This is one of my favorite places to eat in all of San José. Even if there is no show at the Teatro Nacional during your visit, you can enjoy a meal or a cup of coffee here and soak up the neoclassical atmosphere. The theater was built in the 1890s from the designs of European architects, and the art nouveau chandeliers, ceiling murals, and marble floors and tables are purely Parisienne. There are changing art displays by local artists to complete the très chic cafe atmosphere. The menu includes such continental dishes as quiche, Hungarian goulash soup, and wiener schnitzel, but the main attractions here are the specialty cakes and tortes which are displayed in a glass case. Ice cream dishes are raised to a high art form here with names such as "passionate love" and "spaghetti" ice cream. The ambience is classic French cafe, but the marimba music drifting in from outside the open window will remind you that you are still in Costa Rica. The same folks run restaurants with similar menus at the Contemporary Art Museum in the Sabana Park and on Avenida Central in Los Yoses.

La Esmeralda. Avenida 2 between calles 5 and 7. ☎ **506/221-0530.** Main courses $3.50–$6.50. AE, DC, MC, V. Mon–Sat 11am–5am. COSTA RICAN.

No one should visit San José without stopping in at La Esmeralda at least once, the later at night the better. This is much more than just a restaurant serving Tico food: It is the Grand Central Station of Costa Rican mariachi bands. In fact, mariachis and other bands from throughout Central America and Mexico hang out here every night waiting for work. While they wait they often serenade diners in the cavernous open-air dining hall of the restaurant. Friday and Saturday nights are always the busiest, but you'll probably hear lots of excellent music any night of the week. A personal concert will cost you anywhere from $3–$7 per song depending on the size of the group, but if you're on a tight budget you will still be able to hear just fine eaves-dropping on your neighbors. The classic Tico food is quite good. Try the coconut flan for dessert.

Manolo's Restaurante. Avenida Central between calles 0 and 2. ☎ **506/221-2041.** All items $3–$9.15. MC, V. Daily 11:30am–3pm and 6–10:30pm upstairs; 24 hours downstairs. COSTA RICAN.

Spread out over three floors, on a busy corner on Avenida Central, you'll find this roomy restaurant popular with Ticos and tourists alike. You can view the action in the street below, or catch the live folk-dance performance which is staged nightly. The open kitchen serves up steaks and fish, but there is also a popular buffet that includes several tipico dishes, such as platános and black-bean soup, for about $5.50. Down-stairs you'll find Manolo's Churreria, a good place for a quick sandwich—and they have espresso.

Pasteleria Francesa Boudsocq. Calle 30 at Paseo Colón. ☎ **506/222-6732.** Pastries $1.05–$2.75; main courses $3.50–$7.20. MC, V. Mon–Sat 8am–7pm. PASTRIES/FRENCH.

Ticos love their pastries and bakeries, and pastry shops abound all over San José. However, this little place on Paseo Colón is one of the best I've found. They have savory meat-filled pastries that make good lunches, as well as plenty of unusual sweets that are great afternoon snacks. Recently they've begun serving sit-down lunches. You can get a traditional *casado*, or a daily special with a French flair, such as *coq au vin*. There are only a couple of tables here.

La Perla. Avenida 2 and Calle Central. ☎ **506/222-7492.** Reservations not accepted. Main courses $1.75–$6.90, MC, V. Daily 24 hours. INTERNATIONAL.

It's easy to walk right past this place (I did) the first time you try to find it. The en-trance is right on the corner looking across at the National Cathedral, and the restau-rant itself is a little bit below street level. This place isn't long on atmosphere but the food is good and the portions are large. The special here is *paella*, a Spanish rice-and-seafood dish, for only $5. Other good choices are *sopa de mariscos*, which is a seafood soup with mussels and clams in a delicious broth, or *huevos à la ranchera*, which is prepared a bit differently than in Mexico and makes a filling meal any time of the night or day. This is a good place to come after a show at the Melico Salazar Theater.

Restaurante Campesino. Calle 7 between avenidas 2 and 4. ☎ **506/255-1356.** Main courses $2.25–$5.50; whole chicken $5; half chicken $2.70. MC, V. Daily 11am–midnight. COSTA RICAN/CHINESE.

This little restaurant serves delicious chicken, so don't even think about ordering any of the Chinese dishes on the menu. The secret of this delectable chicken is in the wood fire over which the chicken is roasted. Depending on how hungry you are, you can get a quarter, half, or full chicken; and you might also try the palmito (hearts of palm) salad. You can eat here, or if you must, take an order to go. You can't miss this place—watch for the smoking chimney high above the roof, or at street level watch for the window full of chickens roasting over an open fire.

Soda B y B. Calle 5 and Avenida Central. ☎ **506/222-7316.** Sandwiches $1.25–$3.50; breakfasts $1.15–$2.50; main courses $1.75–$3.50. DC, MC, V. Daily 8:30am–10pm. COSTA RICAN.

Located on the corner across from the Tourist Information Center on the Plaza de la Cultura, this spot is popular with downtown shoppers and office workers. Service is promt, prices (and noise level) are low, and the food is surprisingly good for a sandwich shop. Slide into a high-backed wooden booth and order the *chalupa de pollo B y B*—it's a sort of tostada piled high with chicken salad and drenched with sour cream and guacamole.

Soda Coppelia. Paseo Colón between calles 26 and 28. ☎ **506/223-8013.** Reservations not accepted. Most items $1.75–$4.50. No credit cards. Mon–Sat 8am–7pm. COSTA RICAN.

If you're looking for a filling, cheap, and quick breakfast in the Paseo Colón area, I recommend this soda. You'll find it near the Universal movie theater. The wooden booths and a few tables on a covered walkway (noisy) are frequently full of local businesspeople because the meals are so reasonably priced. A thin steak will run you $2.20, and for lighter fare, try the burgers, sandwiches, or some of the good-looking pastries such as flaky empanadas or carrot bread.

Soda Vishnu. Avenida 1 between calles 1 and 3. ☎ **506/222-2549.** Reservations not accepted. Main courses $1.25–$2.50. No credit cards. Daily 7am–9:30pm. VEGETARIAN.

Vegetarians will most certainly find their way here. There are booths for two or four people and photo murals on the walls. At the cashier's counter you can buy natural cosmetics, honey, and bags of granola. However, most people just come for the filling *plato de dia* that includes soup, salad, veggies, an entree, and dessert for around $2. There are also bean burgers and cheese sandwiches on whole-wheat bread. There is another Vishnu around the corner on Calle 3 between Avenida Central and Avenida 1.

IN SAN PEDRO/LOS YOSES
EXPENSIVE

✪ **Bijahua.** 50 meters west and 300 meters south of Mas X Menos in San Pedro. ☎ **506/225-0613.** Reservations recommended. Main courses $6.80–$19.80. AE, MC, V. Mon–Fri noon–2:30pm and 7–10:30pm; Sat 6:30–11pm. COSTA RICAN.

This restaurant is almost single-handedly seeking to erase Costa Rica's historical culinary infamy. Using traditional ingredients, chef Isabel Campabadal has created an exotic and innovative menu. Instead of potato, the gnocchi here are made from ñampi, an indigenous tubor, and the tamale appetizer is made from pejibaye, a diminutive palm nut. Main dishes include red snapper stuffed with green plantain puree and shrimp croquettes topped with a maracuyá sauce. Whatever you do, save room for the passion fruit soufflé. The service and setting here are both elegant, and it pays to come here for lunch, when the atrium ceiling and an entire wall of orchids are in full splendor.

Le Chandelier. 100 meters west and 100 meters south of the ICE office in San Pedro. ☎ **506/225-3980.** Reservations recommended. Main courses $7.50–$24.50 lunch, $10.50–$28.50 dinner; fixed-price lunch $16.25, fixed-price dinner $34.50. AE, MC, V. Mon–Sat 11am–2pm and 6–11pm. FRENCH.

Located in a large older house in a quiet residential neighborhood east of downtown San José, Le Chandelier is one of the most elegant restaurants in town. The neighborhood, landscaping, and architectural styling give it the feel of an older Hollywood or Beverly Hills restaurant. The menu includes delicious renditions of French classics such as onion soup, escargots bourguignon, and chicken à l'orange. There are also such less familiar and unexpected dishes as tenderloin with cranberry sauce, carpaccio with smoked salmon and palmito, and roast duck in green pepper sauce. The set dinner is a true feast and might start with an appetizer of carpaccio, followed by gratin of Camembert with shrimp, sorbet, tournedos in cabernet sauvignon and green pepper, cheese and fruit, and a dessert of tiramisu.

MODERATE

✪ Il Pirón. Sabanilla, in front of the UNED. ☎ 506/234-7851. Reservations recommended on weekends. Main courses $3.75–$12.50. MC, V. Tue–Sat 11am–3pm and 6–11pm; Sun 11am–3pm. ITALIAN.

When fire destroyed its first home, Il Pirón's owners moved the restaurant to the other side of the University, in Sabanilla. Service is formal, but not overbearing. Il Pirón feels like a quiet, neighborhood restaurant should—with great food and not much pretense. Towards the rear, the room opens on to a small interior garden with flowering heliconia and hanging orchids. The meat and fish dishes here are wonderful, but don't pass on the pasta. Try the *spaghetti creola,* which contains shrimp in a fresh tomato sauce, with hints of curry and vodka. The tagliatelle is homemade and the foccacio with rosemary is divine. Whenever I go, it seems the conversation at the tables around me is mostly in Italian—always a good sign.

IN ESCAZÚ
EXPENSIVE

Atlanta Dining Gallery. Tara Resort Hotel, 600 meters south of the San Antonio de Escazú cemetary. ☎ 506/228-6992. Reservations recommended. Main courses $7.20–$21.50. AE, MC, V. Daily 7am–11pm. CONTINENTAL.

For elegance, excellent service, delicious food, and fabulous views, you just can't beat the Atlanta Dining Gallery. Located in a reproduction antebellum mansion, this place is straight out of the Deep South, except for that view of the Central Valley out the windows. Elegant dark-wood furnishings and a hardwood floor set the tone, but it is the view that keeps grabbing your attention. Scarlett O'Hara never had it so good. Most nights of the week such dishes as filet mignon with mushrooms, shrimp scampi, chicken with a mango and avocado sauce, and corvina with a red-pepper and wine sauce, accompany the views. A tempting assortment of desserts accompanies a choice of after-dinner aperitifs and cognacs. Breakfasts are also a treat here, with all-you-can-eat Sunday pancake extravaganzas.

INEXPENSIVE

Muy. One kilometer above the Pico Blanco Inn. ☎ 506/254-6281. Reservations recommended on weekends. Main course $3.25–$7.25. MC, V. Mon–Fri 5–11pm; Sat–Sun noon–11pm. BBQ/TEX-MEX.

Located high on a hill above Escazú, this casual restaurant combines a great view with classic barbeque and Tex-Mex cooking. You'll get the best views if you sit outdoors on the small deck, though you'll be sitting on plastic lawn chairs. The atmosphere may be light, but the portions are hefty. Stick to the standards—chicken fajitas or barbeque ribs—and wash it all down with a tangy margarita.

IN THE HEREDIA/ALAJUELA/AIRPORT AREA
EXPENSIVE

Oceanos. 50 meters south of the Hotel Herradura Conference Center. ☎ 506/293-0622. Reservations recommended. Main courses $13.25–$27.50. AE, MC, V (5% surcharge added). SEAFOOD/NOUVELLE CUISINE.

Specializing in fresh seafood preparations, chef Jeff Brosman calls his cuisine "fusion food." Service is formal. Waiters in tuxedo shirts and bow ties toss salads tableside and keep you stocked with a steady supply of fresh breads and herb butter. The menu is so varied and eclectic that it's almost best to order by whim and fancy. Still, you can't go wrong with the Singapore-style curried fish and jumbo shrimp, which comes wrapped in a banana leaf, or the yellowfin tuna Tariq, prepared with olive oil, fennel, and garlic in a Sambuca-and-vermouth flambé. There are also plenty of meat and chicken dishes, as well as wonderful pastas. The homemade cheesecake—Brosman is from New York—is the best I've had in Central America.

STREET FOOD & LATE-NIGHT BITES

On almost every street corner in downtown San José you'll find a fruit vendor. If you're lucky enough to be in town between April and June, you can sample more varieties of mangoes than you ever knew existed. I like buying them already cut up in a little bag; they cost a little more this way but you don't get nearly as messy. Be sure to try a green mango with salt and chili peppers. That's the way they seem to like mangoes best in the steamy tropics—guaranteed to wake up your taste buds. Another common street food that you might be wondering about is called *pejibaye*, a bright orange palm nut about the size of a small apple. They are boiled in big pots on carts. You eat them in much the same way you would an avocado, and they taste a bit like squash.

If it's 1am and you've just got to grab a bite, you're in luck. San José has quite a few all-night restaurants including **La Perla**, **La Esmeralda,** and **Café Parisien,** all of which are described above. Another popular place, which is almost exclusively for men, is the **Soda Palace** on Avenida 2 and Calle 2 (see "San José After Dark," for more information).

5 Attractions

Most visitors to Costa Rica try to get out of the city as fast as possible so they can spend more time on the beach or off in the rain forests. However, San José is the country's main metropolis and there are quite a few attractions here to keep you busy for a while. Some of the best and most modern museums in Central America are in San José, and together these museums have a wealth of fascinating pre-Columbian artifacts. New additions include a modern and expansive children's museum, as well as a centrally located National Arts Center, featuring yet another museum and several performing arts spaces. There are also several great things to see and do just outside San José in the Central Valley. If you start doing day trips out of the city, you can spend quite a few days in this region.

SUGGESTED ITINERARIES

If You Have 1 Day

Start your day on the Plaza de la Cultura. Visit the Gold Museum and see if you can get tickets for a performance that night at the Teatro Nacional. From the Plaza de la Cultura stroll up Avenida Central to the Museo Nacional. After lunch head over to the Jade Museum or the neighboring National Arts Center (if you have the energy for another museum). After all this culture, a stroll through the chaos of the Mercado Central is in order. Try dinner at La Cocina De Leña before going to the Teatro Nacional. After the performance you absolutely must swing by La Esmeralda for some live mariachi music before calling it a day.

If You Have 2 Days

Follow the itinerary above. On Day Two visit the Serpentarium, the Children's Museum (a must if you've brought the kids along), or the Spirogyra Butterfly Garden, do a bit of shopping, and then head out Paseo Colón to the Museo de Arte Costarricense and La Sabana Park.

If You Have 3 Days

Follow the itinerary for the two days outlined above. On Day Three, head out to Irazú Volcano, Orosi Valley, Lankester Gardens, and Cartago. Start your day at the volcano and work your way back toward San José.

If You Have 5 Days

Follow the itinerary for three days outlined above. Then spend Days Four and Five on other excursions from San José. You can go white-water rafting, hiking in a cloud forest, or horseback riding for a day if you are an active type. If you prefer less strenuous activities, try a cruise around the Gulf of Nicoya and a trip to the Rain Forest Aerial Tram.

THE TOP ATTRACTIONS

Ⓢ Centro Nacional de Arte y Cultura (National Arts Center). Calle 13 between avenidas 3 and 5. ☎ 506/255-2468. Free admission. Tue–Sun 10am–4:30pm. Any downtown bus.

Occupying a full city block, this was once the National Liquor Factory (FANAL). Now, it houses the offices of the Cultural Ministry, several performing arts centers, and the Museum of Contemporary Art and Design. The latter has featured several impressive traveling international exhibits since its inception, including large retrospectives by Mexican painter Jose Cuevas and Ecuadorean painter Oswaldo Guayasamin. If you're looking for modern dance, experimental theater or a lecture on Costa Rican video, this is the place to check.

Museo de Arte Costarricense. Calle 42 and Paseo Colón, Parque la Sabana este. ☎ 506/222-7155. Admission $1.50 adults, children and students free. Tue–Sun 10am–4pm. Bus: Sabana–Cementerio.

This small museum at the end of Paseo Colón in Parque la Sabana was formerly an airport terminal. Today, however, it houses a collection of works in all media by Costa Rica's most celebrated artists. On display are some exceptionally beautiful pieces in a wide range of artistic styles, demonstrating how Costa Rican artists have interpreted and imitated the major European artistic movements over the years. In addition to the permanent collection of sculptures, paintings, and prints, there are regular temporary exhibits. If the second floor is open during your visit, be sure to go up and have a look at the conference room's unusual bas-relief walls, which chronicle the history of Costa Rica from pre-Columbian times to the present with evocative images of its people. On weekends local artists sell their work out on the plaza in front of the museum. The Ruiseñor Café here makes a wonderful pit stop.

✪ Museo de Jade Marco Fidel Tristan (Jade Museum). Avenida 7 between calles 9 and 9B, 11th Floor, INS Building. ☎ 506/223-5800, ext. 2584. Admission $2 adults, children and students free. Mon–Fri 8am–4:30pm. Any downtown bus.

Among the pre-Columbian cultures of Mexico and Central America, jade was the most valuable commodity, worth more than gold. This modern museum displays a huge collection of jade artifacts from throughout Costa Rica's pre-Columbian archeological sites. Most of the jade pieces are large pendants that were parts of necklaces, and are primarily human and animal figures. A fascinating display illustrates how the primitive peoples of this region carved this extremely hard stone. Most of the jade pieces date from 330 B.C. to A.D. 700.

There is also an extensive collection of pre-Columbian polychromed terra-cotta vases, bowls, and figurines. Some of these pieces are amazingly modern in design and exhibit a surprisingly advanced technique. Particulary fascinating is a vase that incorporates real human teeth, and a display that shows how jade was imbedded in human teeth merely for decorative reasons. Most of the identifying labels and explanations are in Spanish but there are a few in English.

Before you leave be sure to check out the splendid view of San José from the lounge area.

✪ **Museo de Los Niños (Children's Museum).** Calle 4 and Avenida 9. ☎ **506/233-2734.** Admission $5 adults, $2.50 students, $1.50 children under 12. Tue–Sun 9am–5pm. Any downtown bus.

This museum is located a few blocks north of downtown, on Calle 4. It's easy walking distance, but you might want to take a cab, as you'll have to walk right through the worst part of the red-light district.

This recently converted prison houses an extensive collection of exhibits designed for the edification and entertainment of children of all ages. Experience a simulated earthquake, make music by dancing across the floor. Many of the exhibits encourage hands-on play. If you have children with you, you will definitely want to come here, and you may want to visit even if you don't. Be careful: This museum is large and spread out, and it's easy to lose track of a family member or friend.

✪ **Museo de Oro Banco Central (Gold Museum).** Calle 5 between Avenida Central and Avenida 2, underneath the Plaza de la Cultura. ☎ **506/223-0528.** Admission $5 adults, $1.50 students, 75¢ children under 12. Tue–Sun 10am–4:30pm. Any downtown bus.

Located directly beneath the Plaza de la Cultura, this unusual underground museum houses one of the largest collections of pre-Columbian gold in the Americas. On display are more than 20,000 troy ounces of gold in more than 2,000 objects. The sheer number of small pieces can be overwhelming and seem redundant. However, the unusual display cases and complex lighting systems show off every piece to its utmost. This museum also includes a gallery for temporary art exhibits, and a numismatic and philatelic museum.

✪ **Museo Nacional de Costa Rica.** Calle 17 between Avenida Central and Avenida 2, on the Plaza de la Democracia. ☎ **506/257-1433.** Admission $1 adults, students and children under 10 free. Tue–Sun 8:30am–4:30pm. Closed Dec 25 and 31. Bus: San Pedro.

Costa Rica's most important historical museum is housed in a former army barracks that was the scene of fighting during the civil war of 1948. You can still see hundreds of bullet holes on the turrets at the corners of the building. Inside this traditional Spanish-style courtyard building, you will find displays on Costa Rican history and culture from pre-Columbian times to the present. In the pre-Columbian rooms, you'll see a 2,500-year-old jade carving that is shaped like a seashell and etched with an image of a hand holding a small animal. Among the most fascinating objects unearthed at Costa Rica's numerous archeological sites are many *metates,* or grinding stones. This type of grinding stone is still in use today throughout Central America. However, the ones on display here are more ornately decorated than those that you will see anywhere else. Some of the metates are the size of a small bed and are believed to have been part of funeral rites. A separate vault houses the museum's small collection of pre-Columbia gold jewelry and figurines. In the courtyard, you'll be treated to a wonderful view of the city and see some of Costa Rica's mysterious stone spheres.

Museo Nacional de Ciencias Naturales "La Salle." Across from the southeast corner of Parque la Sabana. ☎ **506/232-1306.** Admission $1 adults, 50¢ children. Mon–Fri 8am–4pm, Sat 8am–noon, Sun 9am–4pm. Bus: Escazú or Pavas from Avenida 1 and Calle 18.

Before heading out to the wilds of the Costa Rican jungles, you might want to stop by this natural-history museum and find out more about the animals you might be seeing. There are stuffed and mounted anteaters, monkeys, tapirs, and many others. However, the collection includes animals from all over the world as well. There are also 1,200 birds and 12,500 insects displayed. A collection of 13,500 seashells is another highlight.

Museo de Entomologia. In the basement of the University of Costa Rica's School of Music, San Pedro. ☎ **506/207-5647.** Admission $1.50. Mon–Fri 1–4pm. Bus: San Pedro from Avenida 2 between calles 5 and 7.

The tropics have produced the world's greatest concentrations and diversity of insects, and at this small museum you can see more than one million mounted insects from around the world. The butterfly collection is the star attraction here.

MORE ATTRACTIONS

Parque Zoologico Simon Bolívar. Avenida 11 and Calle 7, in Barrio Amón. ☎ **506/233-6701.** Admission $1 adults, children under 10 free. Tue–Fri 8am–3:30pm, Sat–Sun 9am–5pm. Any downtown bus, then walk.

I don't think I have ever seen a sadder zoo than this little park tucked away beside the polluted Río Torres. It is a shame that a country that has preserved so much of its land in national parks would ignore this zoo. The cages here are only occasionally marked, and many are dirty and small. The collection includes Asian, African, and Costa Rican animals. For many years, there have been plans to build a new zoo with more modern displays, and while some minor improvements have been made, there's still a long way to go.

Serpentarium. Avenida 1 between calles 9 and 11. ☎ **506/255-4210.** Admission $2.50 adults, 75¢ children between ages 6–13. Daily 9am–6pm. Any downtown bus.

The tropics abound in reptiles and amphibians, and the Serpentarium is an excellent introduction to all that slithers and hops through the jungles of Costa Rica. The live snakes, lizards, and frogs are kept in beautiful, large terrariums that simulate their natural environments. Poisonous snakes make up a large part of the collection with the dreaded fer-de-lance pit viper eliciting the most gasps from enthralled visitors. Also fascinating to see are the tiny, brilliantly colored poison arrow frogs. Iguanas and Jesus Christ lizards are two of the more commonly spotted of Costa Rica's reptiles, and both are represented here. Also on display is an Asian import—a giant Burmese python, which is one of the largest I have ever seen. This little zoological museum is well worth a visit, especially if you plan to go bashing about in the jungles. It will help you identify the numerous poisonous snakes you'll want to avoid. If you show up around 3pm you may catch them feeding the piranhas and perhaps some of the snakes.

Spyrogyra Butterfly Garden. 100 meters east and 100 meters south of El Pueblo Shopping Center. ☎ **506/222-2937.** Admission $5. Daily 8am–3pm. Calle Blancos bus from Calle 3 and Avenida 5.

Butterflies have been likened to self-propelled flowers, so it comes as no surprise that butterfly gardens are becoming all the rage throughout the tropics these days. If you'd like to find out why, drop in here at Spyrogyra. Though this butterfly garden is smaller and less spectacular than the other two listed below, it is a good introduction to the life cycle of butterflies. You'll find Spyrogyra near El Pueblo, a 20-minute walk from the center of San José.

ATTRACTIONS OUTSIDE SAN JOSÉ

The Butterfly Farm. In front of Los Reyes Country Club, La Guácima de Alajuela. ☎ **506/438-0400.** Admission $10 adults, $5 students and children under 12. Daily 9am–3pm. Bus: San Antonio/Ojo de Agua on Avenida 1 between calles 20 and 22.

At any given time, you may see around 30 of the 80 different species of butterflies raised at this butterfly farm south of Alajuela. The butterflies live in a large enclosed garden similar to an aviary, and flutter about the heads of visitors during tours of the gardens. When we visited we saw glittering blue morphos and a butterfly that mimics the eyes of an owl. In the demonstration room you'll see butterfly eggs, caterpillars, and pupae. Among the latter, there are cocoons trimmed in a shimmering gold color and cocoons that mimic a snake's head in order to frighten away predators. The farm also offers a bee tour during which you can observe bees at work in glass observation hives.

Butterfly Paradise. On the road from San Joaquín to Santa Barbara, 1 kilometer north, and 350 meters west, on the right-hand side. ☎ **506/265-6694.** Admission $10 adults, $5 children under 12. Daily 9am–3pm. First take a bus to Heredia from Calle 1 between avenidas 7 and 9 in San José. In Heredia, transfer to a bus bound for either San Joaquín or Santa Barbara. In San Joaquín, you can get a taxi.

This butterfly garden is similar to the other two and offers the same experience—a guided walk through the screened-in butterfly habitat. You'll see dozens of beautiful butterflies and learn all about their feeding, mating, and egg-laying habits. In the museum collection there are more butterflies to marvel over, and many other insects as well.

Café Britt Farm. North of Heredia on the road to Barva. ☎ **506/260-2748.** Admission $19–$25 per person, including transportation from downtown San José. Three tours daily 9am, 11am, and 3pm. Tours Nov–Feb during the harvest season; store open daily 8am–5pm all year.

Though bananas are the main export of Costa Rica, people are far more interested in the country's second most important export crop—coffee. Café Britt is one of the leading brands of coffee here, and the company has put together an interesting tour and stage production at its farm, which is 20 minutes outside of San José. Here, you'll see how coffee is grown. You'll also visit the roasting plant to learn how a coffee "cherry" is turned into a delicious roasted bean. Tasting sessions are offered for visitors to experience the different qualities of coffee. There is also a store here where you can buy very reasonably priced coffee.

✪ Lankester Gardens. Paraíso de Cartago. ☎ **506/551-9877** or 506/552-3247. Admission $2.50 adults, 25¢ children. Daily 8:30am–3:30pm. Closed on all national holidays. Cartago bus from San José, then the Paraíso bus from the south side of the Parque Central in Cartago.

There are more than 1,200 varieties of orchids in Costa Rica, and no less than 800 species are on display at this botanical garden in Cartago province. Created in the 1940s by English naturalist Charles Lankester, the gardens are now administered by the University of Costa Rica. The primary goal of the gardens is to preserve the local flora, with an emphasis on orchids and bromeliads. Paved trails wander from open, sunny gardens into shady forests. In each environment, different species of orchids are in bloom. There is an information center, and the trails are well tended and well marked.

Museo Joyas del Tropico Humedo (Jewels of the Rain Forest). 100 meters east of the cemetery of Santa Domingo de Heredia. ☎ **506/244-5006.** Admission $5 adults, $2.50 children under 12. Mon–Sat 9am–5pm; Sun 10am–6pm. At Calle 1 between avenidas 7 and 9, take the Heredia/Tibás/Santo Domingo bus, then a taxi from Santo Domingo.

Far more than just another bug collection, this exhibit takes the position that insects are works of art, tiny tropical jewels. The displays are artistically arranged and include more than 50,000 arthropods and insects (including thousands of different butterflies), collected from around the world by former Oregon biologist Richard Whitten and his wife Maggie.

✪ Zoo Ave. La Garita, Alajuela. ☎ **506/433-8989.** Admission $7.50 adults, $1 children under 12. Daily 9am–5pm. Bus: Catch an Alajuela bus on Avenida 2 between calles 12 and 14. In Alajuela, transfer to a bus for Atenas and get off at Zoo Ave before you get to La Garita.

Dozens of scarlet macaws, reclusive owls, majestic raptors, several different species of toucans, and a host of brilliantly colored birds from Costa Rica and around the world make this place an exciting one to visit. Birdwatching enthusiasts will be able to get a closer look at birds they may have seen in the wild. There are also large iguana, deer, and monkey exhibits—and look out for the 12-foot-long crocodile. Zoo Ave only houses injured, donated, or confiscated animals.

WALKING TOUR
Downtown San José

Start: Plaza de la Cultura.
Finish: Plaza de la Cultura.
Time: Allow a full day for this tour, though most of your time will be spent touring the four museums mentioned.
Best Time: Any day of the week, except Monday, when the Gold Museum is closed.
Worst Time: Monday, see above.

Because San José is so compact, it's possible to visit nearly all of the city's major sites in a single day's walking tour. Begin your tour on the Plaza de la Cultura, perhaps after having breakfast at the Gran Hotel Costa Rica.

Begin by walking to the:

1. Teatro Nacional, which faces the entrance to the Gran Hotel Costa Rica. Be sure to take a walk around inside this baroque masterpiece. The cafe here is another great place to have a meal or a pastry and coffee. Around the back of the theater is the:

2. Gold Museum, which is built beneath the Plaza de la Cultura to the left of the Teatro Nacional. This museum houses the largest collection of pre-Columbian gold in Central America. From the Gold Museum, walk two blocks west on Avenida 2 to reach the:

3. National Cathedral, a neoclassical structure with a tropical twist. The roof is tin, and the ceiling is wood. A statue of the Virgin Mary is surrounded by neon stars and a crescent moon. Diagonally across the street is the:

4. Melico Salazar Theater. This theater has an impressive pillared facade. Though the interior is not nearly as ornate, there are often interesting art and photo exhibits in the lobby. Continue west on Avenida 2 and turn right on Calle 6. In two blocks, you will be in the:

5. Mercado Central, a fragrant (not necessarily pleasantly so) district of streets crowded with produce vendors. A covered market, with its dark warren of stalls, takes up an entire block and is the center of activity. Beware of pickpockets in this area. Head back toward the Teatro Nacional on Avenida Central, and in seven blocks you will come to an excellent place for lunch.

☕ **TAKE A BREAK**   One of the best lunches in San José is at the **Ruiseñor Café** inside the National Theater. I know this is where you started, but the soups,

Walking Tour—San José

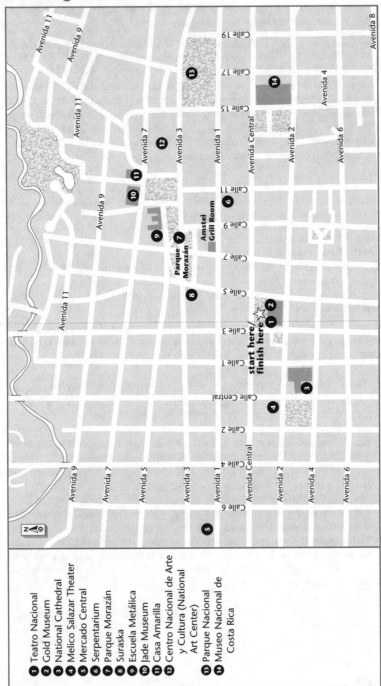

1 Teatro Nacional
2 Gold Museum
3 National Cathedral
4 Melico Salazar Theater
5 Mercado Central
6 Serpentarium
7 Parque Morazán
8 Suraska
9 Escuela Metálica
10 Jade Museum
11 Casa Amarilla
12 Centro Nacional de Arte y Cultura (National Art Center)
13 Parque Nacional
14 Museo Nacional de Costa Rica

start here/ finish here

Amstel Grill Room

Parque Morazán

2362

sandwiches, and main dishes are excellent, and not heavy enough to spoil your walking mood. You'll be well fed and perfectly positioned to continue your tour.

After lunch head over to the corner of Avenida 1 and Calle 9 where you'll find the:

6. **Serpentarium.** This indoor zoo offers a fascinating look at the reptiles and amphibians of Costa Rica and other parts of the world. When you leave the Serpentarium, head north on Calle 9 and you will come to:

7. **Parque Morazán,** a classically designed park that was restored to its original configuration in 1991. This is a good place for people-watching. At the center of the park is a large bandstand modeled after a music temple in Paris. Across the street from the west side of the park you'll find:

8. **Suraska,** a handcrafts shop with a good selection of products made from local woods, as well as ceramics and jewelry. Retrace your steps back to the far side of the park, and across the street to the north you will see the:

9. **Escuela Metálica,** Avenida 5 and Calle 9, which is one of the most unusual buildings in the city. It is made of metal panels that are bolted together, and was premanufactured, then shipped over from Europe late in the 19th century. One block north, on Avenida 7, you'll come to the:

10. **Jade Museum,** which is located in a high-rise office building. The cool, dark exhibit halls are filled with jade pendants, and there are also great views of the city. Across Calle 11 from the Jade Museum is the:

11. **Casa Amarilla,** which is an attractive old building that now houses the Ministry of Foreign Affairs. This building, along with the recently remodeled park directly across the street, were donated to Costa Rica by Andrew Carnegie. The grounds on the east side of the Casa Amarila house a section of the Berlin Wall. From here, walk through the bamboo groves of the Parque España to the entrance of the:

12. **Centro Nacional de Arte y Cultura (National Art Center).** You can just use this as a shortcut to your next destination, or take a tour of the Museum of Contemporary Art and Design. Make sure to exit the center at its southeast entrance, which will place you right across from the:

13. **Parque Nacional,** which has an large bronze monument to the nations that defeated Tennesseean William Walker's attempt to turn Central America into a slave state in the 19th century. Across Avenida 1 is a statue of Juan Santamaría, who gave his life to defeat Walker. If you continue south on Calle 17, you will find the:

14. **Museo Nacional de Costa Rica,** between Avenida Central and Avenida 2. This museum is housed in a former army barracks that still shows signs of the 1948 revolution. Inside is Costa Rica's largest collection of pre-Columbian art and artifacts. After touring the museum, you need only head west on Avenida Central or Avenida 2 and in seven blocks you will be back at the Plaza de la Cultura.

6 Organized Tours

There are literally dozens of tour companies operating in San José, and the barrage of advertising brochures can be quite intimidating. There really isn't much reason to take a tour of San José since it is so compact—you can easily visit all the major sites on your own (see above). However, if you want to take a city tour, which will run you between $15 and $20, here are some companies: **Otec Tours,**

Edeficio Ferencz, Calle 3 between avenidas 1 and 3, Apdo. 323-1002, San José (☎ 506/256-0633); **TAM,** Calle Central between Avenida Central and Avenida 1 (☎ 506/256-0203 or 506/222-3866); **Vic-Vic Tours,** Calle 3 between avenidas 5 and 7 (☎ 506/233-3435); **San Jose Travel,** Calle 11 and Avenida 2, (☎ 506/257-4511), and **Swiss Travel Service,** (☎ 506/232-7188), which has several offices around San José including locations in the lobbies of the Hotel Corobicí and the Hotel Amstel. These same companies also offer a whole range of day trips out of San José.

7 Outdoor Activities

Due to the smog and pollution, you'll probably want to get out of the city before undertaking any strenuous or aerobic activity. However, there are some options available in and around San José, if you want to brave the natural and man-made elements.

La Sabana Park (at the western end of Paseo Colón), formerly San José's international airport, is the city's center for active sports and recreation. Here you'll find everthing from jogging trails, soccer fields, and a few public tennis courts to the National Stadium. All the facilities are free and open to the public. If you really want to experience the local culture, try getting into a pick-up soccer game here.

For information on **horseback riding, hiking,** and **white-water rafting** trips from San José, see "Easy Excursions from San José," at the end of this chapter.

BIKING

Bicycle riding in and around San José is suicidal and I don't recommend it. If you want to jog, you should try the La Sabana Park mentioned above, or head to Parque del Este, which is east of town, in the foothills above San Pedro. Take the San Ramón/Parque del Este bus from Avenida 2 between calles 9 and 11. It's never a good idea to jog at night, on busy streets, or alone. Women should be particularly careful about jogging alone.

GOLF & TENNIS

If you want to play tennis or golf, check with the hotels Herradura and Cariari (see listings above).

SWIMMING

If you aren't going to get to the beach anytime soon and want to cool off, check out the new **Agua Mania** (☎ 506/293-2890) on the road to San Antonio de Belén, near the Hotel Herradura. This modern water theme park has water slides, tube rides, and a wave pool, as well as miniature golf and go-carts. Open Tuesday though Thursday and Sunday from 9:30am to 5:30pm; on Saturday until 10pm. Admission is $7.50 for adults, $5 for children under 12. Buses that pass Agua Mania leave almost every hour from Avenida 1 between calles 18 and 20.

Alternately, if you'd prefer to spend an afternoon relaxing in a spring-fed swimming pool, head out to **Ojo de Agua** (☎ 506/441-2808)**,** which is on the same road to San Antonio de Belén. The crystal-clear waters are cool and refreshing, and even if it seems a bit chilly in San José, it is always several degrees warmer out here. This place is very popular with Ticos and can get quite crowded on weekends, but you do have to keep an eye on your valuables. Admission is 75¢. Buses leave almost hourly for Ojo de Agua, departing from Avenida 1 between calles 18 and 20.

8   Spectator Sports

Ticos take their *fútbol* seriously. Although not up to European or World Cup standards, Costa Rican professional soccer is some of the best in Central America. The soccer season runs from September through June, with the finals spread out over several weeks in late June and early July. You don't need to buy tickets in advance. Tickets generally run between $2.50–$12.50. It's worth paying a little extra for *sombra numerado* (reserved seats in the shade). Other options include *sombra* (general admission in the shade), *palco* and *palco numerado* (general admission and reserved mezzanine), and *sol general* (general admission in full sun). The main San José team is Saprissa (affectionately called *El monstro*, or The Monster). Saprissa's stadium is in Tibás (take any Tibás bus from Calle 2 between avenidas 3 and 7). Games are usually held on Sunday at 11am, but occasionally they are scheduled for Saturday afternoon or Wednesday evening. Check the local newspapers for game times and locations.

The **Vuelta de Costa Rica** is a Central American version of the Tour de France. Bicycle racers from around the region spend several weeks each December battling each other up and over the mountains on the roads of Costa Rica. If you're traveling around the country during December, check the local papers for routes and racing times, and you may be able to watch the pack pass by.

During the first week of January, Costa Rica hosts the **Copa del Café (The Coffee Cup),** which is an important international event on the junior tennis tour. Matches are held at the Costa Rica Country Club (☎ 506/228-9333) in Escazú. Admission $5 and you can buy tickets at the box office.

Although I hesitate to call it a sport, **Las Corridas a la Tica** (Costa Rican bullfighting) is a popular and frequently comic stadium event. Instead of the blood-and-gore/life-and-death confrontation of traditional bullfighting, Ticos just like to tease the bull. In a typical *corrida,* anywhere from 50–150 *toreadores improvisados* (literally, improvised bullfighters) stand in the ring waiting for the bull. What follows is a slapstick scramble to safety whenever the bull heads towards a crowd of bullfighters. The braver bullfighters try to slap the bull's backside as the beast chases down one of his buddies. You can see a bullfight during the Festejos Populares in Zapote, a suburb east of San José. The corridas run all day and well into the night during Christmas week and the first week in January. Admission is $2–$5. Take the Zapote bus from Calle 1 between avenidas 4 and 6.

9   Shopping

Serious shoppers will be disappointed in Costa Rica. Aside from coffee, there isn't much that is distinctly Costa Rican that you can buy. In fact, you probably won't be overwhelmed by the desire to buy things the way you might be in other countries that have indigenous handcrafts. To compensate for its own relative lack of handcrafts, Costa Rica does a brisk business in selling crafts and clothes imported from Guatemala and Panama. Still, there are are some interesting and unique items to buy, as discussed under "Best Buys," below (see also "The Best Places to Shop," in chapter 1).

THE SHOPPING SCENE

Shopping in San José centers around an area marked by the parallel streets of Avenida 1 and Avenida 2, from about Calle 14 in the west to Calle 13 in the east.

For several blocks west of the Plaza de la Cultura, Avenida Central is a pedestrians-only street where you'll find store after store of inexpensive clothes for men, women, and children.

Most shops in the downtown district are open Monday through Saturday from about 8am to 6pm. You'll find that some shops close for lunch while others remain open. When you do purchase something, you'll be happy to find that there is no sales tax.

International laws prohibit purchasing endangered wildlife—visitors to Costa Rica should not buy any wildlife or plants, even if they are readily for sale. The Audubon Society does not tolerate sales of any kind of sea turtle product (including jewelry), wild birds, lizard or snake skin, coral, or orchids (except those grown commercially). It's especially hard to capture the subtle shades and colors of the rain and cloud forests, so to avoid getting home only to discover that the photos you took on your trip don't do justice to the beauty of Costa Rica, you might want to buy one of the picture books on Costa Rica mentioned in the "Recommended Books" section of chapter 2.

BEST BUYS

Two words of advice—buy coffee. Buy as much as you can carry. Coffee is the best shopping deal in all of Costa Rica. Although the best Costa Rican coffee is supposedly shipped off to North American and European markets, it's hard to beat the coffee that's roasted right in front of you here. **Café Britt** is the big name in Costa Rican coffee. The most expensive brand, it is not necessarily the best. For good flavor and value, visit **Café Trebol,** on Calle 8 between Avenida Central and Avenida 1. I highly recommend buying your coffee here. They'll pack the beans for you in whatever size bag you want. Be sure to ask for whole beans; Costa Rican grinds are too fine for standard coffee filters. Best of all is the price: One pound of coffee sells for about $1.75. It makes a great gift and keeps for a long time in your refrigerator or freezer. If you should happen to buy prepackaged coffee in a supermarket in Costa Rica, be sure the package is marked *puro;* otherwise, it will likely be mixed with a good amount of sugar—the way Ticos like it.

One good coffee-related gift to bring home is a coffee sock and stand. This is the most common mechanism for brewing coffee beans in Costa Rica. It consists of a simple circular stand, made out of wood or wire, which holds a sock. Put the ground beans in the sock, place a pot or cup below, and pour boiling water through. You can find the socks and stands at most supermarkets, and in the Mercado Central. Depending on its construction, a stand will cost you between $1.50 and $5; socks run around 30¢, so buy a few spares.

If your interest is in handcrafts, there are many places for you to visit. As I've said, the quality of Costa Rican handcrafts is generally very low, and the offerings are limited. The most typical item you'll find are handpainted wooden oxcarts. These come in a variety of sizes and the big ones can be shipped to your home for a very reasonable price.

You may also run across carved masks made by the indigenous Boruca people of southern Costa Rica. These full-sized balsa wood masks come in a variety of styles, both painted and unpainted, and run anywhere from $10 to $70, depending on the quality of workmanship.

SUBURBAN MALLS

In recent years, large suburban malls have been springing up all around San José and its neighboring suburbs. There's **Multiplaza** in Escazú, there's **Plaza del Sol** in Curridabat, and there's the unfinished—but already bustling—**Mall San Pedro.** Inside, you'll find all the familiar name-brand favorites from Victoria's Secret lingerie to Benetton jeans and shirts. Due to high import taxes, prices are substantially higher here than in North America or Europe. Since fakes are always possible, it's best to examine merchandise carefully to be sure you're getting the quality you're paying for.

MARKETS

There are several markets near downtown, but by far the largest is the **Mercado Central,** which is located between Avenida Central and Avenida 1 and calles 6 and 8. Inside this dark maze of stalls you'll find all manner of vendors. Although this is primarily a food market, you can find a few vendors selling Costa Rican souvenirs, crude leather goods, and musical instruments. Be especially careful about your wallet or purse because this area is frequented by very skillful pickpockets. All the streets surrounding the Mercado Central are jammed with produce vendors selling from small carts or loading and unloading trucks. It is always a hive of activity, with crowds of people jostling for space on the streets. In the hot days of the dry season, the aromas can get quite heady.

There is also a daily street market on the **west side of the Plaza de la Democracia.** Here you'll find two long rows of temporary stalls selling t-shirts, Guatemalan handcrafts, small ceramic *ocarinas* (a small musical wind instrument), and handmade jewlery. You may be able to bargain the price down a little bit, but bargaining is not a traditional part of the vendor culture here, so you'll have to work hard to save a few dollars.

SHOPPING A TO Z
ART GALLERIES

Amir Art Gallery. Calle 5 between avenidas 1 and 3. ☎ **506/255-3261.**

This gallery carries original artworks in a variety of mediums featuring Central American themes. Some of it is pretty gaudy, but this is a good place to find Nicaraguan and Costa Rican "primitive" paintings. The gallery has a second location nearby at Avenida 5 between calles 3 and 5.

Galleria Andromeda. Calle 9 at Avenida 9. ☎ **506/223-3529.**

This small, personal gallery features contemporary national artists of good quality. There are usually prints and paintings by several artists on display, and prices are very reasonable.

Galleria 11-12. Calle 19 and Avenida 11, in Barrio Aranjuez. ☎ **506/222-4345.**

This gallery deals mainly in high-end Costa Rican art, from neoclassical painters like Teodorico Quirós to modern stars like Rafa Fernandez and Fabio Herrera.

HANDCRAFTS

The most appealing artisans' market close to San José is the **La Garzas Handicraft Market** in Moravia (see below). If you want to stick to downtown San José, try the **outdoor market on the Plaza de la Democracia,** though prices here tend to be high and bargaining can be difficult. If you prefer to do your craft shopping in a flea-market atmosphere, head over to **La Casona** on Calle Central between Avenida Central and Avenida 1. Also be sure to visit the excellent **Annemarie Souvenir Shop** in the lobby of the Hotel Don Carlos.

Several other shops around San José sell a wide variety of crafts—from the truly tacky to the divinely inspired. Here are some of the places to look for such items.

Angie Theologos's Gallery. San Pedro; call for directions. ☎ **506/225-6565.**

Angie makes sumptuous handcrafted jackets from handwoven and embroidered Guatemalan textiles. Her work also includes boleros, and t-shirts made with Panamanian molas (appliquéd panels). Her colorful gallery of clothing may soon be located at the airport as well.

Annemarie Souvenir Shop. Calle 9 between avenidas 7 and 9. ☎ **506/221-6063.**

Now occupying two floors at the Hotel Don Carlos, this shop has an amazing array of wood products, leather goods, papier-mâché figurines, paintings, books, cards, posters, and jewelry, to mention just a few of the things you'll find here. You'll see most of this stuff at the other shops, but not in such a relaxed and unpressured environment. Don't miss this shopping experience.

Asociacion Nacional Pro Desarrollo De La Artesania (ANDA). Avenida Central between calles 5 and 7. ☎ **506/233-3340.**

If you're looking for Guatemalan clothing and they're asking too much at the Plaza de la Cultura, you might try this shop in the center of town. They also carry Boruca masks, carved gourds, t-shirts, and other souvenir-type items.

✪ **Atmosfera.** Calle 5 between avenidas 1 and 3. ☎ **506/222-4322.**

This place has high-quality Costa Rican arts and crafts, from primitivist paintings and sculpture to skilled turned-wood bowls. It consists of several small rooms spread over three floors, so be sure you explore every nook and cranny—you'll see stuff here that is not available anywhere else in town.

La Galeria. Calle 1 between Avenida Central and Avenida 1. ☎ **506/221-3436.**

This small store features some of the best of modern Costa Rican handcrafts. There is a fine selection of wood carvings and gold and silver pre-Columbian jewelry reproductions, paintings, and prints with Latin American themes, metalware, and rugs. The little boxes and bowls of native Costa Rican hardwoods are particularly attractive.

❸ **Las Garzas Handicraft Market.** In Moravia, 100 meters south and 50 meters east from the Red Cross Station. ☎ **506/236-0037.**

This artisans' market is a short ride out of San José, and includes more than 25 shops which sell wood, metal, and ceramic crafts, among a large variety of other items.

Madera Magia. Calle 5 between avenidas 1 and 3. ☎ **506/233-2630.**

What you'll notice here is that almost everything is made of wood. The shop is filled with elegant, thin bowls of native hardwood, a big selection of wooden boxes, mirrors framed in wood, and very handsome handmade furniture. All items are high quality, created by artisans under the guidance of designer J. Morrison.

Maya-Quiche. Avenida Central between calles 5 and 7. ☎ **506/223-5030.**

Located across the street from the handcraft shop ANDA (in the Galería Central Ramírez Valido shopping mall), this shop sells handcrafts from Central American countries, including gaily painted boxes, letters, and animals from El Salvador, and molas from Panama.

Mercado De Artesanos Canapi. Calle 11 and Avenida 1. ☎ **506/221-3342.**

This store carries a wide variety of typical Costa Rican handcrafts, including large, comfortable woven-rope hammocks; reproductions of pre-Columbian gold jewelry and pottery bowls; coffee-wood carvings; and many other carvings from rare Costa Rican hardwoods. In general, however, the crafts you'll find here are of low quality.

Mercado Nacional De Artesanias. Calle 11 and Avenida 4 Bis. ☎ **506/221-5012.**

Located only a couple of blocks away from the above-mentioned Mercado de Artesanos Canapi store, this shop offers similar crafts at similar prices.

✪ **Suraska.** Calle 5 and Avenida 3. ☎ **506/222-0129.**

If you haven't been impressed with the quality of the handcrafts you've seen, save your money for a visit to this store. Among the selections here are ceramics, mobiles, and jewelry. Of particular note are the wood carvings of North American artist Barry Biesanz, who turns out exquisite pieces of finely worked hardwood. Be forewarned, however, that these pieces are expensive.

JEWELRY

Esmeraldas Y Diseños. Avenida Las Americas, Sabana Norte, from the Restaurante Chicote, 100 meters north, 50 meters west and 150 meters north. ☎ **506/231-4808** or 506/231-5428.

Notice the location given above for this jewelry store—it is truly a classic San José address. You'll find here copies of pre-Columbian jewelry designs in gold, and jewelry including semiprecious stones from Brazil and emeralds from Columbia.

LEATHER GOODS

Malety. Avenida 1 between calles 1 and 3. ☎ **506/221-1670.**

The quality of leather products found in Costa Rica is not as good as in North America and prices are high, but take a look and see for yourself. This is one of the outlets in San José where you can shop for locally produced leather bags, briefcases, purses, wallets, and other such items. A second store is located on Calle 1 between Avenida Central and Avenida 2.

LIQUORS

Café Rica, similar to Kahlua, and Salicsa, a cream liqueur, are two delicious liqueurs made from coffee in Costa Rica. You can buy these liqueurs in government liquor stores and tourist shops, but just about the best prices I have seen are at the supermarket chain **Mas X Menos.** There is a Mas X Menos outlet on Paseo Colón and another on Avenida Central at the east end of town, just below the Museo Nacional de Costa Rica.

10　San José After Dark

With the rise in numbers of people who choose to visit Costa Rica, San José has been making strides to meet the nocturnal needs of tourists and residents alike. You'll find plenty of interesting clubs and bars, a wide range of theaters, and some very lively discos.

To find out what's going on in San José while you're in town, pick up a copy of the *Tico Times* (English) or *La Nación* (Spanish). The former is a good place to find out where local expatriates are hanging out; the latter's "Viva" section has extensive listings of everything from discos to movie theaters to live music.

THE PERFORMING ARTS

Theater is very popular in Costa Rica; downtown San José is studded with small theaters. However, tastes tend towards the burlesque and the crowd pleasers are almost always simplistic sexual comedies. The **National Theater Company** (☎ 506/ 257-8305) is one major exception, tackling works from Lope de Vega to Lorca to Mamet. Almost all of the theater offerings are in Spanish, though there are two amateur theater groups that stage works in English periodically. Check the *Tico Times* to see if anything is running during your stay.

Aside from theater, Costa Rica has a surprisingly strong modern dance scene. Both the University of Costa Rica and the National University have modern dance companies that perform regularly in San José. Two independant companies— **Los Denmedium** and **Diquis Tiquis**—are of excellent calibre. Sadly, however, you're almost more likely to catch these troupes performing in New York or Caracas than in San José.

The **National Symphony Orchestra** is a respectable orchestra by regional standards, though their repertoire tends to be rather conservative. The symphony season runs from March through November, with concerts roughly every other week at the **Teatro Nacional,** Avenida 2 between calles 3 and 5 (☎ 506/221-1329). Tickets cost between $2.50 and $15 and can be purchased at the box office.

Visiting artists also stop in Costa Rica from time to time. Recent concerts have featured Spanish tenor Jose Carreras, romantic crooner Julio Iglesias, and classic rockers Jethro Tull. Many of these concerts and guest performances take place in San José's two historic theaters: the **Teatro Nacional** and the **Teatro Melico Salazar,** Avenida 2 between Calle Central and Calle 2 (☎ 506/222-2653).

Costa Rica's cultural panorama changes drastically every March, when the country hosts large arts festivals. On odd-numbered years the festival features purely local talent, but on even numbered years the month-long fête offers up a nightly smorgasbord of dance, theater, music, and monologue from around the world. Most nights of the festival you will have between four and ten shows to chose from. Many are free, and the most expensive ticket is $5.

THE CLUB & MUSIC SCENE

If you like to dance, you'll find plenty of places to get down in San José. Salsa and merengue are the main beats that move people here and many of the dance clubs, discos, and salons feature live music on the weekends. However, if you're looking to catch some jazz, rock, or blues in a small club there's not nearly the selection.

The "Viva" section of the *La Nación* newspaper has weekly performance schedules. A couple of dance bands to to watch for are **Marfil** and **Los Brillanticos. Liverpool** is a popular rock cover band, and if you're looking for jazz, check out **Expresso** or pianist **Manuel Obregon.**

A good place to sample a range of San José's nightlife is in **El Pueblo,** a shopping, dining, and entertainment complex done up like an old Spanish village. It's just across the river to the north of town. The best way to get here is by taxi; all the drivers know El Pueblo well. Within the alleyways that wind through El Pueblo are a dozen or more bars, clubs, and discos; there is even a roller-skating rink. **Cocoloco** (☎ 506/ 222-8782) features nightly "fiestas," and **Discoteque Infinito** (☎ 506/221-9134) has three different ambiences under one roof. Across the street you'll find **La Plaza** (☎ 506/222-5143), one of my favorite dance spots.

Only in the Central Valley: Dining Under the Stars on a Mountain's Edge

While there are a myriad of unique experiences to be had in Costa Rica, there's just one that can only be experienced in San Jose's Central Valley: dining on the side of a volcanic mountain. These hanging restaurants, called *miradors,* are a resourceful response to San Jose's topography. Because the city is set in a broad valley surrounded on all sides by volcanic mountains, people who live in these mountainous areas on the edges of the valley have no other place to build roadside cafés—so vertically they build. Many of the roads through these mountains are studded with these hillside hanging restaurants.

While the food at most of these establishments is not usually spectacular, the views often are, particularly at night, when the whole wide valley sparkles in a wash of lights. The town of **Aserri,** 6 miles south of downtown San José, is the king of miradors and **Mirador Ram Luna** (☎ 506/230-3060), is the king of Aserri. Grab a window seat and, if you've got the fortitude, order a plate of *chicharrones* (fried pork rinds). There's often live music at Ram Luna, just in case the whole thing makes you feel like dancing. You can hire a cab for around $8 or take the Aserri bus at Avenida 6 between Calle Central and Calle 2. Just ask the driver where to get off.

LIVE MUSIC

Akelarre. Calle 21 between avenidas 4 and 6. ☎ **506/223-0345.**

This popular club is located in a renovated old house near the Museo Nacional. There are several rooms in which to check out the action, as well as a garden out back. There are frequent live music performances by hot Costa Rican groups.

Casa Matute. Calle 21 and Avenida 10. ☎ **506/222-6806.**

This historic old house just south of the Supreme Court has been converted into a sprawling club complex, with an assortment of theme rooms ranging from a Whiskey Bar to a French Left Bank–style cafe. It's become immensely popular with young Ticos, who like flitting around between environments. There's almost always live music here, with most of the same bands you'd find on another night at Akelarre.

La Esmeralda. Avenida 2 between calles 5 and 7. ☎ **506/233-7386.**

A sort of mariachi Grand Central Station, La Esmeralda is a cavernous open-air restaurant and bar that stays open 24 hours a day. In the evenings, mariachi bands park their vans out front and wait to be hired for a moonlight serenade, or perhaps a surprise party. While they wait, they often fill the restaurant with loud trumpet blasts and the sound of the big bass guitarón. If you've never been serenaded at your table before, this place is a must. A song will cost you anywhere from $3 to $10 depending on the size of the group you hire.

DISCOS & SALONS

El Tobogan. 200 meters north and 100 meters east of the La Republica main office, off the Guapiles highway. ☎ **506/257-3396.**

The dance floor in this place is about the size of the football field and yet it still fills up. This is a place where Ticos come with their loved ones and dance partners. There's always a live band here, and sometimes they're very good.

Salsa 54. Calle 3 between avenidas 1 and 3. ☎ **506/221-3220.**

This is the place to go to watch expert salsa dancers and to try some yourself. In addition to the informal instruction you'll soak up just by watching, you might even be able to take a Latin dance class here.

Las Tunas. Sabana North, 500 meters west of the ICE office. ☎ **506/231-1802.**

This happening place serves Mexican food and barbecue, but where it really cooks is in the bar and discotheque, where live Costa Rican pop music is featured weekly.

THE BAR SCENE

There seems to be something for every taste here. Lounge lizards will be happy in most hotel bars in the downtown area, while students and the young at heart will have no problem mixing in at the livelier spots around town. Sports fans can even find a place to catch the most important games of the day.

The best part of the varied bar scene in San José is something called a *boca,* the equivalent of a *tapa* in Spain, a little dish of snacks that arrives at your table when you order a drink. In most bars, the bocas are free; but in some, where the dishes are more sophisticated, you'll have to pay for the treats. You'll find drinks reasonably priced, with beer costing around $1–$1.50 and mixed drinks around $2–$3.50.

Charleston. Avenida 4 between calles 7 and 9. ☎ **506/255-3993.**

This relaxed bar has a 1920s theme. Businessmen like to unwind here after a grinding day. Great recorded jazz music plays on the stereo and sometimes there are even live bands.

El Cuartel De La Boca Del Monte. Avenida 1 between calles 21 and 23. ☎ **506/221-0327.**

This popular bar began life as an artist and bohemian hangout. Over the years it's become the leading meat market for the young and well-heeled. However, artists still come, as do foreign exchange students, visiting tourists and, for some reason, many of the river-rafting guides, so there's always a diverse mix. There's usually live music here on Wednesday and Friday nights, and when there is, the place is packed shoulder to shoulder.

Nashville South. Calle 5 between avenidas 1 and 3. ☎ **506/233-1988.**

As it name implies, this is a country-and-western bar. It's very popular with homesick expatriates, and has a friendly atmosphere and fun music. The television here will usually have on some sort of professional sports event or CNN.

Rio. Avenida Central, Los Yoses. ☎ **506/253-5088.**

This bar and restaurant is close to the University of Costa Rica, and consequently attracts a younger clientele. At night Rio is always packed to overflowing with the wealthy and the wanna-be's of San José.

Risa's Bar. Calle 1 between Avenida Central and Avenida 1. ☎ **506/223-2803.**

This second-floor bar is in a beautiful old building in the heart of downtown San José. There's a big dug-out canoe over the bar, but the exposed brick walls and the U.S. rock videos give Risa's a very North American urban atmosphere. The music is loud! At the end of the night, you can either walk back down the stairs, or take the curving slide out.

Shakespeare Bar. Avenida 2 and Calle 28. ☎ **506/257-1288.**

Located next to the Sala Garbo movie theater, this classy little spot is a good place to meet after a movie or a show at the Sala Garbo or Laurence Olivier Theater next door.

Soda Palace. Calle 2 and Avenida 2. ☎ **506/221-3441.**

Mostly a men's hangout, this dingy but brightly lit bar hardly lives up to its name, but is a Costa Rican institution. It opens directly onto busy Avenida 2 and is open 24 hours a day. Men of all ages sit at the tables conversing loudly and watching the world pass by. You never know what might happen at the Palace. Mariachis stroll in, linger for a while, then continue on their way. Legend has it that the revolution of 1948 was planned right here.

HANGING OUT IN SAN PEDRO

The two-block stretch of San Pedro just south of the University of Costa Rica is the closest thing to the Left Bank or the East Village you'll find in Costa Rica. Bars and cafes are mixed in with bookstores and copy shops. It's one of the few places in town where you can sit calmly at an outdoor table or walk the streets, without constantly checking over your shoulder and reaching for your wallet. You can just stroll the strip until someplace strikes your fancy, or try one of the following.

La Maga. 100 meters east of the Church in San Pedro. ☎ **506/283-5040.**

This artsy cafe is named after a character in Julio Cortázar's novel *Hopscotch*. Inside, you'll find comfortable wooden tables and racks of magazines and newspapers for perusing. La Maga just took over and remodeled the building next door, turning it into a cavernous performing space for Costa Rica's avant-garde and experimental theater and dance troupes.

La Villa. 200 meters east and 100 meters north of the Church in San Pedro. ☎ **506/225-9612.**

This converted Victorian house holds the ghosts of Che Guevara and Camilo Cienfuegos, or at least you'll see posters of them and other Latin American revolutionaries on the walls. Around the tables you'll find poets and painters mixing with a new generation of student activists, all in a lively atmosphere. There's even a foosball table in the far back.

THE GAY & LESBIAN SCENE

Because Costa Rica is such a conservative Catholic country, the gay and lesbian communities here are rather discreet. Homosexuality is not generally under attack, but many gay and lesbian organizations jealously guard their privacy, and the club scene is not entirely stable. Women should definitely check in with **Casa Yemaya** (☎ 506/223-3652 or 506/257-8529) for suggestions on clubs and community connections, while both men and women can call **The International Gay and Lesbian Association** (☎ 506/234-2411).

As of press time, the happening gay and lesbian bars and dance clubs were **Deja Vu,** Calle 2 between avenidas 14 and 16 (no phone) and **La Avispa,** Calle 1 between avenidas 8 and 10 (☎ 506/223-5343). The former is predominantly a guy's bar, while the latter is popular with both men and women, although they sometimes set certain nights of the week or month aside for specific communities.

MOVIES AND MORE

Most of the movies shown in San José are first-run U.S. productions (in English with Spanish subtitles) that get here about 3 months after originally opening in the States. Ticos tend toward action flicks, so there's almost always a Schwarzenegger or Van Damme film to choose from. Even if you aren't interested in what's playing, it's worth the $2.50 admission just to see a movie in an old-style theater with a full-sized screen. Try out the **Cine Magaly,** Calle 23 between Avenida Central and

Avenida 1 (☎ 506/223-0085); **Cine Rex,** Calle Central between avenidas 2 and 4, just off the Parque Central (☎ 506/221-0041); or **Cine Variedades,** Calle 3 between Avenida Central and Avenida 1 (☎ 506/223-0085). These theaters even have balconies. Check the "Viva" section of *La Nación* or the *Tico Times* for movie listings and times.

Sala Garbo, 100 meters south of the Pizza Hut on Paseo Colón (☎ 506/222-1034) shows foreign and art films, usually with Spanish subtitles, but sometimes with English subtitles.

GAMBLING CASINOS   Gambling is legal in Costa Rica and there are casinos at virtually every major hotel. However, as in Tico bullfighting, there are some idiosyncracies involved in *gambling a la tica*. If blackjack is your game, you'll want to play "rummy." The rules are almost identical, except the house doesn't pay double on blackjack—instead it pays double on any three-of-a-kind, or three-card straight flush. If you're looking for roulette, what you'll find here is a bingo-like spinning cage of numbered balls. The betting is the same, but some of the glamour is lost. You'll also find a version of five-card draw poker, but the rule differences are so complex that I advise you sit down and watch for awhile, and then ask some questions before joining in. That's about all you will find. There are no craps tables or baccarat. There's some controversy over slot machines—one-armed bandits are currently outlawed—but you will be able to play electronic slots and poker games. Most of the casinos here are quite casual and small by international standards. You may have to dress up slightly at some of the fancier hotels, but most are accustomed to tropical vacation attire.

11   Side Trips from San José

San José makes an excellent base for exploring the beautiful Meseta Central and the surrounding mountains, and in fact, it is possible to explore much of the country on day tours from San José. Probably the best way to make the most of these excursions is on guided tours, but if you rent a car you'll have greater independence. There are also some day trips that can be done by public bus. Below is information on many of the day tours that are offered by tour companies in San José. I have arranged these by type of activity. In addition to the tours listed below, there are many other tours, some of which combine two or three different activities or destinations. Companies offering a wide variety of primarily nature-related day tours out of San José include: **Costa Rica Expeditions** (☎ 506/257-0766 or 506/222-0333); **Costa Rica Sun Tours** (☎ 506/255-3418); **Ecole Travel** (☎ 506/223-2240); **Fantasy Tours** (☎ 506/220-2393); **Geotour** (☎ 506/227-4029); **Otec Tours** (☎ 506/256-0633); and **Swiss Travel Service** (☎ 506/231-4055).

Before signing on for a tour of any sort, find out how much time will be spent in transit and eating lunch, and how much time will actually be spent doing the primary activity. I've had complaints about tours that were rushed, or that spent too much time on secondary activities.

RECREATIONAL DAY TRIPS

BICYCLING   Narrow mountain roads with spectacular views make for some great, though strenuous, bicycling in Costa Rica. As yet there are only a few companies offering cycling trips, however. **Rios Tropicales** (☎ 506/233-6455) offers a day-long mountain-bike trip to Tapantí National Park. Most of the riding on this trip is downhill, and there are numerous opportunities to birdwatch and explore nature trails. The cost of $70 includes transportation, use of cycling equipment, breakfast, and lunch.

Rios Tropicales also offers multiday biking and rafting trips.

Other companies offering bicycling trips include **El León Viajero** (☎ 506/ 233-9398), which has three different tours ranging in price from $70 to $95, and **EcoTreks** (☎ 506/289-8191), which rents mountain bikes and designs custom tours for travelers.

BUNGEE JUMPING There's nothing truly unique about bungee jumping in Costa Rica, but it's a little bit less expensive than a similar experience farther north. If you've always had the bug, **Tropical Bungee** (☎ 506/233-6455) will let you jump off a 265-foot bridge for $45; two jumps cost $70. Transportation is $7 each way.

CRUISES Several companies offer cruises to the lovely Tortuga Island in the Gulf of Nicoya, and these excursions include gourmet buffet meals and stops at a deserted (until your boat arrives) beach. Companies offering these trips include **Bay Island Cruises** (☎ 506/296-5551), **Calypso Tours** (☎ 506/233-3617), and **Sea Ventures** (☎ 506/257-2904). The cruises cost around $70 per person and include transportation from San José to Puntarenas and back.

HIKING If you do not plan to visit Monteverde or one of Costa Rica's other cloud-forest reserves, consider doing a day tour to a cloud forest. Guided hikes through these misty, high-altitude forests provide an opportunity to visit one of the tropics' most fascinating habitats. Birdwatching and a chance to learn about the ecology of the cloud forest are the main attractions of these trips. One of the most popular and highly recommended hiking tours is to the Los Angeles Cloud Forest Reserve. This tour is operated by **Hotel Villablanca** (☎ 506/228-4603) and includes a 3-hour guided walk through the cloud forest. The cost is $75, which includes transportation, breakfast, and lunch. Another cloud forest day hike is offered by **Senderos de Iberoamérica** (☎ 506/255-2859). This trip takes you to the Los Juncos Biological Reserve for a total of 5 hours of guided walks. Transportation, breakfast, and lunch are all included in the $70 fee.

HORSEBACK RIDING If you enjoy horseback riding, you have your choice of many fascinating locations near San José for day-long trips. The going rate for a day trip out of San José to go horseback riding is around $70 per person, including transportation, lunch, and a 4-hour guided ride. **L.A. Tours** (☎ 506/221-4501) offers rides through pastures and along the beach. **Sacramento Horseback Ride** (☎ 506/ 237-2116) offers rides through mountain forests and pastures. Great view! **La Paz** (☎ 506/221-3060 or 506/222-5005) offers a trip through the cloud forest on the flank of Poás Volcano. The ride visits two different waterfalls. **El León Viajero** (☎ 506/233-9398) offers three different horseback-riding tours, each in a different part of the country.

HOT-AIR BALLOONING One of the most fascinating ways to see Costa Rica is from a balloon floating above the forest. **Serendipity Adventures** (☎/fax 506/ 450-0328 or 800/635-2325 in the U.S.) offers a half-day tour above the countryside around Naranjo (25 miles from San José). Serendipity will pick you up at your hotel room at 4:30am—that's right—and bring you to the ballooning site. After a several-hour soar, you will be treated to a tipico breakfast and an optional tour of a coffee farm, before the return to San José. Price is $235 per person with a minimum of two persons. Other trips include overnight accommodations and are more expensive.

PRE-COLUMBIAN RUINS Though Costa Rica lacks such massive pre-Columbian archeological sites as can be found in Mexico, Guatemala, or Honduras, it does have Guayabo National Monument, a small excavated town, which today is but a collection of building foundations and cobbled streets. If you have a car, or are an intrepid bus hound, you can do this tour on your own. If not, **Senderos de Iberoamérica** (☎ 506/255-2859) offers trips to Costa Rica's most extensively excavated pre-Columbian archeological site for $70 per person.

RAFTING, KAYAKING & RIVER TRIPS Cascading down Costa Rica's mountain ranges are dozens of tumultuous rivers, several of which have become very popular for white-water rafting and kayaking. For between $65 and $90, you can spend a day rafting through lush tropical forests; longer trips are also available. Some of the more reliable rafting companies are **Aventuras Naturales** (☎ 506/225-3939 or 800/308-3394 in the U.S.); **Costa Rica White Water** (☎ 506/257-0766 or 506/222-0333); **Costa Sol Rafting** (☎ 506/293-2151 or 800/245-8420 in the U.S.); and **Rios Tropicales** (☎ 506/233-6455). If I had to choose just one day trip to do out of San José, it would be a white-water rafting trip.

There are also some raft and boat trips on calmer waters. These trips usually focus on the wildlife and scenery along the river.

Sarapiquí Aguas Bravas (☎ 506/292-2072) offers tours that include a boat trip down the Sarapiquí River, a quiet river fed by clear mountain streams. The scenery along this river is a combination of rain forest and farms, and these tours pass through the lush Braulio Carrillo National Park before reaching the put-in spot. Sarapiquí Aguas Bravas also runs rougher sections of the same.

Perhaps the best-known river tours are those that go up to Tortuguero National Park. Though it is possible to do this tour as a day trip out of San José, it is a long and expensive day. You're much better off doing it as a one- or two-night trip. See chapter 10, "The Caribbean Coast," for details.

RAIN FOREST AERIAL TRAM When you first see the Aerial Tram (☎ 506/257-5961), you may wonder where the slopes are. Built on a private reserve bordering Braulio Carillo National Park, the tramway is the fruition of rain-forest researcher Dr. Donald Perry, whose cable-car system through the forest canopy at Rara Avis helped establish him as an early expert on rain-forest canopies. The tramway takes visitors on a 90-minute ride through the rain-forest tree tops, where they have the chance to glimpse the complex web of life that makes these forests so unique. There are also well-groomed trails through the rainforest and a restaurant on site, so it can easily turn into a full day trip. The cost for tours, including transportation from San José, is $65. Alternately, you can pay $47.50 and take a bus from Calle 12 between avenidas 7 and 9. Buses leave every half hour and cost $2.

VOLCANO TRIPS Poás, Irazú, and Arenal volcanoes are three of Costa Rica's most popular destinations. For more information on the Arenal Volcano, see chapter 7, and for more information on Poás and Irazú, see below. Numerous tour companies in San José offer trips to all three volcanoes, and though the trips to Poás and Irazú take only half a day, the trips to Arenal take all day. I don't recommend these latter trips because you usually arrive when the volcano is hidden by clouds, and leave before the night's darkness shows off its glowing eruptions. Tour companies offering trips to Poás and Irazú include **Costa Rica Expeditions** (☎ 506/257-0766 or 506/222-0333); **Costa Rica Sun Tours** (☎ 506/255-3418), **Otec Tours,** Edeficio Ferencz, Calle 3 between avenidas 1 and 3, Apdo. 323-1002, San José (☎ 506/256-0633); **TAM,** Calle Central between Avenida Central and Avenida 1 (☎ 506/256-0203 or 506/222-3866); **Vic-Vic Tours,** Calle 3 between avenidas 5 and 7 (☎ 506/233-3435); **San Jose Travel,** Calle 11 and Avenida 2, (☎ 506/257-4511), and **Swiss Travel Service,** (☎ 506/232-7188). Prices range from $25–$30 for a half-day trip to $50–$70 for a full-day trip.

CARTAGO, THE OROSI VALLEY & IRAZÚ VOLCANO

Located about 15 miles southeast of San José, Cartago is the former capital of Costa Rica. Founded in 1563, it was Costa Rica's first city—and was in fact its only city for almost 150 years. Irazú Volcano rises up from the edge of town, and although it is quiescent these days, it has not always been so peaceful. Earthquakes have damaged Cartago repeatedly over the years, so that today there are few of the old colonial buildings left standing. In the center of the city a public park winds through the ruins of a large church that was destroyed in 1910, before it was ever finished. Construction was abandoned after the quake, and today the ruins are a neatly manicured park, with quiet paths and plenty of benches.

Cartago's most famous building, however, is the **Basilica de Nuestra Señora de Los Angeles** (the Basilica of Our Lady of the Angels), which is dedicated to the the patron saint of Costa Rica and stands on the east side of town. Within the walls of this Byzantine-style church is a shrine containing the tiny figure of La Negrita, the Black Virgin, which is nearly lost amid its ornate altar. Legend has it that La Negrita first revealed herself on this site to a peasant girl in 1635. Miraculous healing powers have been attributed to La Negrita, and over the years thousands of pilgrims have come to the shrine seeking cures for their illnesses and difficulties. The walls of the shrine are covered with a fascinating array of tiny silver images left as thanks for cures affected by La Negrita. Amid the plethora of diminutive arms and legs, there are also hands, feet, hearts, lungs, kidneys, eyes, torsos, breasts, and—peculiarly—guns, trucks, beds, and planes. There are even dozens of sports trophies which I assume were left in thanks for helping teams win big games. August 2 is the day dedicated to La Negrita. On this day tens of thousands of people walk to Cartago from San José and around the country in devotion to this powerful statue.

If you'd like to soak in a warm-water swimming pool, head 2.5 miles south of Cartago to **Aguas Calientes.** A little over a mile east of Cartago, you'll find **Lankester Botanical Garden** (☎ 506/551-9877), a botanical garden known for its orchid collection. See "Attractions," above, for details.

Buses for Cartago leave San José every 10 minutes from Calle 5 and Avenida 18. The length of the trip is 45 minutes; the fare is about 35¢.

Located 20 miles north of Cartago, 11,260-foot-tall Irazú Volcano is one of Costa Rica's more active volcanoes, although at this time it is relatively quiet. It last erupted on March 19, 1963, on the day that President John F. Kennedy arrived in Costa Rica. The eruption showered ash on the Meseta Central for months after, destroying crops and collapsing roofs, but enriching the soil. There is a good paved road right to the rim of the crater, where a desolate expanse of gray sand nurtures few plants and the air smells of sulfur. The landscape here is often compared to that of the moon. There are magnificent views of the fertile Meseta Central and Orosi Valley as you drive up from Cartago, and if you're very lucky you may be able to see both the Pacific Ocean and Caribbean Sea at the same time. Clouds usually descend by noon, so schedule your trip up here as early in the day as possible. From the parking area, a short trail leads to the rim of the volcano's two craters, their walls a maze of eroded gullies feeding onto the flat floor far below. This is a national park, and admission is $6 at the gate (see "Costa Rica's National Parks & Bioreserves," in chapter 4 for more information). Don't forget to wear warm clothes: This may be the tropics, but it can be cold up at the top. On you way back down, stop for breakfast at **Restaurant Linda Vista** (☎ 506/225-5808). It's on the right as you come down the mountain. Located at an elevation of 10,075 feet, it claims to be the highest restaurant in Central America; there are walls of windows looking out over the valley far below. A hearty Tico breakfast of gallo pinto with ham will cost about $2.50.

Buses leave for Irazú Volcano Saturday, Sunday, and holidays from Avenida 2 between calles 1 and 3 (in front of the Gran Hotel Costa Rica). The fare is $3.90 and the trip takes about 1¹/₂ hours. To make sure the buses are running, phone 506/ 272-0651. If you are driving, head northeast out of Cartago toward San Rafael, then continue driving uphill toward the volcano, passing the turnoffs for Cot and Tierra Blanca en route.

The **Orosi Valley,** southeast of Cartago and visible from the top of Irazú on a clear day, is called the most beautiful valley in Costa Rica. The Reventazon River meanders through this steep-sided valley until it collects in the lake formed by the Cachí Dam. There are scenic overlooks near the town of Orosi, which is at the head of the valley, and in Ujarrás, which is on the banks of the lake. Near Ujarrás are the ruins of Costa Rica's oldest church (built in 1693), whose tranquil gardens are a great place to sit and gaze at the surrounding mountains. Across the lake is a popular recreation center, called Charrarra, where you'll find a picnic area, swimming pool, and hiking trails. In the town of Orosi there is yet another colonial church built in 1743. A small museum here displays religious artifacts.

It would be difficult to explore this whole area by public bus, since this is not a densely populated region. However, there are buses from Cartago to the town of Orosi. During the week, these buses run every half hour and leave from a spot one block east and three blocks south of the church ruins in Cartago. Saturday and Sunday, a bus runs every hour from the same vicinity and will drop you at the Orosi lookout point. The trip takes 30 minutes, and the fare is 30¢. If you are driving, take the road to Paraíso from Cartago, head toward Ujarrás, continue around the lake, then pass through Cachí and on to Orosi. From Orosi, the road leads back to Paraíso. There are also guided day tours of this area from San José (call any of the companies listed under Organized Tours above).

POÁS VOLCANO

This is another active volcano accessible from San José in a day trip. It is 23 miles from San José on narrow roads that wind through a landscape of fertile farms and dark forests. As at Irazú, there is a paved road right to the top. The volcano stands 8,800 feet tall and is located within a national park, which preserves not only the volcano but also dense stands of virgin forest. Poás's crater is over a mile across and is said to be the second-largest crater in the world. Geysers in the crater sometimes spew steam and muddy water 600 feet into the air, making this the largest geyser in the world. There is an information center where you can see a slide show about the volcano, and there are marked hiking trails through the cloud forest that rings the crater. About 20 minutes from the parking area, along a forest trail, is an overlook onto beautiful Botos Lake, which has formed in one of the volcano's extinct craters.

Because the sulfur fumes occasionally become dangerously strong at Poás, the park is sometimes closed to the public. This is a national park and admission is $6 at the gate. For more information see "Costa Rica's National Parks & Bioreserves," in chapter 4.

There is an excursion bus on Sundays and holidays leaving from Calle 12 and avenidas 2 and 4 at 8:30am and returning at 2:30pm. The fare is $3 for the round-trip. The bus is always crowded, so arrive early. Other days, take a bus to Alajuela, then a bus to San Pedro de Poás. From there you will have to hitchhike or take a taxi ($20 round-trip), which makes this alternative almost as costly as a tour. All the tour companies in San José offer excursions to Poás, although they often don't arrive until after the clouds have closed in. If you're traveling by car, head for Alajuela and continue on the main road through town toward Varablanca. Just before reaching Varablanca, turn left toward Poasito and continue to the rim of the volcano.

HEREDIA, ALAJUELA, GRECIA, SARCHÍ & ZARCERO

All of these cities and towns are northwest of San José and can be combined into a long day trip (if you have a car), perhaps in conjunction with a visit to Poás Volcano. The scenery here is rich and verdant, and the small towns and scattered farming communities are truly representative of Costa Rica's agricultural heartland. If you're relying on buses, you'll be able to visit any of the towns listed below, but probably just one per day.

Heredia was founded in 1706. On its central park stands a colonial church dedicated in 1763. The stone facade leaves no questions as to the age of the church, but the altar inside is decorated with neon stars and a crescent moon surrounding a statue of the Virgin Mary. In the middle of the palm-shaded park is a music temple, and across the street, beside several tile-roofed municipal buildings, is the tower of an old Spanish fort. Of all the cities in the Meseta Central, this is only one with some colonial feeling to it; you'll still see adobe buildings with Spanish tile roofs along narrow streets. Heredia is also the site of the National Autonomous University, so you'll find some nice coffee shops and bookstores near the school. Buses leave for Heredia almost every 5 minutes from Calle 12 and Avenida 2, and from Calle 1 between avenidas 7 and 9. Bus fare is 30¢.

Alajuela is one of Costa Rica's oldest cities, and is located only 12 miles from San José. Although it is an attractive little city filled with parks, there isn't much to see or do here. The **Juan Santamaría Historical Museum,** Avenida 3 between Calle Central and Calle 2 (☎ 506/442-1838), commemorates Costa Rica's national hero, who gave his life defending the country against a small army led by William Walker, a U.S. citizen who invaded Costa Rica in 1856. Walker was trying to set up a slave state in Central America. The museum is open Tuesday through Sunday from 10am to 6pm; admission is free. Buses leave for Alajuela every 10 minutes from Avenida 2 between calles 10 and 14; fare is 45¢.

From Alajuela, a narrow, winding road leads to the town of **Grecia,** which is noteworthy for its unusual metal church, which is painted a deep red and has white gingerbread trim. The road to Sarchí is to the right as you go around the church.

Sarchí is Costa Rica's main artisan town. It is here that the colorfully painted miniature oxcarts you see all over Costa Rica are made. Oxcarts such as these were once used to haul coffee beans to market. Today, though you may occasionally see oxcarts in use, most are purely decorative. However, they remain a well-known symbol of Costa Rica. In addition to miniature oxcarts, many other carved wooden souvenirs are made here with rare hardwoods from the nation's forests. There are dozens of shops in town, and all have similar prices. The other reason to visit Sarchí is to see its unforgettable church. Built between 1950 and 1958, the church is painted pink with aquamarine trim and looks strangely like a child's birthday cake. Buses leave for Sarchí every 25 minutes from Calle 8 between Avenida Central and Avenida 1. Bus fare is 65¢.

Beyond Sarchí, on picturesque roads lined with cedar trees, you will find the town of **Zarcero.** In a small park in the middle of town is a menagerie of topiary sculptures (sculpted shrubs) that includes a monkey on a motorcycle, people and animals dancing, an ox pulling a cart, a man wearing a top hat, and a large elephant. It's worth the drive to see this park, or better yet, you can stop here on the way to La Fortuna and Arenal Volcano. Buses for Zarcero leave from San José daily at 9:30am and 12:15, 4:15, and 5:15pm from Calle 16 between avenidas 1 and 3.

The road to Heredia turns north off the highway from San José to the airport. To reach Alajuela from Heredia, take the scenic road that heads west through the town of San Joaquín. To continue on to Sarchí, it is best to return to the highway south of Alajuela and drive west toward Puntarenas. Turn north to Grecia and then west to Sarchí.

TURRIALBA

This attractive little town 33 miles east of San José is best known as the starting point and home base for many popular white-water rafting trips. However, it is also worth a visit if you have an interest in pre-Columbian history or tropical botany. **Guayabo National Monument** is one of Costa Rica's only pre-Columbian sites that has been excavated and is open to the public. It's located 12 miles northeast of Turrialba and preserves a townsite that dates to between 1000 B.C. and A.D. 1400. Archeologists believe that Guayabo may have supported a population of as many as 10,000 people, but there is no clue yet as to why the city was eventually abandoned only shortly before the Spanish arrived in the New World. Excavated ruins at Guayabo consist of paved roads, aqueducts, stone bridges, and house and temple foundations. There are also grave sites and petroglyphs. The monument is open daily from 8am to 4pm. This is a national park and admission is $6 at the gate. For more information see "Costa Rica's National Parks & Bioreserves," in chapter 4.

Botanists and gardeners will want to pay a visit to the **Center for Agronomy Research and Development (CATIE),** which is located 5 kilometers southeast of Turrialba on the road to Siquerres. This center is one of the world's foremost facilities for research into tropical agriculture. Among the plants on CATIE's 2,000 acres are hundreds of varieties of cacao and thousands of varieties of coffee. The plants here have been collected from all over the world. In addition to trees used for food and other purposes, there are also plants grown strictly for ornamental purposes. CATIE is open Monday through Friday from 8am to 4pm. For information on guided tours, phone 506/556-6431.

While you are in the area, don't miss an opportunity to spend a little time at **Turrialtico** (☎ 506/556-1111) a lively open-air restaurant and small hotel high on a hill overlooking the Turrialba Valley. The view from here is one of the finest in the country, with the lush green valley far below and volcanoes in the distance. Meals are quite inexpensive and a room will cost you only $20. This place is popular with rafting companies who bring groups here for meals and for overnights before, after, and during multiday rafting trips. You'll find Turrialtico about 6 miles out of Turrialba on the road to Siquierres.

Guanacaste & the Nicoya Peninsula

Guanacaste province is Costa Rica's sunniest and driest region. The rainy season starts later and ends earlier here, and overall it is more dependably sunny than in other parts of the country. Combine this climate with a coastline that stretches from the Nicaraguan border to the southern tip of the Nicoya Peninsula and you have an equation that yields beach bliss. Beautiful beaches abound along this coastline. Some are pristine and deserted, some are lined with luxury resort hotels, and still others are backed by little villages where you can still get a double room for under $30 a night. These beaches vary from long, straight stretches of sand to tiny coves bordered by rocky headlands. Whatever your passion in beaches, you're likely to find something that comes close to perfection.

There is, however, one caveat. During the dry season, when sunshine is most reliable, the hillsides in Guanacaste turn browner than the chaparral of southern California. Dust from dirt roads blankets the trees in many areas and the vistas are far from tropical. Driving these dirt roads without air-conditioning and hermetically sealed windows can be extremely unpleasant. However, if you can't tolerate the least bit of rain on your holiday in the sun, the beaches up here are where you'll want to be.

On the other hand, if you happen to visit this area in the rainy season, the hillsides are a beautiful rich green, and the sun usually shines all morning, giving way to an afternoon shower, when a nice siesta is often in order. So, if you want your beaches backed by greenery, and you're coming down between December and May, head south or over to the other side of the country. The beaches of the south Pacific coast and the Caribbean coast are much lusher and have more of a tropical feel, though they also are more humid and rainy.

Guanacaste is also Costa Rica's "Wild West," a dry landscape of cattle ranches and cowboys, who are known here as *sabaneros,* a name that derives from the Spanish word for savannah or grassland. This is big country, with big views and big sky. If it weren't for those rain forest–clad volcanoes in the distance, you might swear you were in Texas. However, Guanacaste hasn't always looked this way. At one time this land was covered with a dense, though fairly dry, forest that was cut for lumber to create pasturelands for grazing cattle. Today, that dry tropical forest exists only in remnants preserved in several national parks. Up in the mountains, in Rincón de la Vieja National

Park, not only will you find forests and wildlife, but you'll also find hot springs and bubbling mudpots similar to those in Yellowstone National Park in the United States.

1 Liberia

232 kilometers NW of San José; 133 kilometers NW of Puntarenas

Founded in 1769, Liberia is the capital of Guanacaste province, and though it can hardly be considered a bustling city, it does have the distinction of having a more colonial atmosphere than almost any other city in the country. Narrow streets are lined with charming old adobe homes, many of which have ornate stone accents on their facades, carved wooden doors, and aged red-tile roofs.

Liberia is best looked upon as a base for exploring this region. From here it is possible to do day trips to nearby beaches and three national parks, although only two of them have facilities for visitors. Several moderately priced hotels are located on the outskirts of Liberia at the intersection of the Interamerican Highway and the road to the Nicoya Peninsula and its many beaches. See "Where to Stay," later in this section, for detailed descriptions of the area's lodging options.

ESSENTIALS

GETTING THERE & DEPARTING   By Plane   The airstrip in Liberia has finally been cleared to accept commercial international flights. However, at press time, no airlines have instituted regular flights to Liberia. Check with your travel agent, as this is expected to change.

Sansa (☎ 506/233-0397, 506/233-3258, or 506/233-5330) has flights to Liberia leaving daily at 11:15am from the Juan Santamaría International Airport. This flight stops first in Tambor. The one-way fare is $25.

Travelair (☎ 506/220-3054 or 506/232-7883) has flights daily to Liberia at 12:30pm from San José's Pavas International Airport. This flight stops first in Tamarindo. Fares are $82 one-way; $136 round-trip.

By Bus   Express buses leave **San José** daily at 7, 9, and 11:30am and 1, 3, 4, 6, and 8pm from Calle 14 between avenidas 1 and 3. The ride is 4 hours. A one-way fare costs $2.80. From **Puntarenas,** buses leave at 5:30, 7, and 9:30am and 12 and 5pm. The ride takes $2^{1}/_{2}$ hours. A one-way fare costs $1.80.

Buses depart for Monteverde and San José from the Liberia bus station on the edge of town, 200 meters north and 100 meters east of the main intersection on the Interamerican Highway. Express buses for San José leave daily at 4:30, 6, 7:30, and 10am and 12:30, 2, 4, 6, and 8pm. To reach Monteverde, take any Puntarenas or San José bus leaving before 1pm. Get off at the Río Lagarto Bridge and catch the Puntarenas/Santa Elena bus which departs at approximately 3:15pm. For information on getting to various beaches, see the sections below.

By Car   Take the Interamerican Highway west from San José, and follow the signs for Nicaragua. It takes approximately 4 hours to get to Liberia.

ORIENTATION   Arriving   The highway passes slightly to the west of town. At the intersection with the main road into town, there are several hotels and gas stations. If you turn east into town, you will come to the central square in less than a kilometer.

Information   There is a small **tourist information center** (☎ 506/666-1606) three blocks south of the modern white church on Liberia's central park. While you're here gathering information, you can quickly tour the center's little museum of

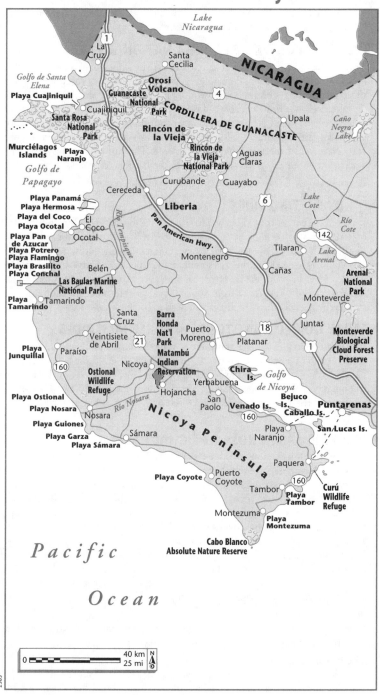

Lake Nicaragua

La Cruz

Golfo de Santa Elena

Playa Cuajiniquil

Cuajiniquil

Santa Rosa National Park

Murciélagos Islands

Playa Naranjo

Golfo de Papagayo

Playa Panamá

Playa Hermosa

Playa del Coco

Playa Ocotal

El Coco

Ocotal

Playa Pan de Azucar

Playa Potrero

Playa Flamingo

Playa Brasilito

Playa Conchal

Las Baulas Marine National Park

Belén

Playa Tamarindo

Tamarindo

Playa Junquillal

Paraíso

Santa Cruz

Veintisiete de Abril

(160)

Ostional Wildlife Refuge

Nicoya

Playa Ostional

Playa Nosara

Nosara

Playa Guiones

Playa Garza

Playa Sámara

Sámara

Hojancha

Santa Cecilia

Orosi Volcano

Guanacaste National Park

CORDILLERA DE GUANACASTE

Upala

Caño Negro Lake

(4)

Rincón de la Vieja

Rincón de la Vieja National Park

Aguas Claras

Curubande

Guayabo

Cereceda

Liberia

Pan American Hwy.

Río Tempisque

(6)

Lake Cote

Río Cote

(142)

Tilaran

Lake Arenal

Montenegro

Cañas

Arenal National Park

Monteverde

Monteverde Biological Cloud Forest Preserve

Juntas

(1)

Platanar

Puerto Moreno

(18)

Barra Honda Nat'l Park

Matambú Indian Reservation

Yerbabuena

Chira Is.

Golfo de Nicoya

San Paolo

Venado Is.

Bejuco Is.

Caballo Is.

Puntarenas

(160)

Playa Naranjo

San Lucas Is.

Nicoya Peninsula

Playa Coyote

Puerto Coyote

Paquera

(160)

Tambor

Playa Tambor

Curú Wildlife Refuge

Montezuma

Playa Montezuma

Cabo Blanco Absolute Nature Reserve

Pacific

Ocean

0   40 km

25 mi

N

NICARAGUA

2363

Guanacaste culture. The emphasis is on the life of the *sabanero*. The center is open Monday through Saturday from 8am–12pm and 1–5pm.

EXPLORING RINCÓN DE LA VIEJA NATIONAL PARK

This national park has an area of geothermal activity similar to Yellowstone National Park in the United States. Fumaroles, geysers, and hot pools cover a small area of this park, creating a bizarre, other-worldly landscape. Its main entrance is situated 25 kilometers northeast of Liberia down a badly rutted dirt road. There are several lodges located around the perimeter of the park, and all offer guided hikes and horseback rides into the park. In addition to hot springs and mudpots, there are waterfalls, a lake, and a volcanic crater to be explored. The birdwatching here is excellent, and the views out across the pasturelands to the Pacific Ocean are stunning.

Entry Passes & Camping   The entrance fee for this park is $6 per person.

NEARBY RAFTING TRIPS

Leisurely raft trips (no white water) are offered by **Safaris Corobici** (☎ 506/ 669-1091) about 40 kilometers south of Liberia. They have 2-hour ($35), 3-hour ($43), and half-day ($60) trips that are great for families and birdwatchers. Along the way you may see many of the area's more exotic animal residents—howler monkeys, iguanas, Caiman, coatimundis, otters, toucans, parrots, mot-mots, trogons, and many other species of birds. Aside from your binoculars and camera, a bathing suit and sunscreen are really the only things you need to bring on these trips.

NEARBY GUIDED BOAT TOURS & HORSEBACK RIDES

If you are staying in Liberia and want to tour the surrounding countryside with a guide, contact **Guanacaste Tours** (☎ 506/666-0306) in nearby Cañas. This company offers boat tours down the Bebedero River to **Palo Verde National Park,** which is south of Cañas and is best known for its migratory bird populations. They also lead a horseback trip up through the cloud forest on Miravalles Volcano, which is north of Cañas.

EXPLORING SANTA ROSA NATIONAL PARK

Best known for its remote, pristine beaches, reached by several kilometers of hiking trails or a four-wheel-drive vehicle, Santa Rosa National Park is a fine place to ramble, watch sea turtles nest, and surf. Located 30 kilometers north of Liberia on the Interamerican Highway, it covers the Santa Elena Peninsula and has the distinction of being Costa Rica's first national park. Unlike other national parks, it was founded not to preserve the land but to preserve a building, known as La Casona, which played an important role in Costa Rican independence. It was here, in 1856, that Costa Rican forces fought the decisive Battle of Santa Rosa forcing the U.S.-backed soldier of fortune William Walker and his men to flee into Nicaragua. Inside the restored ranch house you'll find relics from and representations of that historic battle. This small museum and monument is open daily from 8am until 4:30pm. It costs $6 per person to enter the park.

Camping   Camping is allowed at several sites within the park, but generally you must reserve in advance. A campsite costs $1.50 per person per day.

The Beaches   Eight kilometers west of La Casona down a rugged road that is impassable during the rainy season is **Playa Naranjo.** Four kilometers north of Playa Naranjo along a hiking trail that follows the beach you'll find **Playa Nancite. Playa Blanca** is 21 kilometers down a dirt road from Caujiniquil, which itself is 20 kilometers north of the park entrance. Playa Nancite is known for its *arribadas* (grouped egg-layings) of olive Ridley sea turtles, which come ashore to nest by the tens of thousands each year in October. Nearby Playa Naranjo is best known for its perfect surfing waves, which break at Witch's Rock just offshore. On the northern side of the peninsula is the even more remote Playa Blanca, which can be reached in the dry season if you have a four-wheel-drive vehicle. This beach is reached by way of the village of Caujiniquil.

WHERE TO STAY
IN TOWN
Expensive
Hotel Las Espuelas. Apdo. 88-5000, Liberia, Guanacaste. ☎ **506/293-4544,** 305/539-1630, or 800/245-8420 in the U.S. Fax 506/293-4839 or 305/858-7478 in the U.S. 44 rms. A/C TV TEL. $80 double; $90 triple. AE, MC, V.

This hotel is located on the Interamerican Highway, 2 kilometers south of Liberia. The name means "spurs" and is a reference to this being cowboy (*sabanero*) country, but despite the rugged epithet, this is the most luxurious hotel in Liberia. The open-air lobby and adjacent dining room and bar all have the feel of a modern hacienda. Surrounding the hotel are spacious gardens that are shaded by huge old Guanacaste trees. The trees and garden together give this hotel an oasis-like feel. The guest rooms are attractive, though a bit small, and have polished tile floors. In the bathroom, you'll find a basket of toiletries, which is a rarity in Costa Rican hotels. Overall, however, the amenities here are only slightly more upscale than at other similar, and less expensive, hotels in Liberia.

Dining/Entertainment: There's a large and attractive dining room serving moderately priced international and Costa Rican meals. There is a small bar adjacent to the restaurant and a modest casino open nightly from 7pm until the last bettor calls it quits.

Facilities: Small swimming pool, tour desk, and conference room.

Moderate
Hotel El Sitio. Liberia, Guanacaste. ☎ **506/666-1211.** Fax 506/666-2059. 52 rms. A/C TV TEL. $65 double; $75 triple; $85 quad. AE, DC, MC, V.

Located about 80 yards west of the fire station on the road to Santa Cruz and the beaches, this hotel follows the same basic Spanish-influenced hacienda style as Las Espuelas and offers similar amenities, but is considerably less expensive. Throughout the hotel, there are red-tile floors and original paintings of local Guanacaste scenes on the walls. The rooms have all been remodeled and now have cool tile floors instead of carpeting, and newer air-conditioning units. The pool area is shady (a welcome relief from the strong Guanacaste sun), and there is even one of those famous pre-Columbian basalt spheres in the garden. Beside the pool, there is a rancho-style bar/restaurant. Other amenities and services include horseback riding, bike rentals, a children's play area, a whirlpool tub, tour arrangements, and a car-rental desk.

Nuevo Hotel Boyeros. Apdo. 85, Liberia, Guanacaste. ☎ **506/666-0722** or 506/666-0995. Fax 506/666-2529. 70 rms. A/C TEL. $42 double; $54 triple. AE, MC, V.

You'll find this economical hotel just before the main Liberia intersection on the Interamerican Highway, and though it isn't as attractively landscaped as other hotels in town, it's all right in a pinch. Arches with turned wooden railings and a red-tile roof give this two-story, motel-style building a Spanish feel. In the courtyard of the hotel are two pools—one for adults and one for children—and a rancho bar/snack bar. All the rooms have a private balcony or patio overlooking the pool. The best and coolest rooms are on the second floor of the east wing. The small restaurant serves meals ranging in price from $3.80 to $7.50. Guests also have access to a gym/fitness center two blocks away.

Inexpensive

Hotel Bramadero. Carretera Interamericana, Libera, Guanacaste. ☎ **506/666-0371.** Fax 506/666-0203. 25 rms (all with bath). $19–$28 double; $23–$32.50 triple; $27–$37 quad (higher prices are for A/C rooms). AE, MC, V.

This roadside motel lacks ambience, but the rates are good and the rooms are generally clean. Rooms without air-conditioning can be a bit musty and most rooms are crammed wall-to-wall with beds, so ask to see a couple first. Behind the restaurant is the hotel's small pool, which is wonderfully cooling in an area that is the hottest, driest, and dustiest in Costa Rica. Rooms closest to the road and the hotel's attached restaurant and bar can be noisy at night, especially on the weekends, when families from San José flee the cool elevations for the warmth of the lowlands. The restaurant here is quite popular, despite the fact that it gets a lot of traffic noise and serves mediocre, though filling, meals.

Hotel Guanacaste. 25 meters west and 100 meters south of the bus station, Liberia, Guanacaste. ☎ **506/666-0085.** Fax 506/666-2287. 29 rms (all with private bath). $14.75 double; $20.50 triple; $23 quad. MC, V.

This very economical little hotel is primarily a hostel-type establishment catering to young travelers on a tight budget. In addition to the simply furnished rooms, there's a basic soda serving cheap Tico meals. The management here can help arrange trips to nearby national parks and tell you about other interesting budget accommodations, including campgrounds, in the area. The two newest rooms here are doubles with air-conditioning and cost slightly more. You'll find this basic hotel around the corner from Hotel Bramadero.

NEAR CAÑAS

Moderate

✪ **Hotel Hacienda La Pacífica.** Apdo. 8-5700, Cañas, Guanacaste. ☎ **506/669-0266** or 506/669-0050. Fax 506/669-0555. 33 rms. $67 double; $77 triple; $87 quad. AE, MC, V.

If you want a central location for exploring the national parks of this region, there are few better choices than the Hacienda La Pacífica. Originally started as a research facility and wild-animal rehabilitation center, the hotel is now a spacious mini-resort hotel with attractive grounds, organized tours and activities, marked trails, and an inviting pool. The hotel is located on the banks of the gentle Corobici River, which is a good place for birdwatching. Though the hotel is 40 kilometers south of Liberia, it is still convenient for visiting Santa Rosa and Rincón de la Vieja national parks, as well as Palo Verde National Park and the Lomas Barbudal Biological Reserve. Rooms vary in size, though all have tile floors and a patio of some sort. The larger rooms have private sun patios, as well as another patio. These rooms also have sliding-glass doors that make the rooms quite bright; high ceilings keep them cool. The open-air restaurant is shady and cool, and serves moderately priced meals. The lodge offers a number of services, including horseback riding ($10 per hour), bike rentals ($3 per hour), guided walks ($10), rafting trips ($35 for 2 hours), and tours to the different national parks. On the grounds, you'll also find a restored 19th-century adobe house, and nearby there is a small, privately owned zoo.

NEAR RINCÓN DE LA VIEJA NATIONAL PARK
Moderate

✪ **Los Inocentes Lodge.** Apdo. 1370-3000, Heredia. ☎ **506/265-5484.** Fax 506/265-6431. 11 rms. $53.50 per person (includes three meals). AE, V.

Set on a ranch 14 kilometers from La Cruz, near the Nicaraguan border, Los Inocentes is popular with naturalists interested in exploring the nearby forests. Horseback rides ($26 per day) through the ranch are the most popular activities, and in fact, the ranch does a brisk business in tours coming up here from various Nicoya Peninsula beaches to do some riding. The rooms are comfortable, though basic, and have tile floors. Some have high ceilings, and all open onto large verandahs with hammocks and wicker rocking chairs. Meals are simple but filling. In addition to horseback riding, there are nature trails and a swimming pool. There's a great view of Orosi Volcano from the lodge.

✪ **Rincón De La Vieja Mountain Lodge.** Apdo. 114-5000, Liberia, Guanacaste. ☎ **506/225-1073** or 506/234-8835. Fax 506/234-1676. 27 rms (all with private bath). $48.40 double; $66 triple; $81.40 quad. AE, MC, V.

This is the closest lodge to the Las Pailas mudpots and the Azufrale hot springs. The rustic lodge is surrounded by grasslands that conjure up images of the African savannah. It's at the end of the road and feels very remote (the road here is really, really bad). The polished-wood main lodge looks like a cross between a ranch hacienda and a mountain cabin. There's a long verandah set with chairs, and inside is a small lounge and dining room with long tables for communal meals. Some of the rooms are quite small, while others have lots of space. Some have hammocks on their verandahs and others back up to a small stream. Meals, which are simple but hearty Tico fare, will cost you $26 to $30 a day. The lodge offers numerous day-long tours either on foot or on horseback. Transportation from Liberia can be arranged at additional cost. If you are driving, follow the directions to the Hacienda Lodge Guachepelin and continue driving on this dirt road for another 7 kilometers, passing the turnoff for the park entrance.

Santa Clara Lodge. Apdo. 17-5000, Quebrada Grande de Liberia, Guanacaste. ☎ **506/223-7141** or 666-0473. Fax 506/666-0475. 7 rms (none with bath), 1 cabin (with bath). $27–$30 double; $41 cabin. Meals are an additional $17 per person per day. No credit cards.

Santa Clara Lodge is located in the foothills of Guanacaste's volcanic mountains on a working dairy farm where guests are even invited to participate in the morning milking. With shady grounds on the banks of a small river, the setting is quite tranquil. You can sit beneath the palapa sipping a drink and listen to the chickens clucking in the yard, or go for a swim in the mineral-water pool. The lodge is well suited for exploring the region if you have your own car or want to arrange tours. Santa Rosa, Guanacaste, and Rincón de la Vieja national parks are all within an hour's drive. You can also hike through field and forest to four different waterfalls. Guided hikes ($10) and horseback rides ($20 to $50) can be arranged, and the trip to the hot springs is particularly recommendable. Rooms are simply furnished, as you might expect on a working ranch, and only the cabin has a private bath. Meals are filling Tico fare such as rice and beans, steaks, chicken and fries, salads, and fruits. It is also possible to camp here. To reach the lodge, head north from Liberia for about 23 kilometers and turn right on the road to Quebrada Grande. In Quebrada Grande, turn right at the soccer field and continue for another 4 kilometers. You can also arrange free daily transportation from Liberia to the lodge if you phone in advance.

Inexpensive

Hacienda Lodge Guachepelin. Apdo. 636, Alajuela. ☎ **506/442-2864** or 506/442-2818. Fax 506/442-1910. 6 rms (none with private bath), 2 dorms. $32–$35 double; $9 per person dorm. Meals are an additional $17 per person per day. No credit cards.

Located 23 kilometers northeast of Liberia on the edge of Rincón de la Vieja National Park, this rustic lodge is housed in a 112-year-old ranch house. The rooms are pretty basic, and the dorms are actually the old bunkhouse. The ranch is still in operation today, and in addition to exploring the park, you can ride horses and commune with the pigs, dairy cows, and beef cattle. It isn't easy to get to the lodge, and once you arrive you'll need a few days to explore the park, so plan on taking all your meals here and going on a few guided tours. A horseback tour with a bilingual guide will cost around $24 per person for a half-day ride. This is one of the closest lodges to the thermal springs (10 kilometers) and bubbling mudpots (5 kilometers) of Rincón de la Vieja National Park. Horseback rides can be arranged to the geothermal areas, as well as to various lakes, the top of a nearby dormant volcano, and some beautiful waterfalls. If you're driving a car, you'd better have four-wheel-drive or high clearance (though in the dry season it's sometimes passable in a regular car). To reach the lodge, drive about 5 kilometers north of Liberia and turn right on the dirt road to Curubande, which you will pass through in about 12 kilometers. Continue on this road for another 6 kilometers, passing through the ranch's gate, before arriving at the lodge. When you contact the lodge to make a reservation, you can arrange to be picked up in Liberia for $7 per person ($14 round-trip).

WHERE TO DINE

There aren't many dining choices in Liberia, so most visitors choose to eat in their hotel's dining room. In town, the most popular alternative is **Pizzeria Pronto,** which is located 100 meters west of the tourist information center and serves a wide range of pizzas baked in a clay oven. Other choices include:

Restaurante Pókopí. 100 meters west of the gas station on the road to Santa Cruz. ☎ **506/ 666-1036.** Main courses $3.15–$10.15. AE, MC, V. Daily 11am–10pm. CONTINENTAL.

It doesn't look like much from the outside, but this tiny restaurant has a surprising amount of class inside. An even more pleasant surprise is the unusual (for rural Costa Rica) variety of continental dishes on the menu. Order one of their delicious daiquiris while you peruse the menu, which is on a wooden cutting board. You have your choice of dolphin (the fish, not the mammal) prepared five different ways, pizza, chicken Cordon Bleu, chicken in wine sauce, and other equally delectable dishes. However, for a real surprise, order the chateaubriand. It comes to your table with great flare, surrounded by succulent fresh vegetables and a tomato stuffed with peas. Be sure to dine early if you want a quiet meal; attached to the restaurant is a disco that swings into action at 9pm, Wednesdays through Sundays. And you thought you were out in the sticks.

Ⓢ **Restaurant Rincón Corobici.** Interamerican Highway, 4 kilometers north of Cañas. ☎ **506/669-1234.** Reservations not accepted. Main courses $2.50–$15.50. MC, V. Daily 8am–10pm. COSTA RICAN/INTERNATIONAL.

The food here is decidedly mediocre, but the setting, particularly during the day, more than makes up for it. While there is plenty of covered seating in the main open-air dining room, you'll want to choose a table on the wooden deck, which overlooks a beautiful section of the Corobici River. The sound of rushing water tumbling over the rocks in the riverbed is soothing accompaniment to the simple-but-filling meals.

The whole fried fish is your best choice here, though they also have steaks, lobster, shrimp, and sandwiches. This restaurant makes an ideal lunch stop if you are heading to or from Liberia, or have just done a rafting trip on the Corobici River. Be sure to try the fried yuca chips. You may never go back to french fries.

2 Playa Hermosa & Playa Panamá

258 kilometers NW of San José; 40 kilometers SW of Liberia

Playa Hermosa means "beautiful beach," which is a very appropriate name for this crescent of sand. Surrounded by dry, rocky hills, this curving gray-sand beach is long and wide and rarely crowded, despite the presence of the Condovac La Costa condominium development on the hill at the north end of the beach. Fringing the beach is a swath of trees that stay surprisingly green right through the dry season. The shade provided by these trees is a big part of the beach's appeal—it gets hot here and some shade is always appreciated at the beach. At both ends of the beach rocky headlands jut out into the surf, and at the base of these rocks, you'll find tide pools that are fun to explore.

Beyond Playa Hermosa, you'll find Playa Panamá, which has recently been transformed from one of the most remote and underdeveloped beaches in Guanacaste to the first to host, not one, but two major resort hotels. Since these resorts are located slightly north of Playa Panamá proper, it is still possible to enjoy the quiet beauty of this big, calm beach.

ESSENTIALS

GETTING THERE & DEPARTING   By Plane   The nearest airports with regularly scheduled service are **Liberia** and **Tamarindo.** From either of these places you can arrange a taxi to bring you the rest of the way.

By Bus   Express buses leave San José daily at 3:20pm from Calle 12 between avenidas 5 and 7, stopping first at Playa Hermosa and next at Playa Panamá, 3 kilometers farther north. The trip takes 5 hours. One-way fare costs $3.80.

Alternately, you can take a bus from San José to Liberia (see "Liberia," above, for details) and then take a bus from Liberia to Playa Hermosa or Playa Panamá. Buses leave Liberia for these two beaches daily at 7:30 and 11:30am, and 3:30, 5:45, and 7pm. The trip lasts 45 minutes. A one-way fare costs $1.

One bus departs for San José daily at 5am from Playa Panamá, with a stop in Playa Hermosa along the way. Buses to Liberia leave Playa Panamá at 5am and 4pm, stopping in Playa Hermosa a few minutes later. Ask at your hotel for where to catch the bus.

By Car   Follow the directions for getting to Liberia, then head west toward Santa Cruz. Just past the village of Comunidad, turn right. In about 11 kilometers you will come to a fork in the road. Take the right fork. These roads are relatively well marked, and a host of prominent hotel billboards should make it easy enough to find the beach. It takes about 5 hours from San José.

ORIENTATION   Arriving   There are no real towns here, just a few houses and hotels on and near the beach. You will come to Playa Hermosa first, followed by Playa Panamá a few kilometers farther along the same road.

Information & Water Sports–Equipment Rental   In the middle of Playa Hermosa, you'll find **Aqua Sport** (☎ 506/670-0353), the tourist information and water-sports equipment rental center for Playa Hermosa. Kayaks, sailboards, canoes, bicycles, beach umbrellas, snorkel gear, and parasails are all available for rental at fairly reasonable rates. This is also where you'll find the local post office, public phones, and a restaurant (see "Where to Dine" below).

SWIMMING & DIVING

Either beach is usually good for swimming, although Playa Panamá is slightly more protected. If you want to do some diving while you're here, check in at the dive shop at **La Costa Hotel & Villas** at the north end of the beach. A two-tank dive should run around $60 per person.

GUIDED NATIONAL PARK TOURS

Ecotours (☎ 506/670-0458) is located just south of Aqua Sport near the middle of Playa Hermosa. This small operation organizes guided tours to most of the national parks and natural attractions in the region.

WHERE TO STAY
VERY EXPENSIVE

Costa Smeralda Hotel. Apdo. 12177-1000, San José. ☎ **506/670-0044.** Fax 506/670-0379. 74 rms, 4 suites. A/C TV TEL. $140 double; $160 triple; $180 quad; $240 suite. AE, MC, V.

Although there's no real connection to their Italian namesake, this resort hotel does have a Mediterranean feel to it. With plans for further expansion, this new hotel already covers nearly 10 acres. Low red-tile roofed buildings are spread across a gentle hillside overlooking the sea. The rooms are all new and immaculate, with cool tile floors, flowing transparent drapes, spacious bathrooms, and giant covered patios. The suites are even larger, with a comfortable sitting room and private jacuzzi. The windows here, including the large full-wall front windows, do not open, so you must use the air-conditioning. There's a semi-private small patch of beach about 500 meters from the hotel.

Dining/Entertainment: Meals are served in a large open-air dining room, with Italian and French chefs serving a wide range of international dishes. There is also a palapa snack bar rancho out by the pool. The hotel recently inaugurated its casino, which opens nightly at 6pm and closes when the last gambler calls it quits.

Facilities: A large, amoeba-like, free-form pool, tennis court.

Malinche Real Beach Resort. Playa Arenilla, Guanacaste. ☎ **506/670-0033.** Fax 506/670-0300. 100 rms. A/C TV TEL. Dec 1–Apr 30, $258.25 double; $333.75 triple; $409.32 quad; May 1–Nov 30, $223.50 double; $300 triple; $375.50 quad; children under 12 are $18 per day. Rates are all-inclusive (including drinks). AE, MC, V.

Just a few kilometers north of the Costa Smeralda, this is the first hotel in the massive Papagayo Project and the first all-inclusive resort in the Guanacaste region. Each of the 50 independent villas can be separated into two rooms or shared by a family. Inside, one room is equipped with a king-sized bed; the other with two queen-sized beds. All rooms have marble floors, pine ceilings, large bathrooms, and private patios or balconies. The resort is quite spread out, so if you don't want to do a lot of walking or wait for the golf cart shuttles, ask for a room near the pool and restaurants. For those seeking more isolation, there are rooms located in the dry forest behind the resort, and others overlooking the somewhat removed Bahía Culebra (Snake Bay). The hotel has a host of organized sports and activities, including daily programs for children. All nonmotorized sports equipment, activities, and classes are included. The hotel has its own small crescent-shaped swath of beach, which is very calm and protected for swimming.

Dining/Entertainment: The hotel's most formal dining option has been dubbed Da Vinci, which serves northern Italian cuisine in an elegant indoor setting. Reservations and proper attire are required. Breakfasts and more casual meals can be taken at the open-air La Fonda restaurant, overlooking the pool. There is also a pool-side bar.

Services: Concierge, room service, laundry service, and valet parking.

Facilities: A playful three-tiered main pool, a small lap pool, and a wave-resistant pool; a well-equipped fitness center, with Nautilus machines, free weights, jacuzzis, a steam room, sauna, health bar, and daily classes. There is also a tennis court, volleyball courts, water-sports equipment, nature trails, children's programs, a conference center, tour desk, beauty salon, and boutique.   ·

EXPENSIVE

La Costa Hotel & Villas. Playa Hermosa, Guanacaste. ☎ **506/290-0565** or 506/290-0561. Fax 506/290-0566. 54 rms, 101 villas. A/C TV TEL. Dec–Apr and July, $110 double; May–June and Aug–Nov, $81 double. AE, DC, MC, V.

For a long time this was the only full-service resort around, and it remains the lone major hotel on Playa Hermosa. Set on a steep hillside at the north end of the beach, La Costa was built with Mediterranean styling. The best rooms are those at the top of the hill and farthest from the beach—you'll need to be in good shape to stay here. Unfortunately the resort was not designed for walking, and there are no sidewalks and little shade. Luckily, the two pools are both at the top of the hill, so if you are staying up high, you don't have to walk down to the beach to take a swim. The villas have kitchens, satellite TVs, and lots of space, and while these rooms are the closest to the beach, very few have any view to speak of. The newer hotel rooms have the best views, attractive furniture, and tile floors.

Dining/Entertainment: The hotel has numerous eating establishments. La Pampa is the hotel's most formal dining room and specializes in steaks. Frutas y Flores is more casual and is open throughout the day. El Pelícano is a snack bar by the pool. Bars include Las Lapas, on the beach; Chico & Pepe, by the main pool; Bayview, by the second pool; and La Carretera, an indoor lounge. There is also a disco that can really get packed on the weekends.

Services: Diving-equipment rentals, scuba classes, dive trips, jet-ski rentals.

Facilities: Two freshwater swimming pools, tennis court, dive shop, tour desk, mini-market, gift shop.

MODERATE

Ⓢ **Cabinas Playa Hermosa.** Apdo. 117, Liberia, Guanacaste. ☎/fax **506/670-0136.** 22 rms (all with bath). $32.60 double; $40.75 triple; $48.90 quad. No credit cards.

This little hotel, tucked away under shady trees, is a sprawling beachfront spread at the south end of Playa Hermosa. Each large room has a pair of Adirondack chairs on its front porch, and the beach is only a few steps away. Rooms 1 through 4 directly front the ocean, but they are also very close to the restaurant and bar, so can be noisy. The rest are located in several low buildings that run perpendicular to the beach. Even though most of the rooms are rather dark, they are large and have a lot of closet space. Each has two double beds. Horseback riding and boat trips can be arranged. The open-air restaurant has a rustic tropical feel to it, with unfinished tree trunks holding up the roof. Seafood and homemade pasta are the specialties. Menu prices range from $3.75 to $10.50; service can be quite slow and inattentive. To find the hotel, turn left at the first road into Playa Hermosa. The hotel's white archway gate is just after the curve.

✪ El Velero Hotel. Playa Hermosa, Guanacaste. ☎ **506/670-0330.** Fax 506/670-0310. 13 rms. $54 double; $68 triple; $80 quad (rates slightly higher during Christmas and Easter, and slightly lower during off-season). AE, MC, V.

This small Canadian-owned hotel is the nicest moderately priced place on Playa Hermosa. It's located right on the beach and has its own small swimming pool beside an open-air bar. White walls and polished tile floors give El Velero a Mediterranean flavor. The guest rooms are large and most have high ceilings. The upper third of each room's walls are screens, so there is plenty of cross-ventilation. Fans also help keep the rooms cool. Bathrooms are small and have showers only. When I last visited, construction had started on eight new rooms. Various tours, horseback riding, and fishing trips can be arranged through the hotel, however, the most popular excursions are the full-day and sunset cruises on the hotel's namesake, a 38' sailboat. The hotel has its own restaurant, which offers a good selection of meat, fish, and shrimp dishes in the $6.50 to $12.50 range.

WHERE TO DINE

Aqua Sport. On the beach. ☎ **506/670-0353.** Reservations not accepted. Main courses $4.50–$15.50. MC, V. Daily 9am–9pm (12–9pm in rainy season). CONTINENTAL.

Part of the Aqua Sport market and equipment-rental shop is a small open-air restaurant with tables of polished hardwood. The beach is only steps away, and the atmosphere is very casual. The food, however, is much better than what you would expect from such a place. The focus is on seafood—grilled lobster for $15.50, shrimp à la diabla for $7.50, and huge paella or assorted seafood platters that feed four for $45 and $50 respectively.

3 Playa del Coco & Playa Ocotal

253 kilometers NW of San José; 35 kilometers W of Liberia

Playa del Coco is one of the most easily accessible beaches in Guanacaste, with a paved road right down to the water, and has long been a popular destination with middle-class Ticos from San José. Unfortunately, most of the hotels right in town are quite run-down, and the water is neither very clean or appealing (this is a busy fishing port). The crowds that come here like their music loud and constant, so if you're in search of a quiet retreat, stay away. On the other hand, if you're looking for a beach with cheap hotels and plenty of cheap food and beer close at hand, you may enjoy Playa del Coco.

The beach, which has grayish-brown sand, is quite wide at low tide and almost nonexistent at high tide. In between high and low, it's just right. Trash is a bit of a problem right in town. However, if you walk down the long, curving beach to the north of town, you're bound to find a nice, clean spot to unfold your blanket. Better still, if you have a car, head over to Playa Ocotal, which is a couple of kilometers down a dirt road. This is a tiny pocket of a cove bordered by high bluffs, and is quite beautiful.

ESSENTIALS

GETTING THERE & DEPARTING   By Plane   The nearest airport with regularly scheduled flights is in Liberia. From there you can take a bus or arrange for a taxi to take you to Playa del Coco.

By Bus   An express bus leaves San José at 10am daily from Calle 14 between avenidas 1 and 3, stopping first in Playa del Coco. Allow 5 hours for the trip.

A one-way ticket is $2.80. From Liberia, buses leave at 5:30 and 8:15am, and 12:30, 2, 4:30, and 6:15pm. The trip takes 45 minutes. A one-way ticket costs $1.10.

One bus departs daily from Playa Ocotal for San José at 9:15am, stopping in Playa del Coco a few minutes later. Buses for Liberia leave at 7 and 9:15am, and 2, 3, and 6pm.

By Car Follow the directions for getting to Liberia and Playa Hermosa, but take the left fork instead. It takes about 5 hours from San José.

ORIENTATION **Arriving** Playa del Coco is a small but busy beach town. Most of its hotels and restaurants are either on the water or on the road leading into town. Playa Ocotal is south of Playa del Coco on a dirt road that leaves the main road just before the beach. Playa Ocotal is a collection of vacation homes, condos, and hotels, and has one bar on the beach.

FUN ON AND OFF THE BEACH

There is not much to do here except lie on the sand, hang out in the sodas and bars, or go to the discos. If you're interested, you might be able to join a soccer match (the soccer field is in the middle of town). Over at nearby Playa Ocotal there are often pickup volleyball games by the soda on the beach. It's also possible to arrange horseback rides; ask at your hotel.

SCUBA DIVING Scuba diving is the most popular watersport in the area and dive shops abound. **Bill Beard's Diving Safaris** (☎ 506/670-0012), **Mario Vargas Expeditions** (☎ 506/670-0351), and **Rich Coast Diving** (☎ 506/670-0176) all offer equipment rentals and dive trips. A two-tank dive, with equipment, should cost between $60 and $80 per person. Both Mario Vargas and Diving Safaris also offer PADI certification courses.

SPORTFISHING Full- and half-day sportfishing excursions can be arranged through **Papagayo Sportfishing** (☎ 506/670-0354) or the **Hotel Flor de Itabo** (☎ 506/670-0011).

WHERE TO STAY
EXPENSIVE

El Ocotal Beach Resort. Apdo. 1, Playa del Coco, Guanacaste. ☎ **506/670-0321.** Fax 506/670-0083. 43 rms, 12 bungalows, 3 suites. A/C TV TEL. Dec 16–Aug 15, $90 double, $105 bungalow, $130–$170 suite; Aug 16–Dec 15, $80 double, $105 bungalow, $120–$150 suite. AE, DC, MC, V.

This is the most luxurious hotel in the Playa del Coco area, although, unfortunately, I have received complaints about the quality of service here. The guest rooms vary in age, though all are fairly spacious and attractively furnished. The older rooms are closer to the beach, while the rooms with the best views and greatest comfort are atop a hill overlooking a dramatic stretch of rocky coastline. Scuba diving and sportfishing are the main draws here, though diminutive Playa Ocotal is one of the prettiest little beaches along this stretch of coast and offers good swimming.

Dining/Entertainment: El Ocotal's primary restaurant is one of its greatest assets. The large room is surrounded on three sides by walls of glass and has a stunning view of Playa Ocotal and miles of coastline. There is also patio dining. Seafood is the specialty and the prices are moderate. El Ocotal also runs the Father Rooster restaurant on the beach, with more casual meals and service.

Services: Scuba classes, rentals, and trips are some of the hotel's most popular services. There are also boat excursions, fishing charters, surfing excursions, a car-rental desk, and a tour desk.

Facilities: The hotel's main swimming pool is quite attractive and has a little artificial waterfall. Ranchos beside the pool provide shady shelter when the sun gets too strong. There are also two other pools, tennis courts, a hot tub, and a dive shop.

MODERATE

Hotel La Flor De Itabo. Apdo. 32, Playa del Coco, Guanacaste. ☎ **506/670-0292** or 506/670-0011. 16 rms, 8 apts. $31–$57 double; $70 apartment for one to four people. AE, DC, MC, V.

This is the most luxurious of the hotels right in Playa del Coco, and though it is not on the beach, the pool is large and the grounds are lushly planted. Toucans and parrots squawk and talk amid the flowers, adding their own bright colors to an already colorful garden. Stone reproductions of pre-Columbian statues provide a touch of the mysterious at this quiet retreat. With fewer than two dozen rooms, the service here is reliably good. The most inexpensive rooms are in four bungalows, with screened-in windows and fans. The standard rooms are more spacious, have air-conditioning, and are attractively decorated with wood carvings and Guatemalan textiles. The apartments are located a little bit away from the main building. While they are larger than the standard and bungalow rooms, have air-conditioning, and include kitchenettes, they tend to feel a bit spartan. Italian dishes are the specialty of the restaurant, with main courses ranging from $6.10 to $10.15. The bar is decorated with flags from all over the world and is a popular hangout with sport fishermen. There is even a small casino here. In addition to a pool, the hotel has a volleyball court, children's play area, and a small park.

INEXPENSIVE

☉ Cabinas Chale. Playa del Coco, Guanacaste. ☎ **506/670-0036.** Fax 506/670-0303. 25 rms (all with bath). $23.40 double; $26.85 triple; $30.20 quad. No credit cards.

Located down a dirt road to the right as you are coming into town, this small hotel is quite a bit better than those directly on the beach, and is also much quieter. Your only company as you stroll down to the beach, which is only 150 feet away, may be a herd of grazing cattle. The rooms are simply furnished with double beds, overhead fans, tile floors, and refrigerators, and each comes with a Tico clothes-washing sink called a *pila*. Some larger rooms have just been added and these are a bit nicer than the older rooms. There is a spartan, screen-walled bar that is open only during the busy season (November to April), and a small pool on a raised patio in back.

☉ La Luna Tica. Playa del Coco, Guanacaste. ☎ **506/670-0279.** 31 rms (all with bath). $17–$22 double; $23–$28 triple; $31.50–$36.50 quad. Rates include breakfast. No credit cards.

This is a good budget choice if you want to be close to the the beach. It's located just south of the soccer field and its 15 oldest rooms are located right on the beach. These are very basic, have polished concrete floors, and are kept very clean. The newer rooms are in the annex just across the street. Three of these have air-conditioning. The nicest rooms are on the second floor; each has hardwood floors and is flanked by a cool verandah. La Luna Tica also has a traditional soda right on the beach, serving inexpensive Tico meals and fish dishes. Considering that the room rates include breakfast, this is the best deal in town.

A BED-AND-BREAKFAST

✪ Hotel Villa Casa Blanca. Apdo. 176-5019, Playa del Coco, Guanacaste. ☎/fax **506/670-0448.** 10 rms, 4 suites. $50–$55 double; $60–$65 triple; $80–$85 suites. Rates include breakfast. AE, MC, V (add 6% surcharge).

With friendly, helpful owners, beautiful gardens, and attractive rooms, this bed-and-breakfast inn is my favorite spot in the area. The inn is located in a new development about 500 meters from the beach and is built in the style of a Spanish villa. All the guest rooms have their own distinct characters, and though some are a bit cramped, others feel quite roomy. One room has a canopy bed and a beautiful bathroom with a step-up bath. The suites are higher up and have ocean views. My favorite has a secluded patio with lush flowering plants all around. A little rancho serves as an open-air bar and breakfast area, and beside this is a pretty little lap pool with a bridge over it. Villa Blanca also represents several rental houses and condos in the area, so if you plan to stay for a week or more, or need lots of room, ask about these.

WHERE TO DINE

There are dozens of cheap open-air restaurants at the traffic circle in the center of El Coco village. These restaurants serve Tico standards, with an emphasis on fried fish. Prices are quite low, and so too is the quality for the most part. For better food, try the two places listed below. For views, you can't beat the restaurant at **El Ocotal Beach Resort** and for desserts, lunch, or snacks, there's **San Francisco Treats.**

Helen's. 100 meters south of the ice factory. ☎ **506/670-0121.** Reservations not accepted. Main courses $4.85–$12.50. No credit cards. Daily 11am–10pm. COSTA RICAN/SEAFOOD.

This is a local favorite, and because Helen's husband is a fisherman, the seafood is always absolutely fresh. The **ceviche** comes in a big bowl and is enough for a meal. Be sure to try the lobster soup if it's on the menu.

El Rancho De Ocotal. Playa Ocotal. ☎ **506/670-0429.** Reservations not accepted. Pizzas $5–$7.50; main courses $7.50–$15. MC, V. Daily 8am–10pm. INTERNATIONAL.

This open-air restaurant near the beach at Playa Ocotal specializes in wood-oven pizzas, but is also popular for its swimming pool. You can order a meal or just a drink, and use the pool for as long as you like. There are also steaks and seafood on the menu.

4 Playas Flamingo, Potrero, Brasilito & Conchal

280 kilometers NW of San José; 66 kilometers SW of Liberia

These beaches were among the first in Costa Rica to attract international attention, and today Playa Flamingo remains the most highly developed beach on this stretch of coast. This isn't surprising when you see the blue water and narrow strand of white sand that is Playa Flamingo. The views from Playa Potrero are beautiful; on Playa Brasilito, budget travelers have a chance at some fun in the sun without spending a fortune; and, until quite recently, Playa Conchal was the exclusive find of a select group of beachcombers. What makes this grouping of beaches so memorable are the little, rocky islands offshore and the long sweeps of beach that are separated by a rugged peninsula.

On Playa Brasilito you will find one of the only two real villages in the area. The soccer field is the center of the village, and around its edges you'll find a couple of little *pulperias* (general stores). There's a long stretch of beach, and though it is of gray sand, it still has a quiet, undiscovered feel to it (at least on weekdays). Playa Brasilito is rapidly becoming popular both with Ticos and budget travelers from abroad. There's now a disco here and on weekends it can get pretty crowded and noisy.

Just south of Brasilito is the small, crushed-shell beach of Conchal. At press time, finishing touches were being put on a major 300-room resort, which should drastically change the feel of this former beachcomber's secret retreat.

Only a few miles away is the luxury resort beach called Playa Flamingo. This is one of Costa Rica's top resort beaches, with luxury hotels, a marina, a private airstrip, retirement and vacation homes, and, best of all, one of the only white-sand beaches in the area. In fact, the old name for this beach was Playa Blanca, which made plenty of sense. When the developers moved in, they needed a more romantic name than "White Beach," so it became Playa Flamingo, even though there are no flamingos.

You'll probably want to spend plenty of time on this beautiful beach. Playa Flamingo is on a long spit of land that forms part of Potrero Bay, or Bahia Flamingo, as the developers wish it to be known. On the ocean side of the peninsula, there is the long white-sand beach, behind which is a dusty road and then a mangrove swamp. At the end of the sand spit is a fortresslike rock outcropping upon which most of Playa Flamingo's hotels and vacation homes are built. There are great views from this rocky hill. If you are not staying on Playa Flamingo, you should know that there are parking spots all along the beach road where you can park your car for the day. There is, however, little shade on the beach, so be sure to use plenty of sunscreen and bring an umbrella if you can. The bay side of the peninsula is where the marina is located.

If you continue along the road from Brasilito without taking the turn for Playa Flamingo, you will soon come to Playa Potrero. The sand here is a brownish gray, but the beach is long, clean, and deserted. You can see the hotels of Playa Flamingo across the bay. Drive a little further and you will find the still underdeveloped Playa La Penca and Sugar Beach.

ESSENTIALS

GETTING THERE & DEPARTING   By Plane   The nearest airport with regularly scheduled flights is in **Tamarindo.** From there you can arrange for a taxi to drive you to any one of these beaches.

By Bus   Express buses leave San José daily at 8 and 10:30am from the corner of Calle 20 and Avenida 3, stopping at Playas Brasilito, Flamingo, and Potrero, in that order. The ride takes 6 hours. A one-way ticket costs $4.50.

Express buses depart Playa Potrero for San José at 9am and 2pm, stopping a few minutes later in Playa Brasilito and Playa Flamingo. Ask at your hotel where the best place is for catching the bus. Buses to Santa Cruz leave Potrero at 9am and 5pm. If you are heading north toward Liberia, get off the bus at Belén and wait for a bus going north. Buses leave Santa Cruz regularly for San José.

By Car   There are two major routes to these beaches. The most direct route is by way of the Tempisque River ferry. Take the Interamerican Highway west from San José. 47 kilometers past the turnoff for Puntarenas, turn left for the ferry. After crossing the Tempisque River, follow the signs for Nicoya, continuing north to Santa Cruz. About 16 kilometers north of Santa Cruz, just before the village of Belén, take the turnoff for Playas Flamingo, Brasilito, and Potrero. After another 20 kilometers, take the right fork to reach these beaches. The drive takes about 6 hours.

It is often slightly quicker, particularly on Fridays and Saturdays when beach traffic is heavy, to drive north all the way to Liberia and then come back south, thus avoiding the lines of cars waiting to take the ferry. This also applies if you are heading back to San José on a Sunday. After you reach Liberia, follow the directions for reaching Playa Hermosa, but continue on the main road past the town of Filadelfia, until the village of Belén. Turn right here until you reach Huacas, where there will be signs pointing you toward Playa Flamingo.

ORIENTATION   Arriving   These beaches are strung out over several miles of dirt roads. Playa Flamingo is by far the most developed. It is located down a side road, while the villages of Brasilito and Potrero are right on the main road.

FUN ON AND OFF THE BEACH

Though Playa Flamingo is the prettiest beach in this area, Playa Potrero has the gentlest surf, and therefore is the best swimming beach. Playa Conchal, which is nearly legendary for its beach of crushed pink seashells, is a short walk south of Brasilito. Though it is beautiful, the drop-off is quite steep and known for its dangerous riptides. The water at Playa Brasilito is often fairly calm, which makes it another good swimming choice. However, my favorites are Playas La Penca and Sugar Beach.

SCUBA DIVING   Scuba diving is quite popular here. The following companies can all take you out for a day of underwater exploration. The **Quicksilver/Holiday Scuba** (☎ 506/654-4010) operates out of the Hotel Aurola Playa Flamingo, **Eco Treks** (☎ 506/654-4141) is based at the Flamingo Marina Hotel and Club, and **Costa Rica Diving** (☎ 506/654-4148) is located on the road to Playa Potrero. All of them offer trips out to the Catalina and Bat Islands for between $60 and $90. Both Quicksilver/Holiday and Eco Treks also offer PADI certification courses.

SPORTFISHING   If you want to go sportfishing, you'll have plenty of options here. The **Marina Flamingo Yacht Club** (☎ 506/654-4203) can hook you up with a variety of boats based along its docks. A full-day fishing excursion can cost between $450 and $1,200, depending on the size of the boat. Half-day trips cost between $250 and $550.

Alternately you can contact the **Bahia Potrero Resort Hotel & Club** (☎ 506/654-4183), **Flamingo Marina Hotel & Club** (☎ 506/290-1858), **Club Villas Pacífica** (☎ 506/654-4137), or Tom Bradwell at **Blue Marlin Sport Fishing** (☎ 506/654-4043). The choices are many and competition is fierce here, so shop around to find the boat, skipper, and price that best fit your needs.

HORSEBACK RIDING   If you'd rather stay on dry land, you can arrange a horseback ride with **Jalisco Tours** (☎ 506/654-4106). They charge approximately $10 per hour for their rides.

MOUNTAIN BIKING   You can rent a mountain bike from **Eco Treks** (☎ 506/654-4141) at the Flamingo Marina Hotel and Club. Ask the folks at Eco Treks and they'll point you to a ride suited to your ability and conditioning level.

WHERE TO STAY
EXPENSIVE

Flamingo Marina Hotel & Club. Playa Flamingo (Apdo. 321-1002, Paseo de los Estudiantes, San José), Guanacaste. ☎ **506/654-4141** or 506/290-1858 in San José. Fax 506/654-4035 or 506/231-1858 in San José. 23 rms, 8 suites, 13 condos, 4 apts. A/C TV TEL. $105 double; $140–$160 suite; $180–$240 apt or condo. All rates include continental breakfast. AE, DC, MC, V.

Located up the hill from the beach, the Flamingo Marina Hotel offers one of the most attractive settings at Flamingo Beach. A big open-air lobby is done up to resemble an old village and overlooks both the swimming pool and the bay. There are a variety of room types to choose from, all of which have air-conditioning and refrigerators. The standard rooms have tile floors and lots of wood accents, while the suites have tiled whirlpool tubs, and wet bars in the seating area. All the rooms have patios or balconies, and most have bay views.

Dining/Entertainment: The Sunrise Cafe serves continental dishes with an emphasis on seafood. The bar beside the pool has seating in a big, cold-water whirlpool tub.

Services: Tour desk, sportfishing charters; mountain bike, sea kayak, and boogie board rentals; snorkeling and diving trips and classes.

Facilities: There are two swimming pools (one with a swim-up bar), a tennis court, and a gift shop.

Hotel Aurola Playa Flamingo Holiday Inn. Playa Flamingo (Apdo. 7802-1000, San José), Guanacaste. ☎ **506/654-4010** or 800/HOLIDAY in the U.S.; 506/233-7233 in San José. Fax 506/654-4060. 88 rms. A/C TV TEL. $75–$160 double; $150–$260 suite. AE, DC, MC, V.

This hotel, right across the road from the beach at Playa Flamingo, has long been a favorite of vacationing gringos. In late 1995, it received a total facelift that has spruced it up quite a bit. The hotel is constructed in a horseshoe shape around a large pool and opens out on the ocean. Rooms have a clear view of the ocean, across a narrow dirt road. All the rooms are clean and cool, with tile floors, modern bathrooms, and many amenities, including VCRs. The pool- and beach-view rooms are slightly nicer, and you'll pay more for them. The suites all have a sitting room, wet bar, two TVs, and two balconies. There's a modest gym, a large game room, and a children's play room. The most popular meeting and eating place here is the poolside Sand's Restaurant.

✪ **Hotel Sugar Beach.** Playa Pan de Azucar (Apdo. 90), Guanacaste. ☎ **506/654-4242** or 307/733-2904 in the U.S. Fax 506/654-4329 or 307/733-1058 in the U.S. 29 rms, 2 suites. $80–$125 double, $150–$200 suite. AE, MC, V.

Just as the name implies, the Hotel Sugar Beach is located on a white-sand beach—one of the few in the area and therefore one of the most attractive in my opinion. So far, this hotel is the only thing out here, giving it a strong measure of seclusion and privacy. The beach is on a small cove surrounded by rocky hills. Unfortunately, the hills become very brown and desolate in the dry season (which is when most tourists come to visit), so don't expect the verdant tropics if you come down here in March or April. The hotel itself is perched above the water. Nature lovers will be thrilled to find wild howler monkeys and iguanas almost on their doorsteps. Snorkelers also should be happy here; this cove has some good snorkeling in the dry season. The newest rooms are set back amid the trees and are quite large. Tile floors, wicker furniture, beautiful carved doors, and big bathrooms all add up to first-class comfort. The oldest rooms are the most basic, though they are in an interesting circular building. Hammocks under the trees provide a great way to while away a hot afternoon. The open-air dining room is in a circular building with a panoramic vista of ocean, islands, and hills. There are daily specials with prices from $6 to $15 for entrees. Scuba-diving and snorkeling trips, horseback riding, and fishing-boat charters can be arranged. The hotel rents masks and fins, sea kayaks, and boogie boards.

Villas Flamingo. Playa Flamingo, Guanacaste. ☎/fax **506/654-4215**. 24 condos. $81.50 double; $97.80 triple; $105.95 quad. AE, MC, V.

Villas Flamingo, a condominium development, is down at the south end of Playa Flamingo, which is much shadier and more attractive than the more developed north end of the beach. You're also closer to the beach than at any other hotel except the Holiday Inn. The condos here are two stories with two bedrooms, two bathrooms, full kitchens, tile floors throughout, and attractive decor. The grounds are well landscaped and cared for, and there are some big, old shade trees around. The living rooms are fronted by a wall of glass, though only the rooms very close to the beach or high up have much of a view. White walls and red-tile roofs give this place a very Mediterranean feel. You can also rent a larger villa that sleeps up to six people at the adjacent Flamingo Park development.

MODERATE

Hotel Bahia Potrero Beach Resort. Playa Potrero (Apdo. 45-5051, Santa Cruz), Guanacaste. ☎ **506/654-4183.** Fax 506/654-4093. 14 rms (all with bath). $69 double; $76 triple. All rates include continental breakfast. AE, MC, V.

This comfortable little beach hotel is on Playa Potrero and, from the beach in front, has a view of Playa Flamingo across the bay. Set in a green garden with a white wooden fence surrounding the property, the Bahia Flamingo feels like a private home in the country. A laid-back atmosphere prevails—with hammocks for dozing, a pool, and miles of nearly deserted beach for strolling and swimming. The rooms are large and cool, though a little dark. They all have refrigerators and a small patio. Fishing and snorkeling trips can be arranged. To find this hotel, watch for the sign pointing down a road to the left a mile or so after you pass the turnoff for Playa Flamingo. The hotel's restaurant is a breezy, high-ceilinged room and has a nice view of green lawns, white fence, and blue ocean. Meals of fresh seafood and hearty steaks average $5 to $10.

INEXPENSIVE

⑤ Cabinas Conchal. Playa Brasilito (Apdo. 185-5150, Santa Cruz), Guanacaste. ☎/fax **506/654-4257.** 8 rms (all with private bath). $19 double; $23 triple; $29 quad. No credit cards.

Located on the south edge of Brasilito, Cabinas Conchal consists of several yellow buildings inside a walled compound. The stucco-and-stone construction gives the buildings a bit of character, as well as added security. Some rooms have just a double bed, while others have a double and a pair of bunk beds. All are quite clean. Table fans help keep the rooms cool. The beach is about 200 meters away.

⑤ Cabinas Cristina. Playa Potrero (Apdo. 121, Santa Cruz), Guanacaste. ☎ **506/654-4006.** Fax 506/654-4128. 5 rms (all with bath). $25.25 double; $28.50 triple; $33.40 quad. No credit cards.

This little place is located on Playa Potrero across the bay from Playa Flamingo and a few kilometers north of Brasilito. Although Cabinas Cristina isn't right on the beach, it's still a great value in this area of high-priced hotels. The rooms are spacious and very clean (they fill up fast), with hot plates, refrigerators, dressers, bars with stools, tiled baths, and double and bunk beds. On the verandah there are large rocking chairs. The friendly owner, Daniel Boldrini, speaks some English. There is a small pool in the middle of a grassy green yard and a thatched-roof palapa. Playa Potrero is just a 5-minute walk down a dirt road.

Hotel Brasilito. Playa Brasilito, Santa Cruz, Guanacaste. ☎ **506/654-4237.** Fax 506/654-4247. 15 rms (all with private bath). $28–$36 double. V.

This hotel, right in Brasilito and just across a sand road from the beach, offers basic, small rooms that are generally quite clean. There's also a bar and big open-air restaurant serving economical meals. This is still one of the best values in town, though the building across the street is a disco, which makes it difficult to go to bed early on the weekends. The higher prices are for rooms with air-conditioning; rates also rise during Christmas and Easter. Rooms "A" and "B" each have a nice balcony and ocean view. The hotel also rents snorkeling equipment, bodyboards, and horses, and can arrange a variety of tours.

CAMPING ON THE BEACH

It's possible to camp on Playa Potrero, but there's no camping on the other beaches. Contact **Maiyra's** (☎ 506/654-4213), where sites are available for $2 per person. Maiyra's also has some basic cabins.

LONG-TERM STAYS: RENTING A CONDO OR PRIVATE HOME

If you plan to be here for a while or are coming down with friends or a large family, you might want to consider renting a condo or house. They rent for anywhere between $100 and $300 per day in the high season (slightly less during the low season). For information and reservations, contact **Sea View Rentals,** Apdo. 77, Santa Cruz, Guanacaste (☎ 506/654-4007; fax 506/654-4009).

WHERE TO DINE

Amberes. Playa Flamingo near the Flamingo Marina Hotel. ☎ **506/654-4001.** Reservations recommended in high season. Main courses $5.90–$16.50. MC, V. Daily 6:30–10pm. CONTINENTAL.

This is the happening spot in Flamingo. Not only is it the most upscale restaurant outside of a hotel, but it also boasts a bar, a disco, and even a tiny casino. So, you can come for dinner and make it an evening. Though the menu changes daily, you'll always find a wide selection of interesting dishes, with the accent on seafood. Fresh fish served either meùniere or provence style are two of the best dishes here. One drawback is that they play their music way too loud at dinner. Luckily the open-air disco doesn't get cranking until 10pm. The bar opens at 5pm.

✪ **Marie's.** Playa Flamingo near the Flamingo Marina Hotel. ☎ **506/654-4136.** Reservations not accepted. Sandwiches $2–$5.50, main courses $4–$15. V. Daily 6:30am–9pm.

Right in the middle of all the luxury hotels at Playa Flamingo is a great little place for a snack or a full meal. The menu is primarily sandwiches and other lunch foods, but on the blackboard behind the bar you'll find daily specials such as mahi-mahi (called "dorado" down here) and, from August to December, lobster and conch. You'll also find such Tico favorites as casados and ceviche. Tables in the open-air restaurant are made from slabs of tree trunks. Be sure to try the three-milks cake (a Nicaraguan speciality), which just might be the moistest cake on earth.

5 Playa Tamarindo

295 kilometers NW of San José; 73 kilometers SW of Liberia

Tamarindo is growing rapidly, but so far the development remains a mixture of mostly small hotels in a variety of price ranges and an eclectic array of restaurants. The beach itself is a long, wide swath of white sand that curves gently from one rocky headland to another. Behind the beach are low, dry hills that can be a very dreary brown in the dry season, but instantly turn green with the first brief showers of the rainy season. The dust that turns the hills brown can also make the main street through Tamarindo extremely unpleasant to walk along, so stick to the beach.

Though there is only one major resort hotel in town, the abundance of stylish smaller hotels have made Tamarindo one of the most popular beaches on this coast. Fishing boats bob at their moorings at the south end of the beach, and brown pelicans fish just outside the breakers. A sandy islet offshore makes a great destination if you are a strong swimmer; if you're not, it makes a great foreground for sunsets. Tamarindo is popular with surfers, who ply the break right here, or use it as a jumping-off place for Playas Grande, Langosta, Avellana, and Negra.

Nearby is Playa Grande, one of the last nesting sites for the giant leatherback turtle, the largest turtle in the world. This beach is usually too rough for swimming, but the beach break is becoming very popular.

ESSENTIALS

GETTING THERE & DEPARTING   By Plane   Sansa (☎ 506/233-0397, 506/233-5330, or 506/233-3258 in San José) flies nonstop to Tamarindo from San José's Juan Santamaría International Airport at 7am Monday through Saturday. The flight takes 45 minutes. Sansa also has a daily 11:15am flight that stops first in Tambor and Liberia before touching down in Tamarindo. This takes 1 1/2 hours. The one-way fare for either flight is $50.

Travelair (☎ 506/220-3054 or 506/232-7883) flies to Tamarindo daily at 7:40am and 12:30pm from San José's Pavas International Airport. The first flight makes one stop en route, the second is nonstop. The flights' durations are 1 hour 15 minutes and 50 minutes, respectively. Fare is $82 one-way, $136 round-trip.

Sansa flights leave Tamarindo for San José at 7:55am Monday through Saturday and daily at 1pm. Travelair flights leave for San José at 9:05am and 1:30pm daily.

By Bus   Two express buses leave San José daily for Tamarindo. The 3:30pm bus departs from Calle 14 between avenidas 3 and 5 and takes 5 1/2 hours. The one-way fare is $4.20. The 4pm departure leaves San José from Calle 20 between avenidas 1 and 3, takes 6 hours, and costs $4.10 for a one-way ticket.

Alternately, you can catch a bus to Santa Cruz from the Calle 20 station. Buses leave San José for Santa Cruz daily at 7:30 and 10:30am, and 2, 4, and 6pm. The trip's duration is 5 hours; one-way fare is $3.50. Buses leave Santa Cruz for Tamarindo daily at 4:30, 6:30, 8:30 and 11:30am, and 1 and 8:30pm. The trip's duration is 1 1/2 hours; one-way fare is $1.40.

If you are coming from Liberia, you can take a Santa Cruz or Nicoya bus (which run almost hourly), get off in the village of Belén, south of Filadelfia, and wait for the next Tamarindo-bound bus. However, since buses to Tamarindo are infrequent, you may have a long wait. It's generally best to go to Santa Cruz and pick up the Tamarindo-bound bus there.

A direct bus leaves Tamarindo for San José daily at 5:45am. Buses to Santa Cruz leave at 6, 6:30, 7, and 9am, and 12 and 3pm. In Santa Cruz you must transfer to a San José bus.

By Car   The most direct route is by way of the Tempisque River ferry. Take the Interamerican Highway west from San José, and 47 kilometers past the turnoff for Puntarenas, turn left toward the ferry. After crossing the Tempisque River, follow the signs for Nicoya, continuing north to Santa Cruz. About 16 kilometers north of Santa Cruz, just before the village of Belén, take the turnoff for Tamarindo. In another 20 kilometers take the left fork for Playa Tamarindo. The drive takes about 6 hours.

On Fridays and Saturdays, when beach traffic is heavy, it is often quicker to drive all the way north to Liberia and then come back south, thus avoiding the lines of cars waiting to take the ferry. This also applies if you are heading back to San José on a Sunday. See the section "Playas Flamingo, Potrero, Brasilito & Conchal," above, for more specific directions.

ORIENTATION   Arriving   The unpaved road leading into town runs parallel to the beach and dead-ends just past Cabinas Zully Mar. There are a couple of side roads off this main road that lead further on to Playa Langosta, where several of the newer hotels are to be found.

FUN ON AND OFF THE BEACH

Tamarindo is a long beach and though it can be great for swimming at times, it is often too rough. You also have to be careful when and where you swim on Tamarindo Beach. There are rocks just offshore in several places, some of which are exposed only at low tide. An encounter with one of these rocks could be nasty, especially if you are bodysurfing. Also, you should avoid swimming near the estuary mouth, where the currents can carry you out away from the beach.

If you want to just laze on the beach, you can pick up beach chairs, umbrellas, and mats at **Tamarindo Tour/Rentals** (☎ 506/654-4078), located on the right as you come into town. It is open daily, and doubles as the local information center and ICT office.

SNORKELING, SURFING & SEA KAYAKING   If you want to try any of these water sports while in Tamarindo, **Iguana Surf** (☎ 506/654-4019) is your one-stop source for equipment. To get there, head up the main road, turning left before the Zully Mar cabins (in the direction of the Hotel Pasatiempo) and then follow this road as it turns right and the shop will be prominently on your left. These folks are open daily and rent snorkeling equipment ($15 per day), boogie boards ($10 per day), sea kayaks ($35 per day), and surfboards ($20 per day). They also have half-day and hourly rates for many of these items.

You can also rent similar equipment at slightly lower rates from **Tamarindo Tour/ Rentals** (☎ 506/654-4078), open daily, and located on the right as you enter town.

SPORTFISHING   **Papagayo Excursions** (☎ 506/654-4254), which has its office at the Hotel Tamarindo Diria, offers folks a chance to go after the "big ones" that abound in the waters offshore. From here it takes only 20 minutes to reach the edge of the continental shelf and the waters preferred by marlin and sailfish. Although fishing is good all year, the peak season for billfish is between mid-April and August. Rates for the boat are $250 to $450 for a half day and $350 to $700 for a full day. Alternatively, you can contact **Tamarindo Sportfishing** (☎ 506/653-0090), which offers half-day trips for between $250 and $500 and full-day trips for between $350 and $800.

WATCHING NESTING SEA TURTLES   On nearby Playa Grande, leatherback sea turtles nest between August and February. One of the best times to see this activity is at night. For optimal viewing, join a night tour—they usually cost $12 per person. Only a few guides are licensed to operate these tours, and all groups are required to use only red-light flashlights. No flash photography is allowed because any sort of light can confuse the turtles and prevent them from laying their eggs. Before going on one of these tours, make sure that your guide will be following all precautions aimed at protecting the turtles. Playa Grande is just north of Tamarindo across a small river mouth. The trips simply ferry tourists across in small pangas, and then it is a 5- to 10-minute walk up Playa Grande.

BIKING, HORSEBACK RIDING & OTHER ACTIVITIES   Bikes are available for rent at **Tamarindo Tour/Rentals** (see above for phone and location), and you can arrange to go horseback riding through **Papagayo Excursions** (☎ 506/ 654-4254). Rates for horse rental, with a guide, are $25 for 2 hours. This company also offers 2-hour boat tours of the nearby estuary for $20 per person, and full-day trips to Palo Verde National Park for $75. The estuary tours, which head back into the mangrove swamp near Tamarindo, are very popular and are offered by several companies around town. Ask at your hotel, and you should be able to arrange one of these boat trips for under $13.

WHERE TO STAY
IN TOWN
Expensive

⚙ **Hotel El Jardín Del Eden.** Playa Tamarindo (Apdo. 1094-2050, San Pedro), San José. ☎/fax **506/653-0111.** 20 rms. A/C FAN. $80–$140 double. All rates include breakfast buffet. AE, MC, V.

Though it isn't right on the beach, this is the most luxurious and comfortable hotel in Tamarindo. It also offers the best service and some of the best meals in town. There are excellent views from the guest rooms, which are in Mediterranean-style buildings on a hill 150 yards from the beach. The owners of the hotel are French and have brought to their hotel a touch of sophistication that is often lacking at beach hotels in Costa Rica. Almost all the guest rooms have a balcony or private terrace with views of the Pacific. The large stone-tiled terraces, in particular, give you the sense of staying at your own private villa. The honeymoon room has a huge bathroom with a tub, while other rooms have showers only. Service here is very personal, and the staff can help you arrange various tours and excursions.

Dining/Entertainment: The thatched-roof, open-air dining room features excellent French and Italian meals with nightly specials.

Facilities: There are two swimming pools, one of which has a swim-up bar. There's also a whirlpool tub. The terraces surrounding the pools and tub have thatched palapas for shade, and there's even a little artificial waterfall flowing into the pool.

Hotel Capitan Suizo. Playa Tamarindo, Guanacaste. ☎ **506/653-0353** or 506/653-0075. Fax 506/653-0292. 22 rms, 8 bungalows. TEL. $95–$103 double; $130 bungalow. All rates include breakfast buffet; lower rates in off-season. AE, MC, V.

This quiet, luxurious hotel is located on the southern end of Tamarindo. The rooms are located in a series of two-story duplex buildings. The lower rooms have air-conditioning and private patios; the upper units have plenty of cross-ventilation and small balconies. All have large bathrooms and sitting rooms with a fold-down futon couch. The spacious bungalows are spread around the shady grounds, near the large free-form pool. Meals are all served in the open-air rancho. The hotel can arrange a wide variety of tours and activities.

⚙ **Sueño del Mar.** Playa Tamarindo, Guanacaste. ☎/fax **506/653-0284.** 3 rms, 1 suite. $75–$95 double; $95–$165 suite. All rates include breakfast. AE, MC, V.

This place is such a gem I hesitate to let the secret out. Located at the south end of Tamarindo beach on Punta Langosta, it's the little touches and innovative design that set Sueño del Mar apart. The rooms are actually small, but feature four-poster beds made from driftwood, African dolls on the window sills, Kokopeli candle holders, and open-air showers with sculpted anglefish, hand-painted tiles, and lush tropical plants. Fabrics are from Bali and Guatemala. Somehow, all this works well together, along with the requisite hammocks nestled under shade trees right on the beach. The suite is a separate small *casita* with its own kitchen, verandah, and sleeping loft. Breakfasts here are earning local renown. The beach right out front is rocky and a bit rough, but does reveal some nice, quiet tidal pools at low tide.

Tamarindo Diriá. Playa Tamarindo (Apdo. 6762-1000, San José), Guanacaste. ☎ **506/653-0031** or 506/290-4340. Fax 506/653-0032 or 506/290-4367. 70 rms. A/C TV TEL. $108 double; $134 triple. All rates include breakfast buffet. AE, MC, V.

This is Tamarindo's old reliable beachfront resort, and recent remodeling and steady upkeep have kept the hotel in pretty good shape. Wedged into a narrow piece of land between a dusty road and the beach, the Diriá manages to create its own little world of tropical gardens and palm trees. The remodeled rooms are done in contemporary pastel colors with red-tile floors. Some rooms have separate seating areas, and most have hair dryers, clock radios, and a basket of toiletries in the small bathroom. It is the beachfront location and attractive gardens that make this hotel a worthwhile place to stay. There are plans to add 125 new rooms on a plot of land across the street.

Dining/Entertainment: The big open-air bar/restaurant beside the pool features a different menu nightly, with prices for main dishes ranging from $5 to $10. The new Matapalo restaurant serves a continental menu out by the beach under an immense matapalo tree. There is also a lunch buffet in the garden most days.

Services: Tour desk, beach-equipment rentals, car-rental desk.

Facilities: Swimming pool, gift shop, game room. Across the street, there is a small commercial center, with a mini-mart.

Moderate

Hotel El Milagro. Playa Tamarindo (Apdo. 145-5150, Santa Cruz), Guanacaste. ☎ **506/653-0042** or 506/441-5102. Fax 506/441-8494. 33 rms. $45–$60 double with fan; $55–$70 double with A/C. Additional persons $10. All rates include continental breakfast. AE, MC, V.

This place started out as a restaurant but has expanded into an attractive little hotel on the edge of town. It's located across the road from the beach, and the rooms are lined up in two long rows facing each other behind the restaurant. The front wall of each room is made of louvered doors that can be opened up to give the room plenty of air. These doors open onto small semicircular patios. Rooms are comfortable and have high ceilings. Pretty gardens and some big, old, shade trees make El Milagro even more attractive. The restaurant serves excellent continental dishes, and there is a swimming pool with a swim-up bar. There's also a children's pool. Various tours and excursions can be arranged through the hotel.

Hotel Pasatiempo. Playa Tamarindo, Santa Cruz, Guanacaste. ☎/fax **506/653-0096.** 10 rms. Nov–Mar, $59 double; Apr–Oct, $39–$49 double. AE, MC, V.

This newer hotel is set back from the beach a couple of hundred yards in a grove of shady trees. The guest rooms are housed in duplex buildings with thatch roofs, and each room has its own patio with a hammock. There's plenty of space in every room and some even sleep five people. Each room bears the name of a different beach, and the bedroom walls all have hand-painted murals. In the center of the five duplexes is a small pool. There is also a popular rancho-style, open-air bar that has an evening happy hour and good snacks. The adjacent restaurant serves excellent pastas and fresh fish and is one of the best restaurants in town. There is also a small boutique here.

Inexpensive

In addition to the cabinas and hotel listed below, there are two campgrounds in Tamarindo: a private campground on the beach just before Tamarindo Tour/ Rentals on the outskirts of town; and **Tito's Camping** out by the Hotel Capitan Suizo. Tito's charges $2 per person.

Ⓢ Cabinas Marielos. Playa Tamarindo, Guanacaste. ☎ **506/653-0041.** 14 rms (all with bath). $18.80 double; $20.90 triple; $25 quad. No credit cards.

This place is located down a palm-shaded driveway across the road from the beach. Rooms are clean and fairly new, though small and simply furnished. There are tile floors and wooden chairs on the patios. Some of the bathrooms do not have doors, but they are clean. There is even a kitchen that guests can use, and the garden provides a bit of shade. The hotel provides a laundry service and can arrange turtle tours.

Cabinas Zully Mar. Tamarindo, Guanacaste. ☎ **506/226-4732.** Fax: 506/286–0191. 27 rms (all with bath). $18.67–$36.58 double; $23.55–$42.55 triple. AE, MC, V.

The Zully Mar has long been a favorite of budget travelers staying in Tamarindo. The newer rooms, which are in a two-story, white-stucco building with a wide, curving staircase on the outside, have air-conditioning and are more comfortable. The doors to these guest rooms are particularly interesting; they're hand-carved with pre-Columbian motifs. There are also high ceilings with fans, tile floors, a long verandah, and large bathrooms. The older rooms are much smaller and more spartan. Although there are mango trees out front for shade, there is little other landscaping, and the sandy grounds look a bit unkempt. Don't let this bother you: Miles of beach are just across the street, as are a popular restaurant and bar.

Hotel Pozo Azul. Playa Tamarindo, Santa Cruz, Guanacaste. ☎ **506/653-0280** or 506/653-0286. 27 rms (all with bath). $22.60–$28.60 double or triple; $35.80 quad. No credit cards.

This is one of the first hotels you'll spot as you drive into Tamarindo proper. It's on the left side of the road and therefore not on the beach. There isn't much shade on the grounds, but there are swimming pools for adults and kids. In the 17 rooms with air-conditioning, there are also hot plates, refrigerators, tables and chairs, large windows, and *pilas* (sinks) for washing clothes. Some rooms have covered parking to keep your car out of the blistering heat. There is no restaurant here, so you'll have to either cook your own meals or walk into town to one of the restaurants. In recent years, the Pozo Azul has become a surfer hangout.

IN PLAYA GRANDE
Expensive
♥ **Las Tortugas Hotel.** Playa Grande, Guanacaste. ☎/fax **506/680-0765.** 11 rms, 2 suites. A/C. Nov–Mar, $85 double, $125 suite; Apr–Oct, $50 double, $75 suite. No credit cards.

Playa Grande is best known for the leatherback turtles that nest here, and much of the beach is now part of Las Baulas National Park, which was created to protect the turtles. However, this beach is also popular with surfers, who make up a large percentage of the clientele at the beachfront Las Tortugas Hotel. The rooms here are all quite large and most have interesting stone floors and semicircular shower stalls. High ceilings help keep the rooms cool, but there is also air-conditioning in many rooms. The upper suite has a curving staircase that leads up to its second room. The owners led the fight to have the area declared a national park, and also do everything possible to protect the turtles. The hotel's restaurant is on the second floor, giving it a view of the waves and beach. There is also a small bar, a turtle-shaped swimming pool, and a jacuzzi.

WHERE TO DINE
MODERATE
♥ **Coconut Café.** On the left as you come into town. No phone. Reservations not accepted. Main courses $6.45–$16.60. No credit cards. Daily 6–10pm. INTERNATIONAL.

This is one of Tamarindo's more atmospheric restaurants. A thatch roof, wicker furniture, and fresh flower arrangements all set on a raised deck add up to a gringo fantasy of the tropics, but isn't that what you came down here for anyway? The Coconut Café serves some of the most imaginative food in town, including such dishes as red chicken curry, mahi-mahi macadamia, shrimp brochettes, and fondue. However, because the menu changes daily, you can expect other equally enticing dishes when you visit. Below the dining room there is a comfortable lounge. The only drawback here is that the very dusty road is only a few feet away.

El Milagro. On the left as you enter town. ☎ **506/653-0042.** Reservations not accepted. Main courses $5.10–$14.50. AE, MC, V. Daily 7am–11pm. CONTINENTAL/COSTA RICAN.

Lush gardens and wide terraces make this the most attractive restaurant in town, and you might even be able to go for a swim in the adjacent pool if you're so inclined. Reproductions of pre-Columbian stone statues stand in the gardens and the bar has carved-wood columns. On those rare occasions when it is raining, you can retreat to one of the indoor dining rooms. Though the emphasis here is on seafood, you'll also find such unexpected offerings as chicken Cordon Bleu, fried Camembert, banana flambé, crêpes with ice cream, and hot fruits in amaretto sauce.

INEXPENSIVE

In addition to the places listed below, there's an unnamed restaurant in a basic wooden shack, next to the Sunrise Café, where I've had some of the freshest fish dinners of my life. The **Soda Natural,** next to Cabinas Marielos, is also a good, inexpensive spot for breakfasts and lunch.

Fiesta del Mar. At the end of the main road. No phone. Reservations not accepted. Main courses $3.95–$14. No credit cards. Daily 8am–11pm. STEAK/SEAFOOD.

Located across the circle from the beach, the Fiesta del Mar specializes in steaks and seafood cooked over a wood fire. Try the grilled steak in garlic sauce for $8 or the whole fried fish for $4.50. The open-air dining area is edged with greenery and has a thatched roof, so it feels very tropical. There's also live music several nights a week.

Ⓢ **Restaurant Zully Mar.** At the end of the road. No phone. Most items $3–$12.50. No credit cards. Daily 7am–11pm. COSTA RICAN.

This restaurant, opposite the hotel of the same name, is right on the beach at the end of the road that leads into Tamarindo. It's definitely a step above the average Tico-style open-air restaurant. The food is good, and the view can't be beat. Sit and watch the boats bob in the swells just offshore while you dine on fresh fish sautéed in garlic. The bar is a popular hangout with locals and tourists, and a big bowl of ceviche accompanied by a few drinks is a favorite order. Be forewarned: This place is often mobbed, especially on weekends, when they sometimes set up a huge stereo system and blast dance music.

✪ **Panadería Johann.** On the road into town. No phone. Reservations not accepted. Prices: $2–$9. No credit cards. Daily 6am–8pm. BAKERY/PIZZA.

There are always fresh-baked goodies at this Belgian-run bakery on the outskirts of Tamarindo, although what you might find on any given day is never certain. Possibilities include buttery croissants, vegetarian pizzas, chocolate éclairs, and different types of bread. A whole pizza goes for around $9. If you are heading out to the beach for the day, be sure to stop by and pick up some bread or pastries. There are a few tables out back where you can eat your pizza. There is also a separate open-air restaurant, El Cocodrillo, right next door.

6 Playa Junquillal

30 kilometers W of Santa Cruz; 20 kilometers S of Tamarindo

Playa Junquillal (pronounced hoon-key-*awl*) is a long, windswept beach that, for most of its length, is backed by grasslands. This gives it a very different feel from other beaches on this coast. There is really no village to speak of here, so if you're heading out this way, plan on getting away from it all. It's not a cliché—Junquillal is truly off the beaten path. Once here, your options for what to do are limited to whatever is on offer at your chosen hotel. However, the long beach is good for strolling, and the sunsets are superb.

ESSENTIALS

GETTING THERE & DEPARTING   By Plane   The nearest airport with regularly scheduled flights is in Tamarindo. You can arrange a taxi from the airport to Playa Junquillal.

By Bus   An express bus leaves San José daily at 2pm from the corner of Calle 20 and Avenida 3. The trip's duration is 5 hours; one-way fare is $2.40.

Alternately, you can take a bus to Santa Cruz (see "Playas Flamingo, Potrero, Brasilito & Conchal" for details) and from there, take the 6:30pm bus to Playa Junquillal. The ride takes 1^1/$_2$ hours, and the one-way fare is $1.20.

The one express bus to San José departs Playa Junquillal daily at 5am. There is also a daily bus to Santa Cruz that departs at the same time.

By Car   Take the Interamerican Highway from San José. 47 kilometers past the turnoff for Puntarenas, turn left toward the Tempisque ferry. After crossing the Tempisque River, continue north through Nicoya to Santa Cruz. In Santa Cruz, head west 14 kilometers to the town of 27 de Abril, which is where the pavement ends. From here it is another 18 kilometers to Playa Junquillal.

FUN ON THE BEACH

Other than walking on the beach, swimming when the surf isn't too strong, and exploring tide pools, there isn't much to do here, which is just fine with me. This beach is ideal for anyone who just wants to relax without any distractions. Bring a few good books. Actually, the larger hotels here—Antumalal, Iguanazul, and Villa Serena—all offer plenty of activities and facilities, including volleyball, swimming pools, tennis courts, and even a disco (at Hotel Antumalal). Sportfishing trips can also be arranged at most hotels. At the Iguanazul, guests can rent bikes, which is a good way to get up and down this beach.

WHERE TO STAY & DINE
EXPENSIVE

✪ **Hotel Antumalal.** Playa Junquillal (Apdo. 49-5150, Santa Cruz), Guanacaste. ☎/fax **506/680-0506.** 23 rms. Dec–Apr, $85 double, $95 triple; May–Nov, $55 double, $60 triple. AE, DC, MC, V.

Located at the end of the road into Playa Junquillal, the Antumalal is the lushest and oldest hotel on the beach. The owners are Italian, so don't be surprised if you encounter Italian tour groups. The big, old shade trees and lush gardens create a world of tropical tranquility that is perfect for romance and relaxation. Guest rooms are all in duplex buildings with stucco walls and beautiful murals on inside walls. Out front you'll find a big patio with a hammock, while inside there are brick floors, colorful Guatemalan bedspreads, and big bathrooms. When I last visited, construction was well underway on nine new suites.

Dining/Entertainment: The dining room is housed under a huge, high-peaked rancho that has a fascinating driftwood chandelier hanging from the ceiling. The menu includes plenty of good Italian dishes. There's a bar here in the restaurant, plus another beside the pool. There is also a small discotheque.

Services: Horseback riding, boat charters for fishing and scuba diving.

Facilities: The swimming pool, with its swim-up bar, is only a few steps from the beach and is beautiful at night when the underwater lights are on. Other facilities include a tennis court and modest exercise room.

MODERATE

✪ **Iguanazul Hotel.** Playa Junquillal (Apdo. 130-1550, Santa Cruz), Guanacaste. ☎/fax **506/680-0783** or 506/232-1423. 24 rms. Dec–Apr, $60–$80 double, $70–$85 triple; May–Nov, $45–$65 double, $52–$70 triple. AE, MC, V.

Though the gravel road leading up to this hotel doesn't make Iguanazul seem too promising, once you step through the entryway and see the resortlike pool, you may well be captivated. Set on a windswept, grassy bluff above a rocky beach, Iguanazul is far from the madding crowd. This is definitely a spot for sun worshippers who like to have a good time, and the clientele tends to be young and active. The pool is large, as is the surrounding patio area. There's a volleyball court, and the bar plays lively classic rock throughout most of the day. Don't, however, expect a tropical setting; grasslands surround the hotel, which gives the area the feel of Cape Cod or the Outer Banks. Guest rooms are beautifully decorated with basket lampshades, wicker furniture, red-tile floors, high ceilings, and blue-and-white tile bathrooms. The higher prices are for air-conditioned rooms.

There are also plenty of things to do around here. You can rent horses, bikes, and body boards. Captain Gene runs sportfishing charters out of the hotel, and there are board games, dartboards, and table tennis for those who find the sun and sea monotonous. The hotel also maintains a well-stocked gift shop, and the food here is excellent.

⑤ **Hotel Villa Serena.** Playa Junquillal (Apdo. 17, Santa Cruz), Guanacaste. ☎/fax **506/680-0573.** 10 rms. $65 double; $75 triple; $85 quad. Rates are substantially lower during off-season. AE, MC, V.

Each of these individual bungalows is surrounded by neatly manicured lawns and gardens. The hotel is directly across the street from the beach, which is free of rocks and excellent for swimming most of the time. The hotel's main building houses the second-floor dining room, which serves filling and tasty European-style meals and has an enticing view of the beach. Art nouveau decorations and European art abound throughout the building, giving the hotel a very sophisticated feel for such a remote location. The rooms are quite spacious and have ceiling fans, dressing rooms, and large bathrooms. Each has its own covered patio, and only steps away is the small pool. The German owner is very friendly and helpful, and can arrange horseback riding or fishing tours.

INEXPENSIVE

In addition to the lodgings listed below, **Camping Los Malinches** has wonderful campsites on fluffy grass, amidst manicured gardens, set on a bluff above the beach. Camping will run you $7 per tent, but the fee entitles you to bathroom and shower privileges.

⑤ **Hotel El Castillo Divertido.** Playa Junquillal, Santa Cruz, Guanacaste. ☎ **506/680-0015** in Santa Cruz. 7 rms. Dec–Apr, $30 double; May–Nov, $23 double. No credit cards.

Quite a few people have moved to Costa Rica from around the world in hopes of living out fantasy lives impossible in their home countries. This fanciful hotel is just such a creation. Built by a young German, the hotel is a tropical rendition of a classic medieval castle (well, sort of). Ramparts and a turret with a rooftop bar certainly grab the attention of passersby. Guest rooms here are fairly small, though rates are also some of the lowest in the area. Ask for an upstairs room with a balcony. The hotel is about 500 meters from the beach.

Hibiscus Hotel. Playa Junquillal (Apdo. 163-5150, Santa Cruz), Guanacaste. ☎ **506/ 780-0737.** 5 rms (all with private bath). $32.50 double, $37 triple. No credit cards.

Though the accommodations here are very simple, the German owner makes sure that everything is always clean and in top shape. The grounds are pleasantly shady, and the beach is just across the road. The rooms have cool Mexican-tile floors and firm beds.

7 Playa Sámara

35 kilometers S of Nicoya; 245 kilometers W of San José

Playa Sámara is a pretty beach on a long horseshoe-shaped bay. Unlike most of the rest of the Pacific coast, the water here is excellent for swimming, since an offshore island and rocky headlands break up most of the surf. Because Playa Sámara is easily accessible by bus or car, and because there are several cheap cabinas, sodas, and discos here, this beach is popular with young Ticos out for a weekend of beach partying, and families seeking a quick and inexpensive getaway. In the wake of this heavy traffic, the beach can get trashed. However, the calm waters and steep cliffs on the far side of the bay make this a very attractive spot, and the beach is long and wide. Directly behind the main beach is a wide, flat valley that stretches inland and to the north.

ESSENTIALS

GETTING THERE & DEPARTING   By Plane   Sansa (in San José: ☎ 233-0397, 233-3258, or 233-5330) flies to Carillo (15 minutes south of Sámara) at 7am Monday through Saturday, and at 11:15am on Sunday, from San José's Juan Santamaría International Airport. The flight makes two stops en route. The flight's duration is 1 hour and 30 minutes; fare is $50 each way.

Travelair (in San José: ☎ 220-3054 or 232-7883) flies to Carillo daily at 7:40am from San José's Pavas International Airport. The flight's duration is 40 minutes; fare is $75 one-way, $122 round-trip.

The Sansa flight leaves Carillo for San José at 8:50am Monday through Saturday, and at 1:30pm on Sunday. Travelair flies out of Carillo daily at 9:40am.

By Bus   An express bus leaves San José daily at noon from Calle 14 between avenidas 3 and 5. The trip's duration is 6 hours; one-way fare is $4.75.

Alternately, you can take a bus from this same San José station to Nicoya and then catch a second bus from Nicoya to Sámara. Buses leave San José for Nicoya daily at 6, 8, and 10am, and 12, 1, 2:30, 3, and 5pm. The trip's duration is 6 hours; fare is $3.90. Buses leave Nicoya for Sámara and Carillo daily at 8am, and 2 and 3pm. The trip's duration is 1¹/₂ hours. The fare to Sámara is $1.05; fare to Carillo is $1.25.

The express bus to San José leaves daily at 4am. Buses for Nicoya leave daily at 5:30 and 6:30am. Buses leave Nicoya for San José daily at 4, 7:30, and 9am, and 12, 2:30, and 5pm.

By Car   Follow the directions for Playa Junquillal above, but in Nicoya, follow the signs south to a road that has recently been paved all the way to the beach. Rumor has it an important government official has a beach house here.

ORIENTATION   Arriving   Sámara is a busy little town at the bottom of a steep hill. The main road heads straight into town, passing the soccer field before coming to an end at the beach. Just on the edge of town is a road to the left that leads to several of the more expensive hotels listed below. This road also leads to Playa Carillo and the Guanamar Resort.

FUN ON AND OFF THE BEACH

Aside from sitting on the sand and soaking up the sun, the main activities in Playa Sámara seem to be hanging out in the sodas and dancing into the early morning hours. If you stay close to the center of town (by the soccer field), expect to stay up until the disco closes down.

You'll find that the beach is nicer and cleaner down at the south end near Las Brisas del Pacifico hotel. For fewer crowds, head south to Playa Carillo, a long, flat beach about 20 minutes from Sámara.

SPELUNKING   Spelunkers will want to head 62 kilometers northeast of Playa Sámara on the road to the Tempisque ferry. Here, at Barra Honda National Park, there is an extensive system of caves.

WHERE TO STAY

EXPENSIVE

✪ **Villas Playa Sámara.** Playa Sámara (200 meters north of Centro Colón, Avenida 5 and Calle 38, San José), Guanacaste. ☎ **506/256-8228.** Fax 506/221-7222. 56 rms. $125 double; $185 quad. Low season rates available. AE, MC, V.

Located 5 minutes south of town, this is the newest luxury hotel in Sámara, and consequently the gardens are still a bit sparse. Other than that, this beachfront resort is a great place. Built to resemble a village, the resort consists of numerous bungalows varying in size from one to three bedrooms. Attractive though not overly luxurious, the villas are outfitted with bamboo furniture, and there are tiled baths (hot water is provided by rather noisy water heaters). All the villas have kitchens and patios, and some of the nice touches include colorful bedspreads and artwork, basket lampshades, and vertical blinds on the windows. White-stucco exterior walls and red-tile roofs give the villas a Mediterranean look.

Dining/Entertainment: The open-air restaurant overlooks the pool and serves good seafood. There is also a casino above the restaurant.

Services: Horse and bicycle rentals.

Facilities: The swimming pool here is beautiful at night and has a swim-up bar and adjacent cold-water whirlpool tub. Other facilities include volleyball and badminton courts.

MODERATE

✪ **Hotel Las Brisas del Pacífico.** Playa Sámara (Apdo. 11917-1000, San José), Guanacaste. ☎/fax **506/680-0876** or 506/233-9840 in San José. 36 rms. Nov–Apr, $60–$95 double, $70–$105 triple; May–Oct, $45–$75 double or triple. AE, MC, V.

Located on the same road as the Marbella, this hotel is set amid very shady grounds right on a quiet section of the beach, and backs up a steep hill. Most of the rooms are up a long and steep flight of stairs at the top of the hill. However, in exchange for climbing the stairs, you do get an excellent view of the bay. These hilltop rooms have large balconies and walls of glass that take in the views. The third-floor rooms are the largest here, but due to the design, the second-floor rooms actually have the best views. At the base of the hill, there are rooms in stucco duplexes with steeply pitched tile roofs and red-tile patios. These rooms have cold-water showers only, but it's never cool enough here to warrant hot showers. Only a few steps from the beach, there is a small pool with a cold-water whirlpool. The main dining room is a breezy open-air restaurant surrounded by lush garden plantings. The menu changes daily, but the emphasis is always on German and European cuisine. Entree prices range from $6.50 to $12.50. There is also a second pool and bar at the top of the hill.

Hotel Marbella. Playa Sámara (Edificio Cristal, Avenida 1a, San José), Guanacaste. ☎ /fax **506/ 233-9980.** 14 rms, 6 apts. Nov–Mar, $44 double, $57 triple, $63.50 apt; Apr–Oct, $37 double, $47 triple, $53 apt. Weekly discounts available on apartment rentals. AE, MC, V.

Though it is a bit of a walk to the beach and the immediate surroundings are none too appealing, this small German-run hotel is properly tropical in decor. You'll find the Marbella just around the corner from the road that leads down to the soccer fields and the beach. Guest rooms are fairly large and have red-tile floors and woven mats for ceilings. There are open closets and modern bathrooms with hot water. The apartments are a good choice for families or long-term stays. There's a small swimming pool in a gravel courtyard, and a second-floor dining room with rattan chairs and a bamboo-fronted bar. All the rooms have a small balcony or porch, though not necessarily any sort of a view. You can inquire here about the three A-frame chalets across the street. The dining room only serves breakfast these days, but you'll also find a bar and snack bar here.

INEXPENSIVE

In addition to the accommodations listed below, you'll find a slew of very inexpensive places to stay along the road into town and around the soccer field. Many of the rooms at these places are less accommodating than your average jail cell. However, you can pitch a tent right by the beach for a few dollars at **Camping Cocos,** where you can also use their basic showers and bathrooms.

🟢 **Cabinas Belvedere.** Playa Sámara, Guanacaste. ☎ **506/685-5004.** 3 rms (each with private bath). $24.50 double. Rate includes continental breakfast. No credit cards.

This tropical Swiss chalet is located on the hillside across the street from the Hotel Marbella on the inland edge of town. The rooms are rather small, but they are immaculate and have fans and mosquito nets. The clinchers for me, though, are the framed velvet paintings on the walls.

🟢 **Hotel Giada.** Playa Sámara, Nicoya, Guanacaste. ☎ **506/222-7553** or 506/222-7443. Fax 506/223-5426. 13 rms (all with bath). $31 double; $39 triple; $45 quad. All rates include continental breakfast. MC, V.

This new Italian-owned hotel is located on the left-hand side of the main road into town, about 150 meters before the beach. The rooms are all very clean and comfortable, and even have a small balcony. Breakfasts are served in a cool, shady central gazebo. The management is very helpful and can arrange dive or fishing expeditions and horseback riding trips.

WHERE TO DINE

There are numerous inexpensive **sodas** in Sámara, and most of the hotels have their own dining rooms. In town, try the following.

Colochos Bar. On the main street through town. ☎ **506/680-0445.** Reservations not accepted. Main courses $4.90–$15.50. No credit cards. Daily 11am–10pm. COSTA RICAN/ SEAFOOD.

This open-air rancho restaurant on the main road into town offers a wide selection of seafoods. There are four different types of ceviche, lobster dishes, paella, and plenty of shrimp plates. Prices are very reasonable and portions are large. Though there's a thatch roof over your head, you'll find lace doilies on the tables.

NEARBY PLACES TO STAY & DINE

✪ **Guanamar Beach & Sportfishing Resort.** Puerto Carillo, Guanacaste (Apdo. 7-1880-1000, San José; or in the U.S: Costa Sol International, 1717 North Bayshore Dr., Suite 3333, Miami, FL 33132). ☎ **506/293-4544** or 800/245-8420 in the U.S. Fax 506/293-4839 or 305/858-7478 in the U.S. 42 rms. A/C TV TEL. $110–$120 double; $165 suite. MC, V.

About 20 minutes south of Sámara you'll find the Guanamar resort, which is set on a hillside above long, flat Playa Carillo. The location provides some spectacular views, but it is a long walk down to the beach and a hot walk back up. However, you can spend your time on the extensive hardwood decks that surround the hotel's pool. These decks give the resort's main public areas the feel of a huge treehouse. For many years this was a private sportfishing resort, and fishing for marlin and sailfish is still one of the main attractions of Guanamar. Guest rooms are spacious, though not overly attractive. However, the views from the decks and patios make up for any lack in the interior decor. Try to get one of the newer bungalow rooms.

Dining/Entertainment: The dining room is housed in a large rancho at one end of the deck that passes by the swimming pool. At the other end of the deck is a second rancho that houses another bar area. In the dining room, there are trunks of palm trees growing up through the wooden floor. The menu includes international dishes, including some Japanese dishes, with prices ranging from $6.80 to $15.50 for entrees.

Services: Room service, tour arrangements, fishing-boat charters, and boat tours. Bicycle, boogie-board, horse, snorkeling-equipment, and water-ski rentals.

Facilities: The swimming pool is built up and out from the hillside and is surrounded by an attractive hardwood deck. There is also a gift shop.

✪ **Hotel Punta Islita.** Apdo. 6054-1000, San José. ☎ **506/296-3817.** Fax 506/231-0715. 20 rms, 4 suites. A/C TV. $132 double; $175 suite. All rates include breakfast. AE, MC, V.

Set on a high bluff between two mountain ridges that meet the sea, Punta Islita is isolated. Although it is possible to drive here, most guests opt to fly into the nearby airstrip. Punta Islita is just one beach down from Guanamar, but if you do drive, it is best to come over on the Naranjo ferry from Puntarenas, and then up through Jicarral and Coyote. The rooms here are done in a Santa Fe style, with red Mexican floor tiles, neo-Navajo print bedspreads, and calm, adobe-colored walls offset with sky-blue doors and trim. Each room has a king-size bed, stocked minibar, and a private patio with a hammock. The suites also come with a separate sitting room and a private two-person jacuzzi. The hotel also rents one larger villa, with a fully equipped kitchenette, for longer stays. The beach below the hotel is a small crescent of gray-white sand with a calm protected section at the northern end. The hotel will shuttle you up and back. Otherwise, it's about a 10 minute walk away.

Dining/Entertainment: Meals are all served in the large, thatched rancho, which also houses the hotel's bar and sitting area. When you're this isolated, the meals had better measure up, and so far Punta Islita has met the challenge. The emphasis is on fresh seafood in light nouvelle French sauces, but the steak in two-pepper sauce is also excellent.

Services: Laundry service and nightly turndown.

Facilities: The small tile pool and adjoining jacuzzi are set on the edge of the bluff and create the illusion of blending into the ocean far below. The hotel also has two tennis courts, a small gym, a golf driving range, water-sports equipment, bicycle and 4x4 rentals, a conference center, a tour desk, and a small gift shop.

8 Playa Nosara

55 kilometers SW of Nicoya; 266 kilometers W of San José

Playa Nosara is actually several beaches, almost all of which are nearly deserted most of the time. Because the village of Nosara is several kilometers from the beach, and because the land near the beach has been turned into a large, spread-out resort community, Nosara has been spared the sort of ugly, uncontrolled growth characteristic of many other Guanacaste beaches. All of the hotels are spread out, and most are tucked away down side roads. There is not the hotels-on-top-of-hotels feeling that you get at Playa Flamingo. In fact, on first arriving here, it's hard to believe there are any hotels around at all. Nosara has long been popular with North American retirees, and they too have made sure that their homes are not crammed cheek-by-jowl in one spot. Their houses are hidden amongst all the trees that make Nosara one of the greenest spots on the Nicoya Peninsula. So, if you are looking for reliably sunny weather and a bit of tropical greenery, this is a good bet.

The best way to get to Nosara is to fly; however, with everything so spread out, that makes getting around once you've arrived difficult. The roads to and in Nosara are in horrendous shape, and though there has long been talk of some sections being widened and paved, it will probably still be quite a few years before the blacktop reaches Playa Nosara.

ESSENTIALS

GETTING THERE & DEPARTING   By Plane   Sansa (in San José: ☎ 506/233-0397, 506/233-3258, or 506/233-5330) flies one flight a day to Nosara, departing from San José's Juan Santamaría International Airport at 7am. The flight makes one stop en route. Flight duration is 1 hour and 10 minutes; fare is $50 each way.

Travelair (in San José: ☎ 506/220-3054 or 506/232-7883) also makes one flight a day to Nosara. It departs from San José's Pavas International Airport at 10:45am and makes one stop en route. The flight's duration is 1 hour; fare is $82 one-way, $122 round-trip.

One Sansa flight a day departs Nosara at 8:25am. Travelair flights take off daily at 11:55am.

By Bus   An express bus leaves San José daily at 6:15am from Calle 14 between avenidas 3 and 5. The trip's duration is 7 hours. One-way fare is $4.25.

You can also take a bus from San José to Nicoya (see "Playa Sámara" for details), and then catch a second bus from Nicoya to Nosara. A bus leaves Nicoya for Nosara daily at 1pm. Trip duration is 3 hours; one-way fare is $1.10.

The bus to San José leaves daily at 4pm. The bus to Nicoya leaves daily at 6am. Buses leave Nicoya for San José daily at 4, 7:30, and 9am, and 12, 2:30, and 4pm.

By Car   Follow the directions above for getting to Playa Sámara, but watch for a fork in the road a few kilometers before you reach that beach. The right-hand fork leads, after another 22 kilometers of terrible road, to Nosara.

ORIENTATION   Arriving   The village of Nosara is about 5 kilometers inland from the beach, however, most of the hotels listed here are on the beach itself.

FUN ON AND OFF THE BEACH

There are several beaches at Nosara, including the long, curving Playa Guiones, Playa Nosara, and, my personal favorite, diminutive Playa Pelada. This latter is a short, white-sand beach lined with sea grasses and mangroves. However, there isn't too much sand at high tide, so you'll want to hit the beach when the tide's out. At either end of the beach there are rocky outcroppings that reveal tide pools at low tide. Surfing and bodysurfing are both good here; Playa Guiones in particular is garnering quite a reputation as a consistent and rideable beach break. Because the village of Nosara is several miles inland, these beaches are very clean, secluded, and quiet.

When evening rolls around, don't expect a major party scene. Nightlife in Nosara seems to be centered around the two bars located across from each other by the town's soccer field.

FISHING CHARTERS Most of the hotels in the area can arrange fishing charters for $250 to $300 for a half day or $400 to $600 for a full day. These rates are for one to four people. You can also contact **Pesca Bahia Garza** (☎ 506/680-0856) and arrange a half-day or full-day fishing trip.

BIRD AND SEA TURTLE WATCHING Birdwatchers should explore the mangrove swamps around the estuary mouth of the Río Nosara. Just walk north from Playa Peleada and follow the river bank; explore the paths into the mangroves.

If your timing is right, you can do a night tour to nearby Playa Ostional to watch nesting olive Ridley sea turtles. These turtles come ashore by the thousands in a mass egg-laying phenomenon known as an *arribada*. These arribadas take place 4 to 10 times between July and November, with each lasting between 3 and 10 days. Consider yourself very lucky if you should happen to be around during one of these fascinating natural phenomena. Even if it is not turtle-nesting season, you may want to look into going up to Playa Ostional. During the dry season, you can usually get there in a regular car, but during the rainy season, you'll need four-wheel drive. This beach is part of Ostional National Wildlife Refuge. At the northwest end of the refuge is India Point, which is known for its tidepools and rocky outcrops.

WHERE TO STAY
MODERATE

Estancia Nosara. Playa Nosara (Apdo. 37, Bocas de Nosara), Guanacaste. ☎/fax **506/680-0378.** 10 rms. $42–$51 double; $50–$59 triple; $58–$67 quad. MC, V.

Although this hotel is a mile or so from the beach, it's set amid shady jungle trees and has a swimming pool and tennis court, which together make Estancia Nosara a good value. There's a man-made waterfall tumbling from a small hill of stones near the pool and reproductions of pre-Columbian stone statues in the lush garden. The guest rooms are in two buildings and have red-tile floors, kitchenettes, high ceilings, overhead fans, showers with hot water, and plenty of closet space. There's a large open-air restaurant serving moderately priced meals. The hotel rents out horses, boogie boards, snorkling equipment, and bikes. A full day of fishing arranged through the hotel will cost $400 for the boat, which can take up to four people.

Hotel Villa Taype. Playa Nosara (Apdo. 8-5233, Bocas de Nosara), Guanacaste. ☎/fax **506/680-0763.** 12 rms, 6 bungalows. $55–$75 double; $75–$95 triple. V.

Although a relatively new hotel, this place has already changed its name and management once. Construction is underway on additional bungalows, and the gardens still have a few years to go before they fill in the bare spots left over from the initial building. The room decor is very simple, but quite attractive. There are white-tile floors, high ceilings, overhead fans, and well-designed bathrooms. The least expensive rooms are those without air-conditioning. All have patios, but the bungalows have their own little ranchito, with a sitting area and hammock. The dining room, with its wood ceiling and arched windows overlooking the pool, serves moderately priced meals; the swimming pool itself has a swim-up bar. There is also a tennis court here, and you can rent bodyboards, surfboards, tennis rackets, and snorkeling gear. Best of all, the beach is only 100 yards away.

Hotel Playas De Nosara. Playa Nosara (Apdo. 4, Bocas de Nosara), Guanacaste. ☎ /fax **506/680-0495.** 20 rms. $75 double; $85 triple. Rates higher during Christmas and Easter weeks. No credit cards.

Perched high on a hill above both Playa Pelada and Playa Guiones, this older hotel has the best views in the area, if not necessarily the best accommodations. In the 5 years I've been visiting, the place has always had the feeling of someone's unfinished backyard project. After years of delays, the large kidney-shaped pool may finally be near completion, but the unfinished construction all around it will probably continue for some time. So far, all the rooms overlook Playa Guiones and have balconies so you can take in the great view. The gardens, though fairly lush, seem untended. The circular restaurant holds a high perch over Playa Pelada and is an excellent spot to take in the sunset.

INEXPENSIVE

A Bed-and-Breakfast

✪ **Almost Paradise.** Playa Nosara (Apdo. 15, Bocas de Nosara), Guanacaste. No phone. Fax 506/685-5004. 6 rms (each with bath). $36.50 double, including breakfast. No credit cards.

Located on the hill above Playa Pelada, this delightful bed-and-breakfast is aptly named. This older wood building is a welcome relief from all the concrete and cinder block so common in Costa Rican construction. The rooms are simple and clean, and feature colorful local artwork. All have access to an inviting covered verandah, with strung hammocks and an ocean view. The attached restaurant has gone through several incarnations over the years, yet has remained a local favorite.

A Cabina

🟢 **Cabinas Chorotega.** Nosara, Guanacaste. ☎ **506/680-0836.** 8 rms (two with private bath). $13–$16 double. No credit cards.

Located on the outskirts of Nosara village, Cabinas Chorotega is about 5 kilometers from the beach, so you'll need to have some sort of transportation if you stay here and want to go the beach. The rooms are very basic but clean, and the rooms with private baths are a particularly good value. Some rooms have more windows and are quite a bit brighter than others, so look at a couple of rooms if you can.

A NEARBY PLACE TO STAY & DINE

Villaggio La Guaria Morada. Playa Garza (Apdo. 860-1007, Centro Colón, San José), Guanacaste. ☎ **506/680-0784** or 233-2476 in San José. Fax 506/680-0784. 30 bungalows. $75 double; $90 triple; $105 quad. All rates include continental breakfast. MC, V.

This is the most expensive and luxurious hotel in this part of the peninsula and cultivates an exclusive, clublike ambience. Though the landscape all around is cattle pastures, once you pass through the guarded gate, you enter a tropical fantasy compound. A huge, three-story thatched-roof building serves as a restaurant, bar, and casino, and surrounding this impressive building are the smaller thatched-roof bungalows. The overall impression is of a tropical Indian village. Directly in front of the resort is a three-quarter-mile curving beach, and a short walk away is a smaller beach of pink sand. When I last visited, the staff spoke of a recent ownership change and plans to focus on selling time-shares to the bungalows.

The guest rooms, in either individual or duplex bungalows, are simple, yet comfortable. The louvered walls open up to connect the patio with the bedroom, creating a single large living area. There are interesting bamboo ceilings and overhead fans, and in the bathroom you'll find hot water provided by showerhead heaters. The overall effect is of a tropical-Mediterranean fusion.

Dining/Entertainment: The menu here is heavy on seafood and Italian dishes, and the food is quite good, though you'll probably spend most of your meal admiring the impressive thatched roof. Prices range from $6.25 to $21.65 for entrees. In the same building, you'll find a very comfortable bar and a small open-air casino.

Services: Horse rentals, fishing charters, tour arrangements.

Facilities: The swimming pool, made with small blue tiles, is quite lovely. There are also some *palapas* for shade, and a gift shop.

WHERE TO DINE

Doña Olga's. On the beach at Playa Pelada. No phone. Reservations not accepted. Main courses $1.75–$16. No credit cards. Daily 6:30am–10pm. COSTA RICAN.

Little more than a roof with some tables under it, Olga's is still one of the most popular restaurants in Nosara. Gringos and Ticos alike hang out here savoring fried-fish casados, sandwiches, and breakfasts that include huge helpings of bacon. On the weekends the cavernous structure beside the restaurant becomes a lively disco.

9 Playa Tambor

150—168 kilometers W of San José (not including ferry ride); 20 kilometers S of Paquera; 38 kilometers S of Naranjo.

Once a sleepy fishing village, Tambor became, in 1993, the site of Costa Rica's first all-inclusive beach resort. Though the original plans called for a sprawling mega-resort with several hotels, controversy and shifting fortunes have apparently stalled work on any future development. Playa Tambor Resort currently has 402 rooms, which still makes it, for the moment, the largest beach resort in Costa Rica. Playa Tambor is a long scimitar of beach protected on either end by rocky headlands. These headlands give the waters a certain amount of protection from Pacific swells, making this a good beach for swimming. However, the sand is a rather hard-packed dull gray-brown color, and I find this beach far less attractive than those located farther south along the Nicoya Peninsula.

Aside from the two resorts listed here, there are a few inexpensive cabinas available near the town of Tambor, at the southern end of the beach.

ESSENTIALS

GETTING THERE & DEPARTING   By Plane   Air Sansa (☎ 506/233-0397, 506/233-3258, or 506/233-5330) flies one flight a day to Tambor from San José's Juan Santamaría International Airport. From Monday through Saturday, the flight departs at 7am and makes three stops before arriving 2 hours later; on Sunday, it departs at 11:15am and flies nonstop, getting to Tambor 30 minutes later. Fare is $40 each way.

Travelair (☎ 506/220-3054 or 506/232-7883) flies to Tambor daily at 10:45am from San José's Pavas International Airport. Flight duration is 30 minutes. Fare is $62 one-way, $98 round-trip.

By Bus and Ferry   If you are traveling from San José by public transportation, it takes two buses and a ferry ride to get to Tambor. This can require spending a night in Puntarenas, so don't plan on heading out this way unless you have plenty of time.

Buses leave San José for Puntarenas daily every 30 minutes between 5am and 7pm from the corner of Calle 12 and Avenida 9. The trip's duration is 2 hours; fare is $2. From Puntarenas take the *lancha* or *Paquereña* (☎ 506/661-2830), which leaves from the pier behind the market at 6 and 11am, and 3pm. This passenger launch should not be confused with the two car ferries that also leave from Puntarenas, and you should always check the schedule before making plans. Ferry trip duration is 1¹/₂ hours; fare is $1.10. The bus south to Tambor will be waiting to meet the lancha when it arrives in Paquera. Bus ride duration is 55 minutes; fare is $1.80.

When you're ready to head back, the Paquera bus, which originates in Montezuma, passes through Tambor at 6:15am, 10:45am, and 2:45pm to meet the Paquereña ferry, which leaves for Puntarenas at 8am, and 12:30 and 5pm. Total trip duration is 3¹/₂ hours. Total combined bus and ferry fare is $2.90.

The car ferry from Paquera leaves four times daily: at 6 and 10:30am, and 2:30 and 7pm. The car ferry from Naranjo leaves at 5:10 and 8:50am, and 12:50 and 5pm.

By Car   Take the Interamerican highway from San José to Puntarenas and catch either the Naranjo ferry or the Paquera ferry.

The Naranjo ferry leaves daily at 3, 7, and 10:50am, and 2:50 and 7pm. The trip's duration is 1¹/₂ hours. Fare is $9.50 for cars, $1.40 for adults, and 75¢ for children. The Naviera Tambor ferry to Paquera leaves daily at 4:15 and 8:45am, and 12:30 and 5:30pm. The trip's duration is 1¹/₂ hours. Fare is $11.50 for a car; $1.50 for adults, $4 for adults in first class; $1 for children, and $2 for children in first class.

ORIENTATION   **Arriving**   Tambor is about 45 minutes south of Paquera and 2 hours south of Naranjo. The road from Paquera to Tambor was upgraded when the resort was built, and taking the Paquera ferry will save you time and some very rough, dusty driving. The Naranjo road, until Paquera, is all dirt and gravel and in very bad shape.

Though there is a small village of Tambor, through which the main road passes, the hotels themselves are scattered along several kilometers. You'll see signs for these hotels as the road circles around Playa Tambor.

FUN ON AND OFF THE BEACH

Playa Tambor Beach Resort is an all-inclusive, full-service resort, so if you are staying here, you'll have access to all manner of beach toys. If you're staying at Hotel Tango Mar, you won't have access to so many toys, but you will have the Nicoya Peninsula's only golf course on the premises. Both Playa Tambor Beach Resort and Hotel Tango Mar offer tours around this part of the peninsula, and horseback riding. Playa Tambor Beach Resort also has a full-service dive shop that offers open-water courses and daily dive trips.

Curú Wildlife Refuge, 16 kilometers north of Tambor, has several pretty, secluded beaches, as well as forests and mangrove swamps. This private reserve is extremely rich in wildlife. Howler and white-faced monkeys are often spotted here, as are quite a few species of birds. Admission is $5.

WHERE TO STAY

✪ **Hotel Tango Mar.** Tambor, Puntarenas (mailing address: Apdo. 3877-1000, San José). ☎ **506/222-3503** or 506/661-2798. Fax 506/221-6551. 18 rms, 12 suites, 6 villas. TV. Dec–Apr, $131 double, $142 triple; $179–$263 villa; May–Nov, $145–$160 double, $175 suite, $195–$395 villa. May–Nov rates include continental breakfast. AE, MC, V.

Before Tambor was built, Tango Mar was the luxury resort in this neck of the woods. Today, it's still a great place to get away from it all. With only 18 rooms and scattered suites and villas, there are never any crowds. The water is wonderfully clear, and the beach is fronted by coconut palms and luxuriant lawns. If you choose to go exploring, you'll find seaside cliffs and even a waterfall that pours into a tide pool. The hotel rooms all have big balconies and walls of glass to soak up the ocean views; some rooms even have their own whirlpool tubs. The suites are set back among shade trees and flowering vegetation. Each has a carved four-poster canopy bed and indoor jacuzzi. The villas are all different, but all are spacious and relatively secluded. Some of the suites and villas are a bit far from the beach and main hotel, but they all come with the use of a golf cart for getting around.

Dining/Entertainment: The small open-air restaurant overlooks the beach and has plenty of patio space. The varied menu includes plenty of fresh fish with prices ranging from $6.95 to $23.95 for entrees. There is also an adjacent bar.

Services: Guided horseback rides ($20 to $40), boat and snorkeling tours ($35 to $70), fishing charters ($250 to $500 for a half day, $795 for a full day for up to six people), limited room service, golf club, bike rentals, massages.

Facilities: The swimming pool, though small, is set in a lush, secluded garden that is reached by way of a sidewalk across a frog pond. Tango Mar's 10-hole golf course is the only golf course on the Nicoya Peninsula (it has a $25 greens fee). There are also tennis courts.

Playa Tambor Beach Resort. Bahia Ballena, Puntarenas (mailing address in the U.S.: Barceló Award Hotels, 150 SE Second Ave., Miami, FL 33131). ☎ **506/661-1915,** 305/539-1167, or 800/858-0606 in the U.S. Fax 506/661-2069 or 305/539-1160 in the U.S. 402 rms. A/C TV TEL. Nov–Apr, $138–$390 double; May–Oct, $115–$138 double. Rates are all-inclusive (including drinks). AE, MC, V.

All-inclusive beach resorts can be found all over the Caribbean, but this is still Costa Rica's only one, although construction is underway on more. The Playa Tambor development has been surrounded by controversy since its inception, and charges of violating Costa Rica's environmental laws were leveled against the Spanish developers.

However, when you pass through the guarded gate of this resort, you would never know there was the slightest whiff of controversy surrounding it. A huge complex of open-air buildings form the lobby, theater, restaurants, and bars. Hundreds of happy vacationers soak up the sun, splash in the pool and the waves, and quietly form lines for their buffet meals. The guest rooms are housed in attractively designed buildings that are reminiscent of banana plantation houses. The rooms themselves are built to international standards, and though they have not even a hint of Costa Rican character, they are quite comfortable.

Dining/Entertainment: The cost of all your meals and bar drinks is included in the room rates here, and when it comes time to eat, you can choose from a buffet at El Tucán, à la carte meals at El Rancho, or fast food from the poolside El Palenque. There are also a couple of different bars, a disco, and a large theater that stages nightly performances.

Services: Tours, cruises, sportfishing and sunset sailboat excursions, and scuba trips can be arranged for an additional cost. Sports equipment available for use by guests free of charge includes sailboards, sea kayaks, snorkeling gear, small sailboats (Hobie Cats and Sunfish), and boogie boards. Table tennis, croquet, and badminton are also available.

Facilities: The beautiful pool, one of the largest in the country, is surrounded by hundreds of lounge chairs and has a swim-up bar. Other facilities include lighted tennis courts, a basketball court, an outdoor exercise facility, and a whirlpool tub.

EN ROUTE TO TAMBOR & MONTEZUMA

Oasis Del Pacífico. Playa Naranjo (Apdo. 200-5400), Puntarenas (mailing address in the U.S.: SJO 1552, P.O. Box 025216, Miami, FL 33102-5216). ☎/fax **506/661-1555.** 36 rms. $36.70 double; $49 up to four people. AE, MC, V.

Located just 3 minutes from the Playa Naranjo ferry dock, this casual resort is a family-run operation that provides a quiet place to relax in the sun. Though the beach here isn't very good for swimming, there is a good-size pool. You'll also find a kiddie pool, a play area, and plenty of lawn for the kids to run around on, should you bring the family. The friendly owners will make sure you feel right at home and introduce you to their various pets—dogs, macaws, and a deer. The guest rooms have tile floors and high ceilings, and vary considerably in size. Along the tiled verandah there are hammocks just waiting for some serious relaxing. You can also try your hand at fishing from the resort's private pier. Meals in the resort's dining room often include exotic dishes prepared by the Singaporean owner. Horseback riding and fishing trips can be arranged. The greatest attraction of this place is that it is very convenient, yet feels remote.

10 Playa Montezuma

166—184 kilometers W of San José (not including the ferry ride); 36 kilometers SE of Paquera; 54 kilometers S of Naranjo

For years Montezuma has enjoyed near legendary status amongst backpackers, hippie expatriates, and European budget travelers. This fame and tourist traffic has had its price. The haphazard collection of budget lodgings which sprung up were generally pretty ratty, long-term campers were trashing the beach, and Montezuma earned a nasty reputation for having a sewage problem. In recent years, local businesspeople and hotel owners have joined together, and most of these problems have been addressed. Now, the town has a well-tended feel, and there are lodgings of value and quality in all price ranges. The local community even passed an ordinance shutting down all loud discos in the town center, so it's possible to get a good night's sleep as well.

Still, it is the natural beauty, miles of almost abandoned beaches, rich wildlife, and jungle waterfalls that first made Montezuma famous, and they are what keep this one of my favorite beach towns in Costa Rica. The water here is a gorgeous royal blue, and beautiful beaches stretch out along the coast on either side of town. Be careful, though: the waves can occasionally be too rough for casual swimming, and you need to be aware of stray rocks at your feet. Be sure you know where the rocks and tide are before doing any bodysurfing. The best places to swim are in front of the El Sano Banano Cabinas, or several kilometers farther north at Playa Grande.

ESSENTIALS

GETTING THERE & DEPARTING   By Bus and Ferry   If you are traveling from San José by public transportation, it will take you two buses and a ferry ride to get to Montezuma. This can require spending a night in Puntarenas, so don't plan on heading out this way unless you have plenty of time.

Buses leave San José for Puntarenas daily every 30 minutes between 5am and 7pm from the corner of Calle 12 and Avenida 9. Trip duration is 2 hours; fare is $2.

From Puntarenas take the *lancha* or *Paquereña* (☎ 506/661-2830), which leaves from the pier behind the market at 6am, 11am, and 3pm. This passenger launch should not be confused with the two car ferries that also leave from Puntarenas, and you should always check the schedule before making plans. Ferry trip duration is 1¹/₂ hours; fare is $1.10.

The bus south to Montezuma will be waiting to meet the lancha when it arrives in Paquera. The trip's duration is 1 hour and 45 minutes; fare is $2.70.

When you're ready to return, the bus for Paquera leaves Montezuma daily at 5:30 and 10am, and 2pm and meets the Paquereña ferry, which leaves for Puntarenas at 8am, and 12:30 and 5pm. Total trip duration is 4 hours. Total combined bus and ferry fare is $3.80.

The car ferry from Paquera leaves at 6 and 10:30am, and 2:30 and 7pm. The car ferry from Naranjo leaves at 5:10 and 8:50am, and 12:50 and 5pm.

By Car   Take the Interamerican highway from San José to Puntarenas and catch either the Naranjo ferry or the Paquera ferry.

The Naranjo ferry leaves daily at 3, 7, and 10:50am, and 2:50 and 7pm. Trip duration is 1¹/₂ hours. Fare is $9.50 for cars, $1.40 for adults, and 75¢ for children.

The Naviera Tambor ferry to Paquera leaves daily at 4:15 and 8:45am, and 12:30 and 5:30pm. Trip duration is 1¹/₂ hours. Fare is $11.50 for a car; $1.50 for adults, $4 for adults in first class; $1 for children, and $2 for children in first class.

Montezuma is about 1¹/₂ hours south of Paquera and 3 hours south of Naranjo. The road from Paquera to Tambor has been upgraded with the arrival of the resort hotel, and taking the Paquera ferry will save you time and some very rough, dusty driving. Beyond Tambor, it's approximately another 50 minutes to Montezuma.

ORIENTATION & INFORMATION   Arriving   The bus stops at the end of the road into the village. From here, hotels are scattered up and down the beach and around the village's few sand streets. You'll be bombarded with opportunities to rent a horse, or take one of the tours to the famous waterfalls.

Before you jump at the first offer, you might want to pay a visit to the tourist information desk in a little kiosk in the center of the village.

Another good resource is **Monte-aventuras** (☎ 506/642-0025), which functions as a tour and information clearinghouse. Located in an office at the entrance to the Hotel El Jardin, Monte-aventuras can arrange boat tours and rafting trips, and offers car and motorcycle rentals, international phone and fax service, and currency exchange.

FUN ON AND OFF THE BEACH

In Montezuma, mostly you just hang out on the beach, hang out in a restaurant, hang out in a bar, or hang out in a hammock at your hotel. However, if you're interested in more than just hanging out, head for the waterfall just south of town. This waterfall is one of those tropical fantasies where water comes pouring down into a deep pool. It's a popular spot, but it's a bit of a hike up the stream. There are actually a couple of waterfalls up this stream, but the upper falls are by far the more spectacular. You'll find the trail to the falls just over the bridge south of the village (just past Las Cascadas restaurant). At the first major outcropping of rocks, the trail disappears and you have to scramble up the rocks and river for a bit. In places a trail will reappear for small sections. Just stick close to the stream and you'll eventually hit the falls.

HORSEBACK RIDING & VISITING A GREAT TIDE POOL   Several people around the village rent horses for around $5 to $7 an hour, though most people choose to do a 4-hour **horseback tour** for $20 to $30. These latter rides usually go to a second waterfall 8 kilometers north of Montezuma. This waterfall cascades straight down into a deep tide pool at the edge of the ocean. The pool here is a delightful mix of fresh and sea water, and you can bathe while gazing out over the sea and rocky coastline. This is one of my favorite swimming holes in all of Costa Rica. You can also ride a horse to Cabo Blanco. Luis, whose rental place is down the road that leads out of town to the left, is a reliable source for horses, as is Roger.

OTHER ACTIVITIES   In the center of the village, there are a couple of rental shops where you can rent a bicycle by the day or hour, as well as boogie boards. If you'd like to get out on the water and visit yet another beautiful beach, ask at the information center about boat trips to **Tortuga Island.** These tours last 5 hours and cost around $25, which is a considerable savings over similar trips offered by companies in San José—although the trips out of San José include a gourmet lunch that isn't a part of the trips from Montezuma.

AN EXCURSION TO CABO BLANCO NATURE RESERVE: PELICANS, HOWLER MONKEYS & BEAUTIFUL BEACHES

As beautiful as the beaches around Montezuma are, the beaches at **Cabo Blanco Absolute Nature Reserve,** 11 kilometers south of the village, are, in many people's opinions, even more beautiful. Located at the southernmost tip of the Nicoya Peninsula, Cabo Blanco is a national park that preserves a nesting site for brown pelicans, magnificent frigate birds, and brown boobies. The beaches are backed by lush tropical forest that is home to howler monkeys that are often seen (and heard!). You can hike through the preserve's lush forest right down to the deserted, pristine beach. This is Costa Rica's oldest official bioreserve and was set up thanks to the pioneering efforts of conservationists Karen Mogensen and Nicholas Wessberg. Admission is $6. There are usually shared taxis heading out this way from Montezuma in the morning. The fare is around $5 per person.

WHERE TO STAY
MODERATE

✪ **Amor de Mar.** Montezuma, Cóbano de Puntarenas. ☎/fax **506/642-0262.** 12 rms (8 with private bath). $30 double with shared bath; $35–50 double or triple with private bath. No credit cards.

It would be difficult to imagine a more idyllic spot in this price range. In fact, it's hard to imagine a much more idyllic spot at all. With its wide expanse of neatly trimmed grass sloping down to the sea, tide pools (one of which is as big as a small swimming pool), and hammocks slung from the mango trees, this is the perfect place for anyone who wants to do some serious relaxing. The owners, who have young children, love to have other families as guests, and there's always a cheerful family atmosphere. However, couples and individuals will also enjoy a stay at Amor de Mar simply for the stunning location and beautifully appointed main building, which abounds in varnished hardwoods. The big porch on the second floor is a great place for reading or just gazing out to sea. Only breakfast is served here, with the specialty being homemade whole-wheat French bread.

Los Mangos. Montezuma, Cóbano de Puntarenas. ☎ **506/642-0259** or 506/642-0076. Fax 506/642-0036. 10 rms (6 with private bath), 10 bungalows. Dec–Mar, $25 double or triple without bath; $40 double or triple with bath; $60 bungalow. Apr–Nov, rates are slightly lower. V.

This is still the only hotel in Montezuma with its own swimming pool. Situated across the road from the water and near Amor de Mar, it takes its name from the many mango trees under which the bungalows are built (May is mango season). The rooms are fairly basic and, in an older building close to the road, a good value. However, it is the octagonal bungalows built of Costa Rican hardwoods that are the most attractively appointed. Each bungalow has a small porch with rocking chairs, a thatched roof, a good amount of space, and ceiling fans. The swimming pool is built to look like a natural pond, and there's even an artificial waterfall flowing into it. Beside the pool is a large rancho-style restaurant and bar serving reasonably priced French and Italian meals.

⭐ **El Sano Banano.** Montezuma, Cóbano de Puntarenas. ☎/fax **506/642-0068.** 3 rms, 12 cabins, 1 apt (all with private bath). Dec–Mar, $35–$45 double, $60–$70 cabin, $60–$120 apt. Rates lower in off-season. AE, MC, V (add 10% surcharge).

El Sano Banano is the sort of tropical retreat many travelers dream about. If you walk up the beach, you'll find it on the left about 10 minutes later. From the front porch of your cabin you can sit and listen to the waves crashing on the beach a few feet away. Please do not try to drive up the beach, even if you have a four-wheel-drive vehicle. Seclusion and quiet are the main offerings of this place, and cars would ruin the atmosphere. If you don't want to carry all your bags, you can leave some of your stuff at the Sano Banano restaurant in the village, and the hotel will bring it to your room. There are two types of cabins here—octagonal, hardwood, Polynesian-style buildings and white, ferroconcrete, geodesic domes that look like igloos—as well as three more standard rooms in the main building. All the rooms are set amid a lush garden planted with lots of banana and elephant-ear plants, and there are big rocks scattered beneath the shady old trees. The rooms and cabins vary in age and style, so have a look at a couple if you can. All have refrigerators, coffee makers, and hot plates, and many guests opt for extended stays. One other thing you should know is that the showers, though private, are outside of the cabins in the trees. This is the tropics. Why not?

INEXPENSIVE

Now that camping on the beach is discouraged, campers will have to make do at **El Rincón de los Monos,** which is near the beach, charges about $3 per tent, and provides showers and bathrooms.

🅢 **Hotel La Aurora.** Montezuma, Cóbano de Puntarenas. ☎ **506/642-0051.** Fax 506/642-0025. 8 rms (all with private bath). Dec–Mar, $16.30–$24.50 double ($5 each additional person); Apr–Nov, $8.15–$16.30 double ($3 each additional person). No credit cards.

Just to the left as you enter the village of Montezuma, you'll see this large, white house. The rooms are spread around the spacious three-story building, which also features a small library of books, some hammocks and comfortable chairs, and flowering vines growing up the walls. In fact, there are vines all over La Aurora, which give it a tropical, yet gothic feel. Most rooms are of average size and have wood walls that don't go all the way to the ceiling, which improves air circulation but reduces privacy. There are two new rooms up on the third floor with balconies and an ocean view over the tree tops. Fresh coffee and tea are provided every morning. There is also a kitchen available to guests, and lunch and dinner are served at reasonable prices.

Hotel Moctezuma. Montezuma, Cóbano de Puntarenas. ☎/fax **506/642-0058.** 22 rms (15 with private bath). $8.50 double without bath, $14.50 double with bath; $16.75 triple with bath; $19 quad with bath. V (add 10% surcharge).

Located right in the center of the village and overlooking the small bay, the Hotel Moctezuma offers basic but clean rooms with fans, in two facing buildings. Some of the rooms are upstairs from the hotel's noisy bar and restaurant. It's noisy here, but you get a verandah with an ocean view. If you like to go to sleep early, try to get a room at the back of the building across the street instead. The walls don't go all the way to the ceiling, which is great for air circulation, but lousy for privacy.

WHERE TO DINE

Las Casadas. On the road out of town toward Cabo Blanco. ☎ **506/642-0049.** Reservations not accepted. Main courses $2.80–$9.80. No credit cards. Daily 9am–9pm. COSTA RICAN/ SEAFOOD.

This little open-air restaurant is built on the banks of the stream just outside of the village and takes its name from the nearby waterfalls. The short menu sometimes includes fresh fish filets, whole red snapper, or shrimp in salsa ranchera. There are few more enjoyable places in Costa Rica to have a meal. You can sit for hours beneath the thatched roof listening to the stream rushing past.

✪ Playa de Los Artistas. Across from Hotel Los Mangos. No phone. Reservations not accepted. Main courses $4–$12.50. No credit cards. Daily 6–10:30pm. ITALIAN/MEDITERRANEAN.

If you're craving Italian food for dinner, this is the place to find it in Montezuma. The open-air restaurant is beside an old house fronting the beach, and there are only a few tables. Arrive early if you want to be sure of getting a seat; this place is popular. Meals are served in large, broad ceramic bowls, set on wooden-ringed coasters, and come with plenty of fresh bread for soaking up the sauces. The menu changes nightly, but always features several fish dishes. The fresh grouper in a black pepper sauce is phenomenal.

✪ El Sano Banano. On the main road into the village. ☎ **506/642-0272.** Reservations not accepted. Main courses $3.25–$6.50. V (with a 10% surcharge). Daily 7am–10pm. VEGETARIAN.

Delicious vegetarian meals including nightly specials, sandwiches, and salads are the specialty of this ever-popular Montezuma restaurant, although fish and chicken dishes are also served. You can even order a sandwich with cheese from the cheese factory in Monteverde. The day's menu specials are posted on a blackboard out front early in the afternoon so you can be savoring the thought of dinner all day. Any time at all, the yogurt-fruit shakes are fabulous. El Sano Banano also doubles as the local movie house. They show nightly videos projected on a large screen and have a library of more than 300 movies. The movies begin at 7:30pm and require a $2.50 minimum purchase.

MONTEZUMA AFTER DARK

Ever since the local bars were required to turn down their music at 10pm, most of Montezuma's raging nightlife has moved to the **Kaliolin Disco,** 1.5 kilometers south of town. Kaliolin's is open Wednesday, Friday, and Saturday nights, and even provides a free taxi back into town at the end of the evening or, more likely, early the following morning (they're open until 2 or 3am).

If your evening tastes are a bit mellower, one of the restaurants in town, **El Sano Banano,** also doubles as the local movie house. See their listing under "Where to Dine," above, for more information.

7 The Northern Zone

If you like your eco-tourism rough and gritty, but don't think you can take the heat and humidity of the Osa Peninsula, this is the area for you. The northern zone, roughly defined here as the area north of San José and between Guanacaste province on the west and the low-lands of the Caribbean coast on the east, is a naturalist's dream come true. There are rain forests and cloud forests, jungle rivers, and an unbelievable diversity of birds and other wildlife. In addition to its reputation for muddy hiking trails and crocodile-filled rivers, the northern zone also claims one of the best windsurfing spots in the world (on Lake Arenal, which is free of crocodiles, by the way) and Costa Rica's most active volcanos. Arenal Volcano, when free of clouds, puts on spectacular nighttime light shows and by day is reflected in the waters of nearby Lake Arenal. Adding a touch of comfort to a visit to the northern zone are several hot springs that vary in their levels of luxury.

1 Puerto Viejo de Sarapiquí

82 kilometers N of San José; 102 kilometers E of La Fortuna

The Sarapiquí region, named for the river that drains this area, lies at the foot of the Cordillera Central mountain range. To the west is the rain forest of Braulio Carrillo National Park, and to the east are Tortuguero National Park and Barra del Colorado National Wildlife Refuge. In between these protected areas lie thousands of acres of banana, pineapple, and palm plantations. It is here that you can see the great contradiction of Costa Rica. On the one hand, the country is known for its national parks, which preserve some of the largest tracts of rain forest left in Central America, but on the other hand, nearly every acre of land outside of these parks has been clear-cut and converted into plantations (and the cutting continues today).

Within the remaining rain forests, there are several lodges that attract naturalists (both amateur and professional) who are interested in learning more about the rain forest. Two of these lodges, La Selva and Rara Avis, have become well known for the research that is conducted on their surrounding reserves.

ESSENTIALS

GETTING THERE & DEPARTING   By Bus   Express buses leave San José daily at 6:30, 7, 9, and 10am, and 12, 1, 3, 3:30, and

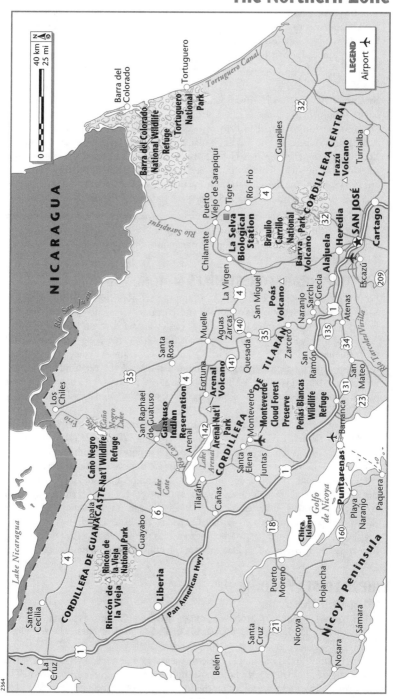

4pm from Avenida 11 between Calle Central and Calle 1. If you are heading to La Selva, Rara Avis, or El Gavilán lodges, be sure you are on a bus going through Las Horquetas. Trip duration is 4 hours; fare is $3.75.

Express buses for San José leave Puerto Viejo daily at 4, 6, 8, and 10:30am, and 2, 3, and 4pm. Buses leave Las Horquetas for San José daily at 7 and 11:30am, and at 3 and 5:15pm.

By Car   The Guápiles Highway, which leads to the Caribbean coast, heads north out of downtown San José on Calle 3 before heading east. Turn north before reaching Guápiles on the road to Río Frio and continue north through Las Horquetas, passing Rara Avis, La Selva, and El Gavilán lodges, before reaching Puerto Viejo. An alternative route goes through Heredia, Barva, Varablanca, and San Miguel before reaching Puerto Viejo. This is a more scenic route, but the road is in very bad condition in certain stretches. If you want to take this route, head west out of San José and then turn north to Heredia and follow the signs for Varablanca.

ORIENTATION   Arriving   Puerto Viejo is a small town, at the center of which is a soccer field. If you continue past the soccer field on the main road and stay on the paved road, you will come to the Río Sarapiquí and the dock where you can look into arranging a boat trip.

BOAT TRIPS, RAIN-FOREST HIKES & MORE

For the adventurous, Puerto Viejo is a jumping-off point for trips down the Río Sarapiquí to Tortuguero National Park and Barra del Colorado National Wildlife Refuge on the Caribbean coast. Boat trips can be arranged at most hotels in town. A boat for up to ten people will cost you $100 to Oro Verde Lodge and back, $300 to Tortuguero, and $275 to Barra del Colorado. Alternatively, you can head down to the town dock on the bank of the Sarapiquí and see if you can arrange a less expensive boat trip on your own. A trip down the Sarapiquí, even if it's only for an hour or two, provides opportunities to spot crocodiles, Caiman, monkeys, sloths, and dozens of species of birds.

Another option is to do a kayak trip down the Sarapiquí. These trips are offered by **Rancho Leona,** La Virgen de Sarapiquí, Heredia (☎ 506/761-1019), a small stained-glass workshop, kayaking center, and guest house on the banks of the Río Sarapiquí in the village of La Virgen. The trips are done as a package that includes two nights lodging in simple, dormitory-style accommodations and an all-day kayak trip with some basic instruction and lunch on the river. The cost for the two-day trip is $75 per person. No experience is necessary, and the river is very calm. Other more extensive trips, and trips for experienced kayakers, can be arranged.

All of the lodges listed below arrange excursions throughout the region, including boat trips on the Sarapiquí, guided hikes in the rain forest, and horseback or mountain bike rides.

WHERE TO STAY & DINE
IN PUERTO VIEJO

Hotel El Bambú. Apdo. 1518-2100, Puerto Viejo, Sarapiquí. ☎ **506/253-2308.** Fax 506/225-8860. 11 rms. TV. $55 single or double; $65 triple; $75 quad. All rates include continental breakfast. AE, MC, V.

This is the most luxurious hotel in Puerto Viejo and is surprisingly attractive. I still haven't figured out why such a hotel exists in this remote and untouristed town. The guest rooms and lobby are all up on the second floor of a modern building, and to reach them you must first walk through the big open-air restaurant that overlooks the dense grove of bamboo for which the hotel is named. The rooms have high ceilings, tile floors, and attractive bamboo furniture. You'll find the hotel directly across the street from the soccer field in the middle of town. Tours around the region, as well as boat trips down the Río Sarapiquí as far as Barra del Colorado and Tortuguero, can be arranged.

Mi Lindo Sarapiquí. Puerto Viejo, Sarapiquí. ☎ **506/766-6281.** 6 rms (each with private bath). $16.50 double; $24.80 triple. No credit cards.

This little family-run lodging is located in the center of town overlooking the soccer field. The comfortable and clean rooms are on the second floor, above the large restaurant and bar.

SOUTH OF PUERTO VIEJO

El Gavilán Lodge. Apdo. 445-2010, Zapote, San José. ☎ **506/234-9507.** Fax 506/253-6556. 15 rms (12 with private bath). $50 double; $75 triple. Lower rates during off-season. All rates include breakfast. MC, V.

Located on the banks of the Río Sarapiquí just south of Puerto Viejo on the road to Río Frio, El Gavilán is surrounded by 250 acres of forest reserve (secondary forest) and 25 acres of gardens planted with lots of flowering ginger. If you're interested in orchids, plan a visit in March when these beautiful flowers are in bloom. Guest rooms are simply furnished, but do have fans and hot water, and there are always fresh flowers. The rooms in the main building are fairly basic, but have huge bathrooms with two sinks. Other rooms are in rustic duplexes with cement floors. There is also a whirlpool spa in the garden. Tico meals are served buffet style, and there are always plenty of fresh fruits and juices (though no alcohol is served, so bring your own). Lunch and dinner each cost $8. Those interested in the outdoors and nature are the ones who will most enjoy a stay here. There's a kilometer-long nature trail at the lodge, and various excursions can be arranged. Guided hikes through the forest ($15 per person), horseback rides ($15 per person), and river trips ($20) are all offered.

La Selva Biological Station. South of Puerto Viejo (U.S. mailing address: Interlink 341, P.O. Box 02-5635, Miami, FL 33152). ☎ **506/240-6696** or 506/240-5033. Fax 506/240-6783. 15 rms. $90 per person. Lower rates for researchers; all rates include three meals daily. MC, V.

Located a few kilometers south of Puerto Viejo, La Selva Biological Station caters primarily to students and researchers, but also accepts visitors seeking a rustic rainforest adventure. The atmosphere is definitely that of a scientific research center. La Selva, which is operated by the Organization for Tropical Studies, covers 3,700 acres and is contiguous with Braulio Carrillo National Park. Researchers estimate that more than 2,000 species of flora exist in this private reserve, and 400-plus species of birds have been identified here. Rooms are basic, though they are large and have tiled bathrooms. High ceilings help keep them cool. The dining hall is a big bright place where students swap data over fried chicken and rice-and-beans. Because scientific research is the primary objective of La Selva, researchers receive priority over casual, short-term visitors. If you wish to visit La Selva, you must have a reservation, preferably made several months in advance. January through March, June, and July are the busiest months here. Direct transportation to and from La Selva costs $10 each way, and is only available on Monday, Wednesday, and Friday.

NEAR BARRA DEL COLORADO NATIONAL WILDLIFE REFUGE

Oro Verde Station. Apdo. 7043-1000, San José. ☎ **506/233-6613.** Fax 506/223-7479. 14 rms (8 with private bath). $49.20 double; $64.90 triple. AE (San José office only).

Surrounded by nearly 20,000 acres of private reserve (3,000 acres of which is virgin forest) and bordering the Barra del Colorado National Wildlife Refuge, the Oro

Verde Station is primarily a facility for researchers and students, but is also open to the public. The nearest road is 30 miles away, so the lodge can only be reached by boat. The lodge's several high-peaked, thatched-roof buildings lend a very tropical air to the facilities. Guest rooms are fairly basic, as you might expect at a research facility, and meals are often less than memorable. Both lunch and dinner are in the $5 to $10 range. There are plenty of hiking trails; river trips and guided hikes can be arranged for an additional cost.

NEAR BRAULIO CARRILLO NATIONAL PARK

✪ Rara Avis. Apdo. 8105-1000, San José. ☎/fax **506/764-4187** or 506/256-4876 and fax 506/253-0844 in San José. 19 rms (10 with private bath). $90 double with shared bath, $150 double with private bath. All rates include transportation from Las Horquetas, guided hikes, and three meals daily. MC, V.

Once the exclusive stomping grounds of scientists and students, Rara Avis was made famous by the pioneering canopy research of Dr. Donald Perry, who first erected his famous canopy cable-car system in the rain forest here. Since that time, Rara Avis has become a very popular destination for people with a more casual interest in the rain forest. Though Perry's canopy cable car is no longer here, the rain-forest research facility is still a fascinating place to visit. To get to Rara Avis, you must first travel to the village of Las Horquetas, which is between Guápiles and Puerto Viejo de Sarapiquí. In Las Horquetas, you are met by a tractor that takes 3 hours to cover the 15 kilometers to Rara Avis's more popular lodge (there are two lodges and one cabina here). The road has recently been graded, but the last 3 kilometers are still over a road made of fallen logs and deep, deep mud. The Waterfall Lodge is by far the more comfortable and has rustic rooms and a wraparound porch. The more economical El Plastico Lodge was at one time a penal colony, and though it has been renovated and converted, it is still very spartan. There is a new cabina set deep in the forest beside a river, with two comfortable rooms for those wanting closer communion with nature. (It's a 10-minute walk from the main lodge.) Meals are basic Tico-style dishes with lots of beans and rice. Rara Avis is adjacent to Braulio Carrillo National Park and together the two have many miles of trails for you to explore. Birdwatchers take note: More than 320 species of birds have been sighted here. When making reservations, be sure to get directions for how to get to Las Horquetas.

WEST OF PUERTO VIEJO

✪ Selva Verde Lodge. Chilamate, Sarapiquí. ☎ **506/766-6077** or 506/766-6277. Fax 506/766-6011. 40 rms, 5 bungalows. $126 double; $159 triple. All rates include three meals daily. MC, V.

So, you've been hearing all about eco-tourism and saving the rain forests and you want to see what it's all about, but you're accustomed to comfortable accommodations and good food. No problem. Selva Verde is just what you're looking for. Here at this beautifully designed lodge you can experience the rain forest without being uncomfortable. Located right on the main highway a few kilometers west of Puerto Viejo, Selva Verde is bounded by the Río Sarapiquí, across which is a large rain-forest preserve. The rooms here are all connected by covered walkways that keep you dry even though this area receives more than 150 inches of rain each year. The lodge buildings are all built of varnished hardwoods, inside and out, and are built on pilings so that all the rooms are on the second floor. Because as few trees as possible were cut to build this lodge, you can sit on your verandah looking straight into the branches, which are often alive with birds. As you might guess, this lodge is a birdwatcher's paradise, and in fact, is often filled with Elderhostel tour groups that are busily working on their life lists. The bungalows are as comfortable as the rooms in the main lodge, but are located 500 meters into the forest, and offer a measure more of privacy. Meals are served in a beautiful, large dining room that overlooks the river; they are well prepared and filling, but not too creative. There are several trails on the grounds, and bikes can be rented. Excursions that can be arranged through the lodge include river trips ($25 per person), canoe trips ($45 per person), rafting trips ($45 per person), horseback riding ($20 per person), and guided walks ($15 per person).

2 Arenal Volcano & La Fortuna

140 kilometers NW of San José; 61 kilometers E of Tilarán

If you've never experienced it firsthand, the sight and sound of an active volcano erupting is awesome. Until 1937 when the mountain just west of La Fortuna was first scaled, no one ever dreamed that it might be a volcano. Gazing up at the cinder-strewn slopes of Arenal Volcano today, it is hard to believe that people could not have recognized this perfectly cone-shaped volcano for what it is. However, in July of 1968, the volcano, which had lain dormant for hundreds of years, erupted with sudden and unexpected violence. The nearby village of Tabacón was destroyed and nearly 80 of its inhabitants were killed. Since that eruption more than a quarter century ago, 5,358-foot-high Arenal has been Costa Rica's most active volcano. Frequent powerful explosions send cascades of red-hot lava rocks tumbling down the western slope of the volcano. During the day, the lava flows steam and rumble. However, it is at night that the volcano puts on its most mesmerizing show. If you should be lucky enough to be here on a clear night, you will see the night sky turned red by lava spewing from Arenal's crater. In the past few years, the forests to the south of the volcano have been declared Arenal National Park. Eventually this park should stretch all the way to Monteverde Biological Cloud Forest Preserve.

Lying at the eastern foot of this natural spectacle is the tiny farming community of La Fortuna. In recent years, this town has become a center for volcano watchers from around the world. There are several moderately priced hotels in and near La Fortuna, and it is here that you can arrange night tours to the best volcano-viewing spots, which are 17 kilometers away on the western slope, past the Tabacón Hot Springs.

ESSENTIALS

GETTING THERE & DEPARTING   By Bus   Buses leave San José for La Fortuna daily at 6:15, 8:40, and 11:30am from Calle 16 between avenidas 1 and 3. The trip's duration is $4^1/_2$ hours; fare is $3.35.

Alternatively, you can take a bus to Ciudad Quesada from the same location in San José and then take a local bus from Ciudad Quesada to La Fortuna. Ciudad Quesada buses leave San José daily every hour from 5am to 7:30pm. Trip duration is 3 hours, fare is $2. Buses leave Ciudad Quesada for La Fortuna at 6, 7, and 11am, and 1, 3, and 6pm. Trip duration is 1 hour, fare is $1.10.

Buses depart La Fortuna for San José daily at 5 and 11am, and 2:45pm. Buses to Ciudad Quesada leave at 5, 6:30, 7:20, 9:20, 10, and 11:15am, and 3:30pm daily. From there you can catch one of the hourly buses to San José. There are also buses to Tilarán, at the northern end of Lake Arenal, daily at 8am and 4pm.

By Car   There are several routes to La Fortuna from San José. The most popular is to head west on the Interamerican Highway and then turn north at Naranjo, continuing north through Zarcero to Ciudad Quesada. From Ciudad Quesada one route goes through Jabillos, while the other goes through Muelle. This latter route is the better road. It is, however, a little quicker to go first to Alajuela and then head north to Varablanca before continuing on to San Miguel where you turn west toward Río Cuarto and Aguas Zarcas. From Aguas Zarcas, continue west through Muelle to the turnoff for La Fortuna. Travel time either way is around 3 hours. A new route from San Ramón (west of Naranjo) north through Tigra, though unpaved, is very scenic and passes the Villablanca and Valle Escondido lodges.

ORIENTATION   Arriving   La Fortuna is only a few streets wide with almost all the hotels, restaurants, and shops clustered along the main road that leads out of town towards Tabacón and the volcano. There are several small information and tour-booking offices across the street from the soccer field.

EXPERIENCING THE VOLCANO

The first thing you should know is that you can't climb Arenal Volcano. It is not safe due to the constant activity; several foolish people who have ignored this warning have lost their lives, and others have been severely injured. Watching Arenal's constant eruptions is the main activity in La Fortuna and is best done at night when the orange lava glows against the starry sky. Though it is possible to simply look up from the middle of town and see Arenal erupting, the view is better from the west side of the volcano. If you have a car, you can drive to the west side, but if you have arrived by bus, you will need to take a taxi or tour. **Arenal National Park** constitutes an area of 2,920 hectares, which include the viewing and parking areas closest to the volcano. The park is open from 8am to 10pm daily and charges $6 admission per person. However, unless you need to actually feel the heat of a lava flow, you will probably find the view of the natural fireworks perfectly acceptable on the dirt road just outside the park entrance.

Night tours are offered through every hotel in town and at several tour offices on the town's main street, at a cost of $5 to $10. Almost all of the tours include a stop at one of the hot springs.

OTHER THINGS TO SEE & DO

Aside from the impressive volcanic activity, the area around Arenal Volcano is also packed with other natural wonders.

Leading the list of side attractions is the **Río Fortuna waterfall,** which is located about 5½ kilometers outside of town in a lush jungle setting. There is a sign in town to indicate the road that leads out to the falls. For $3, you can hike or drive (depending on recent rainfall) to within viewing distance of the impressive falls. Once you get to the lookout, it's another 15–20 minute hike down a steep and often muddy path to the pool formed by the waterfall. For $3, you can swim here, but stay away from the turbulent water at the base of the fall—several people have drowned here. Instead, check out and enjoy the calm pool just around the bend.

If this seems like too much exercise, you can rent a horse and guide for transportation. You can arrange this through your hotel or through **Aventuras Arenal** (☎ 506/479-9133), **Jacamar Tours** (☎ 506/479-9010), or **Pura Vida** (☎ 506/479-9045). All of these companies also offer most of the tours listed below.

Another good ride is up to Cerro Chato, an extinct side cone on the flank of Arenal. There is a pretty little lake up here. Either of these tours should cost around $15 to $20 per person.

You can also arrange a tour to the **Venado Caverns,** which are a 45-minute drive from La Fortuna. You'll see plenty of stalactites, stalagmites, and other limestone formations, of course, but you'll also see bats and cave fish. Tours here cost between $25 and $30.

Taking a Soothing Soak in Tabacón Hot Springs

One of the primary fringe benefits that Arenal Volcano has bestowed on the area are several naturally heated thermal springs. Located at the sight of the former village, Tabacón Hot Springs Resort is the most extensive and luxurious spot to soak your tired bones. A series of variously sized pools, fed by natural springs, are spread out among lush gardens. At the center is a large pool with a slide, swim-up bar, and perfect view of the volcano. One of the stronger streams flows over a sculpted waterfall, with a rock ledge underneath that provides a perfect place to sit and receive a free hydrolic shoulder massage. The resort also offers professional massages, mud masks, and an excellent restaurant serving local and Italian dishes. Entrance fees are $14 for adults; $7 for children.

Across the street from the resort and down a gravel driveway is another bathing spot fed by the same springs. You'll find several large pools here, but far more basic facilities and no view. Admission is $2.10.

La Fortuna is also the best place from which to make a day trip to the **Caño Negro National Wildlife Refuge.** This vast network of marshes and rivers is 100 kilometers north of La Fortuna near the town of Los Chiles. This refuge is best known for its amazing abundance of bird life, including roseate spoonbills, jabiru storks, herons, and egrets, but you can also see Caiman and crocodiles. Birdwatchers should not miss this refuge, though keep in mind that the main lake dries up in the dry season, which reduces the numbers of wading birds to be seen. Full-day tours to Caño Negro average between $35 and $45 per person.

You can also go rafting with **Desafio Raft** (☎ 506/479-9464) or **Aguas Brava** (☎ 506/479-9025). Both of these companies offer daily rides of class I-II, III, and IV-V on different sections of the Sarapiquí River. A full day of rafting costs $60 to $80 per person.

Both of the above companies also offer mountain bike rentals and guided tours.

WHERE TO STAY IN LA FORTUNA
MODERATE

✪ **Las Cabañitas Resort.** Apdo. 5-4417, La Fortuna, San Carlos. ☎ **506/479-9400** or 506/479-9343. Fax 506/479-9408. 30 cabins. Dec–Apr, $72.50 double; May–Nov, $65 double. AE, MC, V.

Located 1 kilometer east of town, these rustic mountain cabins are spacious and immaculate inside. About half of the cabins face the volcano and have little porches where you can sit and enjoy the show by day or night. Each cabin is built of varnished hardwoods and has a beautiful floor, a high ceiling, louvered walls to let in the breezes, a modern tile bathroom down a few steps from the sleeping area, and rocking chairs on the porch. There is a small kidney-shaped swimming pool with a snack bar beside it and also a larger, full-service restaurant. Some of the rooms are wheelchair accessible. Various tours can be arranged through the hotel.

⑤ **Hotel-Rancho El Corcovado.** Apdo. 25, El Tanque de La Fortuna, San Carlos. ☎ **506/479-9300.** Fax 506/479-9090. 25 rms. $47 double; $57 triple. MC, V.

This hotel is located 7 kilometers east of La Fortuna. While only the west-facing rooms offer a volcano view (and only from their porches), all rooms are clean and have platform beds. There are good views from the central swimming pool's patio.

The hotel has colorful gardens, its own small lake and forest trails, as well as an inexpensive restaurant serving Tico standards from 6am to 7pm. The owners run an air-taxi service for harrowing flights over the volcano and transportation to other destinations. This hotel isn't quite as attractive as Las Cabañitas up the road, but neither is it as expensive.

INEXPENSIVE

In addition to the inexpensive lodgings listed below, there is **Los Lagos** campground a few minutes west of La Fortuna. It charges $4 per person and has cooking and bathroom facilities, forests, trails, and lakes.

⑤ Hotel Fortuna. La Fortuna, San Carlos. ☎ **506/479-9197.** 15 rms (7 with private bath). $6 double (shared bath); $10 double (private bath); $15 triple (private bath). AE, MC, V.

Located one block south of the gas station, this small hotel is dark and very basic, but the rooms are clean and the prices are great. The second-floor rooms are a bit brighter than those on the ground floor and have a comfortable shared sitting area. There is an open-air restaurant at the front of the hotel.

Hotel Las Colinas. 150 meters south of the National Bank, La Fortuna, San Carlos. ☎/fax **506/479-9107.** 17 rms (all with private bath). $26 double; $33.40 triple. Prices significantly reduced in low season. MC, V.

This three-story building in the center of town offers clean but basic rooms. You'll need to be in good shape if you stay in one of the third-floor rooms, which have the best views, as the stairs are very steep. There are a few rooms on the ground floor, but they don't even have windows to the outside and are very dark. My favorite room is number 33, with a private balcony and an unobstructed view of Arenal Volcano.

Hotel San Bosco. La Fortuna, San Carlos (200 meters north of the gas station). ☎ **506/ 479-9050.** Fax 506/479-9109. 27 rms. $24.45–$37.49 double; $29.34–$40.75 triple; $48.90 suite. MC, V.

Located a block off La Fortuna's main street, the San Bosco has two styles of rooms. The older, cheaper rooms are small and dark and have cement floors. However, the newer rooms are much more attractive and have stone walls, tile floors, air-conditioning, reading lights, and benches on the verandah in front. The suite features a television set. Up on the top floor of the hotel, there is an observation deck for volcano viewing.

WHERE TO STAY & DINE NEAR THE VOLCANO
MODERATE

✪ Arenal Lodge. Apdo. 1139-1250, Escazú. ☎ **506/228-3189.** Fax 506/289-6798. 29 rms. $71.76 double; $83–$95 junior suite; $101–$113 chalet; $120–$135 master. All rates include breakfast. AE, MC, V.

For stunning location and spectacular views, it's hard to beat the Arenal Lodge. Located high on a hillside a mile from Lake Arenal, this lodge has a direct, unobstructed view of Arenal Volcano's most active slope, which is 6 miles away on the far side of a deep valley. If you reserve one of the huge junior suites, you can actually lie in bed and gaze out at the volcano through a wall of glass. The light show on clear nights is enough to keep you awake for hours. These rooms have two queen beds, balconies, clerestory windows, two sinks in the bathroom, and lots of space. The standard rooms, though attractively decorated, have no views at all. However, if you should choose to stay in one of these more economical rooms, it is only a few steps to a large viewing deck. When I last visited, 10 new rooms were being finished in five separate chalets on a hill behind the main building. Each will have a small kitchenette and a view. Meals, which will run you around $30 per person per day, are served in a dining room with a wall of glass, so you can ooh and ahh between bites of corvina or steak. After dinner, you can retire to the library, where there is a huge stone fireplace and a pool table. A separate lounge has a TV and VCR. The lodge can also arrange night tours ($15 per person), trips to the base of Arenal and Tabacón hot springs ($25 to $30 per person), and fishing for rainbow bass in Lake Arenal ($250 for two people with lunch and a guide). Situated on a macadamia plantation between two strips of virgin forest, the lodge has several trails that are great for birdwatching.

Arenal Observatory Lodge. Apdo. 1195-1250, Escazú. ☎ **506/257-9489** or 506/257-3273. Fax 506/257-4220. 26 rms. $40.79–65.20 double; $65.80–$75 triple. AE, MC, V.

This rustic lodge was originally built for the use of volcanologists from the Smithsonian Institution, but is today open to the public as well. The lodge is only $2^1/_2$ miles from the volcano and is built on a high ridge, which gives it the best view of any of the local lodges. Lying in bed at night listening to the eruptions, it is easy to think that the lodge is in imminent danger. The superior rooms feature a floor-to-ceiling window, with a spectacular view of the volcano. Surrounding the lodge is the Arenal National Park, which includes thousands of acres of forest and many kilometers of trails. The lodge offers a number of guided and unguided hiking options, including a free morning trip to a new lava flow. A four-wheel-drive vehicle is recommended for the 9-kilometer dirt road up to the lodge, but two bridges now eliminate the need to ford any major rivers.

Arenal Vista Lodge. Apdo. 818-1200, Pavas, San José. ☎ **506/220-1712.** Fax 506/232-3321. 25 rms. $70 double; $80 triple; $90 quad. AE, MC, V.

This is the newest lodge in the area. It's farther along the same road that leads to the Arenal Observatory Lodge and consequently is even more of an adventure to reach. All the modern rooms have great views of Arenal Volcano, so you can sit back and watch the volcano's fireworks displays in comfort. Meals will cost you an additional $24 per person per day.

INEXPENSIVE

✪ **Montaña De Fuego Inn.** La Palma de la Fortuna, San Carlos. ☎ **506/479-9106.** Fax 506/479-9295. 2 rms, 10 cabinas. $30 double; $38 triple. MC, V.

This hotel offers bed-rattling volcano proximity, at prices far below the fancier eastern slope lodges. Located 8 kilometers outside La Fortuna on the road to Tabacón, these individual cabinas have wonderful volcano views from their spacious glass-enclosed porches. Inside, the cabinas are all varnished wood, with sparse but new appointments. The two rooms are in an older, remodeled home. They have kitchenettes, no view, and are used primarily by larger groups and families.

WHERE TO STAY & DINE EAST OF LA FORTUNA
MODERATE

Hotel La Garza. Plantanar, San Carlos. ☎ **506/475-5222** or 506/222-7355. Fax 506/475-5015. 12 rms. TEL. Nov–Apr, $74 double, $84 triple; May–Oct, lower rates available. MC,V.

This comfortable lodge is set on a large working ranch just south of Muelle. *La Garza* means "the egret" in Spanish, and you will see plenty of these birds here, as they roost nearby. The ranch also includes 750 acres of primary rain forest where many other species of birds can be spotted. Built on the banks of the San Carlos River, the hotel consists of six duplex bungalows, each of which has a deck overlooking the river.

Large trees provide shade, and the sound of the river lulls you to sleep at night. High ceilings and overhead fans help keep the rooms cool. All the rooms are attractively decorated and have views of Arenal Volcano in the distance. When I visited, the restaurant and bar were on the far side of the river, which was crossed by a suspension footbridge. However, there were plans to build a new dining room on the same side of the river as the rooms. Tours of the region can be arranged and you can wander around the ranch observing the day-to-day activity. The hotel also has two pools and a jacuzzi. However, the ranch's rain forest, with all its birds and other wildlife, is the primary attraction here.

Tilajari Hotel Resort. Muelle, San Carlos. ☎ **506/469-9091.** Fax 506/469-9095. 60 rms, 4 suites. A/C. Nov–Apr, $79 double, $100 suite double; May–Oct, discounts available. AE, MC, V.

This sprawling resort just outside the farming community of Muelle (28 kilometers from La Fortuna) is a sort of country club for wealthy Costa Ricans. However, it also makes a good base for exploring this region. Covering 30 acres (unfortunately mostly shadeless lawns) and built on the banks of the San Carlos River, the Tilajari Hotel offers the most luxurious accommodations in the region. The modern buildings are painted a blinding white and have red-tile roofs. About half of the rooms have views of the river, while the others face Arenal Volcano. These latter rooms are slightly larger, but the former rooms have balconies, which makes them a bit more appealing. Large iguanas are frequently sighted on the grounds, as are crocodiles, which live in the San Carlos River.

Dining/Entertainment: There's a large open-air dining room that has both formal and informal sections. The menu consists primarily of moderately priced Tico and international dishes. There is also a bar and disco to round out the entertainment offerings.

Services: The lodge arranges tours around the region, including trips to Caño Negro ($87 per person), Arenal Volcano ($40 per person), Venado Caves ($45 per person), and Fortuna Falls ($45 per person). Trips into the nearby rain forest, either on foot, on horseback, or by tractor, can also be arranged.

Facilities: Swimming pool, tennis courts, racquetball court, soccer field, sauna, game room with pool and table tennis, gift shop.

El Tucano Resort & Spa. Aguas Calientes de San Carlos. ☎ **506/460-6000.** Fax 506/ 460-1692. 90 rms, 2 junior suites, 7 suites. $75 double; $85 triple; $95 junior suite; $105–$185 suite. AE, MC, V.

Located a few kilometers north of Ciudad Quesada (San Carlos) on the road to Aguas Zarcas, El Tucano was Costa Rica's first true spa resort, and though you won't find the sort of services you'd get in Palm Springs, there are natural hot springs and natural steam rooms. The resort is located in a steep-walled valley and faces a lush rain forest. It's more popular with wealthy Tico families than with gringos. The rooms are set into the steep hillside and are connected by narrow, winding alleys and stairways. Most rooms are carpeted and very comfortable, with attractive decorations and tubs in the bathrooms. If you want extra space, ask for one of the suites or junior suites. This is a great place to just kick back and relax for a day or two. Don't miss the natural hot springs that flow into the stream at the back of the property.

Dining/Entertainment: The dining room here is large and formal, with excellent service and a continental menu that includes such dishes as chicken à l'orange and pasta with shrimp. A bar and casino keep adult guests happy after dark.

Services: Room service, shuttle service to San José ($35 per person one-way), horseback riding ($10 per person per hour).

Facilities: Swimming pool, two tennis courts, whirlpool tubs with natural hot-spring waters, natural steam rooms, miniature golf course, gift shop, hiking trails, natural hot springs, and a small zoo.

WHERE TO STAY & DINE SOUTH OF LA FORTUNA
MODERATE

Valle Escondido Lodge. Apdo. 452-1150, La Uruca. ☎ **506/231-0906.** Fax 506/232-9591. 19 rms. $63.50 double; $74.25 triple. AE, MC, V.

South of La Fortuna, just off the road between San Ramón and La Fortuna, is a modest hotel that provides access to some of the region's rain forests. Valle Escondido (Hidden Valley) is situated on a 990-acre farm that includes primary and secondary forest, as well as fields of ornamental plants that are grown for export. The rooms are spacious and comfortable, and all are carpeted. In front of the rooms run long verandahs where you can sit and enjoy the tranquillity of the surroundings. The lodge restaurant serves Tico and Italian meals, which cost $35 per person per day. There is also a small bar. Hiking, horseback riding ($10 per hour), mountain biking ($5 per hour), and birdwatching are the primary activities here; tours are available for an additional charge.

✪ **Villablanca Hotel.** Apdo. 247-1250, San Rafael de Escazú. ☎ **506/228-4603.** Fax 506/228-4004. 5 rms, 54 casitas. $73 double room; $89 double, $104 triple, $152 quad casita. AE, MC, V.

Villablanca is certainly out of the way, and perched as it is, high in the cloud forest, it isn't the sort of place people come to when they want to work on their tans. However, if you are interested in birdwatching or exploring the cloud forest, there is no better place in the country. Owned and operated by a former president of Costa Rica, this lodge consists of 54 Tico-style *casitas,* "little houses," surrounded by 2,000 acres of farm and forest. There are also five new rooms in the main building. While all the rooms are up to par, the casitas are what make this lodge special. Each is built of adobe and has traditional tile floors and whitewashed walls with deep blue trim. This is the classic color scheme of 19th-century adobe homes throughout the country. Inside, you'll find a rounded fireplace in one corner, window seats, comfortable hardwood chairs, colorful curtains, and twin beds covered with attractive bedspreads. Rooms also have electric teapots and small refrigerators. Bathrooms are done in beautiful tiles and have tubs that look out through a wall of windows. In the hacienda-style main lodge, you'll find the dining room, where simple-but-filling buffet meals are served. An unusual atrium garden, library, lounge, gift shop, and small bar round out the amenities. Adjacent to the lodge are 11 kilometers of trails through the Los Angeles Cloud Forest Reserve. Admission to the reserve is $22 per person, and includes a guided hike. You can also rent horses ($10 per hour). Transportation to and from the lodge is $35 each way. Alternatively, you can take a public bus from San José to San Ramón and then take a taxi for around $10. If you are driving, head west out of San José to San Ramón and then head north, following the signs to Villablanca.

3 Tilarán & Lake Arenal

200 kilometers NW of San José; 20 kilometers NW of Monteverde; 70 kilometers SE of Liberia

This remains one of the least developed tourism regions in Costa Rica, but not for lack of resources or charms. Lake Arenal, a man-made lake with an area of 33 square miles, is the largest lake in Costa Rica and is surrounded by rolling hills that are partly pastured and partly forested. At the opposite (east) end of the lake from Tilarán lies the perfect cone of Arenal Volcano. The volcano's barren slopes are a stunning sight from here, especially when reflected in the waters of the lake. The north side of Lake Arenal is a dry region of rolling hills and pastures, distinctly different from the lusher landscape near La Fortuna.

People around here used to curse the winds, which often come blasting across this end of the lake at 60 knots or greater. However, since the first sailboarders caught wind of Lake Arenal's combination of warm freshwater, steady blows, and spectacular scenery, things have been changing quickly. Although the town of Tilarán is still little more than a quiet farm community, out along the shores of the lake hotels are proliferating. Even if you aren't a fanatical sailboarder, you still might enjoy hanging out by the lake, hiking in the nearby forests, and catching glimpses of Arenal Volcano.

The lake's other claim to fame is its rainbow bass fishing. These fighting fish are known in their native South America as *guapote* and are large members of the cichlid family. Their sharp teeth and fighting nature make them a real challenge.

ESSENTIALS

GETTING THERE & DEPARTING   By Bus   Express buses leave San José for Tilarán daily at 7:30 and 9:30am, and 12:45, 3:45, and 6:30pm from Calle 14 between avenidas 9 and 11. Trip duration is 4 hours; fare is $3.

There are also morning and afternoon buses from Puntarenas to Tilarán. The ride's duration is 3 hours; fare is $2.15.

From Monteverde (Santa Elena), there is a bus daily at 7am. Trip duration is 3 hours; fare is $1.25.

Direct buses to San José leave daily at 5, 7, and 7:45am, and 2 and 4:45pm. Buses to Puntarenas leave at 6am and 1pm daily. The bus to Santa Elena (Monteverde) leaves daily at 1pm. Buses also leave regularly for Cañas, where you can catch buses north or south along the Interamerican Highway. Buses for La Fortuna, at the south end of Lake Arenal, leave daily at 7am and 1pm.

By Car   From San José, take the Interamerican Highway west toward Puntarenas and then continue north on this road to Cañas. In Cañas, turn east toward Tilarán. The drive takes 4 hours. If you are thinking of heading up this way from La Fortuna, be aware that for several kilometers the road is unpaved and in very bad shape. The road should not be tried in a regular car, except during the dry season.

ORIENTATION   Arriving   Tilarán is about 5 kilometers from Lake Arenal. All roads into town lead to the central park, which is Tilarán's main point of reference for addresses. If you need to exchange money, check at one of the hotels listed here. If you need a taxi to get to a lodge on Lake Arenal, call 506/695-5324.

WINDSURFING, FISHING & OTHER ACTIVE SPORTS

WINDSURFING   If you want to try windsurfing, you can rent equipment from **Tilawa Windsurfing Center** (☎ 506/695-5050), which has its facilities on one of the lake's few accessible beaches, about 5 miles from Tilarán on the road along the west end of the lake. Boards rent for $40 to $46 per day, and lessons are also available. Over on the other side of the lake you'll find the new **Tico Wind** (fax 506/695-5420 or in the U.S. 800/678-2252), which rents equipment for $50 per day or $275 per week between November and April. Working in conjunction with Tico Wind, **Rio Escondido** is a new mountain bike–rental operation. Use of a top-of-the-line bike will run you around $35 per day. If you can't reach the above rental operations, ask at the **Rock River Lodge,** where you will be outfitted.

FISHING   If you want to try your hand at fishing for rainbow bass, contact **J.J.'s Fishing Tours** (☎ 506/695-5825). A half-day fishing trip will cost between $30 and $100 per person depending on the number of people in your party.

Boating   If you'd just like to go for a boat ride on the lake, check at **Xiloe Lodge** (☎ 506/259-9192).

HORSEBACK RIDING & HIKING   If you're looking for another way to get around on dry land, the folks at Tilawa can arrange for you to rent a horse for $15 per hour. If you feel like strapping on your hiking boots, there are some trails for hiking on the far side of Lake Arenal, near the smaller Coter Lake.

SWIMMING   Up above Lake Arenal on the far side of the lake from Tilarán you'll find the beautiful little heart-shaped **Coter Lake.** This lake is surrounded by forest and has good swimming.

VISITING THE BOTANICAL GARDENS

A taxi to Coter Lake will cost around $12. Continuing south on the road around the lake will bring you to the town of **Nuevo Arenal,** where the pavement ends. If you continue another 4 kilometers on this road, you will come to the **Arenal Botanical Gardens** (☎ 506/694-4273), which is open daily from 9am to 5pm and charges $4 admission. This private garden was only started in 1991, but is already quite beautiful and extensive. Not only are there many tropical plants and flowers to be seen, but there are always butterflies and hummingbirds in the gardens.

WHERE TO STAY
MODERATE

Bahía Azul Lake Resort. Laguna de Arenal, Tilarán, Guanacaste. ☎/fax **506/695-5750.** 15 rms. TV. $40 double; $45 triple. MC, V.

Located 5 kilometers from Tilarán on a small bay of Lake Arenal, Bahía Azul is popular both with windsurfers and vacationing Ticos. Most of the rooms are in a two-story white building that sits on a grassy slope overlooking the lake and green hills beyond. However, my favorite rooms are those down closer to the water. The setting is very tranquil during the week, though on weekends it can get a bit noisy with speedboats racing around the lake. The rooms here are a bit run-down, but all have small refrigerators, ceiling fans, and large windows. There is a bar and restaurant, where main courses range from $4 to $8. The hotel also has fishing gear and water skis for rent, and offers boat trips and excursions to Arenal Volcano and Tabacón Hot Springs. A taxi from Tilarán to Bahía Azul will cost you around $5.

✪ **Hotel Tilawa.** Apdo. 92, Tilarán, Guanacaste. ☎ **506/695-5050** or 800/851-8929 in the U.S. Fax 695-5766. 28 rms. TEL. $65 double; $85 triple. AE, MC, V.

Built to resemble the Palace of Knossos on the island of Crete, the Hotel Tilawa is an avid windsurfer's dream brought to life. The American owners, who have run a windsurfing center on Lake Arenal for years, opened this hotel to provide wealthier windsurfers with a comfortable place to stay. The hotel sits high on the slopes above the lake and has a sweeping vista down the lake. Unusual colors and antique paint effects give the hotel a weathered look (even though it's actually only a few years old). Inside there are wall murals and other artistic paint treatments throughout. Rooms have dyed cement floors, Guatemalan bedspreads, and big windows. Some have kitchenettes. Amenities include a swimming pool and tennis court. There is a bar/disco beside the pool, as well as a moderately priced restaurant in the main building. The Tilawa can arrange windsurfing, mountain biking, horseback riding, and fishing trips.

Lake Coter Eco-Lodge. Apdo. 6398-1000, San José. ☎ **506/221-5075.** Fax 506/221-0794. 37 rms. $48.65–$66.35 double; $57.50–$75.20 triple. AE, DC, MC, V.

Tucked into the forested hills above Lake Arenal is the much smaller, but natural, Lake Coter. Near this pretty lake (up a very bad gravel road), you'll find this rustic lodge. While the older rooms in the main lodge are dark and depressing, there are 12 much nicer rooms on a hill, a short walk from the main lodge. These all have porches and great views. If you are interested in staying here, be sure to request one of these rooms. Surrounding the lodge are more than 1,300 acres of cloud forest and 10 miles of hiking trails.

Meals are served family style in the rustic dining room in the main lodge. Tico standards and some international dishes are the fare here, and meals will run you $25 per person per day. Transportation to and from the lodge can be arranged at additional cost. Activities available include horseback riding, mountain biking, windsurfing, canoeing, and swimming on Lake Coter, as well as hiking. Excursions to Arenal Volcano and Venado Caves can also be arranged.

✪ **Rock River Lodge.** Apdo. 95, Tilarán, Guanacaste. ☎/fax **506/695-5644.** 6 rms; 8 bungalows. $35–$55 double; $45–$65 triple. MC, V.

Set high on a grassy hill above the lake, this small lodge looks as if it might have been transported from Hawaii. The rooms are housed in a long, low lodge set on stilts. Walls and floors are made of hardwood, and there are bamboo railings along the verandah. Wind chimes let you know when the winds are up, and there are sling chairs on the porch. Rooms are of medium size and have one double bed and a bunk bed, as well as modern tiled bathrooms. Though fairly simple in style, this is one of the most attractive lodges in the area. The newer bungalows are further up the hill, offer more privacy, and some even have sculpted bathtubs. It's a long walk down to the lake (not to mention the walk back up), so a car is recommended. Meals will cost you around $25 per person per day and are served in the spacious open-air restaurant where there's a large stone fireplace. This hotel caters to sailboarders and other active travelers. When the wind isn't up, owner Norman List offers mountain biking trips.

A Bed-and-Breakfast

$ **Chalet Nicholas.** Apdo. 72-5710, Tilarán, Guanacaste. ☎/fax **506/694-4041.** 3 rms. $39 double. All rates include full breakfast. No credit cards.

This friendly, American-owned bed-and-breakfast is located 2 kilometers west of Nuevo Arenal and sits on a hill above the road. There are great views from the garden, and one of the three rooms has a view of Arenal Volcano. This modern home is set on 3 acres and has pretty flower gardens, an organic vegetable garden, and an aviary full of toucans and other colorful birds. Behind the property are acres of forest through which you can hike in search of birds, orchids, butterflies, and other tropical beauties. If you don't mind the lack of privacy, the upstairs loft room is the largest. It even has its own private deck. No smoking is allowed in the house or on the grounds. Owners John and Catherine Nichols go out of their way to make their guests feel at home.

INEXPENSIVE

Cabinas Mary. On the south side of the park, Tilarán, Guanacaste. ☎ 506/695-5479. 18 rms (13 with private bath). $20 double with private bath. No credit cards.

Located right on Tilarán's large and sunny central park, Cabinas Mary is a very basic, but fairly clean, lodging. It's upstairs from the restaurant of the same name and has safe parking in back. Rooms are large and have plenty of windows. You even get hot water here, which is a surprise at this price. The restaurant downstairs is a gringo hangout. It's open daily from 6am to 10pm; meals cost between $3 and $7.

$ Hotel Naralit. Tilarán, Guanacaste. ☎/fax **506/695-5393.** 20 rms. $21 double; $26 triple. V.

This newer budget hotel is a good bet in Tilarán. The rooms are clean, and most even have televisions. There are three second-floor rooms that have a nice balcony with a view of the town's church.

Cabinas El Sueño. Tilarán, Guanacaste. ☎ **506/695-5347.** 12 rms (all with private bath). $16 double; $20 triple. MC, V.

Situated in the middle of this small town, Cabinas El Sueño is a simple two-story accommodation, but it is clean and the management is friendly. There is parking in back and a small courtyard complete with a fountain on the second floor of the building. Downstairs, there's a restaurant and bar.

WHERE TO DINE

If you are staying in Tilarán, there are numerous inexpensive eateries, including restaurants at **Cabinas Mary** and **Cabinas El Sueño,** both of which are mentioned above. Also, around the corner from Cabinas Mary is **El Lugar,** a popular restaurant and bar that's worth checking out. If you are staying outside of town, you're likely to eat in your hotel's dining room since there are few restaurants around the shores of the lake. Also worth mentioning is **Equus BBQ,** a small open-air restaurant in front of Xiloe Lodge. It specializes in roast chicken and steaks. If you are staying down near Nuevo Arenal, try the following restaurant.

Restaurant Lajas. On the main street through town. ☎ **506/694-4169.** Reservations not accepted. Main courses $2–$3.90. No credit cards. Daily 11am–9pm. COSTA RICAN.

This surprisingly fancy little restaurant is one of the best values in Costa Rica. There are red tablecloths on every table, waiters in bow ties, and a wall of mirrors to make the tiny dining room look larger than it really is—but these are only the incidentals. The real reason to eat here is for good Tico cooking at rock-bottom prices. The deal of the day is always the casado. You won't walk away hungry or poor.

4 Monteverde

167 kilometers NW of San José; 82 kilometers NW of Puntarenas

To be frank, I have a love/hate relationship with Monteverde. Next to Manuel Antonio, this is Costa Rica's most internationally recognized tourist destination. The fame and accompanying traffic have led me to dub it the Monteverde Crowd Forest. Nevertheless, the preserve itself as well as the extensive network of private reserves around it are incredibly rich in biodiversity, and a well-organized infrastructure helps guarantee a reasonably rewarding experience for first-time eco-adventurers.

Monteverde translates as "Green Mountain," and that is exactly what you will find at the end of the long, rutted dirt road that leads here. Along the way, you'll pass through mile after mile of often dry, brown pasture lands. All of these pastures were once covered with dense forest, but now only small pieces of that original forest remain.

The village of Monteverde was founded in the 1950s by Quakers from the United States who wished to leave behind a constant fear of war as well as an obligation to support continued militarism through paying U.S. taxes. They chose Costa Rica because it was committed to a nonmilitaristic economic path. Although Monteverde's founders came here to farm the land, they recognized the need to preserve the rare cloud forest that covered the mountain slopes above their fields, and to that end they dedicated the largest adjacent tract of cloud forest as the Monteverde Biological Cloud Forest Preserve.

Perched on a high mountain ridge, this tiny, scattered village and surrounding cloud forest are well known both among scientific researchers and eco-travelers. Cloud forests are a mountain-top phenomenon. Moist, warm air sweeping in off the nearby ocean is forced upward by mountain slopes, and as the moist air rises it cools, forming clouds. The mountain tops of Costa Rica are almost daily blanketed in dense clouds, and as these clouds cling to the slopes, moisture condenses on forest trees. This constant level of moisture has given rise to an incredible diversity of innovative life forms and a forest in which nearly every square inch of space has some sort of plant growing. Within the cloud forest, the branches of huge trees are draped with epiphytic plants—orchids, ferns, and bromeliads. This intense botanic competition has created an almost equally diverse poulation of insects, birds, and other wildlife. Monteverde Biological Cloud Forest Preserve covers 26,000 acres of forest, including several different life zones that are characterized by different types of plants and animals. Within this small area are more than 2,000 species of plants, 400 species of birds, and 100 different species of mammals. It is no wonder that the preserve has been the site of constant scientific investigations since its founding in 1972.

The preserve was originally known only to the handful of researchers who came here to study different aspects of life in the cloud forest. However, as the beauty and biological diversity of the area became known outside of academic circles, casual visitors began arriving. For many, the primary goal was a chance to glimpse the rare and elusive quetzal, a bird once revered by the pre-Columbian peoples of the Americas. As the number of visitors began to grow, lodges began opening, word spread, more lodges opened, and so on. Today Monteverde is a prime example of too many people chasing after the same little piece of nature. On a much smaller scale, Monteverde is akin to the Yosemite Valley—a place of great and fragile beauty whose very beauty is threatened by its popularity. However, despite the hordes of eco-tourists traipsing the trails of Monteverde, it is still a beautiful place and offers a glimpse into the life of one of the world's most threatened ecosystems. I urge you, though, to seriously consider visiting another cloud forest area in an effort to lessen the impact of tourism on Monteverde. Other places you could visit include Villablanca and the Los Angeles Cloud Forest Reserve, or the Tapantí National Wildlife Refuge, which has several nearby lodges. At either of these places you will find far fewer crowds and usually better chances of seeing the famed quetzal.

ESSENTIALS

GETTING THERE & DEPARTING   By Bus   Express buses leave San José daily at 6:30am and 2:30pm from Calle 12, 75 meters north of avenida 7. The trip's duration is 3¹/₂ hours; fare is $4.75.

There is also a daily bus that departs Puntarenas for Santa Elena, only a few kilometers from Monteverde, at 2:15pm. The bus stop in Puntarenas is across the street from the main bus station. Trip duration is 2¹/₂ hours; fare is $2.50.

There is a daily bus from Tilarán (Lake Arenal) at 1pm. Trip duration is 3 hours (40 kilometers!); fare is $1.10.

One other option is to take Costa Rica Expeditions's van (☎ 506/257-0766) from San José. You must have a reservation. Fare is $35 each way.

The express bus departs for San José daily at 6:30am and 2:30pm. The bus from Santa Elena to Puntarenas leaves daily at 6am. If you should be heading to Manuel Antonio, take the 6am Santa Elena/Puntarenas bus and transfer in Puntarenas. To reach Liberia, take the 6am Santa Elena/Puntarenas bus and get off at the Río Lagarto Bridge, where the bus reaches the paved road. You can then flag down a bus bound for Liberia (almost any bus heading north). The Santa Elena/Tilarán bus leaves daily at 7am.

By Car   Take the Interamerican Highway toward Puntarenas and follow the signs for Nicaragua. About 31 kilometers past the turnoff for Puntarenas, watch for the Río Lagarto Bridge. It takes about $2^{1}/_{4}$ hours to this point. Take the dirt road to the right just before the bridge. From this turnoff, it's another 38 kilometers ($1^{1}/_{2}$ to 2 hours) to Monteverde. The going is very slow because the road is so bad. Many people are told that this road is not passable without four-wheel drive, but I have been driving it for years, albeit in the dry season, in regular cars. Just don't try it in the rainy season unless you have four-wheel drive. Be sure you have plenty of gas in the car before starting up to Monteverde: This grueling road eats up fuel, and the one gas station in Monteverde doesn't always have gas.

ORIENTATION   Arriving   As you approach Santa Elena, take the right fork in the road if you are heading directly to Monteverde. If you continue straight, you will come into the village of Santa Elena, which has a bus stop, health clinic, bank, general store, and a few simple restaurants and budget hotels.

Monteverde, on the other hand, is not a village in the traditional sense of the word. There is no center of town, only dirt lanes leading off from the main road to various farms. This main road has signs for all the hotels and restaurants mentioned here, and dead-ends at the reserve entrance.

FAST FACTS   In Santa Elena, you'll find the Puntarenas bus stop, a few general stores, a bank, and a little health clinic. There's also a small **information center** (☎ 506/645-5025). It's located across the street from the National Bank and is open Monday through Saturday from 9am to noon and from 1 to 6pm.

GETTING AROUND   A taxi (☎ 506/645-5322) between Santa Elena and either the Monteverde Cloud Forest Reserve or the Santa Elena Rainforest Reserve will cost around $7. Count on paying between $4 to $6 for the ride from Santa Elena to your lodge in Monteverde.

EXPLORING THE WILDLIFE PRESERVE

Don't expect to see all the plants and animals you've been reading about during your visit because many of them are quite rare or elusive. However, with a guide hired through your hotel or on one of the preserve's official guided 2- to 3-hour hikes, you can see far more than you could on your own. At $15 per person, the preserve's tours may seem expensive, especially after you pay the $8 preserve entrance fee, but I strongly recommend that you go with a guide. I went into the preserve twice in the same morning—once on my own and once with a guide—and with the guide I saw much more and learned much more about cloud forests and their inhabitants. On the other hand, while alone I saw a rare bird, a guan, that I didn't see when walking the trails with a dozen other interested but rather noisy visitors. There is much to be said for walking quietly through the forest on your own.

The preserve is open daily from 7am to 4pm. Because only 100 people are allowed into the preserve at any one time, you may be forced to wait for a while before being allowed in. However, if you go the afternoon before you want to visit, you can usually get tickets for early the next morning. Rubber boots are available at the preserve entrance, and rent for $2. The trails can be very muddy depending on the season, so ask at the entrance and these boots may make your hike much more pleasant.

Before venturing into the forest, have a look around the information center. There are several guidebooks available, as well as posters and postcards of some of the preserve's more famous animal inhabitants. Perhaps the most famous resident of the cloud forests of Costa Rica is the quetzal, a robin-sized bird with iridescent-green wings and a ruby-red breast, which has become extremely rare due to habitat destruction. The male quetzal also has two long tail feathers that make it one of the most spectacular birds on earth. The best time to see quetzals is early to midmorning, with February through April (mating season) being the easiest months to spot these magnificent birds.

Other animals that have been seen in Monteverde include jaguars, ocelots, and tapirs. After the quetzal, Monteverde's most beautiful resident was the golden toad (*sapo dorado*). However, following several years of low precipitation, the golden toad seems to have disappeared from the forest, its only known home in the entire world. There has been speculation that the toad was adversely affected by a natural drought cycle, the disappearing ozone layer, pesticides, or acid rain. Photos of the golden toad abound in Monteverde, and I'm sure you'll be as saddened as I was by the disappearance of such a beautiful creature.

To learn even more about Monteverde, stop in at the **Monteverde Conservation League** (☎ 506/645-5003), which is located across the street from the gas station. Their office is open Monday through Friday from 8am to noon and from 1 to 5pm, and from 8am to noon on Saturdays. They sell informative books, T-shirts, and cards, and all proceeds go to purchase more land for the Bosque Eterno de Los Niños (Children's Eternal Forest).

BIRDWATCHING & HIKING OUTSIDE THE PRESERVE

Ample birdwatching and hiking opportunities can also be found outside the preserve boundaries. You can avoid the crowds at Monteverde by heading 5 kilometers north from the village of Santa Elena to the **Santa Elena Forest Reserve.** This 900-acre cloud forest has a maximum elevation of 5,600 feet, which makes it the highest cloud forest in the Monteverde area. There are 8 kilometers of hiking trails as well as an information center. As it borders the Monteverde Preserve, a similar richness of flora and fauna are to be found here. Entry fees at this reserve go directly to support local schools.

The Bajo Tigre Trail is a 2-mile-long trail that's home to several different bird species not usually found within the reserve. The trail starts a little past the CASEM artisans' shop and is open daily from 8am to 4pm. The trail has been undergoing some upkeep and improvements, but the Monteverde Conservation League has promised to keep the entrance fee very low.

You can also go on guided 3-hour hikes at the **Reserva Sendero Tranquilo** (☎ 506/645-5010), which has 200 acres of land, two-thirds of which is in virgin forest. This reserve is located up the hill from the cheese factory, charges $15 for its tours, and is open daily from 5am to 2pm seasonally.

The **Monteverde Eco-Farm** (☎ 506/645-5222) is open daily from 7am to 5pm. More than 100 species of birds have been seen here. There are also good views and two waterfalls. Admission is $5.

CANOPY TOURS, NIGHT TOURS & HORSEBACK RIDING

For an elevated look at the cloud forest, check out the local branch of **Canopy Tours** (☎ 506/645-5423), which has an office across from Hotel El Tucan. The 2^1/$_2$-hour tours run three times daily and cost $40 for adults; $25 for children under 12.

Almost all of the area hotels can arrange a variety of other tour and activity options, including night trips to the Arenal Volcano (a grueling 4-hour ride away), guided night tours of the cloud forest, and, of course, horseback riding. The going rate for horseback rides with a guide is between $7 and $10 per person per hour. **Meg's Riding Stables** (☎ 506/645-5052) is one of the more established operators and offers 4-hour guided rides for around $35.

OTHER THINGS TO SEE & DO IN MONTEVERDE

You can glimpse another part of the area's history at **El Trapiche** (☎ 506/ 645-6054), where the process of making *tapa dulce* is demonstrated on Tuesday, Thursday, and Saturday on an old-fashioned sugar mill. El Trapiche is open Tuesday through Sunday from 11am to 10pm, serves *tipico* food, and sells homemade sugar products. You'll find El Trapiche 1^1/$_2$ kilometers north of Santa Elena on the road to Tilarán.

Because the vegetation in the cloud forest is so dense, most of the forest's animal residents are rather difficult to spot. If you were unsatisfied with your sightings, even with a naturalist guide leading you, you might want to consider attending a slide show of photographs taken in the preserve. These slide shows are presented by the **Hummingbird Gallery** (☎ 506/645-5030) daily at 4:30pm. Admission is $3. The Monteverde Lodge presents a similar slide show at 6:15pm on Monday, and Wednesday through Friday.

You'll find the Hummingbird Gallery just outside the preserve entrance. Hanging from trees around the gallery are several hummingbird feeders that attract more than seven species of these avian jewels. At any given moment, there might be several dozen hummingbirds buzzing and chattering around the building and your head. Inside you will, of course, find a lot of beautiful mounted and unmounted color prints of hummingbirds. There are also many other beautiful photos from Monteverde available in prints or postcards. The gallery is open daily from 9:30am to 5pm.

Birds are not the only colorful fauna in the Monteverde cloud forest. Butterflies abound here, and the **Butterfly Garden,** located near the Pensión Monteverde Inn, displays many of Costa Rica's most beautiful species. Besides the hundreds of preserved and mounted butterflies, there are also gardens and a greenhouse where you can watch live butterflies. The garden is open daily from 9:30am to 4pm, and the admission is $5 for adults and $2.50 for children, which includes a guided tour. The best time to visit is between 11am and 1pm, when the butterflies are most active.

If your taste runs toward the slithery, don't miss the quaint **Serpentarium Santa Elena** (☎ 506/645-5238) on the road to the preserve. It's open daily from 9am to 4pm, and charges $3 for admission.

SHOPPING

If you're in the mood to do some shopping, stop in at **CASEM,** which is on the right just past Restaurant El Bosque. This crafts cooperative sells embroidered clothing, T-shirts, posters and postcards with photos of the local flora and fauna, locally grown and roasted coffee, and many other items to remind you of your visit to

Monteverde. CASEM is open Monday through Saturday from 8am to 5pm, and on Sunday from 10am to 4pm (closed Sunday from May through October). Between November and April, you can also visit the **Sarah Dowell Watercolor Gallery,** which is up the hill from the cheese factory and sells paintings by this local artist.

☕ **TAKE A BREAK** Finally, if all the above has worn you out, stop in at **Chunches** (☎ 506/645-5147), a new coffee/espresso bar and bookstore in Santa Elena, which also doubles as a laundromat.

WHERE TO STAY

When choosing a place to stay in Monteverde, be sure to check whether the rates include a meal plan or not. In the past all the lodges operated on the American plan (three meals a day), but this practice is on the wane. Check before you assume anything.

EXPENSIVE

✪ **Monteverde Lodge.** Calle Central and Avenida 1 (Apdo. 6941), San José. ☎ **506/257-0766.** Fax 506/257-1665. 27 rms. Dec 15–Apr 30, $78 double, $90 triple; May 1–Dec 14, $68 double, $78 triple. AE, MC, V.

Operated by Costa Rica Expeditions, the Monteverde is the most upscale hotel in Monteverde. It's located 5 kilometers from the preserve entrance in a secluded setting near Santa Elena. Guest rooms are large and comfortable and have angled walls of glass, in front of which are set chairs and a table, so avid birdwatchers need not even leave their rooms to do a bit of birding in the morning. However, the gardens and secondary forest surrounding the lodge are also home to quite a few species of birds.

Dining/Entertainment: The hotel's dining room offers excellent formal service (waiters in bow ties), great views, and good Tico and international food. Meals will cost an additional $28 (plus tax and tip) per person per day. The bar adjacent to the dining room is a very popular gathering spot, especially with the many groups that use this lodge. There are regular evening slide shows focusing on the cloud forest.

Services: Bus service to and from San José ($35 each way), shuttle to the preserve ($4 each way), horseback riding, various optional tours.

Facilities: This lodge's most popular feature is a large hot tub in a big atrium garden just off the lobby. After hiking all day, you can soak your bones under the stars.

MODERATE

✪ **Hotel Belmar.** Apdo. 17-5655, Monteverde, Puntarenas. ☎ **506/645-5201.** Fax 506/645-5135. 32 rms. $55 double; $65 triple. Discounts are available in the off-season. No credit cards.

You'll think that you're in the Alps when you stay at this beautiful Swiss chalet–style hotel. Set on the top of a grassy hill, the Belmar has stunning views of the Nicoya Gulf and the Pacific. Afternoons in the dining room or lounge are idyllic, with bright sunlight streaming in through a west-facing wall of glass; sunsets are spectacular. Most of the guest rooms come with wood paneling, French doors, and little balconies that open onto spendid views. Meals usually live up to the surroundings and run around $21 per person per day. The Belmar is up a road to the left of the gas station as you come into the village of Monteverde.

Hotel De Montaña Monteverde. Apdo. 2070-1002, Paseo Los Estudiantes, San José. ☎ **506/224-3050.** Fax 506/222-6184. 22 rms, 5 cabins, 5 suites. Dec–Apr, $60 double, $72 triple, $72–$101 suite; May–Nov, $41 double, $49 triple, $49–$70 suite. AE, MC, V.

This long, low, motel-style building is one of the oldest hotels in Monteverde and is frequently filled with tour groups. The hotel is surrounded by 15 acres of farm and woods, and there are horses available for rent. Older rooms are rustic and have wood paneling. Newer rooms have queen-size beds, more light, and spectacular views of the Nicoya Gulf. There are also several spacious suites, including a honeymoon suite with its own whirlpool tub and a view. For family privacy there are five cabins across the lawn from the main lodge. The rustic glass-walled dining room offers excellent views. Attached to the restaurant is a small bar that is busy in the evening, when people sit around swapping stories of their day's adventures and wildlife sightings. Meals will run you around $30 per person per day. On cold nights, you can warm up in the sauna or hot tub.

Hotel Fonda Vela. Apdo. 70060-1000, San José. ☎ **506/257-1413** or 506/645-5125. Fax 506/257-1416. 28 rms, 8 suites. $59 double; $68 triple; $66–$74 suite double, $75–$83 suite triple. AE, MC, V.

Located on the right after the sign for the Pensíon Flor Mar, the Fonda Vela is one of the more luxurious lodges in Monteverde. Guest rooms are housed in five buildings scattered among the forests and pastures of this former farm, and most have views of the Nicoya Gulf. Lots of hardwood has been used throughout, and there are flagstone floors in some rooms. About half of the rooms have bathtubs, a rarity in Costa Rica. Several large suites—two of which have sleeping lofts—are the most spacious accommodations available, but unfortunately they do not have views. The dining room does have great sunset views and is the site each January of the Monteverde Music Festival, with nightly 5pm concerts of classical, jazz, and Latin music provided by San José's better combos. Meals will run you $22.50 per person per day. You'll also find a bar and a gift shop here, and laundry service and horse rentals ($8 per hour) are available.

Hotel Heliconia. Apartado 10921-1000, San José. ☎ **506/645-5109** or 506/645-5145. Fax 506/645-5007. 22 rms. $60 double; $70 triple. V.

The Heliconia, named after one of the tropics' most fascinating flowers, is one of the most comfortable and luxurious hotels in Monteverde. The main lodge building has varnished wood walls and a hardwood-floored balcony that runs the length of the second floor. Guest rooms in the main building are also done in floor-to-ceiling hardwoods that give them a rustic, mountain-resort feel. Behind the main lodge there are paths that lead through attractive gardens to rooms with more space. These latter rooms have carpeting, and most have full-size baths with bathtubs. There's a hot tub in a bamboo grove, just outside the main building. The hotel's restaurant serves a changing nightly menu with both Tico and international dishes. There's also a small bar and trails that lead from the hotel up to an area of virgin forest with a viewpoint.

Hotel Villa Verde. Apdo. 16-5655, Monteverde, Puntarenas. ☎ **506/645-5025.** Fax 506/645-5115. 16 rms, 5 suites. $45 double; $75 suite. All rates include breakfast. MC, V.

This is the closest hotel to the Preserve and is built on a grand scale. The main lodge features a large dining room with floor-to-ceiling windows that reach all the way to the two-story-high roof. Each suite has a living room, and a fireplace, and is identified not by a number, but by the likeness of a bird that's carved into the door. Standard rooms are spacious and comfortable, although the textured sand bathroom walls and pale blue tiles are an aesthetic disaster. The food here is favored by many of the local residents and guides.

✪ **El Sapo Dorado.** Apdo. 9-5655, Monteverde, Puntarenas. ☎ **506/645-5010.** Fax 506/645-5180. 20 rms (all with bath). $65 double; $77 triple. Sunset Terrace Suites an additional $10. No credit cards.

Located on a steep hill between Santa Elena and the preserve, El Sapo Dorado (named for Monteverde's famous "golden toad") offers attractive cabins with good views. The cabins are built of hardwoods both inside and out, and are surrounded by a grassy lawn. Big windows let in lots of light, and high ceilings keep the rooms cool during the day. The older cabins also have fireplaces, which are a welcome feature on chilly nights. The newer rooms all have spacious terraces, with sunset views. The hotel's restaurant is open to the public and serves three meals daily. The dinner menu changes nightly, but among the regular offerings are chicken with orange sauce, homemade ravioli, and filet mignon with pepper-cream sauce. There is always a vegetarian item, and main courses range from $7 to $12. There is a large patio terrace from which you can watch the sunset while listening to classical music. The bar stays open until 11pm and is usually fairly quiet. To find the hotel and restaurant, watch for the sign on the main road to the preserve.

INEXPENSIVE

El Establo. Apdo. 549-2050, San Pedro. ☎ **506/645-5110** or 506/645-5033. Fax 506/ 645-5041. 20 rms. $35 double; $40 triple; $45 quad. AE, MC, V.

Horses are an integral part of Costa Rican culture and a common sight in Monteverde. El Establo, as its name implies, uses a horse stable theme in its architectural design. Though the hotel is next to the road, there are 120 acres of farm behind it, and half of this area is in primary forest. Most of the rooms are situated off a large enclosed porch that contains plenty of comfortable chairs and a fireplace. Guest-room doors look as if they were salvaged from a stable, but inside, the rooms are carpeted and have orthopedic mattresses and modern bathrooms, though with showers only. The end rooms have a bit more light than others. Of course, the hotel also has plenty of horses for rent at $7 per hour, with a guide. Meals will run you around $21 per person per day.

⑤ **El Bosque.** Apdo. 1165-1000, San José. ☎ **506/645-5129** or 506/645-5158. Fax 506/ 645-5129. 21 rms. $30 double; $36 triple; $40 quad. MC, V.

Hidden down the hill behind El Bosque restaurant (on the main road to the preserve), is one of Monteverde's best values. Though the rooms are very basic, they are clean, fairly large, and have high ceilings, picture windows, and double beds. The cement floors and simple furnishings are what help keep the rates down. The rooms are arranged in a semicircle around a minimally landscaped garden. The setting may not be spectacular, but if you're going to spend all day in the preserve, this shouldn't bother you too much. The hotel also has a camping area ($5 per person per night).

The hotel's restaurant is a hundred yards up a dirt road and down a path that crosses a jungly ravine by footbridge, which turns going for breakfast into a morning birdwatching trip. Tico standards and international dishes are served here, with prices ranging from $4 to $15.40.

Cabinas El Gran Mirador. Monteverde, Puntarenas. ☎ **506/645-5087.** 4 cabins (none with private bath). $17 per person. All rates include breakfast. No credit cards.

If you're looking for a bit more adventure and rusticity than is offered at any of the lodges in Monteverde or Santa Elena, give these friendly folks a call. The rustic wooden cabins are all very simply furnished and have great views of Arenal Volcano (when it's clear). Sleeping is dormitory style and if you're alone, you probably will be grouped with other travelers. The cabins are a long way from the Monteverde

Cloud Forest Preserve, but they are close to the Santa Elena Rainforest Reserve. You can now reach these cabins year round in a four-wheel-drive vehicle, so it's no longer necessary to be taken in by horseback—although you can still rent horses for $8 per hour.

Hotel El Tucan. Santa Elena, Puntarenas. ☎ **506/645-5017.** 14 rms (7 with bath). $10 double without bath, $20 double with bath. No credit cards.

This very basic lodging is located on the edge of Santa Elena (on the back road from the village's main street that leads to Monteverde) and consequently does not have the rural feel of many of the area's other accommodations. Though the rooms without baths are only slightly larger than closets, they are fairly clean. Rooms with a private bath are slightly larger, with some housed in a separate building across the street. Costa Rican–style meals are served in a very basic dining room on the ground floor. Keep in mind that this hotel is 5 kilometers from the preserve. If you don't have a car, transportation to and from the preserve by taxi is going to add a bit to the cost of the room.

⑤ Pensión Flor de Lis. Santa Elena, Monteverde. ☎/fax **506/645-5236.** 8 rms (3 with private bath). $14 double, $21 triple (shared bath); $20 double, $30 triple (private bath). V.

This new pension is my favorite budget option in Monteverde. Located 75 meters up a dirt road, just outside Santa Elena on the way to the preserve, this hotel has an authentic rural feel. The rooms are very simple, but immaculately clean. The owners will make you feel part of the family. They also know and love the area, and are eager to share it with guests. A home-cooked breakfast will cost an extra $3.

Pensión Flor Mar. Apdo. 10165-1000, San José. ☎ **506/645-5009.** Fax 506/645-5011. 13 rms (3 with bath). $26 per person without bath, $30 per person with bath. All rates include three meals daily. No credit cards.

The Flor Mar was one of the first lodges to open in Monteverde and initially catered almost exclusively to professors and students doing scientific research in the preserve. Study groups still make up the bulk of the Flor Mar's business, but casual visitors are also welcome. The rooms are very simply furnished, which means bunk beds in some rooms. There are no views to speak of here. However, this lodge is close to the park entrance—a definite plus if you don't have a car. The dining room is large and rather dark, but there is a much more appealing lounge in the lower of the lodge's two main buildings. The rates include all three meals a day.

⑤ Pensión Monteverde Inn. Apdo. 10165-1000, San José. ☎ **506/645-5156.** 10 rms (8 with private bath). $5 per person with shared bath; $8 per person with private bath. No credit cards.

Of the numerous inexpensive lodgings in the area, this one has the most pleasant surroundings. Located just past the Monteverde Butterfly Garden, the Monteverde Inn is a couple of hundred yards off the main road on a small farm. Owner David Savage and his family have operated this simple, rustic lodge for years. The rooms are small and come with two twin beds or a double bed. Hardwood floors keep the rooms from seeming too spartan. It's a bit of a walk up to the park entrance, but once you reach the main road, you can try hitching a ride. Horse rentals are available for $5 per hour. This is a good choice for those who have to watch their colónes; economical meals are available.

WHERE TO DINE

Most lodges in Monteverde have their own dining rooms, and these are the most convenient places to eat. Because most visitors to Monteverde want to get an early start, they usually grab a quick breakfast at their hotel. It is also common for people to have their lodge pack them a bag lunch to take with them to the preserve. However, there are now several inexpensive restaurants scattered along the road between Santa Elena and Monteverde. Two worth mentioning are the **Pizzeria de Johnny** near the Hotel Heliconia and the **Soda Cerro Verde** across from the gas station.

Alternatively, stop in at **Stella's Bakery** (across the road from the CASEM gift shop) for some fresh bread and maybe a piece of cake or some cookies. Stella's is open daily from 6am to 6pm and also has a small cafe where you can get pizzas, eggplant parmigiana, salads, and deliciously decadent baked goods. Next, stop by the **Monteverde Cheese Factory** and pick up some of the best cheese in Costa Rica (you can even see it being made). The cheese factory is open Monday through Saturday from 7:30am to 4pm, and on Sunday from 7:30am to 12:30pm. Between the two, you should be able to put together a great picnic lunch.

✪ **El Sapo Dorado.** Road to the left as you leave Santa Elena. ☎ **506/645-5010.** Reservations recommended. Main courses $6.60–$13.50. No credit cards. Daily 7am–9pm. INTERNATIONAL.

Located high on a hill above the main road, El Sapo Dorado provides great sunsets and good food. The menu is a little bit more imaginative than at most restaurants in Monteverde, which makes it well worth a visit even if you miss the sunset. A recent menu included such dishes as grilled corvina, fettuccini in peanut-squid sauce, and filet mignon in pepper-cream sauce. In addition to a large, formal dining room, there is a patio that's a great spot for lunch or an early dinner. Taped classical music in the evenings.

The Central Pacific Coast

8

The central Pacific coast offers several of the most easily accessible beaches in Costa Rica. They range from the somewhat seedy Puntarenas and the cut-rate, fun-in-the-sun Jacó, to the jungle-clad hillsides of Manuel Antonio and Dominical. For the most part, this coast is not as spectacular as that of the more rugged Nicoya Peninsula, but neither is it as brown and desolate-looking in the dry season. The climate here is considerably more humid than farther north, but not nearly as steamy as along the south Pacific or Caribbean coasts. Jacó and Manuel Antonio are Costa Rica's two most developed beaches, while Puntarenas, a former seaport, offers the most urban beach setting in the country (it's just a short day trip away from San José). If you're looking to get away from it all and spend as little money as possible, Dominical should be your top choice on this coast.

This is also where you'll find some of Costa Rica's most popular and spectacular national parks and biological reserves: namely, Manuel Antonio National Park, home of three-toed sloths and white-faced monkeys; Chirripó National Park, a misty cloud forest that becomes a barren páramo at the peak of the mountain that lends its name to the park, Mt. Chirripó; and Carara Biological Reserve, one of the last places in Costa Rica where you can see the disappearing dry forest join the damp, humid forests that extend south down the coast, and glimpse an occasional scarlet macaw.

1 Puntarenas

130 kilometers W of San José; 113 kilometers S of Liberia; 60 kilometers N of Playa de Jacó

After decades of decay and neglect, Puntarenas is currently undergoing a major makeover. Plans are in the works to build a modern cruise ship dock that will accommodate up to two ships at a time. A 10-mile-long spit of land jutting into the Gulf of Nicoya, Puntarenas was once Costa Rica's busiest port, but that changed several years ago when the government inaugurated nearby Puerto Caldera, a modern container port facility. After losing its port, the city survived primarily on commercial fishing. Watching the tourist boom bring big bucks to other cities, Puntarenas decided to grab its piece of the pie. To that end, the city built a sewage treatment plant to clean up its water and now has the only beach-cleaning machine in Costa Rica. The town's beachfront Paseo de los Turistas (Tourist Walk), a ten-block promenade of ice cream stands, small restaurants, and arcades will be the next area spruced up. When all the work is finished, Puntarenas should also have a convention and recreation center, a seaside aquarium, a museum, and an artisans' row, where visitors will be able to stock up on regional arts and crafts.

With a good highway leading all the way from San José, Puntarenas can be reached in an hour and a half by car, which makes it the closest beach to San José—at least in elapsed time if not in actual mileage. Because Puntarenas is a city, a former port town and commercial fishing center, this beach has a very different character from any other beach in Costa Rica. The beach itself, a long straight stretch of sand with gentle surf, is backed for most of its length by the Paseo de los Turistas. Across a wide boulevard from the paseo are hotels, restaurants, bars, discos, and shops. It's all very civilized, though the preponderance of cement gives it too much of an urban feel for my taste. The views across the Gulf of Nicoya and the sunsets are quite beautiful, and there is almost always a cooling breeze blowing in off the water. All around town you'll find unusual old buildings, reminders of the important role Puntarenas once played in Costa Rican history. It was from here that much of the Central Valley's coffee crop was once shipped, and while the coffee barons in the highlands were getting rich, so too were the merchants of Puntarenas.

If you're in Costa Rica for only a short time and want to get in some time on the beach, Puntarenas is certainly an option, though swimming here still seems more the exception than the rule. You can even do it in a day trip from San José. Likewise, if you are looking for a base from which to visit national parks up and down the Pacific coast, Puntarenas is one of your best bets. From here you can head north to the national parks in Guanacaste or south to Carara Biological Reserve. Also, if you are heading out to any of the beaches at the southern end of the Nicoya Peninsula, you'll be passing through Puntarenas to catch one of three ferries. Puntarenas is most popular as a weekend holiday spot for Ticos from San José and is at its liveliest on weekends.

ESSENTIALS

GETTING THERE & DEPARTING   By Bus   Express buses leave San José daily every 30 minutes between 5am and 7pm from the corner of Calle 12 and Avenida 9. Trip duration is hours; fare is $2.

The main Puntarenas bus station is a block east of the Hotel Imperial, which is in front of the old main dock on the Paseo de los Turistas. Buses to San José leave daily every 30 minutes between 5am and 7pm. The bus to Santa Elena leaves daily at 2:15pm from a stop across the railroad tracks from the main bus station. Buses to Quepos (Manuel Antonio) leave daily at 5 and 11am, and 2pm. A bus leaves for Liberia daily at 5:30pm.

By Car   Head west out of San José on the Interamerican Highway, passing the airport and Alajuela, and follow the signs to Puntarenas. The drive takes about 1¹/₂ hours.

By Ferry   See the "Playa Tambor" or "Playa Montezuma" sections of chapter 4 for information on crossing to Puntarenas from Paquera or Naranjo on the Nicoya Peninsula and returning.

ORIENTATION   Arriving   Puntarenas is built on a long, narrow sand spit that stretches 3 miles out into the Gulf of Nicoya, and is marked by only five streets at its widest. The ferry docks for the Nicoya Peninsula are near the far end of town, as are the bus station and market. The north side of town faces an estuary, while the

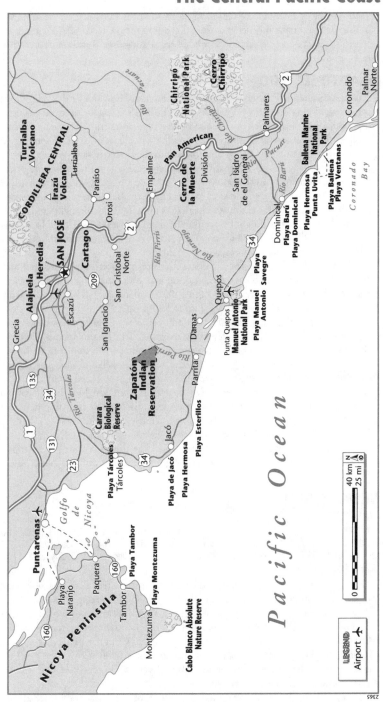

south side faces the mouth of the gulf. The Paseo de los Turistas is on the south side of town, beginning at the pier and extending out to the point. If you need a taxi, call 506/663-2020. Car rentals are available from **Elegante Rent-a-Car** (☎ 506/661-1958).

WHAT TO SEE & DO

Take a walk along the **Paseo de los Turistas** and notice how similar this side of town is to a few Florida beach towns 50 years ago. The hotels across the street range in style from converted old wooden homes with bright gingerbread trim, to modern concrete monstrosities, to tasteful art deco relics needing a new coat of paint. If you want to go swimming, the ocean waters are now said to be perfectly safe (pollution was a problem for many years). Alternatively, you can head out to the end of the peninsula to the **Balneario Municipal,** the public pool. It is huge, has a great view (albeit through a chain-link fence), and is surrounded by lawns and gardens. Entrance is only $1 for adults and 50¢ for children. The pool is open Tuesday through Sunday from 9am to 4pm. If the beach right here in the city doesn't appeal to you, head back down the spit to the **Playa Dona Aña,** a popular beach several kilometers south, with picnic tables, bath and changing rooms, and a restaurant.

Puntarenas isn't known as one of Costa Rica's prime sportfishing ports, but there are usually a few charter boats available. Check at your hotel or at the Hotel Colonial. Rates are usually between $250 and $400 for a half day and between $400 and $600 for a full day. These rates are for up to four people.

The most popular water excursions from Puntarenas are **yacht cruises** among the tiny uninhabited islands of the Guayabo, Negritos, and Pajaros Islands Biological Reserve. These cruises include a gourmet seafood buffet and a stop at beautiful and undeveloped Tortuga Island, where you can swim, snorkel, and sun. The water is clear blue, and the sand is bright white. Several San José–based companies offer these excursions, with round-trip transportation from San José, but if you are already in Puntarenas, you may be able to get a discount by boarding here. Bay Island Cruises (☎ 506/296-5551), Calypso Tours (☎ 506/233-3617), and Sea Ventures (☎ 506/257-2904) are just three of the companies that offer similar tours and will pick you up at your hotel in San José. The price for one of these trips is around $70. Some of these companies also offer sunset cruises with live music, snacks, and a bar.

WHERE TO STAY
EXPENSIVE

Hotel Fiesta. Apdo. 171-5400, Puntarenas. ☎ **506/663-0185** or 506/663-0808; 800/662-2990 or 800/228-5050 in the U.S. Fax 506/663-1516. 268 rms, 7 suites. A/C TV TEL. Dec 16–Apr 15 $95–$115 double, $115–$350 suite; Apr 16–Dec 15 $85–$95 double, $105–$350 suite. AE, MC, V.

There are only a handful of full-service beach resorts in Costa Rica, and only those in Jacó are closer to San José than the Fiesta. So if you're looking for a place in the sun, and you don't want to waste time getting there, this place is worth consideration. Though the resort is right on the beach, it isn't a good swimming beach, so you'll have to confine your water activities to the giant swimming pool. As the name implies, the Fiesta is meant for partying, or at least keeping active. The hotel frequently hosts "beach parties" meant to attract a young Tico clientele, and it is also a convention hotel, so expect crowds.

The hotel is only a few years old, but many of the guest rooms are already showing their age. Though there are large TVs in all the rooms, the bathrooms in the standard rooms are small and have showers only. However, if you opt for a deluxe room or suite, you'll get more comfortable and spacious accommodations.

Dining/Entertainment: A giant rancho at the back of the hotel serves as a restaurant and bar. The latter is done up to resemble a sailboat, complete with sails and rigging. Prices in the restaurant range from $5 to $10 for entrees, though there are also set-price buffets at most meals. A second bar is on an island in the middle of the main pool, and there is also a casino in a large atrium.

Services: Rentals of snorkeling equipment, jet skis, water skis, and sailboards. Tour arrangements and excursions, including scuba trips, sportfishing charters, national-park visits, and day cruises.

Facilities: The free-form main swimming pool is huge, has an island in the middle, and is surrounded by hundreds of lounge chairs. Artificial boulders give it a more natural look. In addition, you'll find a second pool, whirlpool tub, volleyball court, two tennis courts, exercise room, game room, gift shop, and jewelry shop.

Yadran Hotel. At the end of the Paseo de los Turistas (Apdo. 14-5400), Puntarenas. ☎ **506/ 661-2662.** Fax 506/661-1944. 38 rms. A/C TV TEL. $85–$98 double; $105–$118 triple. AE, DC, MC, V.

This is the most luxurious in-town choice and is located at the far end of Puntarenas at the tip of the spit. Because it is in town, you'll have access to other restaurants and can stroll the Paseo de los Turistas. Also, the car-ferry dock is only a few blocks away. The carpeting and appointments seemed a bit run down the last time I visited. The range in room prices reflects whether or not you get an ocean view. I like the upper-floor rooms, with a balcony and a view, best, but even the priciest rooms can seem a bit dreary.

Dining/Entertainment: The hotel has two small restaurants. One is a poolside patio restaurant, and the other is a slightly more formal indoor dining room with a view out over the water. The seafood here is good, if a bit pricey. Entree prices range from $6.50 to $19. A small casino is open every evening from 6pm on. The disco is open on Friday and Saturday beginning at 7pm. It is located underground, so the beat won't keep you awake if you decide not to dance the night away.

Services: Bicycle rentals, sailboat tour and sportfishing arrangements.

Facilities: The pool is small, but it has an attractive patio surrounding it; gift shop.

MODERATE

✪ **Hotel Las Brisas.** Paseo de los Turistas (Apdo. 83-5400), Puntarenas. ☎ **506/661-4040.** Fax 506/661-1487. 19 rms (all with bath). A/C. $50 double; $65 triple (discounts in the off-season). AE, MC, V.

Out near the end of the Paseo de los Turistas, you'll find a very clean hotel with large air-conditioned rooms, a small pool out front, and the beach right across the street. All the rooms have tile floors, double or twin beds, and small tables. Large picture windows keep the rooms sunny and bright during the day. The hotel's small open-air dining room serves some of the best food in town with the emphasis on continental dishes. The bouillabaise is excellent, and if you're lucky you might happen on a Greek-style fish special or homemade moussaka. It's worth staying here just to enjoy the food.

Hotel Porto Bello. Apdo. 108, Puntarenas. ☎ **506/661-1322** or 506/661-2122. Fax 506/ 661-0036. 37 rms. A/C TEL. Dec–Apr, $55 double, $65 triple; May–Nov, $45 double, $55 triple. AE, DC, MC, V.

Located about 7 kilometers before downtown Puntarenas, on the narrow spit behind the soccer field, the Porto Bello is a popular weekend escape for wealthy Ticos. The stucco walls of the hotel are almost blindingly white, but tempered by the lush overgrown gardens that surround the buildings. Most of the rooms have high ceilings, red-tile floors, attractive teak-and-cloth headboards, and balconies or patios that are often hidden by the shrubbery. Watch out—the window unit air conditioners here can be loud. Most of the double rooms have television, but ask first. There are pools for adults and kids, a poolside bar, and even a small beach. You can hire a water taxi for a spin around the bay, or book an all-day cruise to some of the remote and picturesque islands out in the gulf. The open-air restaurant is breezy and cool, with a high ceiling and stucco walls. Grilled meats and seafood are the specialties here—with entrees ranging in price from $6 to $20.

Ⓢ **Hotel Tioga.** Paseo de los Turistas (Apdo. 96-5400), Puntarenas. ☎ **506/661-0271** or 506/255-3115 in San José. Fax 506/661-0127. 46 rms (all with bath). A/C. $30–$45 double (slightly lower rates in the off-season). All rates include breakfast. AE, MC, V.

This 1950s modern-style hotel is Puntarenas's old standard on the Paseo de los Turistas. The beach is right across the street and there are plenty of restaurants within a short walk. When you walk through the front door, you enter a courtyard with a pool that has been painted a brilliant shade of blue. In the middle of the pool, there is a tiny island with a tree growing on it. The four-story hotel is built around this pleasant setting. Rooms vary in size, and some come with cold-water showers only, so if you must have hot water (not really necessary in these hot regions), be sure to request it. The larger rooms are attractive, with huge closets and modern bathrooms. The smaller, less expensive rooms have louvered, frosted-glass windows to let in lots of light and air while maintaining some privacy. The restaurant and bar are on the second floor and there is a breakfast room and lounge on the fourth floor, so you can look out across the water as you enjoy your complimentary breakfast.

INEXPENSIVE

Hotel Ayi Con. 50 meters south of the market (Apdo. 358), Puntarenas. ☎ **506/661-0164**. 44 rms (22 with private bath). $11.85 double without bath, $16.40 double with bath; $20 double with bath and A/C. No credit cards.

Centrally located near the market and the ferry-boat docks, the Ayi Con is your basic low-budget Tico accommodation. It's above a row of shops in a very busy shopping district of Puntarenas and is frequented primarily by Costa Ricans. Backpackers will find that this is probably the best and the cleanest of the cheap hotels in Puntarenas. If you're just passing through and have to spend a night in town, this place is convenient and acceptable.

WHERE TO DINE

Since you are in a seaport, you should be sure to try corvina—the national fish dish of Costa Rica—at least once. The most economical option is to pull up a table at one of the many open-air **snack bars** along the Paseo de los Turistas. They have names like Soda Rio de Janeiro and Soda Acapulco, and serve everything from sandwiches, drinks, and ice cream to ceviche and whole fish meals. Sandwiches are priced at around a dollar, and a fish filet with rice and beans should cost around $3.50. In addition to the restaurants listed below, you might want to try the **Restaurant and Pizzeria La Terraza** (☎ 506/661-3820), which is housed in a lovely wooden house with gingerbread trim on the Paseo de los Turistas.

Ⓢ **Bierstube.** Paseo de los Turistas between calles 21 and 23, Paseo de los Turistas. ☎ **506/ 661-0330**. DC, MC, V. 10am–12pm daily. GERMAN/SEAFOOD.

This German-Tico beer garden also happens to serve excellent seafood. The restaurant is a huge open room with a high ceiling; louvered windows swing open and provide fresh breezes and a view of the bay. There is beer on tap and good hearty meals. The "filete bierstube" is a fresh piece of corvina in a light tomato sauce, with mushrooms and peppers.

La Caravelle. Paseo de los Turistas between calles 21 and 23, Paseo de los Turistas. ☎ **506/ 661-2262.** Reservations recommended in high season and on weekends. Main courses $5.50– $15. MC, V. Wed–Sat noon–2:30pm and 6–10pm, Sun 12–10pm. FRENCH.

For more than 16 years, La Caravelle has been serving fine French dinners amid an eclectic cafe atmosphere. The restaurant's walls are decorated with a curious assortment of paintings, as well as a carousel horse, which give La Caravelle a very playful feel. The menu, however, is strictly traditional French, with such flavorful and well-prepared dishes as tenderloin with bourguignonne sauce or a tarragon béarnaise. There are quite a few good seafood dishes, as well as a salade niçoise. There's a modest assortment of both French and Chilean wines to accompany your meal, though wine prices are a bit high (as they are all over Costa Rica).

2 Playa De Jacó

108 kilometers W of San José; 60 kilometers S of Puntarenas

Playa de Jacó is the closest thing Costa Rica has to Fort Lauderdale during spring break. This long stretch of beach is strung with a dense hodgepodge of hotels in all price categories, cheap souvenir shops, seafood restaurants, pizza joints, and even a miniature golf course. If you're looking for a cheap place to spend a week in the sun that is close to San José, Jacó continues to be the top choice. Charter flights arrive weekly from Montreal and Toronto and consequently many of the hotels here are owned by Canadians, some of whom speak French and Spanish but little English. Jacó is also now gaining popularity with Germans and young Ticos, so if English is your native tongue, you may find yourself in a distinct minority here. This is the most touristy beach in Costa Rica and is a prime example of what happens when rapid growth hits a beach town. However, on the outskirts of town and close to the beach there is still plenty of greenery to offset the excess of cement along the town's main street. In fact, this is the first beach on the Pacific coast that actually has a tropical feel to it. The humidity is palpable and the lushness of the tropical forest is visible on the hillsides surrounding town. In hotel gardens, flowers bloom profusely throughout the year.

ESSENTIALS

GETTING THERE & DEPARTING   By Bus   Express buses leave San José daily at 7:30 and 10:30am, and 3:30pm from the "Coca-Cola" bus terminal at Calle 16 between avenidas 1 and 3. Trip duration is 3 hours; fare is $2.20.

Buses from San José to Quepos also stop in Jacó (they let passengers off on the highway about 1 kilometer from town). These buses leave San José daily at 6, 7, and 10am, and 12, 2, 4, 5, and 6pm. Trip duration is 3 hours; fare is $1.80.

From Puntarenas, you can catch Quepos-bound buses daily at 5 and 11am, and 2pm and get off in Jacó. The trip's duration is 1 hour; fare is $1.50.

The Jacó bus station is at the north end of town about 50 yards off the main road near the Hotel El Jardin. Buses for San José leave daily at 5 and 11am, and 3pm. Buses bound for Quepos stop in Jacó around 6am, and 12 and 4pm. Since schedules can change, it is best to ask at your hotel about current times of departures.

By Car   There are two main routes to Jacó. The easier though longer route is to take the Interamerican Highway west out of San José and get off at the Puntarenas exit. From here, head south on the Costanera, the coast road. Alternatively, you can take the narrow and winding, though more scenic, old highway, which turns off the

Interamerican Highway just west of Alajuela near the town of Atenas. This highway meets the Costanera a few kilometers west of Orotina.

ORIENTATION Arriving Playa de Jacó is a short distance off the southern highway. One main road runs parallel to the beach and it is off these roads that you will find most of the hotels and restaurants.

GETTING AROUND While almost everything is within walking distance in Jaco, you can can rent a bicycle or scooter from several shops on the main street or **call a taxi** (☎ 506/643-3030). For longer excursions, you can **rent a car** from **Ada** (☎ 506/643-3207), **Economy** (☎ 506/643-3280) or **Zuma** (☎ 506/643-3207). Expect to pay approximately $50 for a one-day rental.

FAST FACTS Both the Banco Nacional and Banco de Costa Rica have branches in town on the main road and are open Monday through Friday from 9am to 3pm. Botiquín Garabito, the town's **pharmacy,** is down the street from the Banco Nacional. There is a **gas station** out by El Bosque restaurant at the south end of town. The **health center** and **post office** are at the Municipal Center at the south end of town, across from El Naranjal restaurant. A public phone office, from which you can make international calls, is located in the ICE building on the main road. This office is open Monday through Saturday from 8am to 12pm and from 1 to 5pm. **The Solar Laundry** (☎ 506/643-3096) is located a few blocks in from the center of town, and is open Monday through Friday 8am to 5pm.

FUN ON AND OFF THE BEACH

Unfortunately, the water here has a nasty reputation for riptides, as does most of the water off Costa Rica's Pacific coast. Even strong swimmers have been know to drown in the power rips. At times storms far offshore cause huge waves to pound on the beach, making it impossible to go in the water at all. If this is the case, you'll have to be content with the hotel pool.

After you've spent some time on Playa de Jacó, you might want to visit some of the other nearby beaches, of which there are several. **Playa Esterillos,** 22 kilometers southwest of Jacó, is long and wide and almost always nearly deserted. **Playa Hermosa,** 10 kilometers southeast of Jacó, where sea turtles lay eggs from July to December, is also well-known for its great surfing waves. **Playa Herradura,** about 6¹/₂ kilometers northwest of Jacó, is ringed by lush hillsides and has a campground and a few very basic cabinas. All of these beaches are beautiful and easily reached by car or bicycle (if you've got plenty of energy).

The same waves that often make Playa de Jacó unsafe for swimming make this beach one of the most popular in the country with gringo surfers. In addition, there are a couple of other excellent surfing beaches nearby—**Playa Hermosa** and **Playa Escondida.** Those who want to challenge the waves can rent surfboards for around $2.50 an hour and boogie boards for $1.50 an hour.

BIKING If you would rather stay out of the surf but still want to get some exercise, you can rent a bike for around $8 per day or $1.50 per hour. Both bikes and boards are available from several places along the main road.

DIVING Scuba divers can arrange dive trips through **Viajes Jaguar** (☎ 506/643-3242), which has its office in an older house next door to the phone office on the main road into town. A two-tank drive is a pricey $80 ($100 with equipment rental). They also rent snorkeling gear for $10 a day.

SPORTFISHING If you're interested in doing some sportfishing, **Viajes Jaguar** (☎ 506/643-3242) rents boats and other equipment (see above for office location). A half-day fishing trip for four people will cost $325, and a full day will cost $450.

CARARA BIOLOGICAL RESERVE: A FAMOUS NESTING GROUND FOR SCARLET MACAWS & A PLACE TO SEE CROCODILES

Fifteen per CMS north of Jacó is Carara Biological Reserve, a world-renowned nesting ground for scarlet macaws. It has several miles of trails open to visitors. There is a loop trail that takes about an hour and another trail that is open only to tour groups. The macaws migrate daily, spending their days in the park and nights among the coastal mangroves. It is often best to view them in the early morning when they arrive, or around sunset when they head back to the coast for the evening. Among the other wildlife you might see here are Caimans, coatimundis, armadillo, pacas, peccaries, river otters, kinkajous, and, of course, hundreds of species of birds. Be sure to bring along insect repellent, or, better yet, wear light cotton long sleeves and pants. The reserve is open daily from 8am to 4:30pm. This is a national park so admission is a flat $6 per person at the gate. There are several companies offering tours to Carara Biological Reserve for around $30–$35. Check at your hotel or contact **Fantasy Tours** (☎ 506/643-3231 or 506/643-3383) for schedules and more information.

Just north of the entrance into the Carara Biological Reserve is the bridge over the Tarcoles River. The muddy banks of this river are home to a healthy population of American crocodiles. This bridge is a prime viewing spot for both the crocodiles and the macaw migrations, and thieves and pickpockets work it regularly. Do not leave your car or valuables unguarded, and be wary if yours is the only car parked here.

ORGANIZED TOURS OF NEARBY SITES

If you will be spending your entire Costa Rican visit in Jacó but would like to see some other parts of the country, you can arrange tours through the local office of **Explorica** (☎ 506/643-3586). This company offers day tours to Poás and Irazú volcanoes, white-water rafting trips, cruises to Tortuga Island, trips to Braulio Carillo and Manuel Antonio national parks, and other places. They also offer overnight trips. Rates range from $55 to $75 for day trips. **Horseback-riding tours** are also very popular. These trips give you a chance to get away from all the development in Jacó and see a bit of nature. Contact Fantasy Tours, or **Sanchez Madrigal Bros.** (☎ 506/643-3203) to make a reservation. Tours lasting 3 to 4 hours cost around $25 to $30.

WHERE TO STAY IN PLAYA DE JACÓ

Since Playa Leona and Playa Hermosa de Jacó (not to be confused with Playa Hermosa in Guanacaste) are close by, many people choose accommodations in these beach towns as well. Selected listings for these two towns follow this section. Also note that many of the hotels listed here have good restaurants and quite a few guests choose to dine at their hotel during their stay.

EXPENSIVE

Hotel Jacófiesta. Apdo. 38, Playa de Jacó, Puntarenas. ☎ **506/643-3147** or 506/643-3243. Fax 506/643-3148. 85 rms. A/C TV TEL. $60–$95 double. AE, MC, V.

If you are not coming down to Jacó on a Canadian charter, it is often difficult to find a room in the high season. This is one place to try, since they don't seem to book up completely with tour groups. Located at the south end of the beach, the Jacófiesta has rooms of various types and ages. I like the large cabina rooms, which have kitchenettes and are located near both the pool and the beach. The older buildings have smaller rooms that are adequate but that face a barren-looking garden. These rooms have small refrigerators. Be forewarned: "fiesta" is Spanish for party. If you're looking for a quiet beach retreat, look elsewhere. If you're looking for a pounding pool-side disco, organized beach volleyball contests, and afternoon mass aerobic classes, this might be the place for you.

Dining/Entertainment: The open-air restaurant serves international dishes with an emphasis on seafood. Entree prices range from $6 to $15. The hotel has recently added a very modern-looking building to house its casino and disco.

Service: Tour desk, car-rental desk.

Facilities: Two adult pools, two kids' pools, tennis court, gift shop.

Hotel Cocal. Apdo. 54, Playa de Jacó, Puntarenas. ☎ **506/643-3067** or 800/732-9266 in the U.S. Fax 506/643-3082. 43 rms. $85–$125 double. Rates include breakfast; lower rates in off-season. AE, MC, V.

No children are allowed at this hotel right on the beach, so the atmosphere is usually very peaceful. The building is done in colonial style, with arched porticos surrounding a courtyard that contains two medium-size pools, a few palapas for shade, and a thatched-roof bar. Each guest room is well proportioned with a tile floor, a double and a single bed, a desk, and a porch or balcony. However, the furniture is a bit old and has seen better days. The rooms with ocean views get the best breezes and are equipped with fans. All the other rooms have air-conditioning. The Cocal is on one of the nameless streets leading down to the beach from the main road through Jacó; watch for their sign in the middle of town. There are two dining rooms here (one on each floor) serving three meals a day. It's the upstairs dining room that has the best view of the beach. Service is generally quite good, and so is the food. Prices range from $5.50 to $18 for entrees.

MODERATE

Jacó Beach Hotel. Playa de Jacó (Apdo. 962-1000, San José), Puntarenas. ☎ **506/220-1772**; 800/272-6654 in the U.S. or 800/463-6654 in Canada. Fax 506/232-3159. 130 rms. A/C TV TEL. Nov–Apr, $80 double or triple; May–Oct, $65 double or triple. All rates include continental breakfast. AE, MC, V.

This is Jacó's main Canadian charter-flight hotel and is packed throughout the high season with crowds fleeing the cold in Ontario and Quebec. Situated right on the beach, this five-story hotel is just what you would expect of a tropical beach resort. The open-air lobby is surrounded by lush gardens, and there are covered walkways connecting the hotel's buildings. The hotel underwent remodeling in 1993 and now has a more modern look about it. Rooms are adequate, and have tile floors and walls of glass facing onto balconies. However, not all of the rooms have good views (some face another building). Ask for a view room on a higher floor, if possible. Bathrooms tend to be a bit battered, but they do have bathtubs. If you'd like more space and a kitchen, ask about the Villas Jacó Princess across the road.

El Muelle, the hotel's open-air restaurant, overlooks the pool and serves local and international dishes in the $4.50-to-$20 price range. Out by the beach, there is the Bar Guipipías, which overlooks the water and doubles as a disco. There is also a small casino.

Other facilities include a round swimming pool (which seems small by today's resort standards and is often crowded), a tennis court, a volleyball court, and a gift shop. Room service, a tour desk, car, motorcycle and surfboard rentals, laundry service, and free shuttle service from San José are all available. In addition, bicycles are provided free of charge to guests.

⑤ Apartotel Gaviotas. Playa de Jacó, Puntarenas. ☎ **506/643-?**
12 apts. Dec–Apr, $50.50 one to five people; May–Nov, $24.66 do
quad. AE, DC, MC, V.

Although it's on the inland side of the main road and is
beach, this is one of the nicest places in town. These chee....
intended for families or groups who plan to stay for a week or more, but ...
season they are a great bargain even for two people. Each apartment has a front wall
of windows looking onto the little pool, a cathedral ceiling with clerestory windows,
and a fan. Floors are tile, as are the kitchen counters. The living rooms have built-
in couches, and in the bedrooms you'll find a double bed and a bunk bed. In each
bathroom you'll find an elegant scalloped sink. There is no restaurant on the
premises, but there is a small bar beside the pool.

✪ Hotel Club del Mar. Apdo. 107-4023, Playa de Jacó, Puntarenas. ☎ **506/643-3194.** Fax
506/643-3194. 18 rms. Nov–Apr, $53–$73.50 double; May–Oct, $30–$55 double. MC, V.

Because of its location, friendly owners, and attractively designed new rooms, this is
my favorite Playa de Jacó hotel. The Club del Mar is at the far southern end of the
beach where the rocky hills meet the beach. The best rooms are in two newer two-
story shell-pink buildings, each of which has eight rooms. Each room has a green-
tile floor, pastel bedspreads, fascinating custom-made lampshades, and tile bathroom
counters, plus French doors that open onto private patios. Older rooms are almost
as attractive and have Guatemalan throw rugs, bamboo furniture, kitchens, and front
walls of glass. A small swimming pool is right by the beach and there is a first-class
restaurant on the premises. Owner Philip Edwardes oversees the kitchen and at times
personally prepares such dishes as lemon chicken and chateaubriand. However, it is
the conviviality and helpfulness of Edwardes and his wife, Marilyn, that make a stay
here so enjoyable. The Edwardeses also arrange horseback rides, raft trips, and various other tours.

Hotel Copacabana. Apdo. 150, Playa de Jacó, Puntarenas. ☎/fax **506/643-3131.** 22 rms,
7 suites. $60 double; $70 double with A/C; $90–$120 suite. MC, V.

This Canadian-owned hotel is right on the beach and popular with sport fishermen
and women, and sports lovers in general. The standard rooms are all on the second
floor and have two double beds, a ceiling fan, and little bay windows with bamboo
shades. On the shared verandah, strung hammocks alternate with small tables and
chairs. Although they have air-conditioning and kitchenettes, most of the suites are
located on the first floor and are a bit claustrophobic. If you can get one on the
second floor with an ocean view, it's worth the splurge. Most of the activity here is
centered around the pool and its neighboring bar. A 24-foot satellite dish ensures a
steady stream of televised sports events and the food here is surprisingly good. In
addition to hearty breakfasts, the restaurant also serves up a creative pasta bar, fresh
seafood, and perhaps the best french fries in Costa Rica.

✪ Pochote Grande. Apdo. 42, Playa de Jacó, Puntarenas. ☎ **506/643-3236.** Fax 506/
220-4979. 24 rms. Dec–Apr, $57 double; May–Nov, $40–$45 double. MC, V.

Named for a huge, old pochote tree on the grounds, this very attractive hotel is
located right on the beach at the far north end of Jacó. The grounds are shady and
lush, and there's a small pool. Guest rooms are large enough to sleep four comfortably and have kitchenettes. All the rooms have white-tile floors and a balcony or patio,
and the second-floor rooms are blessed with high ceilings. The restaurant and snack
bar serve a mixture of Tico, German, and American meals (the owners are German

of Africa). Prices for meals range from $3 to $9. There is also a gift shop. This
stays full with charter groups in the high season.

as Estrellamar. Apdo. 3, Playa de Jacó, Puntarenas. ☎ **506/643-3102.** Fax 506/
3-3453. 20 rms. Dec–Apr, $47–$55 double; May–Nov, $22.50–$30 double. MC, V.

This hotel is located on the landward side of Jacó's main road and is a 200-yard walk
to the beach. However, what you give up in proximity to the beach, you make up
in attractive gardens. Estrellamar, which caters primarily to a French- and German-
speaking clientele, consists of bungalows and apartments, most of which have kitchenettes. The rooms also have tile floors and patios. Try to get a room facing the hotel's
attractive pool. In addition to seating around the pool, there is a shady rancho where
you can sit out of the sun. A quiet atmosphere and a pretty garden are the main
attractions here.

Villas Miramar. Playa de Jacó, Puntarenas. ☎ **506/643-3003.** 12 rms. Dec–Apr, $50 double,
$60 triple; May–Nov, $38 double or triple. MC, V.

Located down a narrow lane off the main road through town, the Miramar is about
100 feet from the beach. It has its own small pool surrounded by a terrace and flowing hibiscus. Guest rooms sport a Spanish architectural style with arched doorways,
wrought-iron wall lamps, and red-tile floors throughout. There are large patios and
all of the rooms have kitchenettes. There are also barbecues in the gardens in case
you'd like to grill some fish or steaks. The apartments vary in size; the largest can sleep
up to six people.

INEXPENSIVE

Hotel El Jardin. Playa de Jacó, Puntarenas. ☎/fax **506/643-3050.** 7 rms. Dec–Apr, $37
double; May–Nov, $30 double. V.

Though this hotel's namesake garden is nothing to write home about, the hotel does
offer economical rates, comfortable rooms, and friendly French-speaking management. This combination seems to have made El Jardin one of the more popular small
hotels in Jacó. The guest rooms are large and clean, and have big bathrooms as well.
There is a small pool in the center of the garden. You'll find this hotel at the far north
end of the beach near the San José bus stop.

Ⓢ **Hotel Zabamar.** Playa de Jacó, Puntarenas. ☎ **506/643-3174.** 20 rms. $24.50 double;
$32.60 triple; $36.70 double with A/C; $44.80 triple with A/C. MC, V.

The Zabamar is set back from the beach in an attractively planted compound. The
older rooms have red-tile floors, small refrigerators, ceiling fans, hammocks on their
front porches, and showers in enclosed, private patios. There are also 10 newer rooms
with air-conditioning. There are even *pilas* (laundry sinks) in little gravel-and-palm
gardens behind the older rooms. Some rooms have rustic wooden benches and chairs.
The shallow swimming pool stays quite warm. Travelers on tight budgets will appreciate the size of the older, less expensive rooms. Special rates can be negotiated for
longer stays, and prices for all rooms are lower from April 15 to December 15. A little
open-air bar/restaurant serves inexpensive seafood and burgers.

Ⓢ **Flamboyant Hotel.** Apdo. 18, Playa de Jacó, Puntarenas. ☎ **506/643-3146.** 8 rms. $23–
$34 double; $25–$36 triple; $27–$38 quad. No credit cards.

The Flamboyant doesn't quite live up to its name, but it is still a good value. The
rooms are arranged around a small swimming pool, and are only a few steps from the
beach. All the rooms are spacious and have kitchenettes, but the furnishings are quite
simple. You'll find the Flamboyant down a narrow lane from the Flamboyant Restaurant, which is on the main road in the middle of Jacó.

Cabinas Alice. 100 meters south of the Red Cross, Playa de Jacó, Puntarenas. ☎ **506/ 643-3061** or 506/237-1412. 22 rms (all with bath). $25.35 double; $32.50–$43.95 triple. MC, V.

Cabinas Alice, though a small and modest Tico-run place, is one of the best values in Jacó. The rooms are in the shade of large, old mango trees, and the beach is right outside the gate. Since the rooms vary in age, ask to take a look at a couple before accepting one. The largest rooms have kitchens, and also happen to be closest to the small pool and the beach. The rooms in back each come with a carved wooden headboard and matching nightstand, a tile floor, a large shower, and potted plants. The other rooms are pretty basic, with nothing but a double and a single bed in the room. The road down to Cabinas Alice is across from the Red Cross center. Meals are served in a small dining room where you can get a fish filet fried in garlic and butter for under $5. This place is popular with young Ticos and fills up fast during the high season.

💲 **Cabinas Las Palmas.** Playa de Jacó, Puntarenas. ☎ **506/643-3005.** Fax 506/643-3512. 23 rms (all with bath). $22.85–$54.60 double; $26.10–$64.40 triple. No credit cards.

Although all of the rooms here are acceptable, the newer ones are a bit nicer. Some rooms come with refrigerators, hot plates, kitchen sinks, laundry sinks, and tables with four chairs, so you can set up housekeeping and stay a while. All have tile floors and very clean bathrooms, and most have two double beds. The three rooms with air conditioning are the most expensive, and I'm not sure they're worth the extra $20. There are lots of flowers in the garden, and the location down a narrow lane off the main road makes Las Palmas a quiet place. If you're coming from San José, take the Jacó exit from the Costanera and go straight through the first (and only) intersection you come to. Take a right on the narrow lane just past Cabinas Antonio.

Chalet Santa Ana. Playa de Jacó, Puntarenas. ☎ **506/643-3233.** 8 rms (each with bath). $15–$22 double; $31 for up to five people. No credit cards.

Located at the quiet south end of the beach across from Hotel Jacófiesta, Chalet Santa Ana is a small two-story building. The guest rooms sleep up to five people and half of them have kitchenettes. There's carpeting in some of the rooms, and walls are of varnished wood. The second-floor rooms have the added advantage of high ceilings and access to a large verandah with chairs. Though the surroundings are not too attractive, this is a good deal for Jacó.

CAMPING

There are several campgrounds in or near Playa de Jacó. **Madrigal,** at the south end of town at the foot of some jungly cliffs, is my favorite. The campground is just off the beach and has a bar/restaurant that is open from 7am to 10pm. You can also try **Camping Garibaldi,** which is centrally located or **El Hicaco,** which is close to the beach, but right next door to an open-air disco—don't expect to get much sleep if you stay here. Campsites run between $2–$3 per night.

WHERE TO STAY IN PUNTA LEONA

Punta Leona Hotel & Club. Apdo. 8592-1000, San José. ☎ **506/231-3131** or 800/ 554-4398 in the U.S. Fax 506/232-0791. 108 rms, 72 apts. A/C TV. $58–$82 double; $92–$150 for four to eight people. AE, DC, MC, V.

This gated resort and residential community 10 kilometers north of Jacó boasts the most impressive grounds of any easily accessible hotel in Costa Rica. Rain forest, white-sand beaches (two of them), and a rocky promontory jutting out into the Pacific all add up to a drama rarely encountered in Costa Rican resorts. After passing through the resort's guarded gate, you drive more than a mile down a gravel road that passes through dense primary rain forest before arriving at the grassy lawns that sprawl beneath huge trees. The main guest rooms are not as luxurious as one would hope, but that is a small price to pay for such a setting. The standard hotel rooms are housed in Spanish-style buildings with red-tile roofs and white stucco walls. Inside, you'll find that the beds and bedspreads are a bit dated, but otherwise the rooms are comfortable. In addition to these rooms, there are a variety of different apartment types, including some unusual small chalets.

Dining/Entertainment: Restaurant Léon Marino serves a variety of Costa Rican and international dishes. Prices are moderate. There is also a more informal outdoor restaurant that serves grilled meats and typical meals, as well as two bars. The one on Playa Manatas doubles as a disco.

Services: There is regular daily bus service between the guest accommodations and Playa Blanca. Sportfishing, sunset cruises, and sailboard, jet-ski, and horse rentals are all available. Scuba lessons and rental equipment are also offered (there's good diving at Playa Blanca).

Facilities: Two swimming pools, 4 miles of beach, tennis court, boutique, supermarket, conference room.

WHERE TO STAY IN PLAYA HERMOSA DE JACÓ
EXPENSIVE

✪ **Villa Caletas.** Apdo. 12358-1000, San José. ☎ **506/257-3653.** Fax 506/222-2059. 8 rms, 19 villas, 1 master suite. A/C. $115 double; $136–$163 villa; $200 master suite. AE, MC, V.

It's hard to find a luxury hotel in Costa Rica with a more spectacular setting. Perched 350 meters above the sea, Villa Caletas enjoys commanding views of the Pacific. While the rooms are all elegantly appointed and spacious, you'll want to stay in a villa here. Each individual villa is situated on a patch of hillside facing the sea or surrounding forests. Inside you'll find a main bedroom with a queen-size bed and a comfortable sitting room with couches that convert into two single beds. The villas feature white-tile floors, modern bathrooms, and a private terrace for sitting around and soaking up the views. It's a long way to the beach down below, or a short drive to Jacó or Herradura, but most guests are happy to lounge around and swim in the free-form "infinity" pool that seems to effortlessly blend into the sea below and beyond.

Dining/Entertainment: The hotel has two restaurants featuring French and continental cuisines, however, the food at both was slightly disappointing on my two visits. The hotel also has a Doric Greek-style amphitheater where sunset concerts of jazz and classical music can be heard.

Facilities: Swimming pool, conference room.

MODERATE

✪ **Terraza del Pacifico.** Playa Hermosa de Jacó (Apdo. 168), Jacó, Puntarenas. ☎ **506/643-3222** or 506/643-3444; 212/213-2399 or 212/213-1838 in the U.S. Fax 506/643-3424. 43 rms. A/C TV TEL. $66 double; $72 triple. AE, MC, V.

It may be a bit out of town, but the Terraza del Pacifico is the best beachfront hotel in the Jacó area. Located just over the hill at the start of Playa Hermosa, this hotel seems to have done everything right. Rooms are built so that they all have ocean views, and in the middle of the hotel complex is a circular pool with a swim-up bar and plenty of chaise lounges for sunbathing and siestas. Red-tile roofs and white walls give the buildings a very Mediterranean look (the management is Italian), while hardwood balcony railings add a touch of the tropics. The guest rooms all have either a patio or balcony, and the room curtains are hand-painted with colorful bird and flower images. The hotel's restaurant is located within a few feet of the high-tide mark and serves good Italian food. During the high season, a small casino operates nightly from 6pm to 12am.

INEXPENSIVE

🟢 **Cabinas Las Olas.** Playa Hermosa de Jacó, Puntarenas. ☎/fax **506/643-3687.** 3 rms, 3 cabinas. $35.50–$40.75 double; $45 cabina, sleeps up to six people. No credit cards.

Playa Hermosa is a renowned surfing beach and this is its prime surfer hotel. The main building is on a hill by the road. Two of the rooms are located upstairs and have two double beds, a verandah with a hammock, and ocean views. Downstairs is a smaller budget room that's fine for a single traveler. The rooms are basic, but comfortable. Closer to the beach are three A-frame cabins or ranchos, which have a roomy bedroom on the second floor (in the peak of the A-frame), and a single bed, bunk bed, kitchenette, and bathroom on the ground floor. Between the main building and the cabins is a pool with a small stone waterfall. Out by the ocean there is a simple cafe that serves breakfast and lunch, and a thatch **palapa** strung with hammocks for watching the waves, horseback riders, and sunsets.

WHERE TO DINE

Many of the accommodations in Playa de Jacó and nearby beach towns have good restaurants and quite a few guests choose to eat all their meals at their hotel. Budget travelers who really want to save money on meals can always stay at a hotel that provides kitchenettes for its guests, shop at the local supermercado, and fix their own meals. But even most inexpensive lodgings have small restaurants that serve good, cheap meals.

If you're feeling adventurous and want to eat in town, I recommend the following places. In addition, **The Garden Cafe, Ceviche del Rey,** and **Restaurante Esperanza** are local favorites, and **Pizzeria Verona** has excellent clay-oven pizzas and homemade pastas. Actually, one of the best restaurants in town is the dining room at the **Hotel Cocal,** which is open to the public. The menu includes such dishes as chateaubriand for two, wienerschnitzel, and pepper steak.

✪ **El Bosque.** 27 yards south of the gas station. ☎ **506/643-3007.** Reservations recommended during high season. Main courses $4.50–$12.80. MC, V. Tue–Sun 10:30am–9:30pm. INTERNATIONAL.

Located on the highway leading south to Manuel Antonio, El Bosque (The Forest) is set amid shady mango trees and flowering gardens. The dining room itself is a small open-air building and the furnishings are heavy colonial reproductions. Shrimp or lobster is a bit pricey at $12.80, but you can get a delicious corvina filet for just over $4. If you are not in the mood for seafood, you can order steak or chicken. There's also a long list of fresh juices and fruit shakes from which to choose. El Bosque makes a great meal stop if you are on your way back from Manuel Antonio; if you are staying in Jacó, free transportation to and from the restaurant is provided.

🟢 **Killer Munchies.** 300 meters south of the Hotel Jacó Beach. ☎ **506/643-3354.** Reservations are not accepted. Main courses: $2.05–$10.75. No credit cards. Mon–Fri 5:30–9pm, Sat–Sun 12–10pm.

The name says it all. This restaurant serves hearty burritos, simple pasta dishes, and a wide array of freshly baked pizzas. With vines covering latticed walls and an abundance of potted palms, the ambience is somewhere between an early '80s fern bar and college beer hall. Try to get a table on the covered deck, so you can watch the people passing by and the pizzas being made in the outdoor wood-burning oven. My favorite item is the Greek pizza, with olives, feta cheese, and anchovies, but the barbeque chicken pizza is also delicious.

✪ **La Piraña.** Apdo. 116, Playa de Jacó. ☎ **506/643-3725.** Reservations recommended during high season. Main courses $3.80–$6.50. AE, DC, MC, V. Tue–Sun 6am–2pm and 5–11pm. INTERNATIONAL.

This new restaurant adds a welcome dose of pizzazz to Jacó's culinary scene. The menu can vary nightly, and while the selection is always eclectic, the quality is reassuringly consistent. The owners often organize theme nights featuring haute cuisine from one or another corner of the world, with the most popular dishes finding their way onto the permanent menu. Baked Caribbean red snapper, jerk chicken, blackened steak, and Egyptian pasta Mohammad all happily coexist here, alongside Costa Rican standards prepared with some subtle twists. The restaurant seats 75 in a spacious open room beneath slow-spinning ceiling fans. Just like the dishes, the decor is mix and match—blue-tile floors, yellow walls, red tables, and teal chairs. Note the unusual hours. Breakfasts are equally pleasing, with fresh baked scones and pastries, light and fluffy omelets, and homemade jams.

PLAYA DE JACÓ AFTER DARK

Playa de Jacó is the Central Pacific's party town and there are several discos that are packed every night of the high season, and every weekend during the low season. The most popular is **Disco La Central,** right on the beach near the south end of town. Located in a huge open-air hall, it features the requisite '70s flashing lights and suspended mirrored ball. A garden bar in a thatched-roof building provides a slightly quieter place to have a drink. **Los Tucanes Disco Club** is another happening place located one street over from Disco La Central. Both charge a nominal cover charge of $3. On the north end of town, situated on the road that leads to the airport, is **Upé!,** another favorite nightspot, while **Los Faroles Restaurant** doubles as the **Jacó Rock Cafe** on weekends.

3 Manuel Antonio National Park

140 kilometers SW of San José; 69 kilometers S of Playa de Jacó

No other destination in Costa Rica has received more intentional attention than Manuel Antonio. Many first-time visitors to Costa Rica plan their vacation around seeing it. It's no surprise why the views from the hills overlooking Manuel Antonio are spectacular, the beaches inside the park are idyllic, and its jungles are crawling with white-faced and squirrel monkeys, among other forms of exotic wildlife. The flipside is that you'll have to pay more dearly to see it and you'll have to share it with far more fellow travelers than you might prefer. Still, this is one of the most beautiful locations in the entire country. Gazing down on the blue Pacific from high on the mountainsides of Manuel Antonio, it is almost impossible to hold back a gasp of delight. Offshore rocky islands dot the vast expanse of blue. In the foreground the rich deep green of the rain forest sweeps down to the water. Even cheap Instamatics regularly produce postcard-perfect snapshots. It is this superb view that hotels at Manuel Antonio sell, and this view that keeps people transfixed on decks, patios, and balconies along the 7 kilometers of road between Quepos and the national park entrance.

One of the most popular national parks in the country, it is also one of the smallest, covering fewer than 1,700 acres. Its several nearly perfect small beaches are connected by trails that meander through the rain forest. One of its most striking features is how quickly the mountains surrounding its beaches rise as you head inland from the water. However, Manuel Antonio National Park was created not to preserve its beautiful beaches but its forests—home to endangered squirrel monkeys, three-toed sloths, purple-and-orange crabs, and hundreds of other species of birds, mammals, and plants. Whereas once this entire stretch of coast was a rain forest teeming with wildlife, now just this small rocky outcrop of forest remains.

Unfortunately, the popularity of Manual Antonio has brought about rampant development and ever-growing crowds of beachgoers. In just the last few years, these factors have turned what was once a peaceful and pristine spot into an area full of hastily built, overpriced hotels, packed parking areas, and noisy crowds. Frankly, Manuel Antonio has become completely overburdened with adoring throngs—some of whom have taken to feeding the wild animals—in a dangerous caricature of what eco-tourism should be. In addition, the stream that forms the boundary of the park and through which park visitors must wade is often polluted with garbage and human waste. On weekends the beaches are packed with people and the disco blares its music until early morning, drowning out the sounds of crickets and frogs that once lulled visitors to sleep here. A shanty town of snack shacks lines the road just outside the park, which makes this area look more like a slum than a national park. Supposedly the environs on the edge of the park are soon going to be improved, and a major resort complex is planned, but as yet nothing has happened.

Those views that are so bewitching also have their own set of drawbacks. If you want a great view, you aren't going to be staying on the beach and, in fact, you probably won't be able to walk to the beach. This means that you'll either be driving back and forth, taking a lot of taxis, or riding the public bus a lot. Also keep in mind that it's hot and humid here, and it rains a lot. However, the rain is what keeps Manuel Antonio lush and green, and this wouldn't be the tropics if things were otherwise.

If you're traveling on a budget, you'll likely end up staying in the nearby town of Quepos, which was once a quiet banana port. The land to the north was used by Chiquita to grow its bananas. However, disease wiped out most of the banana plantations, and now the land is planted with oil-palm trees. To reach Quepos by road, you must pass through miles and miles of these oil-palm plantations. Today Quepos is changing its image from that of shipping port to that of cluttered and dirty tourist boom town.

Despite these caveats, Manuel Antonio is still worth visiting. If you plan carefully, you can avoid many of the problems that detract from its appeal. If you avoid the peak months of December to March, you will avoid most of the crowds. If you must come during the peak months, try to avoid weekends, when the beach is packed with families from San José. If you stay at a hotel part way up the hill from the park entrance, you will have relatively easy access to the beach, you may get a view, and best of all, you'll be out of earshot of the disco. If you visit the park early in the morning, you can leave when the crowds begin to show up at midday. In the afternoon, you can lounge by your pool or on your patio.

ESSENTIALS

GETTING THERE & DEPARTING   By Plane   Sansa (☎ 506/233-0397, 506/233-3258 or 506/233-5330 in San José) flies to Quepos, the town nearest the park, at 8am and 3pm Monday through Saturday, and at 10am on Sunday. All flights leave from San José's Juan Santamaria International Airport. The flight's duration is 20 minutes; fare is $30 each way.

Travelair (☎ 506/220-3054 or 506/232-7883 in San José) also flies to Quepos daily at 8:10 and 11:55am, and 3:15pm, but from San José's Pavas International Airport. Flight duration is 20 minutes; fare is $45 one way, $72 round-trip.

There's an airport transfer service that charges $4 per person to any hotel in Manuel Antonio and Quepos. Speak to a gate agent at either **Sansa** or **Travelair** to arrange a ride. Taxis occasionally meet incoming flights as well. Expect to be charged between $7.50–$10 per car for up to 4 people, depending on the distance to your hotel and your bargaining abilities.

Alternatively, you can fly **Sansa** to Palmar Sur or Puerto Jiménez, or **Travelair** to Palmar Sur. From either of these two towns, you can then take a taxi to Manuel Antonio.

When you're ready to depart, Sansa (☎ 506/771-0161 in Quepos) flights to San José leave at 8:35am and 3:35pm Monday through Saturday, and at 10:35am on Sunday.

Travelair flights leave for San José daily at 10:45am, and 12:25 and 3:45pm.

By Bus　Express buses to Manuel Antonio leave San José daily at 6am, and 12 and 6pm from Calle 16 between avenidas 1 and 3. Trip duration is $3^1/_2$ hours; fare is $5.10.

Regular buses to Quepos leave San José daily at 7 and 10am, and 2 and 4pm. Trip duration is 5 hours; fare is $3.20.

Buses leave Puntarenas for Quepos daily at 5 and 11am, and 2pm. The ride's duration is $3^1/_2$ hours; fare is $3.

Many of the buses for Quepos stop to unload and pick up passengers in Playa de Jacó. If you're in Jacó, you can try your luck at one of the covered bus stops out on the Interamerican Highway.

From Quepos, buses leave for Manuel Antonio roughly every hour, daily from 6am to 10pm. Fare is 30¢.

When you're ready to depart, the Quepos bus station is next to the market, which is three blocks east of the water and two blocks north of the road to Manuel Antonio. Express buses to San José (trip duration is $3^1/_2$ hours) leave daily at 6am, and 12 and 5pm (there is an additional departure at 3pm on Sunday). Local buses to San José (duration is 5 hours) leave at 5 and 8am, and 12 and 4pm. In the busy winter months, purchase your ticket several days in advance.

Buses for Puntarenas leave daily at 4:30 and 10:30am, and 3pm. Any bus headed for San José or Puntarenas will let you off in Playa de Jacó.

By Car　From San José, take the Interamerican Highway west to the Puntarenas turnoff and head south on the Costanera, the coastal road through Jacó. This is an excellent road until south of Puerto Caldera. From there until south of Jacó, the potholes are killers. Some are so old they've sprouted grass. At Parrita, 44 kilometers past Jacó, the pavement gives out completely and you spend the next 25 kilometers bumping along on potholed, washboarded, muddy gravel road (although this is better than the potholed paved road). Needless to say, the driving is slow.

An alternative is to take the narrow and winding old highway, which turns off the Interamerican Highway just west of Alajuela near the town of Atenas and joins the Costanera near Orotina, just in time to catch the worst of the potholes. You'll still have to drive that rutted road between Jacó and Quepos.

ORIENTATION　Arriving　Quepos is a dusty little port town at the mouth of the Boca Vieja Estuary. After crossing the bridge into town, take the lower road (to the left of the high road). In four blocks, turn left and you will be on the road to Manuel Antonio. This road winds through town a bit before starting over the hill to all the hotels and the national park.

GETTING AROUND　A taxi between Quepos, any hotel along the road toward the park, and Manuel Antonio costs around $3. The return trip from the park to your hotel should only cost about 50¢. This is a fixed price, so watch out for drivers who try to charge more.

The bus from Quepos to Manuel Antonio, and vice versa, takes 15 minutes and runs roughly every hour from 6am to 10pm daily. Fare is 30¢.

You can also rent a car from **Elegante Rent A Car** (☎ 506/777-0115) for around $50 a day. They are located in downtown Quepos next door to **La Buena Nota.** With advance notice, they'll meet you at the airport with your car for no extra charge.

If you choose to rent a car, never leave anything of value in it unless you intend to stay within sight of the car at all times. Car break-ins are commonplace here. There are now children who offer to watch your car for a small price when you leave it outside the park entrance. Take them up on the offer if you want to avoid damage to your car by thieves trying to find out what's in your trunk.

FAST FACTS   The new **Laundromat Bati** is located out on the edge of town on the road towards Manuel Antonio. They offer both self service and drop-off, and are open Monday through Friday from 8am to noon and from 2 to 6pm. There's a **pharmacy** called Botíca Quepos on the corner of the main street where you make the turn for Manuel Antonio (☎ 506/777-0038); it's open daily from 7am to 7pm.

EXPLORING THE NATIONAL PARK

Many visitors choose to see the park on an organized tour that may include visits to other national parks and biological reserves. See chapter 4 for listings of U.S. and San José–based tour companies you can contact either before leaving the United States or upon arrival in San José, if this interests you. If you are a guest, you can book a day tour through **El Parador**, a resort in Quepos, listed under "Where to Stay" below; or you can arrange a tour through one of the larger hotels or tour agencies based in Playa de Jacó. (**Hotel Club del Mar, Jacó Beach Hotel,** and **Hotel Jacófiesta** are a few such hotels; for more information, see the section on Playa de Jacó above.) A 2- or 3-hour guided hike should cost between $25 to $30 per person. Alternately, you can explore the park on your own. A map is available at the park entrance. While it is in Spanish, all trails are clearly marked on it, making it easy to comprehend even if you do not speak Spanish fluently.

ENTRY POINT, FEES & REGULATIONS   The park entrance is situated on Playa Espadilla, the beach at the end of the road from Quepos. To reach the park station, you must cross a small, sometimes polluted stream that is little more than ankle deep at low tide but can be knee or even waist deep at high tide. Just after crossing the stream, you'll see it. You will have to pay a fee of $6 per person to enter. This is where you can pick up the small map of the park mentioned above. The park is closed on Monday, but open Tuesday through Sunday from 8am to 4pm year-round. Camping is not allowed. The Parks Service only allows 600 visitors to enter each day, which may mean that you won't get in if you arrive in mid-afternoon during the high season.

THE BEACHES   Playa Espadilla, the beach from which you enter the park, is often perfect for board surfing and bodysurfing, but can be a bit rough for casual swimming. There a couple of little shops by the water that rent boogie boards, beach chairs, and beach umbrellas.

Playa Espadilla Sur is the first beach you come to within the park boundaries. This is usually the least-crowded beach in the park, and one of the best places to find a quiet shade tree to plant yourself under. If you want to explore farther, you can walk along this soft sand beach or follow a trail through the forest behind the beach. At the far end there is a short connecting trail to **Playa Manuel Antonio,** which is sometimes clear enough to offer good snorkeling along the rocks at either end. A branch trail from this beach leads up and around **Punta Catedral** (Cathedral Point), a high promontory bluff, where there are some spectacular views. If you take this trail, wear good shoes. Cathedral Point is one of the best places to spot monkeys, though you are more likely to see a white-faced monkey rather than a rare squirrel monkey. At low tide, Playa Manuel Antonio shows a very interesting relic left by its pre-Columbian residents, a circular stone turtle trap. From Playa Manuel Antonio there is another, slightly longer, trail to the **Puerto Escondido** where there is a blowhole that sends up plumes of spray at high tide. Beyond here, at Punta Surrucho, there are some sea caves. Be careful when hiking beyond Puerto Escondido: what seems like easy beach hiking at low tide becomes treacherous to impassable at high tide. Two other trails wind their way inland from the trail between Playa Manuel Antonio and Puerto Escondido. It's great to spend hours exploring the steamy jungle and then take a refreshing dip in the ocean.

HORSEBACK RIDING, KAYAKING & OTHER ACTIVE SPORTS If your tropical fantasy is to ride a horse down a beach between jungle and ocean, contact **Stable Equus** (☎ 506/777-0001), which charges $30 for a 2-hour ride in Manuel Antonio. This stable allegedly treats its animals more humanely than other stables in the area, and is also concerned with keeping horse droppings off the beaches. Full-day horseback riding excursions to a typical Costa Rican farm are provided by **Rancho Savegre Tours** (☎ 506/777-0528). Tours cost $60 per person and include hotel transfers, lunch, and several swimming stops.

If you're interested in kayaking among the rocky islets of Manuel Antonio National Park or up the nearby Isla Damas estuary, contact **High Tide Ocean Kayaking** (☎ 506/777-0403). They charge $60 for a full-day paddle around the estuary (including lunch at La Tortuga restaurant) or through the national park (with a picnic on the beach). **Iguana Tours** (☎ 506/777-1262) offers all the above tour options, as well as white-water rafting trips on the nearby Naranjo and Savegre Rivers ($65 to $70 full day). Large multiperson rafts are used during the rainy season, and single person "duckies" are broken out when the water levels drop. **Amigos del Río** (☎ 506/777-0082), **Rió Loco White Water Rafting** (☎ 506/777-1170), and **Rainforest Expeditions & School** (☎ 506/777-1170) also offer full-day rafting trips for around $65 to $75 for a full-day trip. This latter company also offers dive trips for $70 and guided all-day hikes for $45.

THINGS TO SEE & DO IN QUEPOS

For a closer look at some exotic birds and other assorted wildlife than you may have gotten in the park, check out **Jardin Gaia,** a Wildlife Rescue Center that rehabilitates and breeds injured and confiscated animals, many of them endangered. The center is located on the road between Quepos and Manuel Antonio. Jardin Gaia is open daily from 8am to 4pm and charges $5 per person, which includes a brief, but informative, tour and plenty of print information.

If you're staying in Quepos and don't want to go all the way over the hill to the park, you can swim and lounge at **Nahomi,** Quepos's public swimming pool. You'll find this pool on a tiny peninsula at the end of the road that parallels the water. Admission is around $1 and the pool is open daily from 9am to 7pm. The rocky promontory on which the pool is built feels like an island and is surrounded by the turquoise waters of a small cove.

Quepos is one of Costa Rica's billfish centers, and sailfish and marlin, as well as tuna, are all common in these waters. If you're into **sportfishing** and happen to be here between December and April, see what's being offered at **La Buena**

Nota (☎ 506/777-0345), or try hooking up with **Blue Fin Sportfishing** (☎ 506/777-1676), **Costa Rican Dreams** (☎ 506/777-0593), **Marlin Azul** (☎ 506/777-0191), **Sportfishing Costa Rica** (☎ 506/257-3553), **Sportfishing Quepos** (☎ 506/777-0493), or **Sportfishing Karahé** (☎ 506/777-0170). A full day of fishing should cost between $450 and $850, depending on the size of the boat.

If you'd just like to go for a cruise around the area and maybe do a bit of **snorkeling, diving,** or **fishing,** see if the *Byblos I* (☎ 506/777-0411) is making trips while you are there. Full-day cruises including lunch and the use of fishing and snorkling gear cost $80 per person, while a 3-hour sunset cruise costs $40.

If you're looking for souvenirs, try **La Buena Nota,** which is on the left just over the bridge as you enter Quepos (☎ 506/777-0345), and has recently opened a second shop across from the Hotel Karahé on the road to Manuel Antonio. These little shops are jam-packed with all sorts of beachwear, souvenirs, and U.S. magazines and newspapers, and also act as informal information centers for the area. If you'd like to find out about renting a house, this is a good place to ask.

If you're looking for some place to sit and read the newspaper you just bought at La Buena Nota, check out **Cafe Milagro** next door. One of the few homey coffeehouses I've found Costa Rica, the folks here roast their own beans and also have a mail-order service to keep you in Costa Rican coffee year-round.

WHERE TO STAY

There are very few beachfront hotels in Manuel Antonio, so consequently, if you want to be able to walk out of your room and be on the beach without taking to the road, you're going to have to pay for the privilege. Prices at the Hotel Arboleda are steep for what you get, but if you want a nicer room for the same amount of money, you won't be on the beach.

If you're traveling on a rock-bottom budget, you'll get more for your money by staying in Quepos and taking the bus to the beaches at Manuel Antonio every day. The rooms in Quepos may be small, but they are much cleaner and more appealing than those available in the same price category on the other side of the hill.

VERY EXPENSIVE

✪ **La Mariposa.** Playa Manuel Antonio, Quepos. ☎ **506/777-0456** or 800/416-2747 in the U.S. Fax 506/777-0050. 10 villas, 6 apartments. $240 double; $310 triple; $380 quad villa; $190–$200 double apartment. All rates include continental breakfast and full dinner. No credit cards.

This is one of Manuel Antonio's premier accommodations. It offers spacious, attractively designed and decorated rooms, and the most breathtaking views in Manuel Antonio. Perched on a ridge at the top of the hill between Quepos and Manuel Antonio, La Mariposa (The Butterfly), commands a mountains-to-the-sea vista of more than 270 degrees. Needless to say, the sunsets here are knockouts. La Mariposa is for those people who truly want to get away from it all (no telephones, TVs, or fax machines) and sit back doing nothing at all for a while. Keep in mind, however, that should you decide to abandon the view and the pool, you're a long way from the beach (either a steep hike or a short drive). The rooms here are all bilevel villas that meld the best of the tropics and the Mediterranean. Each villa has a large bedroom and bathroom on the upper floor and a spacious living room and deck on the lower floor. There are stucco walls and painted tiles, bamboo ceilings, and hardwood floors. Behind the two queen beds in the bedroom, there is a huge tropical mural. The bathrooms are spacious and even have small atrium gardens. They also have high ceilings, skylights, blue-and-white–tile counters, and shelves of plants. You just won't want to leave your villa. At press time, La Mariposa was still completing six spacious new apartments, only two of which will have views. Take note: no children under 15 are allowed.

Dining/Entertainment: Both breakfast and dinner are included in the rates at La Mariposa. The open-air restaurant is set on a red-tiled terrace that takes in all the views. The emphasis is on seafood. Nevertheless, on my last visit the food fell far short of the standards set throughout the rest of the hotel. There is also a small bar.

Facilities: The small swimming pool is set on its own terrace.

El Parador. Apdo. 284, Quepos. ☎ **506/777-1414.** Fax 506/777-1437. 50 rms, 9 junior suites, 1 presidential suite. A/C TV TEL. $140 standard; $108 deluxe; $148 junior suite; $391 presidential suite. All rates are based on double occupancy, each additional person is $30 extra.

What is luxurious opulence to one person can seem blindingly ostentatious to another. The jury is out on El Parador. The hotel itself is spread out over more than 12 acres of land on a low peninsula, down a dirt road from La Mariposa. Its design aims to imitate Spanish Mediterranean grandeur and the main building is loaded with antiques, including 17th-century Dutch and Flemish oil paintings, a 300-year-old carved wooden horse, and 16th-century church and castle doors. The standard rooms are new and well appointed. All have private patios, but most look out on the miniature golf course. Deluxe rooms offer slightly more space, and the second-floor units have private balconies. The junior suites are located on the top of a hill, giving those who stay in them a glimpse of the sea and Cathedral Point in the distance. All are equipped with a VCR, jacuzzi, wet bar, and refrigerator. The presidential suite is in the main building and has the amenities of the other suites, plus a fully equipped kitchenette and decorative antiques. The hotel can arrange a wide variety of tours and activities in the area, and runs a shuttle van to the national park. There is also a small secluded beach about 500 meters from the hotel. El Parador shoots for a level of luxury and service not commonly found in Costa Rica, and if this is what you're looking for in Manuel Antonio, then this is the place for you.

Dining/Entertainment: Most of the meals are served in the main dining room and its adjoining terrace. Breakfasts are served buffet style, and dinners are four-course, prix-fixe affairs, chosen from a menu which changes nightly and generally includes eight main-course selections. There are three private dining rooms of varying sizes that can be reserved for special occasions. Sunsets are best enjoyed from the Mirador Lounge, above and behind the main building.

Facilities: The small kidney-shaped pool has a swim-up bar and central fountain. There is also a modest fitness center, jacuzzi, steam room, tennis court, private helicopter landing pad, tour desk, and small gift shop.

EXPENSIVE

Hotel Arboleda. Apdo. 211, Quepos. ☎/fax **506/777-0092.** 38 rms. $75–$95 double. MC, V.

The Arboleda is one of the few beachfront hotels in Manuel Antonio; unfortunately, it is overpriced for what you get. The rooms are located in two areas: high up on a hillside and farther down, closer to the beach (none are located right on the beach). The grounds are rather unkempt and there is an excess of whitewashed concrete that further detracts from the surroundings. This is one of the few hotels I've visited where the cheaper rooms are closer to the water. These rooms are fairly small and have fans only, but they are definitely the better choice. The more expensive rooms have air-conditioning, but are rather dark and have small bathrooms. There are a few very large units with kitchenettes. These are the most run-down rooms here, but they can hold up to six people, at no extra charge.

Dining/Entertainment: There are two restaurants here. One is by the pool near the top of the hill, and the other is down by the beach. Both serve similar, moderately priced meals. The restaurant by the beach also has a bar with a pool table.

Services: Airport shuttle, horse rentals, sportfishing charters.

Facilities: Swimming pool, handball court.

El Byblos. Apdo. 112, Quepos. ☎ **506/777-0411** or 506/777-0217. Fax 506/777-0009. 17 rms. TV TEL. Dec–Apr, $84–$98 double; May–Nov, $50–$70 double. AE, MC, V.

Although its service can be rather unprofessional at times, El Byblos is still one of the best hotels in Manuel Antonio.

Guest rooms vary in age and setting. The newer rooms are luxuriously large and have air-conditioning and partial ocean views. They are graced with tile floors, wicker furniture, seating areas by the windows, and attractively designed bathrooms. The main drawback of these rooms is that the road, which gets a lot of noisy traffic, is just outside the window. I prefer the older rooms, which are set among the forest trees toward the back of the hotel grounds and, although they have no views, are extremely tranquil, with just the sound of a meandering creek to keep you awake.

Dining/Entertainment: The dining room is on a large covered deck that looks out to the forest trees. The open-beamed hardwood construction is evocative of the tropics and sets an exotic mood for the gourmet French dinners that are served here nightly. There's a decent wine selection (French and Chilean), and a small bar to the side where you can have a cocktail before or after dinner. Entree prices range from $8 to $20.50.

Services: Room service, laundry service, beach and airport shuttles, sportfishing charters, diving trips, day cruises. Be aware that there is a telephone charge even if you use a calling-card number.

Facilities: The small swimming pool is set on the edge of the forest.

Karahé. Apdo. 100-6350, Quepos. ☎ **506/777-0170.** Fax 506/777-0175. 24 rms, 9 villas. $65–$100 double; $90–$125 triple. AE, DC, MC, V.

Of the few beachfront hotels in Manuel Antonio, this is also the best. Note that if you opt for one of the cheapest (and oldest) rooms in the hotel, you'll be a steep uphill climb from the beach and won't have air-conditioning. On the other hand, you'll have the best views.

If you choose to stay in one of the more expensive beachfront units, you'll find a room with almost every amenity even the most finicky traveler expects, but less impressive views. With the exception of the cheapest rooms, all rooms have balconies and full bathtubs. The gardens that surround the upper half of the hotel are quite lush and are planted with flowering ginger that often attracts hummingbirds. Down in the lower part of the hotel grounds, the gardens are not nearly as attractive, but this is where you'll find the small pool. The hotel is located on both sides of the road about 500 yards before you reach the end of the road at Manuel Antonio.

Dining/Entertainment: The hotel's restaurant is built at treetop level midway between the hotel's two levels of accommodations. Entree prices range from $5 to $15, and the specialty of the house is shish kebab cooked over an indoor barbecue. There is also a snack bar near the pool, which serves lunch and doubles as the hotel's bar.

Services: Sportfishing charters, laundry service.

Facilities: Swimming pool, whirlpool tub.

✪ **Hotel Villas Si Como No.** Apdo. 5-6350, Quepos. ☎ **506/777-1250** or 800/506-4299 in the U.S. 29 rms. A/C. $85–$125 double; $185 villa. All rates include breakfast. AE, MC, V.

This new complex seeks to combine modern amenities with an ecologically conscious attitude. All the wood used is farm grown, the jacuzzi is solar heated, and although all the rooms have air-conditioning, guests are asked to use it only when necessary. Rooms in the main building are designed to provide easy access for travelers with physical disabilities, and the whole complex is wheelchair accessible. The more expensive rooms are housed in a series of duplex villas, with tree-top views out over the forest and onto the Pacific. These rooms all have a bedroom, living room, private balcony, and either a kitchenette or wet bar. When two of these rooms are combined, you've got your villa. The hotel has bought a large chunk of property for its own private reserve, and nature trails are planned.

Dining/Entertainment: When I visited, only the Rico Tico Boca Bar 'n Grill was open. This is casual poolside bar and grill serves excellent ceviche, fresh fish, grilled meats, and such Mexican snacks as nachos and quesadillas. A more formal restaurant should be finished by press time.

Facilities: A free-form tile pool, with waterfall, jacuzzi, and slide; conference center and 50-seat laser-projection theater. Every night, a movie on laser disc is shown at 8 pm. Non-guests who dine here can watch the movie for free.

✪ **Hotel Casitas Eclipse.** Apdo. 11-6350, Quepos. ☎ **506/777-0408** or 619/753-6827 in the U.S. Fax 506/777-0408. 10 casitas, 25 rms. A/C. Nov 15–Apr 15, $91–$109 double, $193 two-bedroom casita; Apr 16–Nov 14, $51–$65 double, $113 two-bedroom casita. V.

Located close to the top of the hill between Quepos and Manuel Antonio, these beautiful *casitas* (little houses) are some of the most boldly styled structures in Manuel Antonio. While the villas have a distinctly Mediterranean flavor, the owner swears they are inspired by Mesoamerican and Pueblo Indian villages. Their styling makes them seem much larger than they actually are, although they are certainly plenty roomy as well. All are painted a blinding white and are topped with red-tile roofs. Though simply furnished, the rooms are very comfortable and attractive inside. You can rent either the entire casita or just the downstairs, or, if you don't need all the space, just the upstairs bedroom, which has a separate entrance, private bathroom, and balcony of its own. The larger downstairs suites have tile floors, built-in banquettes, high ceilings, large patios, and full kitchens. There are three attractive tiled pools spread out among the lush grounds. Only the restaurant and a couple of villas have ocean views here, but I prefer the units further from the road, where you're more likely to hear and see squirrel monkeys passing by than trucks and buses. Considering what is available in this price range closer to the beach, this is a great deal.

MODERATE

Ⓢ **Apartotel El Colibri.** Apdo. 94, Manuel Antonio, Quepos. ☎ **506/777-0432**. 10 rms. Dec–Apr, $60 double, $70 triple, $80 quad; May–Nov $30 double, $35 triple, $40 quad. V.

If you have dreams of a secluded retreat where you can laze in a hammock and watch hummingbirds sip nectar from crimson flowers, this hotel is for you. The eight basic rooms are set amid a garden that would have kept Monet or Gauguin happy for years. Narrow paths wind up a hill through lush vegetation that completely hides the rooms from the street. You'll feel as though you have the whole place to yourself in these cozy duplex rooms, each of which has a king-size bed with a Guatemalan bedspread, high ceilings with overhead fans, screen-and-cinderblock walls, red-tile floors, framed posters of Costa Rican wildlife, and French doors that lead to a patio. The spacious patios make the rooms seem much larger than they are and come with hammocks, tables and chairs, and barbecues for grilling any fish you might catch. There are even rooms with beautiful kitchenettes with blue-and-white–tile counters and coffee makers. True tropical elegance. There is a small pool and a couple of older rooms close to the road that are not nearly as nice as the others.

Cabinas Espadilla. Manuel Antonio, Quepos. ☎/fax **506/777-0416.** 32 cabinas. $35–$45 cabina with fan; $55–$65 cabina with air-conditioning. V.

There isn't much shade around these cabinas, but they are clean and close to the beach. The rooms are spacious and most have kitchenettes. Although there isn't much in the way of decor or closet space in any of them, there are enough beds to sleep up to four people comfortably (a double bed and a bunk bed). High ceilings and fans keep the older rooms cool, and in the newer, more expensive rooms there is air-conditioning. Bars on the windows ensure security. The older rooms here are over-priced, but the newer rooms are fairly reasonable. You'll find these cabinas down the side road that runs perpendicular to the beach in front of Playa Espadilla.

✪ **Hotel Costa Verde.** Apdo. 106-6350, Quepos. ☎ **506/777-0584** or 506/777-0187. Fax 506/777-0506. 42 rms. Dec–Apr, $65–$90 double; May–Nov, $40–$70 double. AE, DC, MC, V.

The guest rooms at Costa Verde have long been some of my favorite in the area. With their screen walls they seem to sum up the sensual climate of the tropics—no need for walls when they only keep out the breezes. Over the years Costa Verde has con-tinued to add new rooms, and today the original rooms are some of the least expen-sive, but are still quite pleasant. Most of the rooms have ocean views, kitchenettes, and balconies, and the more expensive rooms have loads of space. When I last visited they were finishing the construction of 16 new deluxe suites that will each have air-conditioning and a jacuzzi. There's a very pretty little pool set into the hillside, and up above the pool is an open-air restaurant that looks into the forest trees, where sloths are sometimes seen. To one side of the dining room is a long bar. Costa Verde is more than halfway down the hill to Manuel Antonio, about a 10-minute walk from the beach.

El Dorado Mojado. Apdo. 238-6350, Quepos. ☎ **506/777-0368.** Fax 506/777-1248. 4 rms, 4 villas. A/C. Dec–Apr: $48.90 double; $73.35 villa; May–Nov: $40.75 double; $48.90 villa. All rates include breakfast. MC, V.

The architectural uniqueness of the buildings at this small hotel make it one of the most interesting places to stay in Manuel Antonio. Both the villas (with full kitch-ens) and the smaller standard rooms are very luxurious. The buildings are set back in the forest and are connected by a raised walkway below which grow lush tropical plants. The buildings resemble modernized banana plantation houses, with walls of glass that extend vertically for two stories before angling in to form an atrium effect. Standard rooms are located either upstairs (with hardwood floors and more light) or downstairs (with painted red-tile floors). Other interesting and attractive touches include cane-sided cupboards, open-air showers with walls of glass block, and Guatemalan bedspreads. The villas also have TVs, carved antique headboards, and Murphy beds. Some people might find the forest shade a bit dark, but it is still a beautiful setting. I would request Villa A, which has earned the title "monkey villa" for the frequent visits local primates pay to it, or Villa D, which sits beside a flow-ing stream and offers the most privacy.

El Lirio. Apdo. 123, Quepos. ☎/fax **506/777-0403.** 9 rms. Dec–Apr, $45 double or triple; May–Nov, $28.50 double or triple. All rates include continental breakfast. AE, MC, V.

Although the nicest rooms overlook the road and consequently can be a bit noisy, there are some quieter rooms at the back of the grounds near the swimming pool. A Mediterranean style prevails here, with arches, stucco walls, and red-tile floors and roofs. Rooms have a Southwestern motif, high ceilings, mosquito nets over the beds, and tiled bathrooms. The grounds are quiet and lush and are planted with many tropical flowers and orchids. There are also some large trees that provide much-needed shade. You'll find El Lirio on the left near the top of the hill as you drive from Quepos to Manuel Antonio. All in all, this is a very attractive place and a pretty good deal.

⑤ Hotel Plinio. Apdo. 71, Quepos. ☎ **506/777-0055.** Fax 506/777-0558. 6 rms, 6 suites, 1 jungle house. Dec–Apr, $60–$70 double, $75 standard suite or house; $90 deluxe suite. May–Nov, lower rates are available. All rates include a breakfast buffet. AE, MC, V.

The Plinio was for many years a favorite of budget travelers visiting Manuel Antonio, and although its room rates have crept up over the years, it's still a great value. The hotel is built into a steep hillside, so it's a bit of a climb from the parking lot up to the guest rooms and restaurant (roughly the equivalent of three flights of stairs). Once you are up top, though, you'll think you're in a treehouse. Floors and walls are polished hardwood, and there are even rooms with tree-trunk pillars. The hotel's suites are the best value. These are built on either two or three levels. Both types have sleeping lofts, while the three-story rooms also have rooftop decks. My favorite room is known as the jungle house and is set back in the forest. The restaurant, which is the most popular in Manuel Antonio, serves a variety of good Italian food, with entree prices ranging from $4.90 to $9.50. Behind the hotel there's a forest with 5 kilometers of trails, and, at the top of the hill, a 50-foot-tall observation tower with an incredible view. There's also a snack bar near the pool for lunches. A lap pool, kids pool, and recreation room with library round out the amenities.

Hotel Sula Bya Ba. Apdo. 203, Quepos. ☎ **506/777-0547.** 9 rms. TEL. Dec–Apr, $66 double with fan; $84–$96 double with air-conditioning; May–Nov, slightly lower rates. AE, MC, V.

You're a long way from the beach when you stay at the Sula Bya Ba, but the artistic decor and atmosphere make this one of the most intriguing hotels at Manuel Antonio. Rooms are large and uncluttered, and seem to be a hybrid of pueblo and Japanese motifs. The doors are reminiscent of shoji screens, and there are opaque windows around the showers, which make the bathrooms quite bright. Color schemes are very soothing and there are works of art on display in all the rooms. The bathrooms come stocked with large fluffy cotton towels and linen kimono bath robes. Breakfast is available and is usually served on a patio in the garden. The hotel also has a small pool, and a gift shop specializing in local crafts and natural products.

✪ Villas Nicolas. Apdo. 236, Quepos. ☎ **506/777-0481.** Fax 506/777-0451. 12 rms. $59–$90 double; $75–$105 triple; $90–$150 quad. Weekly, monthly, and low-season rates available. No credit cards.

These large villas pack a big punch for the buck. Built as terraced units up a steep hill in deep forest, they give a real feeling of being in the jungle. Spacious and well appointed, with wood floors, throw rugs, separate living rooms, and large bathrooms, some rooms even have full kitchenettes, which make longer stays comfortable and feasible.

My favorite feature, though, are the huge balconies, with both sitting chairs and a hammock. There's also a small pool. The rooms highest up the hill have views I'd be willing to pay a lot more for.

A BED-AND-BREAKFAST

⑤ La Colina. Apdo. 191, Quepos. ☎/fax **506/777-0231.** 5 rms, 6 suites. Dec–Apr, $32.60 double, $53 suite; May–Nov, $20 double, $36.50 suite. All rates include breakfast. V.

This casual little bed-and-breakfast is operated by a couple of Colorado natives who moved down to Manuel Antonio a few years ago and converted this house into a

B&B. Although the rooms are fairly small, they are stylishly decorated. They have black-and-white–tile floors, louvered French doors, and despite the small size of the rooms, a good writing desk. Outside each room there is a small patio area with a few chairs. Breakfast is served in your room or on the patio.

The six new suites were still under construction when I last visited, but they will all be larger, and have air-conditioning and ocean views. There was also a two-tiered swimming pool in the works, as well as a bar and restaurant.

INEXPENSIVE

Cabinas Pedro Miguel. Apdo. 17, Manuel Antonio, Quepos. ☎/fax **506/777-0035.** 14 rms (all with bath). $21.20–$36.60 double; $43.20 quad. AE, MC, V.

Located a kilometer outside Quepos on the road to Manuel Antonio (across from Hotel Plinio), these cabinas are very basic, with cement floors and cinderblock walls, but at least they're away from the fray and surrounded by forest. The second-floor rooms are newer, cleaner, and have carpeting as well as a glimpse of the water from the verandah they face. One of them is huge, with a kitchen and a back wall made entirely of screen. From it, guests can look out over a lush stand of trees. During the high season a restaurant serving Costa Rican standards opens, and the owners encourage guests to participate in meal preparation. There's a tiny swimming pool that sometimes has water in it. The management here is very friendly.

Cabinas Piscis. Apdo. 219, Quepos. ☎ **506/777-0046.** 18 rms (6 with private bath). $20 double with shared bath, $30 double with private bath; $5 each additional person. V.

If you want to be within walking distance of the park but out of earshot of the booming speakers of the town's disco—and you don't want to spend a lot of money—this is one of the only choices you have left. The rooms are basic but clean, and the management is very friendly. The 12 newer rooms all have shared baths, whereas each of older rooms has a private bath. The beach is just a hundred yards or so down a forest trail. You'll find Cabinas Piscis on the beach side of the road just before you reach the bottom of the hill and Manuel Antonio.

⑤ **Cabinas Ramirez.** Playas Manuel Antonio, Quepos. ☎ **506/777-0003.** 17 rms (all with bath). $18.70–$22.80 double. No credit cards.

These basic beachside cabinas are the most popular budget choices near the park, especially among young Ticos. The hotel is next door to the restaurant/bar and disco Mar y Sombra, so evenings can be loud here. The rooms are basic cinderblock affairs, with concrete floors. Some are quite dark and prisonlike, but all are clean. The owner also allows camping for backpackers with tents, for about $1.

✪ **Cabinas Vela-Bar.** Apdo. 13, Manuel Antonio, Quepos. ☎ **506/777-0413.** Fax 506/777-1071. 9 rms (each with bath), 1 apt, 1 house. $21.20–$31 double; $35–$57.86 triple; $52.20–$73.35 quad. AE, MC, V.

You'll find this unusual little hotel up the dirt road that leads off to the left just before the end of the road to Manuel Antonio National Park. It has a wide variety of room choices. If you're on an exceedingly tight budget, you can stay in a tiny room or, if you have a little more money to spend, you can opt for a spacious one-bedroom house that has tile floors and arched windows. There are double beds and tiled bathrooms in all rooms. The open-air restaurant/bar is deservedly very popular; check the chalkboard for the day's special. Entrees range in price from $5.10 to $11.50.

Hotel Malinche. Quepos. ☎/fax **505/777-0093.** 28 rms (all with bath). $12.50–$30 double. MC, V.

A good choice for backpackers, the Hotel Malinche is located on the first street to your left as you come into Quepos. You can't miss the hotel's arched brick entrance.

Inside you'll find bright rooms with louvered windows but no screens, so be sure to buy some mosquito coils before night falls. (Mosquito-repelling incense coils are available in drugstores and general stores.) The rooms are small but have hardwood floors and clean bathrooms. The more expensive rooms are new and have air-conditioning and carpets.

⑤ Hotel Quepos. Apdo. 79, Quepos. ☎ **506/777-0274.** 24 rms (15 with bath). $10 double without bath, $15 double with bath. No credit cards.

This little budget hotel is both comfortable and clean. There are hardwood floors, ceiling fans, a large sunny TV lounge, even a parking lot and laundry service. The management is very friendly, and downstairs from the second-floor hotel is an interesting souvenir shop and a charter fishing office. This hotel is across from the soccer field on the way out of town toward Manuel Antonio.

WHERE TO DINE

The most expensive meals in Manuel Antonio are at **El Byblos** and **La Mariposa,** but the quality is inconsistent. For the cheapest meals around, head to one of the dozen or so open-air shacks near the side of the road just before the circle at the entrance to the park. The standard Tico menu prevails with prices in the $2.70 to $8.10 range. Though these little places lack atmosphere, they do have a view of the ocean.

In Quepos, both **El Gran Escape** and **La Marquesa** are good bets. If you're staying in Quepos, and you're planning to do your own cooking or just want to pick up a snack, the market (two blocks in from the main road into town) sells lots of delicious fruit and fresh vegetables, among other staples. There are also several all-purpose grocery stores in downtown Quepos.

MODERATE

✪ Barba Roja. Quepos—Manuel Antonio Road. ☎ **506/777-0331.** Reservations not accepted. Main courses $5.10–$11.30; sandwiches $2.50–$3.05. V (with 7% surcharge). Tue–Sun 5am–9:30pm; Monday 4–9:30pm. SEAFOOD/CONTINENTAL.

Perched high on a hill with stunning views over jungle and ocean, the Barba Roja is the kind of restaurant that people discover on the last day of their vacation and wish they had known about the day they arrived. The rustic interior is done with local hardwoods and bamboo, which give the dining room a warm glow. Take a seat at the counter, and you can sit for hours gazing out at the view. If you tire of the view, glance around at some of the original art by local artists. There is even a gallery attached to the restaurant. Best of all, however, is the food. On the blackboard, there are daily specials such as grilled fish steak served with a salad and baked potato. The restaurant is open for breakfast and serves delicious whole-wheat french toast. For lunch, there are a number of different sandwiches, all served on whole-wheat bread. If you are in the mood to hang out and meet interesting people from all over the world, spend some time at the bar sipping piña coladas or margaritas.

Karola's. Quepos—Manuel Antonio Road. ☎ **506/777-0424.** Reservations not accepted. Main courses $3.30–$12.75. No credit cards. Thurs–Tue 7am–10pm. SEAFOOD/CONTINENTAL.

The steep driveway leading down to this open-air restaurant is within a few feet of the Barba Roja parking lot but is easily overlooked. Watch closely when you're up at the top of the hill. The restaurant is across a footbridge from its parking lot and is set against a jungle-covered hillside. Far below you can see the ocean if you are here during the day. Grilled seafoods are the specialty, but they also do peel-and-eat shrimp with a great house sauce. Desserts, such as macadamia pie, are good, and you can order margaritas by the pitcher.

✪ **Plinio Restaurant.** 1 kilometer out of Quepos toward Manuel Antonio. ☎ **506/ 777-0055.** Main courses $4.90–$9.50. AE, MC, V. Daily 7–10am and 5–10pm. ITALIAN/ GERMAN.

This is the most popular restaurant in Manuel Antonio and it is located in one of my favorite hotels. The open-air restaurant is a sort of covered deck about three stories above the parking lot, so be prepared to climb some steps before you get to eat. It's worth it, though. The basket of bread that arrives at your table shortly after you sit down is filled with delicious treats, and the menu is also full of tempting dishes. Italian is the primary cuisine here, but you may also encounter nightly German specials. The last time I visited the owner said they might even begin experimenting with dishes from Thailand and India. Some of my favorite dishes here include the spaghetti with pesto and the broccoli-and-cauliflower parmigiana. There's also a great antipasto platter that includes prosciutto, salami, and cheese.

Restaurant Vela-Bar. 100 meters down side road near the park entrance. ☎ **506/777-0413.** Reservations not accepted. Main courses $5.10—$11.50. AE, MC, V. Daily 7–10am, 11:30am– 2:30pm, 5:30–11pm (closed at lunch June–Nov). INTERNATIONAL.

The Vela-Bar is a small and casual place that serves some of the more creative cookery in Manuel Antonio. This is also the best of the restaurants closest to the park entrance. Seafood and vegetarian meals are the specialties here, and the most interesting dishes are almost always the specials posted on the blackboard. A typical day's choice might include fresh fish in sherry or wine sauce and curried vegetables.

INEXPENSIVE

La Tortuga. Isla Damas. No phone. Reservations not accepted. Main dishes $3.40–$10.80. V. Daily 9am–8pm. SEAFOOD.

This is one of the most unusual restaurants in Costa Rica. Even though it only serves basic Tico fare, it is an experience that should not be missed. To reach it, you must first drive north out of town toward Playa de Jacó. Watch for the "COMPLEJO TURISTICO" sign and turn west for another mile or so. When you reach the water, you'll find a boatman waiting to take you out to the restaurant on a large converted boat. If there is no boatman around, flash your lights and beep your horn; someone will come for you. The menu is primarily fish, and the owner seems to always have the very best catches of the day. The great seafood, exhilarating boat ride, and the view across the estuary to the forested mountains beyond make this place well worth the effort. If the TV is blaring, ask them to turn it down; they'll oblige.

MANUEL ANTONIO AFTER DARK

The main evening entertainment at Manuel Antonio is the disco that appears after dark at **Restaurant Mar y Sombra.** You can also hang out at the **Vela-Bar,** which is up the road to the left just before you reach Manuel Antonio, and seems to be popular with gay men. The bar at the **Barba Roja** restaurant is another good place to hang out and meet people in the evenings. If you are staying in Quepos, check out the **Disco Arco Iris,** which is across the bridge just before entering town and is built over the water. If you just can't stay away from the gaming tables, the **Hotel Kamuk** in Quepos has a small casino and will even foot your cab bill if you try your luck and lay your money down.

EN ROUTE TO DOMINICAL

Playa Matapalo is a long strand of flat beach that is about midway between Quepos and Dominical. Although it is not as spectacular as either of those two beaches, it does have its charms. Unfortunately, the surf is often too rough to allow much swimming here, although boogie boarding can be good. Foremost among this beach's charms are peace and quiet. With only a few places to stay, there are no crowds here, and Matapalo is still basically a little village. The beach itself is about a kilometer from the village. In addition to the hotel listed here, there is an Italian restaurant that serves economical meals, a Tico cabina with a disco, and other projects in the works.

El Coquito del Pacífico. Playa Matapalo (Apdo. 6783-1000, San José). ☎ **506/233-1731.** Fax 506/222-8849. 6 cabinas. $36 double; $42 triple; $48 quad. No credit cards.

This little collection of cabinas is operated by the same people who run the Hotel Ritz/Pension Continental, a budget-travelers' standard in San José. The cabinas are all quite large and have white-tile floors, high ceilings, colorful sheets on the beds, and overhead fans. There is a small restaurant/bar, and you can rent mountain bikes and boogie boards. Horseback rides can also be arranged; there are plans to add a swimming pool. This is one of the first places you come to when you hit the beach.

4 Dominical

29 kilometers SW of San Isidro; 42 kilometers S of Quepos; 160 kilometers S of San José

The secret has started to slip out, but Dominical and the coastline south of Domincial remain excellent places to find isolated beaches, spectacular views, remote jungle waterfalls, and abundant budget lodgings. Dominical has both right and left beach breaks, which means there are usually surfers in town, but, so far, this area is generally undeveloped, spread out, and slow-paced.

Leaving Manuel Antonio, the road south to Dominical runs by mile after mile of oil-palm plantations. However, just before Dominical, the mountains once again meet the sea. From Dominical south, the coastline is dotted with tide pools, tiny coves, and cliff-side vistas, all of which bring Big Sur, California to mind. Dominical is the largest village in the area and has several small lodges both in town and along the beach to the south. The village enjoys an enviable location on the banks of Río Baru, right where it becomes a wide lagoon before emptying into the ocean. There is good birdwatching along the banks of the river and throughout the surrounding forests.

ESSENTIALS

GETTING THERE & DEPARTING **By Plane** The nearest airport with regular service is in Quepos. From there you can hire a taxi, rent a car, or take the bus.

By Bus To reach Dominical, you must first go to San Isidro de El General or Quepos. Buses for San Isidro de El General leave San José daily every hour from 5:30am to 5pm, from Calle 16 between avenidas 1 and 3. Leave no later than 9:30am if you want to catch the 1:30pm bus to Dominical. The trip's duration is 3 hours; fare is $2.70.

From San Isidro de El General, buses leave for Dominical at 7am, and 1:30 and 3pm. The bus station for Dominical is one block south of the main bus station and two blocks west of the church. Trip duration is 1 1/2 hours; fare is $1.50.

From Quepos, buses leave daily at 5:30am and 1:30pm. Trip duration is 3 1/2 hours; fare is $3.50.

When you're ready to leave, note that buses only depart Dominical for San Isidro de El General twice daily: at 7:30am and 3pm. If you want to get to San José the same day, you'll have to catch the morning bus. Buses to Quepos leave at approximately 7am and 1:30pm. Buses leave San Isidro for San José every hour from 5:30am to 5pm.

By Car   From San José, head south (toward Cartago) on the Interamerican Highway. Continue on this road all the way to San Isidro de El General, where you turn right and head down toward the coast. The entire drive takes about 5 hours.

ORIENTATION   Arriving   Dominical is a small village on the banks of Río Baru. The village is to the right after you cross the bridge and centers around the soccer field and general store, where there is a public telephone.

EXPLORING THE BEACHES & BALLENA MARINE NATIONAL PARK

Because the beach in the village of Dominical is unprotected and at the mouth of a river, it is often much too rough for swimming. However, you can go for a swim in the lagoon at the mouth of the Río Baru, or head down the beach a few kilometers to the little sheltered cove at Roca Verde. If you have a car, you should continue driving south, exploring beaches as you go. At the village of Uvita, 16 kilometers south of Dominical, you'll reach the northern end of the Ballena Marine National Park, which protects a coral reef that stretches from Uvita south to Playa Piñuela and includes the little Isla Ballena, just offshore. At low tide an exposed sandbar allows you to walk about and explore the island. This park is named for the whales that are sometimes sighted close to shore in the winter months.

HORSEBACK TOURS & RAIN-FOREST HIKES

Although the beaches stretching south from Dominical should be beautiful enough to keep most people content, there are lots of other things to do. Several local farms offer horseback tours through forests and orchards, and at some of these farms you can even spend the night. **Hacienda Baru** (☎ 506/771-1903, leave message) offers several different hikes and tours, including a walk through mangroves and along the river bank (good birdwatching), a rain-forest hike through 200 acres of virgin jungle, an all-day trek from beach to mangrove to jungle that includes a visit to some Indian petroglyphs, an overnight camping trip, and a combination horseback-and-hiking tour. Tour prices range from $15 to $60 if there is only one person. If you're traveling with a group, you'll be charged a lower per-person rate, depending upon the number of people in your group. Note, however, that each tour can only accommodate six people. Hacienda Baru can also help you arrange various hikes and horseback rides on other nearby farms.

Down near Uvita there are several beautiful waterfalls that make wonderful destinations for hikes or horseback rides. Ask at **Uvita's Cabinas El Cocotico** for Jorge Diaz, who leads people to the Emerald Pools Falls, also a great place to go for a swim.

FARM STAYS

Finca Brian y Milena, Apdo. 2-8000, San Isidro de El General (☎ 506/771-1903, leave message), offers day and overnight trips to their farm in the hills outside of Dominical. Here you can birdwatch, explore the tropical rain forest, and visit a working farm where tropical fruits, nuts, and spices are grown. If you stay for several nights, you can visit the Santo Cristo or Diamante waterfalls by horseback or on foot. At night here, you can soak in the hot tub. Rates begin at $30 per person per day. Horse rentals and overnight excursions are additional.

WHERE TO STAY
MODERATE

Hotel Río Lindo. Dominical. ☎ **506/771-2009.** Fax 506/771-1725. 10 rms (all with private bath). Dec–Apr, $32–$44 double; May–Nov, slightly lower rates. No credit cards.

This two-story hotel is located near the entrance to Dominical, just across the bridge where the road turns into the village. Rooms are simple but clean and all have ceiling fans. The upstairs rooms are definitely the better choice. These rooms are larger, have nicer furnishings, and better ventilation. Adjacent to the hotel is the Restaurant Maui, a moderately priced place that seems to keep the stereo blaring all day long.

Punta Dominical. Apdo. 196-8000, San Isidro de El General. ☎ **506/787-0016** or 506/787-0017. 4 cabins. $50 double; $62 triple; $74 quad. No credit cards.

Located about 4 kilometers south of Dominical on a rocky point, this place has a stony cove on one side and a sandy beach on the other. The cabins and restaurant are set among shady old trees high above the surf, and have excellent views of both coves. The best views are to be had from the cabinas higher up the hill, but all have good views. The cabins, built on stilts and constructed of dark polished hardwood, all have big porches with chairs and hammocks. Screened and louvered walls are designed to catch the breezes. The bathrooms are large and have separate changing areas. The hotel's open-air restaurant, which specializes in seafood, is one of the best in Dominical. Entree prices range from $3.50 to $15.

INEXPENSIVE

In addition to the places listed here, if you continue south another 16 kilometers, you'll find a campground on Playa Ballena and a couple of basic cabinas in Uvita.

✪ **Albergue Willdale.** Dominical (c/o: Selva Mar, Apdo. 215-8000, San Isidro de El General). ☎ /fax **506/771-1903.** 7 rms (each with private bath). $25 double; $30 triple. No credit cards.

The Albergue Willdale is located directly across from the soccer field and is by far the friendliest place in Dominical. Directly behind the lodge is the river, where you can go swimming, fishing, or paddling around. The owners of this lodge are from Virginia, and they'll gladly fill you in on all there is to do in the area. The rooms are large and have big windows and patios. There are reading lights, fans, hot water, and attractive Mexican bedspreads. If you are interested in staying for a while, the Dales also rent a very comfortable house up in the hills for $120 a night. The house even has its own swimming pool.

Bella Vista. Dominical (c/o Selva Mar, Apdo. 215-8000, San Isidro de El General). ☎ /fax **506/771-1903.** 4 cabins. $30–$45 double. All rates include continental breakfast. No credit cards.

Bella Vista means "beautiful view," and that's exactly what you get when you stay at one of these small rustic cabins high in the hills south of Dominical. This is a very basic sort of place, but the owners are friendly and the location is superb. Transportation between Dominical and Bella Vista is $10 per person each way. Simple meals are served ($4 for breakfast and lunch, $5–$7 for dinner), though one of the cabins has its own kitchen. The favorite activity of guests is an all-day horseback ride through the rain forest to a beautiful waterfall. The price of $40 per person includes your horse, guide, and lunch.

Cabinas Nayarit. 200 meters west of Rancho Coco, Dominical. ☎ **506/771-1878.** 18 rms (14 with private bath). $28.50, for up to three people w/shared bath; $33, for up to three people w/private bath. V.

Wedged between the mouth of the Río Baru and the beach, there are several sandy lanes lined with simple houses and some cabinas, which primarily cater to surfers. Of these, Cabinas Nayarit is the best. There are several styles of rooms here including older rooms with fans and lots of beds (crowded), older rooms with air-conditioning, and newer rooms with air-conditioning, skylights, carved wooden headboards, and jalousie windows.

Roca Verde. Dominical. No phone. 12 rms (7 with private bath). $7 double or triple without bath; $15 double with bath; $20 triple with bath. No credit cards.

This hotel has a wonderful location a couple of kilometers south of Dominical. The setting is superb—on a little cove with rocks and tide pools at the near end. If you're driving, you'll only be able to take the back road from town at low tide, since the road actually crosses a section of the beach. The cheaper rooms are very basic, with wooden walls, a fan, one small window, and a couple of beds. The shared toilets and showers are comparable to what you might find at a campground. The more expensive cabins have private baths and a decidedly tropical feel. The Roca Verde's open-air restaurant/bar is popular with tourists and Ticos alike and it often doubles as a disco on weekend nights, so be prepared.

WHERE TO DINE

Right in town, there's the **Soda Laura,** which serves basic Tico meals and has a nice view of the river mouth. Dishes range in price from $1.75 to $8. Other options include **San Clemente Bar and Grill,** a gringo hangout and sports bar specializing in Mexican-American food, and the **Restaurant Maui,** which is next to the Hotel Río Lindo. These latter two places serve meals that cost between $3.50 and $15. However, if you want to sample the best food in the area, hands down, head south of town to the **Hotel Punta Dominical.**

5 San Isidro de El General: A Base for Exploring Chirripó National Park

120 kilometers SE of San José; 123 kilometers NW of Palmar Norte; 29 kilometers NE of Dominical

San Isidro de El General is the largest town in this region and is located on the Interamerican Highway in the foothills of the Talamanca Mountains. Although there isn't much to do right in town, this is the jumping-off point for trips to Chirripó National Park. This is also the transfer point if you are coming from or going to Dominical, and most buses traveling the Interamerican Highway stop here.

ESSENTIALS

GETTING THERE & DEPARTING   By Bus   Express buses leave San José daily at 5:30am and 5pm from Calle 16 between avenidas 1 and 3. Trip duration is 3 hours; fare is $2.70.

Buses from Golfito and Puerto Jiménez will also drop you off in San Isidro (see chapter 9 for schedules).

There are also buses from Quepos to San Isidro daily at 5:30am and 1:30pm. Trip duration is $3^1/_2$ hours; fare is $3.50.

Buses depart San Isidro for San José daily every hour between 5:30am and 5pm. Buses to Dominical leave daily at 7am, and 1:30 and 3pm. Buses to Golfito pass through San Isidro at around 10am, and 2 and 6pm. Buses to Puerto Jiménez leave daily at 9am and 3pm.

By Car   It is a long and winding road from San José to San Isidro; this section of the Interamerican Highway is one of the most difficult sections of road in the country. Not only are there the usual car-eating potholes, but you must also contend with driving over the 11,000-foot-high Cerro de la Muerte (Mountain of Death), which the ICT (Costa Rican Tourism Board) would like to rename Buenavista (Beautiful View). This aptly named mountain (in either case) is legendary for its dense afternoon fogs, blindingly torrential downpours, steep drop-offs, constant switchbacks, and breathtaking views. In other words, drive with care. And bring a sweater; it's cold up at the top. It'll take you about 3 hours to get to San Isidro.

ORIENTATION **Arriving** Downtown San Isidro is just off the Interamerican Highway. The main bus station is two blocks west of the north end of the central park.

EXPLORING CHIRRIPÓ NATIONAL PARK

At 12,412 feet in elevation, Mount Chirripó is the tallest mountain in Costa Rica, and because of the great elevations within the national park named after it, temperatures can dip below freezing, especially at night. If you are headed up this way, come prepared for chilly weather. The elevation and low temperatures have produced a very different sort of environment for Costa Rica. Above about 10,000 feet only stunted trees and shrubs can survive in regions known as *paramos*. If you are driving the Interamerican Highway between San Isidro and San José, you will pass through a paramo on the Cerro de la Muerte (Mountain of Death).

Hiking up to the top of Mt. Chirripó is one of Costa Rica's great adventures. On a clear day (usually in the morning), you can see both the Pacific Ocean and the Caribbean Sea from the summit. You can do this trip fairly easily on your own if you have brought gear and are an experienced backpacker. While it is possible to hike from the park entrance to the summit and back down in two days, it is best to allow four days for the trip to give yourself time to enjoy your hike fully, and still spend some time on top since that's where the glacier lakes and paramo are. (There's a simple but wonderful lodge near the summit where you can stay overnight.) For much of the way you'll be hiking through cloud forests that are home to the spectacular quetzal, Costa Rica's most beautiful bird. These cloud forests are cold and damp, though, so come prepared for rain and fog.

ENTRY POINT, FEES & REGULATIONS Although it's not that difficult to get to Chirripó National Park from nearby San Isidro, it's still rather remote. And to see it fully, you have to be prepared to hike. To get to the trailhead, you have two choices: car or bus. If you choose to drive, take the road out of San Isidro, heading north toward San Gerardo de Rivas. The trailhead is 15 kilometers (9 miles) down the road. Otherwise, you can catch a bus in San Isidro that will take you directly to the trailhead in San Gerardo de Rivas. Buses leave daily at 5:30am from the central park in San Isidro. It costs $1.05 one way and takes 1 1/2 hours. Another bus departs at 2pm from a bus station 200 meters south of the park. Buses return to San Isidro daily at 7am and 4pm. Because the hike to the summit of Mt. Chirripó can take between 6 to 12 hours—depending upon your physical condition—I recommend taking the earlier bus so you can start hiking when the day is still young, or arriving the day before and spending the night in San Gerardo de Rivas (there are a number of inexpensive cabinas there), before setting out early the following morning.

Park admission is $6 per day. If you plan to stay at the lodge near the summit, you must make reservations in advance, since the number of people who can stay there is limited (see "Staying at the Summit Lodge," below). Note that camping is not allowed in the park. Finally, it's possible to have your gear carried up to the summit by horseback during the dry season. A number of guides work outside the park entrance in San Gerardo de Rivas. They charge between $15–$20 per pack depending on size and weight. In the rainy season, the same guides work, but they take packs up by themselves, not by horseback.

STAYING AT THE SUMMIT LODGE Reservations for the lodge on Mt. Chirripó must be prepaid at the National Parks office in San José or San Isidro

(☎ 506/771-3155). The lodge holds only 40 people; 25 of those spaces can be reserved in San José, while 15 are controlled by the San Isidro office. There's no food or bedding at the lodge, so be sure to bring something to eat, a campstove if you want to cook, and a sleeping bag. It costs $2.50 per person per night.

WHERE TO STAY & DINE IN SAN ISIDRO DE EL GENERAL

Hotel Chirripó. South side of church, San Isidro de El General. ☎ **506/771-0529.** 41 rms (20 with private bath). $7.50 double without bath; $13 double with bath; $19 triple with bath. V.

This budget hotel is about the best you'll find right in San Isidro, and is located on the central square within a couple of blocks of all the town's bus stations. Rooms vary considerably. Some have windows (and street noise), and some have no windows or street noise. Stay away from the rooms in front, since these are the noisiest. There's a large restaurant at the front of the lobby.

EN ROUTE TO SAN JOSÉ: TWO PLACES TO SEE QUETZALS IN THE WILD

Between San Isidro de El General and San José, the Interamerican Highway climbs to its highest point in Costa Rica and crosses over the Cerro de la Muerte. This area has recently acquired a newfound importance as one of the best places in Costa Rica to see quetzals in the wild. March, April, and May are nesting season for the quetzals, and this is usually the best time to see them. However, in this area, it is often possible to seem them year-round. On one 2-hour hike here, without a guide, our small group spotted eight of these amazing birds. All of the lodges listed below, along with some new ones, are located along a 20-kilometer stretch of the Interamerican Highway. You'll probably start seeing their billboards and placards with painted quetzals long before you see any birds.

✪ **Albergue De Montaña Savegre.** Kilometer 80 Carretera Interamericana Sur, San Gerardo de Dota (Apdo. 482, Cartago). ☎ **506/771-1732.** 16 cabins. $63 per person. All rates include three meals daily. V.

This working apple and pear farm, which also has over 600 acres of primary forest, has recently acquired quite a reputation as one of the best places in the country to see quetzals. The farm has long been popular as a weekend vacation and picnicking spot for Ticos, but now people from all over the world are searching out the rustic lodge. The rooms here are quite basic, but if you're serious about birdwatching this shouldn't matter. Hearty Tico meals are served, and if you want to try your hand at trout fishing, you might luck into a fish dinner. You'll find this lodge 9 kilometers down a dirt road off the Interamerican Highway.

✪ **Albergue de Montaña Tapantí.** Kilometer 62 Carreter Interamericana Sur, Macho Gaff, Cartago (Apdo. 1237-1000, Pavas). ☎/fax **506/232-0436.** 11 rms. $60 double; $75 triple; $85 quad. MC, V.

If you want to hike around in the cloud forest, see quetzals, and then return to a large, comfortable room with a private bath, this deluxe lodge is what you're looking for in this area. The buildings at Tapantí are built to resemble Swiss chalets, and you may think you're in Switzerland when you feel how cold it gets here at night. The lodge is at 10,000 feet and frost is not uncommon. However, there is a fireplace in the lounge. Most of the guest rooms are actually suites with separate bedrooms and living rooms; luckily, they also have heaters. The lodge's dining room serves such Swiss specialties as beef fondue and raclette, as well as other continental dishes. Guided hikes, horseback rides, and birdwatching walks are all available through the lodge.

9

The Southern Zone

The heat and humidity are more than many people can handle, but this remote southern region of Costa Rica is one of the country's most beautiful and wild areas. Lush forested mountains tumble into the sea, streams still run clear and clean, and scarlet macaws squawk raucously in the treetops. However, this beauty does not come easy; you must have plenty of time (or plenty of money, preferably both), plus a desire for a bit of adventure if you want to explore this region. Because there are few roads, most of the most fascinating spots can be reached only by small plane or boat, although hiking and four-wheeling will get you into some memorable surroundings as well.

Not surprisingly, this region has only very recently opened up to tourism. It is, after all, an 8-hour drive from San José. Despite an increased interest in southern Costa Rica by international travelers and Ticos alike (Corcovado National Park and Caño Island Biological Reserve are here, and a duty-free port just opened in Golfito), there are still relatively few places to stay. It's best to put some forethought into planning a vacation down here, and by all means, book your room or lodge reservations in advance.

1 Drake Bay

145 kilometers S of San José; 32 kilometers SW of Palmar

Located on the northern end of the Osa Peninsula, Drake Bay is what adventure travel is all about. Little more than a collection of lodges catering to naturalists, anglers, scuba divers, and assorted vacationers, the bay can only be reached by boat or chartered sea plane, which makes it one of the more remote destinations in Costa Rica. Because of the bay's remoteness, there has been little development here. Accommodations vary from tents on wooden platforms and cement-walled cabinas to very comfortable lodges that border on the luxurious. There are few conventional phones and no power lines in Drake Bay, so radio and cellular phones and electrical generators stand in. The village of Drake Bay has its own water system, but it is infamous for its unreliability. If you're headed out this way you may occasionally find yourself without water for a shower, but the problem rarely lasts long.

The bay is named after Sir Francis Drake, who is believed to have anchored here in 1579. Emptying into the bay is the tiny Río

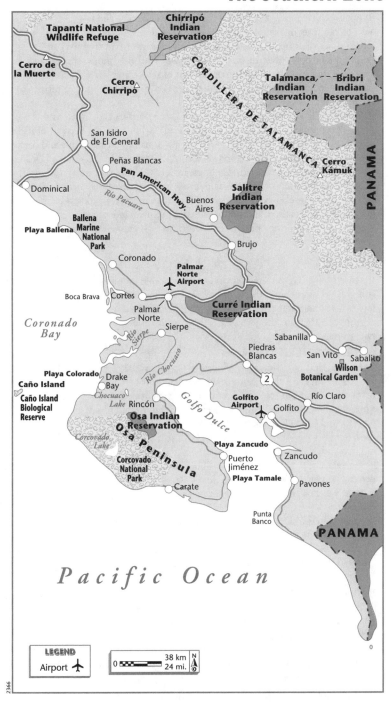

The Southern Zone

Tapantí National
Wildlife Refuge

Chirripó
Indian
Reservation

Cerro de
la Muerte

Cerro
Chirripó

CORDILLERA DE TALAMANCA

Talamanca
Indian
Reservation

Bribri
Indian
Reservation

San Isidro
de El General

Cerro
Kámuk

PANAMA

Peñas Blancas

Pan American Hwy.

Dominical

Río Pacuare

Buenos
Aires

Salitre
Indian
Reservation

Playa Ballena

Ballena
Marine
National
Park

Brujo

Coronado

Palmar
Norte
Airport

Boca Brava

Cortes

Curré Indian
Reservation

Palmar
Norte

*Coronado
Bay*

Río Sierpe

Sierpe

Sabanilla

Piedras
Blancas

San Vito

Sabalito

Playa Colorado

Río Chocuaco

2

Wilson
Botanical Garden

Caño Island

Drake
Bay

Chocuaco
Lake

Rincón

Golfo Dulce

Río Claro

Caño Island
Biological
Reserve

Osa Indian
Reservation

Golfito
Airport

Golfito

*Corcovado
Lake*

Osa Peninsula

Playa Zancudo

Zancudo

Corcovado
National
Park

Puerto
Jiménez

Playa Tamale

Carate

Pavones

Punta
Banco

PANAMA

P a c i f i c   O c e a n

LEGEND

Airport ✈

0 ▭▭▭▭ 38 km
        24 mi.

N

2366

Agujitas, which acts as a protected harbor for small boats and is a great place to do a bit of canoeing or swimming. It is here in the Río Agujitas that many of the local lodges dock their boats. Stretching south from Drake Bay are miles and miles of deserted beaches. Adventurous explorers will find tide pools, spring-fed rivers, waterfalls, forest trails, and some of the best birdwatching in all of Costa Rica. If a paradise such as this appeals to you, Drake Bay makes a good base for exploring the peninsula.

South of Drake Bay lies the wilds of the Osa Peninsula and Corcovado National Park. This is one of Costa Rica's most beautiful regions, yet it is also one of its least accessible. Corcovado National Park covers about half of the peninsula and contains the largest virgin lowland rain forest in Central America. For this reason, Corcovado is well-known among naturalists and researchers studying rain-forest ecology. Take note of the operative words here—rain forest. It does, indeed, rain here. In fact, some parts of the peninsula receive more than 250 inches per year. In addition to producing lush forests, this massive amount of rain also produces more than a few disgruntled visitors. If you're of the opinion that rain ruins a vacation, you might want to consider going elsewhere in Costa Rica.

ESSENTIALS

Because Drake Bay is so remote and only accessible by water or chartered plane, it is highly recommended that you have a room reservation before you arrive. The lodges listed here are scattered along several kilometers of coastline.

Although they are always useful to have on hand in Costa Rica, a flashlight and rain gear are essential in Drake Bay.

GETTING THERE   By Plane   The closest airport to Drake Bay is in **Palmar Sur,** a taxi and boat ride away. **Sansa** (☎ 506/233-0397, 506/233-3258 or 506/233-5330) flies to Palmar Sur at 9am Monday through Saturday, and at 11:15am on Sunday, from San José's Juan Santamaría International Airport. The former flight stops at Coto 47 and Puerto Jiménez en route, and the latter stops at Puerto Jiménez, Golfito, and Coto 47 en route. The former flight duration is 1 hour and 50 minutes; the latter lasts 2 hours and 20 minutes. Both cost $50 each way. Note that this routing may differ, depending on demand.

Travelair (☎ 506/220-3054 or 506/232-7883) has flights to Palmar Sur that depart daily at 8:10am from San José's Pavas International Airport. This flight stops at Quepos en route. Flight duration is 55 minutes; fare is $73 one way, $119 round-trip.

Many hotels in Drake Bay run charter flights to Palmar Sur during the high season (see "Where to Stay" below for details), and it is even possible to charter a sea plane that will fly you directly to the bay. **Alas Anfibias de Costa Rica** (☎ 506/232-9567) charters a 4-passenger sea plane for $750 and an 8-passenger plane for $1,500 (each way).

By Bus   Express buses leave San José daily for Palmar Norte at 5, 7, 8:30 and 11am, and 1, 2:30, and 6pm from Avenida 18 between calles 2 and 4. Bus trip duration is 5 hours; fare is $3.90.

You can also catch a Golfito-bound bus from this same station and get off in Palmar Norte.

Once in Palmar Norte, ask when the next bus goes out to Sierpe. If it doesn't leave for a while (they aren't frequent), consider taking a taxi (see below).

By Taxi and Boat   Once you arrive at either the Palmar Norte bus station or the Palmar Sur airstrip, you'll most likely need to take a taxi to the village of Sierpe. The fare should be between $10 and $15. A seat on a boat from Sierpe downriver to Drake Bay will cost you another $15.

DEPARTING   Have your lodge arrange a boat trip back to Sierpe for you. Be sure the lodge also arranges for a taxi to meet you in Sierpe for the trip to Palmar Sur or Palmar Norte. (If you're on a budget, you can ask around to see if a late-morning public bus is still running from Sierpe to Palmar Norte.) In either of the two Palmars, you can make onward plane and bus connections. At the Palmar Norte bus terminal, almost any bus headed north will take you to San José, and almost any bus heading south will take you to Golfito.

WHAT TO SEE & DO: BEACHES, RAIN FORESTS, WILDLIFE & HIKING

Beaches, forests, wildlife, and solitude are the main attractions of Drake Bay. While Corcovado National Park is the area's star attraction (covered in the next section), there's plenty to soak up in Drake Bay. The Osa Peninsula is home to an unbelievable variety of plants and animals: more than 140 species of mammals, 267 species of birds, and 117 species of amphibians and reptiles. While you aren't likely to see a high percentage of these animals, you can expect to see quite a few, including several species of monkeys, coatimundis, scarlet macaws, parrots, and hummingbirds. The tallest tree in Costa Rica, a 230-foot-tall silk-cotton tree, is located within Corcovado, as is Costa Rica's largest population of scarlet macaws. Other park inhabitants include jaguars, tapirs, sloths, and crocodiles. If you're lucky, you might even see one of the region's *osas.* Though the word means "bear" in English, in this case it refers to the giant anteaters that live on the peninsula.

Around Drake Bay and within the national park there are many miles of trails through rain forests and swamps, down beaches, and around rock headlands. All of the lodges listed below offer guided excursions into the park. It is also possible to begin a hike around the peninsula from Drake Bay.

AN EXCURSION TO CAÑO ISLAND BIOLOGICAL RESERVE

One of the most popular excursions from Drake Bay is a trip out to Caño Island and the Caño Island Biological Reserve for a bit of exploring and snorkeling or scuba diving. The island is located about 12 miles offshore from Drake Bay and was once home to a pre-Columbian culture about which little is known. A trip to the island will include a visit to one of this culture's cemeteries, and you'll also be able to see some of the stone spheres that are commonly believed to have been carved by the people who once lived in this area. The island is most unique for its geological isolation: due to plate tectonics, the island has remained separate from the rest of Central America for more than 40 million years. The dominant tree species is the huge cow or milk tree, which produces a milky sap that can be drunk. Few animals or birds live on the island, but the coral reefs just offshore teem with life and are the main reason most people come here. Most of the lodges listed below offer trips to Caño Island. You can also do some sportfishing while you're in the area; almost any of the lodges can arrange a charter boat for you.

WHERE TO STAY & DINE

I have chosen to list nightly room rates at the following lodges. However, because all but the least expensive places are all-inclusive, the price categories have been shifted to take this into account (a "very expensive" room is classified as "expensive," and so on). Also, please note that these lodges do most of their business in package trips that include several nights' lodging, all meals, transportation, and tours. If you intend to do several tours while you are here, be sure to ask about these packages. They could constitute a significant saving for you.

EXPENSIVE

✪ Aguila De Osa Inn. Apdo. 10486-1000, San José (mailing address in the U.S.: 7500 NW 25 Street, Miami, FL 33122, Cuenta no. 250). ☎ **506/296-2190** or 506/232-7722. Fax 506/232-7722. 14 rms. $180–$225 double; $290–$315 triple. All rates include three meals daily. MC, V.

The most expensive lodge in Drake Bay, it is also the most comfortable. Situated high on a hill overlooking Drake Bay and the Pacific Ocean, the Aguila de Osa Inn offers attractively decorated, comfortable rooms, located a vigorous hike up a steep hillside. There is a bar built atop some rocks on the bank of the Río Agujitas, and a dining room with a good view of the bay. Meals are simply prepared but tasty and filling, and the kitchen leaves a fresh thermos of coffee outside each room every morning. All the guest rooms have hardwood or tile floors, ceiling fans, large bathrooms, and excellent views. Excursions available through the lodge include hikes in Corcovado National Park ($65), trips to Caño Island ($65 per person for snorkelers, $110 per person for scuba divers), horseback rides ($55 per person), and sportfishing ($450 to $850 for a full day's rental depending on the size of the boat and the number of people in your party).

✪ Drake Bay Wilderness Camp. Apdo. 98-8150, Palmar Norte, Osa. ☎ **506/771-2436** or 506/284-4107. Fax 506/771-2436. 4 tents (all with shared bath), 21 rms. Tents, $92 double; rooms, $136 double, $204 triple. All rates include three meals daily. MC, V.

This is one of the most convenient and best-located lodges at Drake Bay. It backs onto the Río Agujitas and fronts onto the Pacific, but because it's on a rocky spit, there isn't a good swimming beach right here. The lodge offers a variety of accommodations of different ages and styles. Travelers who want to rough it a bit or economize can opt for a large tent, while those seeking more comfort can ask for one of the newer rooms. These rooms have ceiling fans, verandahs, and good mattresses on the beds. The older rooms, though smaller, are also very clean and comfortable and were recently remodeled. The family-style meals are filling, with an emphasis on fresh seafood and fresh fruits. The lodge provides free use of its canoes, free same-day laundry service, and fax service for guests. Tours offered by Drake Bay Wilderness Camp include hikes within the national park ($55 per person), trips to Caño Island ($55 per person for snorkelers, $90 per person for scuba divers), horseback riding tours ($35 per person), and sportfishing charters ($250 per day for 1–3 persons).

✪ La Paloma Lodge. Apdo. 97-4005, San Antonio de Belen, Heredia. ☎/fax **506/239-0954** or 506/239-2801 (radio phone at the lodge). 5 rms, 5 cabins. Rooms, $140 double; cabins, $180 double, $210 triple. May–Nov 15, rates are 10% lower. Packages available. All rates include three meals daily. V (7% surcharge added).

Birdwatchers will find no better place to stay in Drake Bay. Situated on a hill that can leave the out-of-shape a bit winded, La Paloma offers expansive ocean views. The main lodge building is a huge, open-air, thatched structure with a long verandah. Over in one corner is a sitting area that makes for a pleasant place to meet other lodge guests. All of the cabins are built on stilts, feature large verandahs, and are set among lush foliage facing the Pacific Ocean. The three older cabins are my favorites simply for their spaciousness and seclusion. Four screen walls keep you in touch with nature and let the ocean breezes blow through. However, the newer cabins do provide wonderful ocean views from their main sleeping lofts. The beach is down at the bottom of the hill, and there is a new tiled pool with superb sunset views. The electricity is shut off each evening at 9:30pm, which might irritate some late-night bookworms, but if you're like me, you'll want to get up at dawn to watch the early-morning birds. The rooms, though much smaller, are still very attractive and have good views from their verandahs, which, like the cabins, have hammocks. Excursions available include hikes in the park ($65 per person), trips to Caño Island ($65 per person), horseback rides ($50 per person), scuba trips ($100 per person), and sportfishing charters ($450 for a full day's boat rental). There are also canoes, kayaks, and snorkeling equipment for rent.

MODERATE

Marenco Biological Reserve. Centro Comercial El Pueblo, Local No. 49-50 (Apdo. 4025-1000), San José. ☎ **506/221-8166.** Fax 506/255-1346. 25 rms. $110–$130 double; $165–$195 triple. All rates include three meals daily. No credit cards.

Marenco is located a few kilometers south of Drake Bay and is consequently the closest lodge to Corcovado National Park. The lodge, which is set on a hillside overlooking the ocean, is surrounded by 1,235 acres of private reserve. There are more than 4 kilometers of trails through the reserve, and the birdwatching here is often excellent. Accommodations are comfortable, albeit fairly simple. All the rooms have ocean views and porches so you can enjoy the sunsets and even birdwatch right from your room. The newer rooms are larger and more comfortable, but the older ones have a lot of style. Rooms are mostly in duplex cabins around the landscaped grounds, and if you get one of the larger rooms, you can lie in bed and gaze out at the forest through walls of screen. The thatched roofs give the compound the feel of a small village. Meals are served family-style in an open-air dining room that has a great view down the hill to the Pacific. Marenco offers the same sorts of tours available at other lodges and charges similar rates.

Corcovado Adventures Tent Camp. Drake Bay, Osa Peninsula. ☎ **506/223-2770.** Fax 506/257-4201. 10 tents (all with shared bathrooms). $90 double. All rates include three meals daily. No credit cards.

If you don't mind camping, this place, midway between the lodges at Drake Bay and Marenco Biological Reserve, is a good choice in the moderate price category. The tents are quite large and are set on wooden decks, and a nice swimming beach is only a few yards away. There are plenty of modern showers and toilets. The large dining room serves simple meals with an emphasis on fresh seafood. Various tours are available, and there are kayaks and snorkeling gear available for rent. With rates comparable to those of the cheapest places in the village and tents as large as some of the village's least expensive rooms, this makes a good choice for anyone who prefers a bit more seclusion and more of an adventurous setting. Excursions you can arrange here include guided hikes ($60), trips to Caño Island ($60), horseback rides ($45), and sportfishing charters ($400 for a full day for up to four people).

☉ Cabinas Jinetes de Osa. Drake Bay, Osa Peninsula. ☎ **506/273-3116** or 506/284-3743. 9 rms (6 with shared bath). $80–$100 double. All rates include three meals daily. MC, V (6% surcharge added).

Although the rooms are small and dark, this is still one of the nicer places at the lower end of the scale in Drake Bay. The wooden construction of the building that houses the rooms, and the long verandah almost directly above the beach are what give this lodge an edge over other moderately priced lodges in Drake Bay. It is also the closest of the less expensive places to the docks on the Río Agujitas, which is nice for those with heavy bags. Basic Tico-style meals are served in a small open-air dining room.

INEXPENSIVE

Cabinas Cecilia. Drake Bay, Osa Peninsula. ☎ **506/382-3299.** 6 rms (2 with private bath). $50 double. All rates include breakfast and dinner.

If cost is a factor to you, this is just about the cheapest place to stay in Drake Bay (of those lodges that include meals in the room rate). Although these cabinas, housed in a cinder-block bunker, are rather stark, they are fronted by a long verandah with a nice view of the bay. Rooms vary in size: some have bunk beds, while others have twin or double beds. Other than the beds, there is no furniture in the rooms. Meals are served in a separate open-air dining room a short distance from the cabinas. The owner also runs a separate bar and restaurant, a short hike up the steep hill above the cabinas.

Cocalito Lodge. Apdo. 63, Palmar Norte, Osa Peninsula. No phone in Costa Rica. ☎ **519/ 782-3978** (in Canada). Fax 506/786-6150 (in Costa Rica). 3 rms, 6 cabins (each with private bath). May–Nov, $37–$60 double; Dec–Apr, $40–$70 double. MC, V (6% surcharge added).

The owners of this little place right on the beach south of La Paloma Lodge are gringos who have been living here for years. Their choice of this remote alternative lifestyle has translated into a rustic and casual beachfront lodge that attracts primarily a younger crowd. Some of the rooms are a bit dark and cramped, but there are also larger and more expensive cabinas that offer plenty of room. In my opinion, Cocalito's greatest attraction is that it is right on a beautiful little cove bordered on both ends by rocky outcrops. At all of the more expensive lodges here in Drake Bay, you have to do a bit of walking (often down muddy trails) to get to a swimmable beach. So, if having the beach right outside your door is more important than having a large luxurious room, Cocalito might be for you. The lodge's dining room offers excellent meals, with many ingredients from the owners' organic garden. Meals cost an additional $30 per day. Electricity is provided by a combination of solar and hydraulic sources, but conserved for the most essential appliances and functions. At night, candles and torches provide most of the lighting. A variety of tours are offered, including trips to Caño Island ($50 per person for snorkelers, $110 per person for scuba divers), guided hikes ($15 to $50 per person), horseback rides ($35 per person), deep-sea fishing ($350 per day for three people), and boat tours of the nearby mangrove swamp ($50 per person).

NEARBY PLACES TO STAY & DINE

Hotel Pargo. Sierpe. ☎/fax **506/788-8032.** 10 rms. A/C. $30 double; $40 triple. No credit cards.

This modern two-story hotel is the only hotel in Sierpe and is located at the dock from which boats leave to head downriver to Drake Bay. So, if you are on your way to Drake Bay and expect to arrive in Sierpe late in the day (when no boats are heading downriver), this is where you should spend the night. Rooms are fairly large, though simply furnished, and are clean. The hotel can arrange most of the same tours that are offered at Drake Bay. These become particularly economical if you can organize a group of at least five people. There is an inexpensive open-air restaurant adjacent to the hotel.

Río Sierpe Lodge. Apdo. 85, Palmar Norte. ☎ **506/257-7010** or 506/220-2121. Fax 506/ 257-7012. 11 rms. $106 double; $159 triple. All rates include three meals daily and transportation to and from Palmar Norte. No credit cards.

This lodge is located on the south bank of the Río Sierpe near the river mouth. You won't have direct access to any beaches if you stay here, but all the same excursions are available at comparable prices. This lodge is best known as a fishing lodge and offers various fishing packages. The lodge is surrounded by forests, and there are hiking trails on the property. Meals in the dining room feature international cuisine with an emphasis on fresh fruits, fish, and chicken. Naturalists, anglers, and scuba divers are all catered to here. Adventurous types can do a two-day horseback trek that includes camping in the rain forest. Note that taxi and river transfers between Palmar and the lodge are included in the rates, which makes this place slightly more economical than the other lodges I've listed.

2 Puerto Jiménez: Gateway to Corcovado National Park

35 kilometers W of Golfito by water (90 kilometers by road); 85 kilometers S of Palmar Norte

Despite its small size and languid pace, Puerto Jiménez is a double boom town, where rough jungle gold panners mix with wealthy eco-tourists, budget backpackers, and a surprising number of celebrities seeking a small dose of anonymity and escape. Located on the southeastern tip of the Osa Peninsula, the town itself is just a couple of gravel streets, with the ubiquitous soccer field, a block of general stores, some inexpensive sodas, a butcher shop, and several bars. Scarlet macaws fly overhead, and mealy parrots provide wake-up calls.

On first glance it is hard to imagine anything ever happening here, but looks are often deceiving. Signs in English on walls around town advertise a variety of tours, with most of the excursions going to nearby Corcovado National Park. The national park has its headquarters here, and this town makes an excellent base or embarkation point for exploring this vast wilderness. If the in-town accommodations strike you as too budget-oriented, you can easily get to more luxurious places farther south on the Osa Peninsula from here. And if the nightlife strikes you as sleepy, don't forget about all those gold miners lurking about. As the home base and resupply station for gold miners—most of them panning illegally—seeking to strike it rich in the jungles in and around the park, Puerto Jiménez's streets can get pretty rowdy at night when panners actually cash in a find. During these times, the bars host some hard drinking that knows few bounds or time limits.

ESSENTIALS

GETTING THERE & DEPARTING   By Plane   Sansa (☎ 506/233-0397, 506/233-3258, or 506/233-5330) has flights departing Monday through Saturday at 9am to Puerto Jiménez, and Sunday at 11:15am, from San José's Juan Santamaría International Airport. The former flight stops at Coto 47 en route; the latter flight is direct. Flight duration for the former flight is 1 hour and 15 minutes; the direct flight is just 45 minutes in duration. Both are $50 each way.

Travelair (☎ 506/220-3054 or 506/232-7883) has flights to Puerto Jiménez departing at 8:15am daily, stopping first in Golfito. Flight duration is 1 hour and 20 minutes; fare is $81 dollars one way, $136 round-trip.

By Bus   Express buses leave San José daily at 6am and 12pm from Calle 12 between avenidas 7 and 9. Trip duration is 9 hours; fare is $7.

Buses depart Puerto Jiménez for San José daily at 5 and 10:30am.

By Boat   There is daily passenger launch service from Golfito to Puerto Jiménez at 11am. The boat leaves from the municipal dock. Trip duration is 1 1/2 hours; fare is $3.

It is also possible to charter a water taxi in Golfito for the trip across to Puerto Jiménez. You'll have to pay around $35 for an entire launch, which can usually hold up to seven people.

One launch a day departs Puerto Jiménez for Golfito from the public dock at 6am.

By Car   Take the Interamerican Highway east out of San José (through San Pedro and Cartago), and continue south on this road. In 3 hours or so, you'll pass through San Isidro de El General. In another 3 hours or so, take the turnoff for La Palma and Puerto Jiménez. This road is paved at first, but at Rincón turns to gravel. The last 35 kilometers are slow and rough, and, if it's the rainy season, too muddy for anything but a four-wheel-drive vehicle.

ORIENTATION   Arriving   Puerto Jiménez is a dirt-laned town on the southern coast of the Osa Peninsula. The public dock is over a bridge past the north end of the soccer field; the bus stop is two blocks east of the center of town. There are several general stores here. Puerto Jiménez is the most popular base for exploring Corcovado National Park.

EXPLORING CORCOVADO NATIONAL PARK

Although a few gringos have, over the years, come to Puerto Jiménez to try their luck at gold panning, the primary reason for coming here these days is to arrange a visit to Corcovado National Park. Within a couple of hours of the town, by four-wheel-drive vehicle, there are several entrances to the park. However, there are no roads into the park, so once you reach any of the entrances, you'll have to start hiking. Exploring Corcovado National Park is not something to be undertaken lightly, but neither is it the expedition that some people make it out to be. The biggest problems of overnight backpacking trips through the park are the heat and humidity. Frequent rainstorms cause the trails to be quite muddy, and should you choose the alternative of hiking on the beach, you will have to plan your hiking around the tides. Often there is no beach at all at high tide. Remember that you can always book a tour of Corcovado from a tour company in Puerto Jiménez or, better yet, through a lodge in Drake Bay (see "Where to Stay & Dine" in "Drake Bay," above) or elsewhere along the Osa Peninsula (see "Where to Stay & Dine around the Osa Peninsula," below)—it's what most visitors do.

GETTING THERE & ENTRY POINTS

There are four primary entrances to the park, which are really just ranger stations reached by dirt tracks. Once you've reached them, you'll have to strap on a backpack and hike. Perhaps the easiest one to reach from Puerto Jiménez is the **La Leona** ranger station, accessible by car, bus, or taxi. If you choose to drive, take the dirt road from Puerto Jiménez to Carate (Carate is at the end of the road). From Carate it is a 3-kilometer hike to La Leona. To travel there by bus, pick up one of the collective buses leaving Puerto Jiménez for Carate daily at 6am and 2:30pm (returning at 8am and 4:30pm). A one-way fare costs $3.15. The bus will pass several campgrounds and small lodges as it approaches the park. Otherwise you can hire a taxi, which will charge approximately $35 each way to Carate.

Alternatively, you can travel to **El Tigre,** about 14 kilometers by dirt road from Puerto Jiménez, where there is another ranger station. But, note that trails from El Tigre go only a short distance into the park. The third entrance is in **Los Patos,** which is reached from the town of La Palma, northwest of Puerto Jiménez. From here, there is a 19-kilometer trail through the center of the park to Sirena, a ranger station and research facility (see "Rain Forest Hikes" below). Sirena has a landing strip that is used by charter flights. The northern entrance to the park is **San Pedrillo,** which you can reach by hiking from Sirena or by boat from Drake Bay or Sierpe (see "Rain Forest Hikes" below). It's 14 kilometers from Drake Bay.

If you're not into hiking in the heat, you can charter a plane in Puerto Jiménez to take you to Carate, Sirena, Drake Bay, or even Tiskita Lodge, which is across the gulf, south of Playa Pavones. Contact **Alfa Romeo Aero Taxi** (☎ 506/775-1515) for details.

FEES & REGULATIONS

Park admission is $6 per person per day. Some of the ranger stations have simple dormitory-style lodgings, cantinas, and campsites, but all must be reserved in advance through the **Parks Service** at their offices in either Puerto Jiménez (☎ 506/735-5036) or San José. (You'll find the Puerto Jiménez office one block east of the main street at the end of town near the soccer field.) Only 35 persons are allowed to camp at each ranger station. For more information about making arrangements while in San José, see chapter 4.

VISITOR INFORMATION

If you plan to hike the beach trails from La Leona or San Pedrillo, be sure to pick up a tide table at the park headquarters' office in Puerto Jiménez. The tide changes rapidly; when it's high, the trails can be impassable.

BEACH TREKS & RAIN-FOREST HIKES

There are quite a few good hiking trails in the park. Two of the better-known ones are the beach routes, starting at either the **La Leona** or **San Pedrillo** ranger stations. None of the park's hikes are easy, but the forest route from the Los Patos ranger station to Sirena, while long, is less taxing than either of the beach treks, which can only be completed when the tide is low. The **Los Patos–Sirena** hike is, as mentioned above, 19 miles through rain forest. It's beautiful, and Sirena is a fascinating place to end up: a research facility, as well as ranger station, it's frequented primarily by scientists studying the rain forest. One of the longest hikes, from **San Pedrillo to Sirena,** can only be done during the dry season. Between any two stations, the hiking is arduous and will take all day, so it's best to rest between hikes, if at all possible. Some distances for reference: It's 16 kilometers from Sirena to La Leona; La Leona is 25 miles along the beach to San Pedrillo; from San Pedrillo, it's another 9 kilometers to Marenco Biological Reserve (see "Where to Stay & Dine" in "Drake Bay" for listing).

WHERE TO STAY & EAT IN THE PARK: CAMPSITES, CABINS & CANTINAS

The **La Leona** ranger station has a campground, some very basic dormitory-style cabins, and a cantina. Reservations are essential at the various ranger stations if you plan on eating or sleeping inside the park. Campsites in the park are $1.50 per person per night. A dorm bed will run you $2.50, and meals are around $13.50 per day. There is camping and a cantina at the **Los Patos** ranger station. **Sirena** has bunks, a campground, and a cantina. Every ranger station has potable water, but it's advisable to pack in your own; whatever you do, don't drink stream water.

ACTIVE SPORTS OUTSIDE THE PARK

Closer to Puerto Jiménez, kayaking trips around the estuary and up into the mangroves and out into the gulf are popular. Contact **Escondido Trex** (☎ 506/

735-5210), which has an office in Soda Carolina. More adventurous multi-day trips are also available.

If you're interested in doing some billfishing or deep-sea fishing, check around the public dock for notices of people with charter boats. Rates are usually around $400 for a full day or $300 for a half day.

WHERE TO STAY IN PUERTO JIMÉNEZ

MODERATE

✪ **Doña Leta's Bungalows.** Apartado 91, Puerto Jiménez. ☎/fax **506/735-5180.** 8 bungalows. $45 double; $55 triple. Discounts in the off-season. No credit cards.

These attractive new cabins are located on a spit of land jutting out into the gulf, just east of town and the airstrip. The smaller cabins are octagonal and have just one double bed, while the larger ones feature a sleeping loft, with a double and single bed above, and a double bed below. All the cabins come with a refrigerator, two-burner stove, private bath, and carved-wood door. There is a large central deck, built under and around a large fig tree that is frequented by scarlet macaws. The grounds also include a couple of volleyball nets, a small patch of beach, and a semi-groomed trail through the mangroves.

INEXPENSIVE

⑤ **Agua Luna.** In front of the public dock, Puerto Jiménez. ☎ **506/735-5034** or 506/735-5108. 14 rms (all with private bath). A/C TV. $30 double or triple. No credit cards.

These very reasonable rooms offer the most luxury of any of the in-town lodgings in Puerto Jiménez. Agua Luna is located right at the foot of the town's public dock and backs up to a mangrove forest. The six older rooms directly face the gulf, across a fenced-in gravel parking area. The most surprising feature in each of these rooms is the huge bathroom, which includes both a shower and a tub facing a picture window that looks into the mangroves. There are two double beds in each room, and on the tiled verandah out front, you'll find hammocks for lounging. The newer rooms were still under construction when I last visited. These are located a half block away, and will be slightly smaller, and slightly cheaper than those in the original building.

Cabinas Marcelina. Puerto Jiménez. ☎ **506/735-5007.** Fax 506/735-5045. 6 rms (each with private bath). $10 double; $14.20 triple. No credit cards.

Located at the southern end of Puerto Jiménez's main street, these basic rooms are a good choice for anyone on a shoestring budget. The owner keeps the tile-floored rooms clean, and there is surprisingly little mildew (always a problem in cinder-block buildings). Bathrooms are basic but adequate.

⑤ **Cabinas Puerto Jiménez.** 50 meters north of Bar y Restaurant El Rancho, Puerto Jiménez. ☎ **506/735-5090** or 506/735-5152. 10 rms (all with private bath). $12 double; $18 triple. No credit cards.

Located right on the waterfront at the north end of the soccer field, this inexpensive accommodation even offers a few rooms with views of the bay. The exterior of the building, with its varnished wood, is probably more appealing than the rooms themselves. Though large, the guest rooms have cement floors and are very basic. However, they are kept very clean and are the best choice in town for travelers on a tight budget.

Hotel Manglares. Apdo. 55-8203, Puerto Jiménez. ☎ **506/735-5002.** Fax 506/735-5121. 10 rms. $30 double. MC, V.

This hotel was once the best choice in town, but it's been resting on its laurels for a while now; consequently, the rooms are a bit run-down. Located on the edge of the mangrove forest, some of its rooms can only be reached by an elevated walkway through the mangroves. The trees, and several bird feeders, assure good birdwatching. The rooms in front are a bit small and can be musty. The rooms in back are slightly larger and more attractive, and surprisingly don't cost any extra. These latter rooms are surrounded by a small, groomed garden and back up on the mangroves. All the rooms have fans to keep you cool, and there is a restaurant serving inexpensive Tico standards, as well as seafood and pizza.

WHERE TO STAY & DINE AROUND THE OSA PENINSULA

As with most of the lodges in Drake Bay, the accommodations listed in this section include three meals a day in their rates and do a large share of their business in package trips. Per-night rates are listed, but the price categories have been downshifted to take into account the fact that all meals are included. Ask about package rates if you plan to take several tours and stay a while; they could save you money.

EXPENSIVE

✪ **Lapa Rios.** Apdo. 100, Puerto Jiménez, Osa Peninsula. ☎ **506/735-5130.** Fax 506/735-5179. 14 bungalows. Mid-Apr to mid-Nov, $208 double, $297 triple; mid-Nov to mid-Apr, $232 double, $331.50 triple. Discounts for children up to 10 years old. All rates include three meals daily and round-trip transfers between Puerto Jiménez and the lodge. AE, MC, V (add 6% surcharge).

Though there are hotels in Costa Rica with more amenities, there is no place more luxurious or private. If you are looking for the ultimate luxury getaway, this may be the place for you. However, keep in mind that there are no TVs, no telephones, no air-conditioning, no discos, no shopping, no paved roads, no other nearby hotels to visit, and no crowds. In fact, other than a beautiful little pool and a tropically exotic bar, there is nothing around to distract your attentions from the stupendous views of the forest and ocean far below. Lapa Rios is surrounded by its own 1,000-acre private rain forest reserve, which is home to scarlet macaws, toucans, parrots, hummingbirds, monkeys, and myriad other wildlife. To give you a closer look at the rain forest, there are several miles of trails, and the resident naturalist can be hired for guided walks. However, if birdwatching is your thing, you need go no further than the lodge's parking lot, which seems to be a popular spot with numerous avian species.

The hotel consists of seven duplex buildings perched along three ridges. Each spacious room is totally private and oriented toward the view. Walls have open screening, and the ceiling is a high-peaked thatched roof. In true *Arabian Nights* fashion, mosquito nets drape languidly over the queen-size beds. A large deck and tiny tropical garden, complete with outdoor shower, more than double the living space of each room. The buildings are constructed of local materials such as palm thatch, bamboo, mangrove wood, and other hardwoods. Perhaps the most surprising aspect of each room is the screen-walled shower that lets you drink in the views while you bathe.

Dining/Entertainment: The centerpiece of the open-air dining room is a 50-foot-tall spiral staircase that leads to an observation deck tucked beneath the peak of the building's thatch roof. In one corner of the dining room is the tropical bar. Each evening there is a choice of three meals, which though well prepared, frequently lack creativity. Breakfasts, on the other hand, are large and delicious.

Services: Guided walks; horseback riding; boat trips; sportfishing; sea kayaking; jungle camping trips; day trips to Corcovado National Park, Caño Island, and Wilson Botanical Gardens; snorkeling-equipment, bodyboard, and surfboard rentals. Tours range from $20 to $40 per person.

Facilities: Swimming pool, hiking trails.

MODERATE

✪ Bosque del Cabo Wilderness Lodge. Osa Peninsula (mailing address in the U.S.: Interlink 528, P.O. Box 025635, Miami, FL 33152). ☎/fax **506/735-5206.** 6 cabins. $140–$160 double; $150 triple. All rates include three meals daily. No credit cards.

This simple yet tasteful lodge is located 500 feet above the water at the southern tip of the Osa Peninsula, where the Golfo Dulce meets the Pacific Ocean. It is surrounded by 300 acres of land that the owners purchased in order to preserve a piece of the rain forest. The thatched-roof cabins are attractively furnished and are set amid beautiful gardens. Meals are well prepared and filling, and usually feature fruits grown on the premises. There's a trail down to a secluded beach that has some tide pools. Surfing is a popular activity here, as are hiking and horseback riding. Trips to the national park or out fishing can be arranged. It will cost you around $15 to take a taxi from Puerto Jiménez to the lodge.

INEXPENSIVE

Ⓢ Corcovado Lodge Tent Camp. Costa Rica Expeditions, Apdo. 6941-1000, San José. ☎ **506/257-0766** or 506/222-0333. Fax 506/257-1665. 20 tents. $78.58 double. All rates include three meals daily. AE, MC, V.

At the opposite end of the luxury scale from Lapa Rios—though no less enjoyable for anyone accustomed to camping—is Costa Rica Expeditions' Corcovado Lodge Tent Camp, which is built on a low bluff right above the beach. Behind the tent camp, forested mountains rise up, and just a few minutes' walk away is the entrance to Corcovado National Park. To reach this lodge is an adventure in itself. You can either take a five-seater chartered plane to the gravel landing strip at Carate and then walk for 45 minutes to the lodge, or take the lodge's specially designed pontoon boat from Golfito or Puerto Jiménez. If you have a four-wheel-drive vehicle, you can get as far as the landing strip and then walk the remaining 1.5 kilometers. Once you're here, you have a real sense of being away from it all.

Accommodations are in large tents pitched on wooden decks. Each tent has two twin beds, a table, and a couple of folding chairs on the front deck. Toilets and showers are a short walk away, but there are enough so that there is usually no waiting. Meals are served in a large screen-walled dining room furnished with picnic tables. A separate but similar building is furnished with hammocks, a small bar, and a few board games. Services at the lodge include guided walks and boat excursions, both into the national park and out to Caño Island. The newest addition to the lodge is a canopy platform located 120 feet up an ancient Ajo tree. Package rates that include transportation and tours are also available, and are actually the way most people come here.

WHERE TO DINE IN PUERTO JIMÉNEZ

Bar Restaurant Agua Luna. 25 meters north of the public pier. ☎ **506/735-5033.** Reservations are not accepted. Main courses $2.50–$8.50. No credit cards. Daily 9am–11pm. COSTA RICAN.

The first restaurant you come to after arriving in Puerto Jiménez by boat is also one of the best restaurants in town. Little more than a collection of tiny thatched ranchos (the equivalent of Mexican *palapas*) set amid shady gardens, Agua Luna has a nice view of the water. The bar is popular, and the music is usually loud, so don't expect a quiet, romantic dinner for two. Seafood is plentiful and fresh, and prices for fish dinners are low even for Costa Rica. Enjoy.

Ⓢ Sodita Carolina. On the main street. ☎ **506/735-5185.** Reservations are not accepted. All items $2.15–$8. No credit cards. Daily 6am–10 or 11pm. COSTA RICAN.

This is Puerto Jiménez's budget travelers' hangout and also serves as an unofficial information center. The restaurant is in the center of the town's main street. The walls are painted with colorful jungle and wildlife scenes, to whet the appetites of new arrivals and satisfy the needs of armchair travelers. Once again, seafood is the way to go. They've got good fried fish as well as a variety of ceviches. The black-bean soup is usually good, and the casados are filling and cost less than $3. If you need a place to stay, there are five basic rooms with cement floors and private baths behind the restaurant. The rooms cost $5 per person, are located behind the kitchen, and front a relatively unattractive yard.

3 Golfito: A Place for Sportfishing & Touring Botanical Gardens

87 kilometers S of Palmar Norte; 337 kilometers S of San José

This old banana port is set on the north side of the Golfo Dulce and is at the foot of lush green mountains. The setting alone is beautiful enough to make this one of the most attractive cities in the country, but Golfito also has an undeniable charm all its own. Sure, the area around the municipal park is kind of seedy, but if you go a little bit farther along the bay, you come to the old United Fruit Company housing. Here you'll find well-maintained wooden houses painted bright colors and surrounded by neatly manicured gardens. It's all very lush and green and clean, an altogether different picture than is painted by most port towns in this country. These old homes are experiencing a sort of renaissance as they become small hotels catering to shoppers visiting the adjacent duty-free shopping center.

But sportfishing cognoscenti know that Golfito's real draw is the marlin and sailfish just beyond its bay. Arguably one of the best places to go fishing in Costa Rica, it provides pleasant, uncrowded surroundings in which die-hard sportfishers can indulge their greatest fantasies of catching the great one to end all great ones. Sportfishing widows, take heed: Golfito is also close to some lovely botanical gardens that you can easily spend a day or more touring—not to mention the great opportunties for birdwatching and other activities.

ESSENTIALS

GETTING THERE & DEPARTING   By Plane   Sansa (☎ 506/233-0397, 506/233-3258, or 506/233-5330) has flights to Golfito departing Monday through Saturday at 6am; Wednesday through Friday at 1pm; and Sunday at 11:15am from San José's Juan Santamaría International Airport. Trip duration is 45 minutes; fare is $50 each way.

Sansa returns to San José Monday through Saturday at 7am; Wednesday through Friday at 2pm; and Sunday at 12:15pm.

Travelair (☎ 506/220-3054 or 506/232-7883) has flights to Golfito daily at 8:15am from San José's Pavas International Airport. The flight stops in Quepos and Palmar Sur en route. Flight duration is 1 hour; fare is $76 one way, $129 round-trip.

Travelair returns to San José daily at 9:45am with a stop at Quepos en route.

By Bus   Express buses leave San José daily at 7am and 3pm from Avenida 18 between calles 2 and 4. The trip's duration is 8 hours; fare is $6.50.

Buses depart Golfito for San José daily at 5am and 1pm from the bus station near the municipal dock.

By Boat   A passenger launch leaves Puerto Jiménez, on the Osa Peninsula, daily at 6am. Trip duration is 1¹/₂ hours; fare is $3.

You may also be able to hire a boat to take you across the Golfo Dulce to Golfito. However, as there are not very many available in Puerto Jiménez, you're likely to have to pay quite a bit ($40 to $65 each way) for such a service.

The passenger launch departs Golfito for Puerto Jiménez daily at 11am.

By Car   It is a straight shot down the Interamerican Highway south from San José to Golfito. However, it is a long and arduous road. In the 8 hours it takes to drive the 337 kilometers from San José, you'll pass over the Cerro de la Muerte (Mountain of Death), which is infamous for its dense fog and torrential downpours. Also, for almost the entire length of this road, you will have to contend with potholes of gargantuan proportions. Just remember, if the road is suddenly smooth and in great shape, you can bet that around the next bend there will be a bottomless pothole that you can't swerve around. Take it easy.

GETTING AROUND   If you can't get to your next destination by boat, bus, or car, **Alfa Romeo Aero Taxi** (☎ 506/775-1515 or 506/296-5596) runs charters to most of the nearby destinations, including Carate, Drake Bay, Sirena, and Puerto Jiménez. A taxi ride anywhere in town should cost around 75¢ each way.

FAST FACTS   If you need to exchange money, you can do so at the **gas station,** or "La Bomba," in the middle of town. There is a **laundromat** on the upper street of the small downtown that charges $3 for a 5-pound load. If you drop off your clothes in the morning, they'll be ready in the afternoon.

SPORTFISHING

The waters off Golfito offer some of the best sportfishing in Costa Rica, and if you'd like to try hooking into a possible world-record marlin or sailfish, contact Steve Lino at **Golfito Sportfishing** (☎ 506/382-2716). A full-day fishing trip will cost between $350 and $550. This company operates out of nearby Zancudo Beach and also offers multi-day packages. Other companies to check with are **Leomar Sportfishing & Diving** (☎ 506/775-0230) and **Roy's Zancudo Lodge** (☎ 506/775-0515), which offer trips at similar prices.

Several lodgings in Golfito and the surrounding area offer guided fishing trips or special fishing packages. They are also good places for camaraderie or just to share a drink with like-minded folks. In Golfito, check out Las Gaviotas Hotel; outside Golfito, there's Punta Encanto.

TOURING THE BOTANICAL GARDENS

About 30 minutes by boat out of Golfito, you'll find **Casa Orchideas,** a private botanical garden. Two-hour tours of the gardens cost $5 per person, with a minimum of four people. Most hotels in the region can organize a tour to the gardens, if not, you'll have to hire a boat to get there, which should cost you around $75 for the trip and waiting time.

If you have a serious interest in botanical gardens, consider an excursion to **Wilson Botanical Gardens** (☎ 506/773-3278 or 506/240-6696), which is located in the town of San Vito, about 65 kilometers to the northeast. The gardens are owned by the Organization for Tropical Studies and include more than 2,000 species of tropical plants from around the world. Among the plants grown here are many endangered species, which makes the gardens of interest to botanical researchers. Despite the scientific aspects of the gardens, there are also many beautiful and unusual flowers amid the manicured grounds. A full day in the gardens, including lunch, will cost you $17. A half-day walk around costs $8. If you'd like to stay the night here, there are rustic rooms and cabins. Rates, including three meals, run between

$53 and $71 per person; you need to make reservations beforehand if you wish to spend the night. You'll find the gardens about 6 kilometers before San Vito. To get here from Golfito, drive back out to the Interamerican Highway and continue south toward Panama. In Cuidad Neily, turn north.

EXPLORING THE TOWN

Other than sportfishing off its waters and exploring nearby botanical gardens, there isn't a whole lot to do in Golfito other than make connections to other places. You can walk or drive through town admiring the United Fruit Company buildings, drop in at one of the souvenir shops, and have a drink overlooking the gulf. However, these simple pursuits may be augmented by more tourist-oriented activities as this area gains in popularity. Check the bulletin boards in restaurants around town to see what sort of tours or activities are available when you arrive.

WHERE TO STAY IN GOLFITO
MODERATE

Complejo Turistico Samoa del Sur. 100 meters north of the public dock. ☎ **506/775-0233.** Fax 506/775-0573. 14 rms. TV TEL. $40 double to quad. AE, MC, V.

It's hard to miss the two giant thatched spires that house this new hotel's already established restaurant and bar. The rooms are spacious and clean. Varnished wood headboards complement two firm and comfortable double beds. There are red-tile floors, modern bathrooms and carved-wood doors. The rooms all share a long, covered verandah that is set perpendicular to the gulf, so there aren't any views to speak of here. If you want to watch the water, you're better off grabbing a table at the restaurant.

✪ **Hotel Sierra.** Apdo. 37, Golfito (Apdo. 5304-1000, San José). ☎ **506/775-0666,** 506/233-9693, or 506/224-3300 in San José. Fax 506/775-0087, or 506/224-3399 in San José. 72 rms. A/C TV TEL. $46.80 double; $53.30 triple. AE, DC, MC, V.

Located right beside the airstrip, the Hotel Sierra has become the hotel of choice for people flying in and out of Golfito. It offers the most luxurious accommodations in town, with a courtyard swimming pool, aviaries full of squawking macaws, and a big dining room and bar. The building is constructed to be as open and breezy as possible, though the guest rooms also have modern air conditioners. Covered walkways connect the hotel's various buildings, and lots of tropical plants and cages full of birds lend an exotic flavor to the surroundings. The rooms have pale blue tile floors, and windows on two sides to let in plenty of light. Bathrooms are very large, and there are safes in all the rooms. The swimming pool is fairly large and even has a swim-up bar. For light meals and snacks, there is a casual restaurant on the far side of the pool. Prices in the main dining room are also fairly moderate, and there are several lobster dishes for around $15. All in all, this place offers very good value.

INEXPENSIVE

⑤ **Cabinas Jardin Cervecero Alamedas.** 100 meters south of the Depósito Libre. ☎ **506/775-0126.** 6 rms (each with private bath). $12.25–$14 double or triple. AE, MC, V.

These six new rooms have been built across the gravel driveway from one of the more popular restaurants in the area around the free port. The rooms are clean, and each has one double, one single, and one bunk bed. I prefer the upstairs rooms which have wood (instead of concrete) floors and more air circulation.

Casa Blanca Lodge. 300 meters south of the Depósito Libre, Golfito. ☎ **506/775-0124.** 10 rms (all with private bath). $10–$15 double; $15 triple or quad. No credit cards.

In the old United Fruit Company neighborhood near the airport, there are many pretty, old houses surrounded by attractive, neatly manicured gardens. Several of these old homes have been turned into inexpensive hotels catering to shoppers visiting the free port. This is one of the nicer of the small family-run hotels. The rooms in the new annex are more attractive and more comfortable than those in the main building, which tend to be dark and musty.

Las Gaviotas Hotel. Apdo. 12-8201, Golfito. ☎ **506/775-0062.** Fax 506/775-0544. 18 rms, 3 cabañas. $30–$35 double; $32.50–$45 triple; $70 cabaña. AE, MC, V.

If you want to be right on the water, this is a good option in Golfito. Situated a short taxi ride out of town on the road that leads to the Interamerican Highway, Las Gaviotas has long been the hotel of choice on the Golfo Dulce. There is a long pier that attracts the sailboat and sportfishing crowd. For landlubbers, there's a small pool built out over the gulf water. Guest rooms, which are set amid attractive gardens, all face the ocean, and though they are quite large, they're a bit spartan and are starting to show their age. There are small tiled patios in front of all the rooms, and the cabañas have little kitchens. The more expensive rooms have air-conditioning. A large open-air restaurant looks over the pool to the gulf, while around the corner there is a large open-air bar. In addition, there's a small gift shop. The waterfront location is this hotel's greatest asset.

Golfo Azul. Barrio Alameda, 300 meters south of the Depósito Libre, Golfito. ☎ **506/775-0871.** Fax 506/775-1849. 24 rms. $18.75 double or triple; $23–$32 double, triple, or quad with air-conditioning. MC, V.

Azul offers a quiet location amid the most attractive part of Golfito. Many of the people who stay here are Ticos in town to shop at the nearby Depósito Libre (free port). However, anyone will appreciate the clean rooms. The smallest rooms are cramped, but there are larger rooms, some with high ceilings that make them feel even more spacious. Bathrooms are tiled and have hot water, and rooms have either fans or air-conditioning. The hotel's restaurant is housed in an older building and is brilliantly white inside and out. Meals are quite reasonably priced.

NEARBY PLACES TO STAY
EXPENSIVE

Gulfo Dulce Lodge. Apartado 137, Golfito. ☎ **506/222-2900** or 506/735-5062. Fax 506/222-5173 or 506/735-5043. 1 rm, 5 cabins. $190 double; $255 triple. All rates include three meals daily. No credit cards.

This small, Swiss-run lodge is just down the beach from Casa Orquideas, about a 30-minute boat ride from Golfito. The five separate cabins and main lodge buildings are all set back away from the beach, 500 meters into the forest. The cabins are spacious, airy, and feature either a twin and a single bed, or three single beds. In addition there are large modern bathrooms, solar hot-water showers, a small sitting area, and a porch with a hammock. Meals are served in an open thatch-roofed building beside the small swimming pool. The lone room, attached to the building that houses the kitchen and laundry, is almost an afterthought, but would do in a pinch. The lodge also offers jungle hikes, river trips, and other guided tours.

Punta Encanto. Golfito (mailing address in the U.S.: Dick or Jackie Knowles, P.O. Box 481, Chautauqua, NY 14722). ☎ **800/543-0397** in the U.S. Fax 506/775-0373. 7 rms. $150 double. All rates include three meals daily. No credit cards.

This small lodge is located a 30-minute boat ride up the bay from Golfito, and if you stay for a minimum of three nights, there is no charge for the transfers to and from

Golfito. The star attraction here is the lodge's deserted beach, which is great for swimming. Surrounding the lodge are acres and acres of rain forest. Guided tours into the forest are available for $15 per person. The guest rooms are simply furnished, and several have views of the gulf. The upstairs rooms have either linoleum or indoor/outdoor carpeting on the floors. All rooms are clean and comfortable. Meals, a combination of Tico and American favorites, are served family style. The lodge can also arrange tours of the nearby Casa Orchideas Botanical Gardens for $15 per person. A trip up the Esquinas River to go bird- and monkey-watching will cost $160 for a boat that can hold eight people. For many years, this was a sportfishing camp, and fishing trips are still offered. It will cost you $35 per hour to fish in the bay and $450 for a full day of deep-sea fishing. Fishing packages are also available. This charmingly casual lodge offers a tranquil getaway for anyone who is looking for tropical solitude.

✪ **Rainbow Adventures.** Apdo. 63, Golfito (mailing address in the U.S.: Michael Medill, 5875 N. Kaiser Rd., Portland, OR 97229). ☎ **506/775-0220** or 503/690-7750 in the U.S. Fax 503/690-7735 in the U.S. 4 rms, 3 cabins. $160–$180 double; $45 each additional person. All rates include three meals daily. No credit cards.

If your vision of the perfect tropical hideaway is a luxurious little open-walled cabin overlooking a secluded beach that is backed by tropical jungle, then Rainbow Adventures may just be your pot of gold. This isolated lodge is surrounded by 1,000 acres of rain forest that abuts Corcovado National Park. The grounds immediately surrounding the lodge are neatly manicured gardens planted with exotic fruit trees, flowering shrubs, and palms from around the world. Your adventure begins in Golfito, where the lodge's speedboat picks you up for the 45-minute boat ride to the lodge. Days are spent lounging in hammocks, swimming, sunning, and exploring the jungle, reading, bird- and wild animal–watching, and maybe a bit of fishing. But mostly you get to just do nothing, and not feel guilty about it. Be warned, however, that if you need TV, telephone, crowds, shopping, or discos, you should stay away from Rainbow Adventures.

Rooms in the main lodge, which is made almost completely of polished tropical hardwoods, are all decorated with antiques, stained glass, and oriental carpets. The second-floor rooms are the least expensive and smallest rooms available. However, they still have plenty of room. For just a little more, you can have the penthouse, a large third-floor room with four open walls and treetop views of the gulf. Only slightly more expensive are the spacious cabinas, which are built on stilts and have open living rooms and large bedrooms that can be divided into small rooms.

Meals are generally served buffet style with a set menu each evening. However, the creativity of the chef and the quantities of food guarantee that everyone leaves the table satisfied. Though beer is available, you should bring your own liquor. Fishing trips (barracuda, roosterfish, snook, and red snapper are plentiful), boat charters ($35 per hour for a boat that can carry four passengers), and guided hikes can all be arranged. The lodge has several well-maintained trails through primary rain forest, with jungle waterfalls and wonderful swimming holes. A private beach provides protected swimming and, in the dry season, some good snorkeling (equipment is available at no charge). The best section of the mile-long beach is a few hundred yards from the lodge.

WHERE TO DINE

In addition to the restaurants listed below, **Tingo's** is a new pizza place worth trying, and **Luis Brenes' Restaurant** (across from the gas station) is a popular hangout and a good place to gather information on trips and tours around the gulf.

Jardín Cervecero Alamedas. 100 meters south of the Depósito Libre. ☎ **506/775-0126.** Main courses $2.80–$10. AE, MC, V. Daily 7am–12am (closed Sunday and Monday during the low season). COSTA RICAN/SEAFOOD.

If you are staying at the Hotel Sierra, Golfo Azul, or any of the other hotels near the Depósito Libre, this should be your first choice when deciding where to eat. The restaurant is located underneath an old house that is built on stilts. White chairs and dark green tablecloths provide a sort of fern-bar feel, while outside real tropical gardens surround the house. There are great deals on seafood here, including a long list of ceviches. The only drawback is that they tend to play the stereo too loud.

ⓢ Soda La Cubana. 150 meters east of the gas station, on the upper road through downtown Golfito. No phone. Main courses $2.80–$7.50. No credit cards. Daily 6am–10pm. COSTA RICAN.

This small, open-air restaurant commands a good view of the gulf and serves hearty meals at rock bottom prices. The menu is pretty basic, but a fresh, whole fish in garlic sauce will cost you just $4.

Samoa del Sur. 100 meters north of the public dock. ☎ **506/775-0233.** Main courses $2.80–$17.50. AE, MC, V. Daily 8am–2am. CONTINENTAL.

It's hard to miss the Samoa del Sur. It's that huge circular rancho just north of the public dock. This oversized jungle structure seems out of place in a town where cinder-blocks are the preferred construction material, but its tropical atmosphere is certainly well appreciated. The restaurant's biggest surprise, however, is its extensive menu of familiar continental and French dishes such as onion soup, salade niçoise, filet of fish meunière, and paella. There are also pizzas and spaghetti. There's a good view of the gulf, which makes this a great spot for a sunset drink or dinner. In addition to the food, the giant rancho also houses a pool table, several high-quality dart boards, and a big-screen TV. The bar sometimes stays open all night.

4 Playa Zancudo

19 kilometers S of Golfito (by boat); 35 kilometers S of Golfito (by road)

Although the word is starting to get out, Playa Zancudo remains one of Costa Rica's main backpacker hangouts, which means that there are plenty of cheap rooms, some cheap places to eat, and lots of young gringos around. These factors alone are enough to keep Zancudo jumping through the winter months. The beach itself is long and flat, and because it is protected from the full force of Pacific waves, it's relatively good for swimming. However, it is certainly not one of the most beautiful beaches in the country. Behind the beach, which disappears at high tide, are piles of driftwood and plastic flotsam and jetsam that have washed up on the shore. There is a splendid view across the Golfo Dulce, though, and the sunsets are hard to beat. Because there is a mangrove swamp directly behind the beach, mosquitoes can be a problem; be sure to bring insect repellent.

ESSENTIALS

GETTING THERE **By Plane** The nearest airport is in Golfito. See "Golfito: A Place for Sportfishing & Touring Botanical Gardens," above for details.

By Boat Water taxis can be hired in Golfito to make the trip out to Playa Zancudo. However, trips depend on the tides and weather conditions. You're more likely to get a boat early in the morning before the winds pick up and make the waters choppy. Currently it costs around $7 per person for a water taxi, with a minimum charge of $20. If you can round up any sort of group, be sure to negotiate.

Alternatively, there is a passenger launch from the municipal dock in Golfito, Monday, Wednesday, and Friday at 8am. Because the schedule sometimes changes, be sure to ask in town for the current schedule. The trip's duration is 45 minutes; fare is $2.

By Bus Year-round, there's one bus a day from Golfito to Zancudo at 1:30 pm. It costs $1.25 one-way. Duration: 3–4 hours.

By Car If you've got a four-wheel-drive vehicle, you should be able to make it out to Zancudo even in the rainy season, but be sure to ask in Golfito before leaving the paved road. A four-wheel-drive taxi will cost around $20 from Golfito. It takes about 2 hours when the road is in good condition.

DEPARTING The public launch to Golfito leaves at 6am Monday, Wednesday, and Friday from the dock near the school, in the center of Zancudo. If you're heading to Pavones or the Osa Peninsula next, contact **Zancudo Boat Tours** (see "What to See & Do," below), which is sometimes willing to make the trips to these two places. They charge $10 per person, with a minimum charge of $30 for either trip.

ORIENTATION Arriving Zancudo is a long, narrow peninsula (sometimes only 100 yards or so wide) at the mouth of the Río Colorado. On one side is the beach, on the other is a mangrove swamp. There is only one road that runs the length of the beach, and it is along this road, spread out over several kilometers of long, flat beach, that you will find the hotels mentioned here. It's about a 30-minute walk from the public dock near the school to the popular Cabinas Sol y Mar.

WHAT TO SEE & DO

The main activity at Zancudo is relaxing, and people take it seriously. There are hammocks at almost every lodge, and if you bring a few good books, you can spend quite a few hours swinging slowly in the tropical breezes. Sure, there's a bar that doubles as a disco, but visitors are more likely to spend their time just hanging out in restaurants, meeting like-minded folks or playing board games.

If you're feeling more energetic, consider a boat tour. Susan and Andrew Robertson, who rent out two small houses in Zancudo, also operate **Zancudo Boat Tours** (☎ 506/775-0353; leave a message). Excursions they offer include a trip up the Río Coto to bird- and wildlife-watch, snorkeling trips, and trips to the Casa Orchidia Botanical Garden. Tour prices are $15 per hour for two people, $20 per hour for three people, and $25 per hour for four people.

WHERE TO STAY

✪ **Cabinas Sol Y Mar.** Apdo. 87, Playa Zancudo, Golfito. ☎/fax **506/775-0353.** 4 rms (each with private bath). Dec 1–Apr 30, $23–$30 double; May 1–Nov 30, $17–$25 double. V (add 6% surcharge).

Although owners Bob and Monika Hara have only four rooms, they run the most popular lodging in Zancudo. Two of the rooms are modified geodesic domes with tile floors, verandahs, and tin roofs. The bathrooms have unusual showers that consist of a tiled platform surrounded by smooth river rocks. The bathrooms also have translucent roofs that flood the rooms with light. The other two rooms are larger and newer, but aren't as architecturally interesting. You'll have to decide between space and character. There is an adjacent open-air restaurant that is the best and most popular place to eat in Zancudo. Seafood dishes are the specialty here (the whole fried fish is good), and prices are very reasonable.

Cabinas Zancudo. Playa Zancudo, Golfito. ☎ **506/773-3027.** 20 rms (all with private bath). $10 double; $15 triple. No credit cards.

This is your basic Tico weekend, beach getaway spot. The rooms are small, dark, and musty. There's no cross ventilation, and half of the rooms are in a building facing the back wall of another building. Weekends are crowded and can be noisy, especially in the dry season. However, if you don't have much money to spend, this is a good choice. There is a *pulperia* (general store) on the premises, as well as a restaurant and bar.

Los Cocos. Apdo. 88, Golfito. ☎ **506/775-0353** (leave a message). 2 cabins. $30–$35 per night; $180–$210 per week. No credit cards.

Although owners Susan and Andrew Robertson prefer to rent their two small houses by the month, in a pinch they'll rent by the night. Set under the trees near Cabinas Sol y Mar (which is where you go to check in at Los Cocos), these two houses served as banana-plantation housing in a former life, until the Robertsons salvaged them and placed them in their current location. The houses have big verandahs and bedrooms and large eat-in kitchens. Bathrooms are down a few steps in back and have hot water. If you plan to stay in Zancudo for a while, you'll appreciate the refrigerator and hot plate.

Hotel Los Almendros. Apdo. 41, Playa Zancudo, Golfito. ☎ **506/284-7759.** 14 rms (all with private bath). $25 double; $30 triple; $50 double with air-conditioning. V.

Primarily a fishing lodge, this simple lodging at the north end of Zancudo is also one of the more comfortable and attractive places in town. All of the rooms look out onto a bright green lawn of soft grass, with the waves crashing on the beach a few steps beyond. They have hardwood floors, small clean bathrooms, ceiling and floor fans, and small verandahs. There is a small restaurant that, of course, specializes in fresh fish. Meals run between $4 and $7 per person. The lodge offers many different types of fishing excursions.

WHERE TO DINE

The best restaurant in Zancudo is at **Cabinas Sol y Mar.** This small, open-air spot is a popular hangout for resident gringos as well as travelers.

5 Playa Pavones: A Surfer's Mecca

40 kilometers S of Golfito

Touted as the world's longest rideable left break, Pavones is a legendary surf spot. It takes around 6 feet of swell to get this wave cranking, but when the surf's up, you're in for a long, long ride. So long, in fact, that it's easier to walk back up the beach to where the wave is breaking than it is to paddle back. The swells are most consistent during the rainy season, but you're likely to find surfers here year-round. Other than surfing, nothing much goes on here. However, the beach is quite nice, with some rocky areas that give Pavones a bit more visual appeal than Zancudo has. If you stick around for a while, you'll learn that the beach has been the site of a bitter land dispute. Various lodges are starting to sprout up, but as of yet, most accommodations here are very basic. Pavones is a tiny village with few amenities and no electricity. The one exception is Tiskita Lodge, a jungle getaway several kilometers south of Pavones.

ESSENTIALS

GETTING THERE & DEPARTING   By Plane   The nearest airport is in Golfito. See "Golfito: A Place for Sportfishing & Touring Botanical Gardens," above, for details.

By Bus   There is a bus to Pavones from Golfito daily at 2pm. Trip duration is 3¹/₂ hours; fare is $1.80.

The bus to Golfito departs Pavones daily at 5am.

By Car   If you have a four-wheel-drive vehicle, you should be able to get to Pavones even in the rainy season, but be sure to ask in Golfito before leaving the paved road. A four-wheel-drive taxi from Golfito to Pavones will cost between $30 and $40. It takes around 3 hours from Golfito.

SURFING, SWIMMING, AND HAMMOCK SWINGING

Other than surfing when the surf is up and swimming when it's not, there isn't a whole lot to do. You can walk the beach, swing in your hammock, or if you feel energetic, go for a horseback ride.

WHERE TO STAY & DINE

Right in Pavones, there are several very basic lodges renting rooms for between $10 and $20 per night for a double room. There are also a couple of sodas where you can get Tico meals. South of Pavones, you'll find the following lodge.

✪ **Tiskita Jungle Lodge.** Costa Rica Sun Tours, Apdo. 1195-1250, Escazú. ☎ **506/ 255-3418.** Fax 506/255-4410. 12 cabins. $80 double; $90 triple. Packages, based upon double occupancy, and including round-trip transportation from San José and two guided walks: four days/three nights $575 per person; five days/four nights $620 per person. AE, MC, V.

This small lodge is nearly on the Panamanian border, with the beach on one side and rain forest–covered hills behind. Although primarily an experimental fruit farm growing exotic tropical fruits from around the world, Tiskita is also a great place to get away from it all. There's a dark-sand swimming beach, tide pools, a farm and a forest to explore, and great birdwatching (230 species have been sighted). Of the 400 acres here, 250 are in primary rain forest, while the rest are in orchards and pastures. The lodge itself is set on a hill a few hundred yards from the beach and commands a superb view of the ocean.

Accommodations are in deluxe rustic cabins with screen walls and verandahs. Constructed of local hardwoods, the cabins have a very tropical feel, and if you're a birdwatcher, you'll be happy to know that you can just sit on the verandah and add to your life list. Meals are served family style and cost around $24 per person per day. While they are not fancy, they are certainly tasty and filling.

The lodge is almost 3 hours from Golfito by car, so most guests take advantage of the package tours, which include air transportation to Tiskita's private landing strip. It's also possible to get a boat to take you to Corcovado National Park from here.

10 The Caribbean Coast

Although this was the coast Christopher Columbus discovered in 1502 and christened Costa Rica (Rich Coast), it has until recently remained *terra incognita*. It was not until 1987 that the Guápiles Highway opened between San José and Limón. Prior to that, the only routes down to this region were the famous jungle train (which is no longer in operation), and the narrow winding road from Turrialba to Siquírres. More than half of this coastline is still inaccessible except by boat or small plane. This inaccessibility has helped preserve large tracts of virgin lowland rain forest, which are now set aside as Tortuguero National Park and Barra del Colorado National Wildlife Refuge. These two parks, on the northern reaches of this coast, together form one of Costa Rica's most popular destinations with eco-travelers. Of particular interest are the sea turtles that nest along this stretch of coast. Another intriguing national park in this area is in Cahuita, a beach town. The park was set up to preserve 500 acres of coral reef, but its palm-tree lined beaches are stunning.

So remote was the Caribbean coast from Costa Rica's population centers in the Central Valley that it developed a culture all its own. Until the 1870s, there were few non-Indians in this area. However, when Minor Keith built the railroad to San José and began planting bananas, he brought in black laborers from Jamaica to lay the track and work the plantations. These workers and their descendants established fishing and farming communities up and down the coast. Today dreadlocked Rastafarians, reggae music, Créole cooking, and the English-based patois of this Afro-Caribbean culture give this region a distinctly Jamaican flavor. Many visitors find this striking contrast with the Spanish-derived Costa Rican culture fascinating. However, in beach towns such as Cahuita and Puerto Viejo, some visitors see only a drug-and-surf culture, and there is no denying that surfing and partying are a way of life for many people, local and visitor alike, in these two towns. Although you need not participate in such activities, if this lifestyle is offensive to you, consider heading to one of the many beaches on the Pacific coast.

1 Tortuguero National Park

250 kilometers NE of San José

"Tortuguero" comes from the Spanish name for the giant sea turtles (*tortugas*) that nest on the beaches of this region every year from

The Caribbean Coast

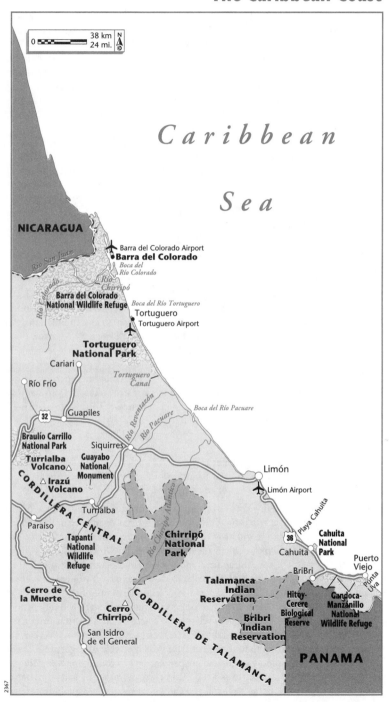

0 | 38 km
24 mi.

N

Caribbean

Sea

NICARAGUA

Río San Juan

Barra del Colorado Airport

Barra del Colorado

Boca del
Río Colorado

Río Colorado

Río Chirripó

Barra del Colorado
National Wildlife Refuge

Boca del Río Tortuguero

Tortuguero

Tortuguero Airport

Tortuguero
National Park

Cariari

Tortuguero
Canal

Río Frío

Río Reventazón

Río Pacuare

Boca del Río Pacuare

32

Guapiles

Braulío Carrillo
National Park

Siquirres

Turrialba
Volcano △

Guayabo
National
Monument

△ **Irazú**
Volcano

Limón

Limón Airport

CORDILLERA CENTRAL

Turrialba

Paraiso

Tapantí
National
Wildlife
Refuge

Río Chirripó Atlántico

Chirripó
National
Park

Playa Cahuita

36

Cahuita
National
Park

Cahuita

Puerto
Viejo

BriBri

Punta
Uva

Cerro de
la Muerte

△
Cerro
Chirripó

CORDILLERA DE TALAMANCA

Talamanca
Indian
Reservation

Hitoy-
Cerere
Biological
Reserve

Gandoca-
Manzanillo
National
Wildlife
Refuge

San Isidro
de el General

Bribri
Indian
Reservation

PANAMA

2367

mid-February to mid-October. The chance to see nesting sea turtles is what attracts many people to this remote region. However, just as many come to explore the intricate network of jungle canals that serve as the main transportation arteries here. This stretch of coast is connected to Limón, the Caribbean coast's only port city, by way of a series of rivers and canals that parallel the sea, often only 100 yards or so from the beach. This aquatic highway is lined for most of its length with a dense rain forest that is home to howler monkeys, three-toed sloths, toucans, and great green macaws. A trip up the canals is akin to cruising the Amazon, though on a much smaller scale.

North of Tortuguero is Barra del Colorado National Wildlife Refuge. This area is better known among anglers than naturalists and is even more remote. You can reach it by continuing up the canals from Tortuguero or by boat from Puerto Viejo de Sarapiquí along the Río Sarapiquí. The waters at the mouth of the Río Colorado offer some of the best tarpon and snook fishing in the world. See chapter 4 for listings of fishing lodges near Barra del Colorado, and chapter 7 for a more detailed description of this protected area.

Overall, remember the climate in this region: It rains a lot here— over 200 inches per year, in fact—so you can expect rain at any time of the year.

ESSENTIALS

GETTING THERE & DEPARTING   By Plane   Sansa (☎ 506/233-0397, 506/233-3258 or 506/233-5330) has flights departing Tuesday, Thursday, and Saturday at 6am for **Barra del Colorado** from San José's Juan Santamaría International Airport. Flight duration is 30 minutes (to Barra del Colorado); fare is $40 one way. From here you will have to take a water taxi ($50), or arrange pickup with your hotel if you're going on to Tortuguero.

Travelair (☎ 506/220-3054 and 506/232-7883) has flights departing daily at 6am for Tortuguero, with an intermediate stop in Barra del Colorado, from San José's Pavas International Airport. Flight duration is 55 minutes (to Tortuguero); fare is $72 one way, $110 round-trip.

In addition, many lodges in this area operate charter flights as part of their package trips.

If you are traveling independently, **Sansa** flights leave **Barra del Colorado** at 6:45am on Tuesday, Thursday, and Saturday for San José. **Travelair** flights depart **Tortuguero** daily at 7:05am and fly directly to San José.

By Boat   Although flying to Tortuguero is convenient if you have only a limited amount of time, a boat trip through the canals and rivers of this region is often the highlight of any visit to Tortuguero. All of the more expensive lodges listed below operate boats, and will make arrangements for you to travel by boat through the canals. However, if you are coming here on the cheap and plan to stay at one of the less expensive lodges or at a budget cabina in Tortuguero, you will have to arrange your own transportation. In this case, you have a couple of options.

The most direct method is to get yourself to the public docks in Moín (just north of Limón), and try to find a boat on your own. There's a bus that runs from a stop 200 meters north of Limón's central park; it costs a quarter. Otherwise, you can take a taxi for $2.50—(for up to four people). You should be able to negotiate a fare between $35–$60, depending on how many people you can round up to go with you. These boats tend to leave between 8 and 10am every morning. Usually, the fare you pay covers the return trip as well, and you can arrange with the captain to take you back across when you're ready to depart.

One boat captain to check with is **Modesto Wilson** (☎ 506/226-0986), who owns a boat named *Francesca*. Wilson offers economical overnight packages to Tortuguero. The trip from Moín to Tortuguero takes between 3 and 4 hours. **Laura's Tropical Tours** (☎ 506/758-2410) also offers boat tours to Tortuguero from Moín.

It is also possible—albeit expensive—to travel to Tortuguero by boat from Puerto Viejo de Sarapiquí (see chapter 7, "The Northern Zone"). Expect to pay $200 to $250 each way for a boat that holds up to 10 people. Check at the public dock in Puerto Viejo de Sarapiquí or ask at the Hotel El Bambú, if you're interested.

ORIENTATION **Arriving** Tortuguero National Park is one of the most remote locations in Costa Rica. There are no roads into this area, so all transportation is by boat or plane. Most of the lodges are spread out over several kilometers to the north of the village of Tortuguero, and the small airstrip is at the north end.

EXPLORING THE NATIONAL PARK

According to existing records, Tortuguero National Park has hosted sea turtles since 1592, largely due to its extreme isolation. Even today, there are no roads into the park. Over the years since, turtles were captured and their eggs harvested by local settlers, but it wasn't until the 1950s that this practice became so widespread that the turtles faced extinction. Regulations controlling this mini-industry were passed in 1963; and in 1970, Tortuguero National Park was established. Today, four different species of sea turtles nest here: the green turtle, the hawksbill, the loggerhead, and the giant leatherback. The prime nesting period is from mid-June to mid-October (with August and September being the busiest months). The park's beaches are excellent places to watch sea turtles nest, especially at night. (Appealingly long and deserted, the beaches are not appropriate for swimming, however. The surf is usually very rough, and the river mouths have a nasty habit of attracting sharks that feed on the many fish that live there.)

Green turtles are perhaps the most common turtle found in Tortuguero, so you are more likely to see one of them than any other species if you visit during the prime nesting season. Loggerheads are very rare here, so don't be disappointed if you don't see one. Perhaps the most spectacular sea turtle to watch laying eggs is the giant leatherback. The largest of all turtle species, the leatherback can grow to 6^1/$_2$ feet long. From mid-February to mid-April it nests, predominately in the southern part of the park.

You can also explore the park's rain forest, either by foot or by boat, and look for some of the incredible varieties of wildlife that live here: jaguars, anteaters, howler monkeys, collared and white-lipped peccaroes, some 350 species of birds, and countless butterflies, among others. There are several trails that branch out from the park entrance.

ENTRY POINT, FEES & REGULATIONS

The Tortuguero National Park entrance and ranger station are at the south end of Tortuguero Village. Admission to the park is $6. Flashlights and cameras are not permitted on the beach, since the lights can deter the turtles from nesting.

ORGANIZED NATIONAL PARK TOURS

Most visitors come to Tortuguero on an organized tour. If you'd like to see several national parks while you're in Costa Rica, you might want to join a tour run by one of the U.S.- or Costa Rican–based tour companies listed in chapter 4. Otherwise, all of the lodges listed below, with the exception of the budget accommodations in

Tortuguero Village, offer various hikes and night tours. See the individual lodge listings for rates. If you choose to stay at one of these lodgings, chances are you'll be on a package that includes a tour of Tortuguero, among other excursions. In addition, there are several tour companies that offer budget two-day/one-night excursions to Tortuguero, which include transportation, all meals, and limited tours around the region. Prices for these trips range between $55 and $80 per person, and guests are generally lodged in one of the basic hotels in Tortuguero Village. These trips are good for travelers who like to be able to say: "Been there, done that." Companies offering these excursions include **Ecole Travel** (☎ 506/223-2240), **Tortuguero Expeditions** (☎ 506/222-2175), and **Tortuguero Odyssey Tours** (☎ 506/758-0824).

BOAT CANAL TOURS

One of the most unique things you can do in Tortuguero is tour its canals by boat. Most of the lodges can arrange a canal tour for you, but you can also arrange a tour through one of the operators in Tortuguero Village. I recommend **Ernesto Castillo,** who can be reached through **Cabinas Sabina**. If he isn't available, ask for a recommendation at **Paraiso Tropical Gift Shop** (☎ 710-0323). Most guides charge between $12-$15 per person for a tour of the canals. If you travel through the park, you'll have to pay the park entrance fee ($6 per person), in addition. Expect to pay $5-$10 per person for an independent night tour of the canals.

FISHING TRIPS & PACKAGES

All of the lodges situated along this coast offer fishing trips and fishing packages. If you want to try your hand at reeling in a monster tarpon, it will generally cost you between $30 and $40 per hour, including boat, guide, and tackle.

EXPLORING THE TOWN

Tortuguero Village is a tiny collection of houses connected by footpaths. The village is spread out on a thin spit of land, bordered on one side by the Atlantic Ocean, and on the other by the main canal. At most points, this spit of land is less than 300 meters wide. In the center of the village you'll find a kiosk that has information on the cultural and natural history of this area.

If you stay at a hotel on the ocean side of the canal, you will be able to walk into and explore the town at your leisure, whereas if you are across the canal, you will be dependent on the lodge's transportation. However, many of the lodges across the canal have their own network of jungle trails that may appeal to naturalists.

The newest attraction in town is the small **Caribbean Conservation Corporation's Visitors' Center and Museum.** While the museum has information and exhibits on a whole range of native flora and fauna, its primary focus is on the life and history of the sea turtles. There is also a small gift shop here, and all the proceeds go toward conservation and turtle protection. The museum is open daily, 10am until noon, and 2 to 5:30pm. Admission is $1.

In the village, you can also rent dugout canoes, known here in Costa Rica as *cayucos* or *pangas*. Be careful before renting and taking off in one of these. They tend to be heavy, slow, and hard to maneuver, and you may be getting more than you bargained for. There are a couple of souvenir shops on the main foot-path near the center of the village—the **Jungle Shop,** which donates 10% of its profits to local schools and is open 9am–5pm (no phone); and **Paraiso Tropical Gift Shop,** which is open from 8:30am–6pm (☎ 710-1323).

WHERE TO STAY & DINE

Although the room rates below appear quite high, keep in mind that they include round-trip transportation from San José (which amounts to approximately $100 per person) and all meals. When broken down into nightly room rates, most of the lodges charge between $40 and $60 for a double room.

EXPENSIVE

Tortuga Lodge. Avenida 3 and Calle Central (Apdo. 6941-1000), San José. ☎ **506/257-0766** or 506/222-0333. Fax 506/257-1665. 25 rms. $657–$685 double, two days/one night; $770–$800 double, three days/two nights. All rates include round-trip transportation from San José and three meals daily. AE, MC, V.

Just a quick glance at the rates listed above will tell you that Tortuga Lodge is quite a bit more expensive than other lodges in the area. If you book a deluxe room, you may find the rates well worth every penny—they are the largest and most comfortable of any lodging nearby. Conversely, standard rooms are small and dark, so you may feel you've overpaid if you book one. In general, what you are paying for is all the years of experience that Costa Rica Expeditions, the lodge's owner, brings to Tortuguero. Service here is generally quite good, as are the meals served in the screen-walled dining room. There are several acres of forest behind the lodge, and a few kilometers of trails wind their way through the trees. This is a great place to look for colorful poison-arrow frogs. Most packages include a couple of different tours, including boat trips through the canals, visits to Tortuguero Village, and trips to see the turtles laying eggs. There are also several optional tours including fishing trips, hikes to Tortuguero Hill, and night hikes. By the time this goes to press, Tortuga Lodge should have completed a major remodeling, slated to include the up-grading of all existing rooms, as well as the construction of 10 new rooms and a new restaurant, bar, and reception area.

MODERATE

Hotel Ilan-Ilan. Apdo. 91-1150, San José. ☎ **506/255-2262** or 506/255-2031. Fax 506/255-1946. 24 rms. $260.80 double, two days/one night; $350 double, three days/two nights. All rates include round-trip transportation from San José and three meals daily. AE, DC, MC, V.

Named after a fragrant tropical flower that grows on the hotel grounds, the Ilan-Ilan is on the opposite side of the canal from the beach. Guest rooms are fairly basic, but large, and are all angled toward the canal so each gets a bit of a breeze. Screened windows in front and back and overhead fans also help keep the rooms cool. Be sure to ask for one of the rooms with a double bed if that's what you prefer; some rooms have only twin beds. Tico meals are served in the small screen-walled dining room, and there is a bar where you can chat with other guests. If you come in by bus and boat, your bus will make a brief stop at Braulio Carillo National Park so you can have a look at the rain-forested mountains before descending into the lowlands. There are bilingual guides to point out wildlife and answer questions, both during the boat trip to the lodge and during outings through the nearby canals and (in season) to the beach at night to watch sea turtles laying their eggs. The lodge also has several acres of forest land through which there are several kilometers of trails.

○ **Jungle Lodge.** Apdo. 1818-1002, San José. ☎ **506/233-0133** or 506/233-0155. Fax 506/233-0778. 34 rms. $389 double, three days/two nights; $486.50 triple, three days/two nights. All rates include round-trip transportation from San José and three meals daily. AE, DC, MC, V.

Located just south of Ilan-Ilan on the same side of the river and about a kilometer from Tortuguero National Park, the Jungle Lodge offers rooms in wooden buildings raised up above the ground on pilings. There are long verandahs set with chairs where you can sit and birdwatch, or just relax and listen to the forest. Most rooms have windows on two sides to let the breezes through, plus ceiling fans. Wooden floors and walls give these rooms an attractive, tropical look. Simple-but-filling meals such as fried chicken or fish with rice and beans are served buffet style at long tables in a screen-walled dining hall. Tours, led by bilingual guides, include boat tours through the canals to look for wildlife, a visit to Tortuguero Village, a hike through the forest, and (in season) trips over to the beach to watch the sea turtles lay their eggs. Optional canoe tours and night tours are also available for $10 and $15, respectively. Fishing trips cost around $35 per hour for two people. This is a big place and can seem crowded and impersonal at times.

✪ **Laguna Lodge.** Apdo. 344, San Pedro, San José. ☎/fax **506/225-3740.** 14 rms. $382 double, three days/two nights. All rates include round-trip transportation from San José, tours, and three meals daily. MC, V.

This is one of the newest and smallest lodges in the area, located 2 kilometers north of Tortuguero Village. The rooms here are all very attractive, with wood walls, waxed hardwood floors, and tiled bathrooms with screened upper walls to let in air and light. Each room also has a little shared verandah. There's a small screen-walled dining room that serves tasty meals. A little covered deck has also been built over the water, and there is even a tiny beach area on the river. Several covered palapa huts have also been built and strung with hammocks. The lodge owners live here year-round, which makes Laguna Lodge a bit more personal than other Tortuguero lodges. Like the Mawamba Lodge (below), this hotel has the added advantage of being on the beach side of the canal. Several different optional tours are available.

Mawamba Lodge. Apdo. 10050-1000, San José. ☎ **506/223-7490,** 506/223-2421 or 506/222-5463. Fax 506/255-4039. 36 rms. $328 double, two days/one night; $410 double, three days/two nights. All rates include round-trip transportation from San José and three meals daily. AE, MC, V.

Located about 500 meters north of Tortuguero Village on the beach side of the canal, Mawamba is a good choice for anyone who would like to be able to wander this isolated stretch of beach at will. Rooms have varnished wood floors, twin beds, cold-water showers, and table fans only. However, there are wide verandahs and plenty of hammocks around for anyone who wants to kick back. The gardens are lush and overgrown with flowering ginger, heliconia, and hibiscus. When I last visited, work was just being completed on a small swimming pool, and there were plans to add hot-water showers. Meals are above average for Tortuguero, and might include pasta and lobster or chicken in béchamel sauce. Plus there is usually good, fresh bread. You can dine either in the screened-in dining room or out on the patio. Tours included in the rates include a 4-hour boat ride through the canals and a guided forest hike. There are also slide shows every other night that focus on the natural history of this area. Optional tours include a night hike ($17 per person) and fishing trips ($40 per hour for two people).

INEXPENSIVE

There are several basic lodges in the village of Tortuguero, offering budget lodgings for between $5 and $15 per person. **Cabinas Miss Junie** (☎ 506/710-0523) and **Cabinas Sabinas** (no phone) are your best bets. If you choose one of these you will have to make your own arrangements for touring the canals, or renting a canoe.

🄢 **El Manati Lodge.** Tortuguero, Limón. ☎ **506/288-1828.** 6 cabins. $28.50 double. No credit cards.

If you'd like to have a Tortuguero jungle lodge experience, but don't have the bucks to spend on the above places, this is your best choice. This lodge is located across the canal and about a kilometer north of Tortuguero Village. The young owners live here, and have slowly built the lodge themselves over the years. The rooms are fairly basic, with cement floors and floor fans, but they have attractive curtains and new fixtures in the bathrooms. There's even warm water. Some accommodations have two separate rooms, one of which has bunk beds. Breakfast ($5) and dinner ($8) are available. Canal tours and turtle-watching walks are $10 per person for 2 hours, and there are canoes that can be rented for $5. Transportation up here and back can be arranged in Moín near Limón for $50 to $60 roundtrip. Piece it all together and you come up with a three-day, two-night trip with tours, meals, and transportation from Limón for around $250 for two people!

A NEARBY LODGE

Parismina Tarpon Rancho. Apdo. 10560-1000, San José. ☎ **506/257-3553**, 506/798-0918, or 800/862-1003 in the U.S. Fax 506/222-1760. 20 rms. $330 double, two days/one night; $430 double, three days/two nights. V.

This lodge is located about midway between Limón and Tortuguero at the mouth of the Río Parismina. For more than 30 years, the American owners have been catering to anglers and other visitors, and today the lodge offers great service, comfortable accommodations, filling meals, and attractive gardens. The rooms all have ceiling fans and good mattresses to assure you a good night's sleep. Outside your door, you'll find a pleasant verandah overlooking the garden. Tortuguero National Park begins a few kilometers to the north of the lodge, and, on an all-day boat tour, you'll get to explore the park's waterways. Other tours included in the package offered by this lodge are a visit to nearby Parismina Village and a night walk to spot nesting turtles or crocodiles. Fishing for tarpon and snook is still a primary attraction here at Parismina, and for an extra $100 per person you can do two half-day fishing trips.

2 Limón: Gateway to Tortuguero National Park and Southern Coastal Beaches

160 kilometers E of San José

It was just offshore from present-day Limón that Christopher Columbus is believed to have anchored in 1502, on his fourth and last voyage to the New World. Although he felt this was potentially a very rich land, and named it Costa Rica, it never quite lived up to his expectations. However, the spot where he anchored has proven over the centuries to be the best port on the Caribbean coast. It was from here that the first shipments of bananas headed to North America in the late 19th century. Today, Limón is a busy port city that ships millions of pounds of bananas northward every year.

ESSENTIALS

GETTING THERE & DEPARTING   By Bus   Buses leave San José daily, every hour between 5am and 7pm from the corner of Avenida 3 between calles 19 and 21. Trip duration is 2¹/₂ hours; fare is $2.40. A slightly more comfortable direct bus leaves from the same block roughly every half hour between 5:30am and 4:30pm; check in San José for a current schedule. Fare is $2.95.

Buses leave Limón for San José roughly every half hour between 5am and 7:30pm. The bus stop is one block east and half a block south of the municipal market. Buses to Cahuita and Puerto Viejo leave daily at 5 and 10am, and 1 and 4pm. The Cahuita bus stop is at Radio Casino, which is one block north of the municipal market. Buses to Punta Uva and Manzanillo, both of which are south of Puerto Viejo, leave Limón daily at 6am and 2:30pm, from the same block.

By Car   The Guápiles Highway heads north out of San José on Calle 3 before turning east and passing close to Barva Volcano and through Braulio Carillo National Park, en route to Limón. The drive takes about 2¹/₂ hours. Alternatively, you can take the old highway, which is equally scenic, though slower. This highway heads east out of San José on Avenida Central, and passes through San Pedro before reaching Cartago. From Cartago on, the road is narrow and winding, and passes through Paraiso and Turrialba before descending out of the mountains to Siquírres where the old highway meets the new. This route will take you 4 hours or more to Limón.

ORIENTATION   Arriving   Nearly all addresses in Limón are measured from the market or from Parque Vargas, which is at the east end of town. The bus stop for buses out to Playa Bonita is just around the corner, to the north of the Cahuita bus stop.

WHAT TO SEE & DO

Limón is not generally considered a tourist attraction. Most travelers use it primarily as a gateway to Tortuguero to the north and the beaches of Cahuita and Puerto Viejo to the south. If you do spend some time in Limón, you can take a seat in Parque Vargas along the sea wall and watch the city's citizens go about their business. There are even supposed to be some sloths living in the trees here. Maybe you'll spot them. Take a walk around town if you're interested in architecture. When banana shipments built this port, many local merchants erected elaborately decorated buildings, several of which have survived the city's many earthquakes. Just be careful after dark, particularly outside of the city center. Limón has earned a reputation for frequent muggings and robberies.

The biggest event of the year in Limón, and one of the most fascinating festivals in Costa Rica, is the annual **Carnival,** which is held for a week around Columbus Day (October 12). For one week of the year, languid Limón shifts into high gear for a nonstop bacchanal orchestrated to the beat of reggae, soca, and calypso music. During the revelries, residents of the city don costumes and take to the streets in a dazzling parade of color. In recent years, however, the central government has tried to reign in Carnival, citing health and safety concerns. If you want to experience Carnival, make hotel reservations early.

If you are planning on heading up to Tortuguero on your own, see "Tortuguero National Park," above, for details on how to get there from Limón.

A NEARBY BEACH

If you want to get in some beach time while you're here in Limón, hop in a taxi or a local bus and head north to **Playa Bonita,** a small public beach. Although the water isn't very clean and usually too rough for swimming, the setting is much more attractive than downtown. This beach is very popular with surfers.

WHERE TO STAY & DINE
MODERATE
Cabinas Cocori. Playa Bonita (Apdo. 1093), Limón. ☎ **506/758-2930.** Fax 506/798-1670. 15 rms, 6 apts (each with bath). $32–$42 double; $41 apt (accommodates up to five people). AE, DC, MC, V.

Located on the water just before you reach Playa Bonita, this hotel and apartment complex commands a fine view of the cove and crashing surf. The grounds are in need of landscaping, but the rooms are quite nice. A two-story white building houses the apartments, each of which has a kitchenette with hot plate and refrigerator, two bedrooms, and a bathroom. A long verandah runs along both floors. The rooms are housed in a new adjacent building. The rooms are small and basic, but clean. The four rooms on the ground floor have air-conditioning; those above make do with a fan and sea breezes. Staying at this location is far preferable to staying in town. You can get here by bus or taxi.

✪ **Hotel Maribu Caribe.** Apdo. 1306-2050, San Pedro. ☎ **506/758-4543**, 506/758-4010, or 506/253-1838 in San José. Fax 506/758-3541, or 506/234-0193 in San José. 52 rms. A/C TEL. $78 double; $88 triple. AE, DC, MC, V.

Located on top of a hill overlooking the Caribbean and built to resemble an Indian village, the Maribu Caribe is a pleasant, if not overly luxurious, choice if you are looking to spend some time in the sun. The hotel is popular with Tico families from San José because it is easy to get to for weekend trips. The guest rooms are in circular bungalows with white tile floors and varnished wood ceilings. The furnishings are a bit old but are still comfortable.

The hotel's restaurant has the best view in Limón, or on the entire Atlantic coast for that matter. It's built out over the edge of a steep hill with tide pools and the ocean almost directly below. In addition to the formal dining room, there are also tables outside on a curving verandah that make the most of the view. Entree prices range from $5 to $16.50, and the emphasis is on seafood prepared in the continental style. There is a bar here, as well as a bar/snack bar by the pool. The Maribu Caribe can help you with tour arrangements and has a gift shop.

✪ **Hotel Matama.** Apdo. 686, Limón. ☎ **506/758-1123** or 506/758-4409. Fax 506/ 758-4499. 16 rms. A/C. $70 double; $85 triple; $100 quad. AE, MC, V.

Almost directly across the street from Cabinas Cocori, the Matama is in a class by itself. The hotel consists of several multiplex buildings set amid dense tropical vegetation across the road from the ocean. The strikingly modern design of the buildings, both inside and out, is a welcome surprise in an area of generally unmemorable accommodations. Each room is decorated with attractive matching drapes and bedspreads, has comfortable wicker furniture, and best of all, large bathrooms with solarium gardens that bring the jungle right into your bath. There are even some units with lofts. Splashing around in the small pool, you'll be surrounded by the sounds of the jungle, and if you want to explore nearby jungles further, you can arrange trips and car rentals here at the hotel. Seafood is the specialty of the large open-air restaurant, with prices ranging from $4.50 to $16.50. The meals are well prepared and elegantly served, but the service can be a bit slow. Room service is also available.

INEXPENSIVE

Hotel Acon. Avenida 3 and Calle 3 (Apdo. 528), Limón. ☎ **506/758-1010.** Fax 506/ 758-2924. 39 rms (all with bath). A/C TEL. $20 double; $24 triple. AE, MC, V.

This older in-town choice is the best you can do in Limón. The rooms, all of which are air-conditioned (almost a necessity in this muggy climate), are clean and have two twin beds and a large bathroom. A television in your room will cost an extra $1.50 per day. The restaurant on the first floor just off the lobby is a cool, dark haven on steamy afternoons, highly recommended for lunch or as a place to beat the heat.

Prices range from $2.75 to $10. The second-floor disco stays open late on weekends, so don't count on a quiet night.

Park Hotel. Avenida 3 between calles 1 and 3, Limón. ☎ **506/758-3476** or 506/798-0555. Fax 506/758-4364. 30 rms, 5 suites (all with bath). $18–$25 double; $22–$28 triple; $40–$50 suites. V.

You can't miss this tall pink, yellow, and turquoise building across the street from the fire station. It's certainly seen better years, but in Limón there aren't too many choices. What makes this place memorable is its aging tropical ambience, so don't expect clean and new. Be sure to ask for a room on the ocean side of the hotel because these are brighter, quieter, and cooler than those on the side of the hotel that faces the fire station. The suites are generally kept in much better condition and have private ocean-view balconies. The large, sunny dining room off the lobby serves standard Tico fare at very reasonable prices.

3 Cahuita

200 kilometers E of San José; 42 kilometers S of Limón

The influx of tourists and an apparently robust drug trade have changed the face and feel of this quiet Caribbean town. A few notorious crimes against tourists have had a serious impact here, and it is highly recommended that you take every possible precaution against robbery and avoid walking alone outside of downtown at night. Nevertheless, Cahuita is still one of the most laid-back villages you'll find anywhere in Costa Rica, and if you spend any time here, you'll likely find yourself slipping into a heat-induced torpor that affects anyone who ends up here. The gravel streets are almost always deserted, and the social heart of the village is the front porches of Salon Vaz and Salon Sarafina, Cahuita's dueling bar/discos. The village traces its roots to Afro-Caribbean fishermen and laborers who settled in this region in the mid-1800s, and today the population is still primarily English-speaking blacks whose culture and language set them apart from other Costa Ricans.

The main reason people come to Cahuita—other than its laid-back atmosphere—are its miles of pristine beaches that stretch both north and south from town. The beaches to the south, as well as the forest behind them and one of Costa Rica's few coral reefs beneath the waters offshore, are all part of Cahuita National Park. Silt and pesticides washing down from nearby banana plantations have taken a heavy toll on the coral reefs, so don't expect the snorkeling to be fantastic. Still, the beaches inside the park are idyllic.

ESSENTIALS

GETTING THERE & DEPARTING   By Bus   Express buses leave San José daily at 10am and 3:30pm from Avenida 11 between Calle Central and Calle 1. Trip duration is 4 hours; fare is $4.50. The Sixaola bus leaves from the same station at 6am and 1:30pm and will leave you on the highway at the entrance to Cahuita, about 1 kilometer from the town center.

Alternatively, you can take a bus to Limón (see above for details), then take a Cahuita- or Puerto Viejo–bound bus from Limón. These latter buses leave Limón daily at 5, 8, and 10am, and 1, 4, and 6pm from Radio Casino, which is one block north of the municipal market. Buses from Limón to Manzanillo depart daily at 6am and 2:30pm and stop in Cahuita. Trip duration is 1 hour; fare is 85¢.

Buses departing Puerto Viejo and Sixaola (on the Panama border) stop in Cahuita at approximately 7, 10, and 11:15am, and 4pm en route to San José. However, these buses are often full, particularly on weekends and throughout the high season. To avoid standing in the aisle all the way to San José, it is better to take a bus first to Limón, and then catch one of the frequent Limón/San José buses. Buses to Limón leave daily at 6:30 and 9am, and 12, 3, 4:30, and 6pm. Another tactic I've used is to take a morning bus to Puerto Viejo, spend the day down there, and board a direct bus to San José at its point of origin, thereby snagging a seat.

By Car Follow the directions above for getting to Limón, and as you enter the outskirts of Limón, watch for a paved road to the right (it's just before the railroad tracks). Take this road south to Cahuita, passing the airstrip and the beach as you leave Limón.

ORIENTATION   Arriving   There are only eight sand streets in Cahuita, so you shouldn't get lost. Three roads lead into town from the highway. Buses usually take the road that leads into the heart of town and drop their passengers at the Salon Vaz bar. An alternate route bypasses town and heads toward Playa Negra, which is just north of town. As you're coming from the north, the first road leads to the north end of Playa Negra. If you come in on the bus and are staying at a lodge on Playa Negra, head out of town on the street that runs between Salon Vaz and the small park. This road will curve to the left and continue a mile or so out to Playa Negra. The village's main street dead-ends at the entrance to the national park (a footbridge over a small stream). The bus stop is in front of Salon Vaz.

FAST FACTS   You can wash your clothes at the self-service **laundromat** in front of Cabinas Vaz. One load in the washer or dryer will cost $1.50. The **police station** is located where the road from Playa Negra turns into town. The **post office,** next door to the police station, is open Monday through Friday from 8am to 5pm. In addition to tours and bicycle rentals, **Cahuita Tours & Adventure Center**, on the main road to Playa Negra about 2^1/$_2$ blocks from Salon Vaz, offers international fax service and allows travelers to exchange money.

EXPLORING CAHUITA NATIONAL PARK

On arrival, you'll immediately feel the call of the long scimitar of beach that stretches south from the edge of town. This beach is glimpsed through the trees from Cahuita's sun-baked main street, and extends a promise of relief from the heat. While the lush coastal forest and picture-perfect palm lines are a tremendous draw, the park was actually created to preserve the 600-acre coral reef that surrounds it. The reef contains 35 species of coral and provides a haven for hundreds of brightly colored tropical fish. You can walk on the beach itself, or follow the trail that runs through the forest just behind the beach to check out the reef.

The best place to swim is beyond the **Peresoso** (Lazy River), a few hundred yards inside Cahuita National Park. The trail behind the beach is great for birdwatching, and if you're lucky, you might see some monkeys or a sloth. The loud whooping sounds you hear off in the distance are the calls of howler monkeys, which can be heard from more than a mile away. Nearer at hand, you are likely to hear crabs scuttling about amid the dry leaves on the forest floor; there are half a dozen or so species of land crabs living in this region. My favorites are the bright orange-and-purple ones. The trail behind the beach stretches a little more than 4 miles to the southern end of the park at **Puerto Vargas,** where you will find a beautiful white-sand beach, the park headquarters, and a primitive campground with drinking water and outhouses. The reef is off the point just north of Puerto Vargas. If you don't dawdle, the hike should take no more than 4 hours.

ENTRY POINTS, FEES & REGULATIONS

The in-town park entrance is just over a footbridge at the end of the village's main street. The main park entrance is at the southern end of the park in Puerto Vargas. The road to Puerto Vargas is approximately 3 miles south of Cahuita on the left. Officially, admission is $6 per person per day, but the last time I visited, the fee was only being collected at the Puerto Vargas entrance and it was possible to enter the park from the town of Cahuita with just a voluntary contribution. This situation is sure to change, and is probably occurring because of a recent confrontation between the town of Cahuita and the government over park fees (two years ago, the government increased all park entrance fees across the board, before 1996's fee standardization). The park is open daily from dawn to dusk, and as stated above, a manned ranger station exists at the Puerto Vargas entrance where there are also campsites.

BEACHES & ACTIVE SPORTS OUTSIDE THE PARK

Outside the park, the best place for swimming is **Playa Negra**. Just keep an eye out for poisonous snakes. On my last visit, I was almost bitten by one on a path on Playa Negra. If you aren't a herpetologist, it's best to assume that all snakes here are poisonous.

If you want to find out where the best diving spots are (there is even a sunken ship you can visit), I suggest a snorkeling trip by boat. **Cahuita Tours & Adventure Center** (☎ 506/755-0232), on the village's main street heading out towards Playa Negra, has glass-bottom boat and snorkeling trips for $15–$20 per person. They also arrange jungle tours ($25–$35), white-water rafting trips ($65–$85), and jeep tours to the Bribri reservation. Cahuita Tours also rents bicycles ($7.50 per day), boogie boards ($12.50 per day), and snorkeling equipment ($7.50 per day). **National Park Tours and Expeditions** (☎ 506/755-0024), located on the left just before the town's park entrance, offers similar tours and rentals at similar prices, as well as three-day boat trips to Bocas del Toro, Panama.

Brigitte (watch for the sign on Playa Negra) rents horses for $5 per hour (you must have prior experience) and also offers guided horseback tours for $25–$35.

BIRDWATCHING & CANOEING ALONG THE ESTRELLA ESTUARY

Birdwatchers who have a car should head north 9 kilometers to the **Aviaros de Caribe** bed-and-breakfast lodge (☎ 506/382-1335) where canoe tours of the Estrella Estuary are available. Nearly 300 species of birds have been sighted in the immediate area. The tour costs $30 per person and leaves throughout the day, but it is best to leave very early or near dusk, and to make reservations in advance.

SHOPPING

At Restaurant Vaz on the main road near the park entrance (not to be confused with Salon Vaz, a bar/disco where buses discharge) and a couple of other places around the village, you can pick up a copy of Paula Palmer's *What Happen: A Folk-History of Costa Rica's Talamanca Coast* (Publications in English, 1993). The book is a history of the region, based on interviews with many of the area's oldest residents. Much of it is in the traditional Créole language, from which the title is taken. It makes fun and interesting reading, and you just might bump into someone mentioned in the book.

You can pick up souvenirs and Caribbean beach clothing at either **Boutique Coco Miko** or **Boutique Bambata**. The latter is also a good place to have your hair wrapped in colorful threads and strung with beads.

EVENING ENTERTAINMENT

The Salon Vaz, a classic Caribbean bar, has traditionally been the place to spend your nights (or days, for that matter) if you like cold beer and very loud reggae and soca music. Now, the **Salon Sarafina**, located just across the street, is giving Vaz a run for its money. There are usually local women hanging out on the front porches of each establishment, selling local pati pies or bowls of run-down stew.

WHERE TO STAY

MODERATE

Cabinas Atlantida. Cahuita, Limón. ☎ **506/755-0115.** Fax 506/755-0213. 30 rms (all with private bath). $53.50 double; $64.20 triple; $74.90 quad. All rates include breakfast. AE, MC, V.

Set amid lush gardens and wide green lawns and run by French Canadians, the Atlantida is one of my favorite lodgings in Cahuita. You'll find it beside the soccer field out by Playa Negra, about a mile out of town. The guest rooms are done in a style reminiscent of local Indian architecture, with thatched roofs, pale yellow stucco walls, and plenty of bamboo trim. All rooms have a patio with a bamboo screen divider for privacy, and when you sit there, you'll be gazing into a flourishing garden. Although only breakfast is included in the room rate, you can also order dinner for under $10 per person. The meals are served in a rancho dining room. Breakfasts include fresh fruit and fresh juice, rolls and homemade marmalade, and there is free coffee all day long. Continental-style dinners are some of the best in town, though they are only available to hotel guests. A host of different tours can be arranged here, from snorkeling to horseback riding to white-water rafting. The beach is right across the street, and the hotel also has a conference room, a small gym, and a nice tile pool.

☺ Chalet Hibiscus. Apdo. 943, Limón. ☎ **506/755-0021.** Fax 506/755-0015. 2 cabins, 1 house (each with bath). Dec–Apr, $32–$40.75 cabin, $81.50 house (can accommodate up to six people); May–Nov, $25–$32 cabin, $61 house. No credit cards.

If you're planning a long stay in Cahuita, I advise checking into this place. Although it is about 2 kilometers from town on the road along Playa Negra, it is well worth the journey. The house has two bedrooms and sleeps up to six people. There is hardwood paneling all around, a full kitchen, hot water, red tile floors, a pila for doing your laundry, and even a garage. A spiral staircase leads to the second floor, where you'll find hammocks on a balcony that looks over a green lawn to the ocean. The attractive little cabins have wicker furniture and walls of stone and wood. If you ever wanted to be marooned on the Mosquito Coast, this is the place to live out your fantasy. You're a kilometer north of Playa Negra here, but there is a tiny swimming pool for cooling off during the day. The chalet is both simple and elegant; the setting, serene and beautiful. Be sure to ring the bell outside the gate—there are guard dogs on the grounds. If the house and cabins here are full, the owner can also arrange rentals of similar accommodations nearby. When I last visited, there were plans to add a simple kitchen, bar, and small recreation area with a billiards table.

Hotel Jaguar Cahuita. Cahuita, Limón (Apdo. 7046-1000, San José). ☎ **506/226-3775** or 506/755-0238. Fax 506/226-4693. 45 rms. $45–$57 double. All rates include breakfast. MC, V.

Located directly across the sandy road from Playa Negra, the Jaguar is Cahuita's largest and most ambitious hotel to date. However, despite the fact that the rooms are the biggest in town and are close to the water, they leave a lot to be desired. When I last visited, there was an untended and run-down feel to the hotel, but I was assured a major sprucing up was in the works. Rooms were designed with solar principles in mind to stay cool and make the most of prevailing breezes. Unfortunately, sometimes the breezes aren't enough, and small table-top fans have had to be added to the rooms. Though half the rooms have views of the water, the rest face only the front rank of rooms. Surrounding the hotel are 17 acres of forest and brush through which a short nature trail has been cut. You're almost certain to see at least one sloth on a morning walk here. There's a small swimming pool here, and the beach is just across the road. The open-air dining room serves very good, moderately priced meals. Many of the ingredients used in the meals come from trees on the hotel property.

✪ **Magellan Inn.** Plaza Víquez, Cahuita (Apdo. 1132, Limón). ☎/fax **506/755-0035.** 6 rms. $55 double; $65 triple. All rates include continental breakfast. AE, DC, MC, V.

This small inn is out at the far end of Playa Negra (about 2 kilometers north of Cahuita) and is the most luxurious hotel in the area. The six large rooms are all carpeted and have French doors, vertical blinds, big tiled bathrooms with hardwood counters, and two joined single beds with attractive bedspreads. Each room has its own tiled verandah with an overhead fan and bamboo chairs. There is a casually sophisticated combination bar/lounge and sitting room that has oriental-style rugs and wicker furniture. However, most memorable are the hotel's sunken pool and garden, both of which are built into a crevice in the ancient coral reef that underlies this entire region. There is often good birdwatching in the hotel gardens. The owners, Jean-Paul Feuillatre and Elizabeth Newton, are from France and Canada, respectively. When I last visited, construction was about to be completed on an adjacent restaurant to be called Casa Créole, where the hotel's excellent chef will continue serving some of the best meals on the coast.

INEXPENSIVE

✪ **Alby Lodge.** Apdo. 840, Limón. ☎/fax **506/755-0031.** 4 cabins (each with bath). $29 double; $33.50 triple; $37.50 quad. No credit cards.

Located about 150 yards down the winding lane to the right just before you reach the park entrance, the Alby Lodge is a fascinating little place hand-built by German owners Yvonne and Alfons Baumgartner. Though these four small cabins are close to the center of the village, they are surrounded by a large lawn and feel secluded. The cabins are all quintessentially tropical with thatch roofs, mosquito nets, hardwood floors and beams, big shuttered windows, tile bathrooms, and a hammock slung on the front porch. You won't find more appealing rooms in this price range.

⑤ **Cabinas Atlantic Surf.** Cahuita, Limón. ☎ **506/755-0086.** 6 rms. $15 double. No credit cards.

These small but attractive rooms are a great choice for budget travelers. In a town where all the newer hotels seem to be built of cement, the rustic, varnished wood walls, floors, and small porches of these rooms are a welcome sight. There are fans and tiled showers within, and Adirondack chairs on the porches. The upstairs rooms have high ceilings but still get pretty warm. The Atlantic Surf is down the lane from the Cabinas Sol y Mar, only 100 yards from the park entrance.

Cabinas Rhode Island. Cahuita, Limón. ☎ **506/755-0264.** 11 rms (all with private bath). $10–$15 double. No credit cards.

These newer cinder-block rooms are down the lane beside the Cabinas Sol y Mar. The rooms are on the left, but the owners live in the house across the street. The rooms are very basic, but they're clean and have a tiled verandah. You're within 100 yards of the park entrance if you stay here.

⑤ Cabinas Tito. 250 meters southeast of G.A.R., Cahuita, Limón. ☎ **506/755-0286.** 6 cabins (each with bath). Dec–Apr, $30 double; May–Nov, $15–$20 double. All rates include continental breakfast. No credit cards.

Located down a grassy path just off the road to Playa Negra, these little cabins are quiet and comfortable. They're surrounded by a shady yard, and the owner's old Caribbean wood-frame house is to one side. The cabinas are made of cement block with tin roofs, but they have tile floors and small front porches with a couple of chairs. Two of the cabins have mini-refrigerators, and at least one has a tiled wall and wicker headboard for the bed. Good value, helpful owners, and pleasant surroundings have made this place an instant hit with budget travelers.

✪ Seaside Jenny's. Cahuita, Limón. ☎ **506/755-0256.** 8 rms (each with bath). $12.50–$20 double; rates slightly lower during off-season. No credit cards.

Located 200 yards straight ahead (toward the water) from the bus stop, Jenny's place has been popular for years, and her newer rooms are some of the best in town in this price range. Best of all, they're right on the water, so you can go to sleep to the sound of the waves. All of the rooms have shuttered windows, and on their porches there are sling chairs and hammocks. The more expensive rooms are on the second floor and have arguably the best views in Cahuita. There is one room in an older building, which, though it has a big porch and plenty of Caribbean atmosphere, is not quite as nice as the others.

Surf Side Cabins. Apdo. 360, Limón. ☎ **506/755-0246.** 23 rms (all with bath). $10–$15 double. No credit cards.

Despite its name, most of the rooms are not right on the water; nonetheless, this is a good budget choice in Cahuita. All the rooms are clean and have jalousie windows that let in a lot of light and air. Only a few are close to the water, and they are always in high demand. The restaurant is popular with locals, who sit and play dominoes for hours—it can get noisy at times. Prices for Tico meals range from $2.75 to $12.50. While I was eating here one night, a large sloth crawled into the open-air restaurant from an adjacent tree. With entertainment like that, it's hard not to recommend this place, although the hotel management can be rather unfriendly.

A NEARBY BED-AND-BREAKFAST

✪ Aviarios del Caribe. Apdo. 569-7300, Limón. ☎ **506/382-1335.** Fax 506/755-0016. 6 rms (each with bath). $60 double; $80 triple; $100 quad. All rates include full breakfast. MC, V.

If you prefer birdwatching to beaching, this is the place to stay on this section of the Atlantic coast. As the name implies, birds are important here. A bed-and-breakfast located on the edge of a small river delta, the lodge's owners have spotted over 300 species of birds within the immediate area. You can work on your life list from the lawns, the second floor, the open-air dining room, and the lounge, or from a canoe, paddling around the nearby canals. This house is built up on stilts and is surrounded by a private wildlife sanctuary that also includes forest trails. The guest rooms are all large and comfortable and have fans, tile floors, potted plants, fresh flowers, and modern bathroom fixtures. Some rooms also have king beds. In the lounge area you'll find a fabulous mounted insect collection, as well as terrariums that house live snakes and poison-arrow frogs. You'll also certainly make friends with Buttercup, the resident three-toed sloth. Only breakfast is served here, so you'll have to take your other meals in Cahuita, or at a roadside soda along the way.

WHERE TO DINE

Coconut meat and milk figure in a lot of the regional cuisine. Most nights, local women cook up pots of various local specialties and sell them from the front porches of the two discos; a full meal will cost you about $2.50. For snacks, there is a tiny bakery on the left side of the main road as you head toward Playa Negra. The coconut pie, brownies, ginger snaps, banana bread, and corn pudding are all delicious. Prices range from 55¢ to $1.

Brigitte's Restaurante. Playa Negra Road, north of Cabinas Atlantida. ☎ **506/755-0053.** Reservations are not accepted. Main courses $3.75–$7.25. No credit cards. Daily 10am–10pm. SWISS/CRÉOLE.

Brigitte is from Switzerland but she's been in Cahuita for quite a few years, so her menu includes an eclectic blend of cuisines. You can get a good Créole run-down stew, but you can also get a steak with mushroom sauce. There are good salads and home-baked breads as well. You never know what might show up as the daily special. Brigitte now also features a wide selection of ice creams for beating the midday heat. The restaurant is located at the back of a house just off the Playa Negra Road. Just follow the signs.

✪ Margaritaville. Playa Negra Road, 2 kilometers north of Cahuita. ☎ **506/755-0038.** Reservations not accepted. Complete meals $5–$7.50. No credit cards. Mon-Sat 6–10pm. INTERNATIONAL.

There's only one dish served each night at this little restaurant, but if you drop by ahead of time and make a special request, the friendly owner may try to accommodate you. However, if you're an adventurous eater, I'm sure you'll enjoy whatever is coming from the kitchen, which might be a local Créole dish made with coconut milk, or roasted chicken or eggplant lasagne. All the breads are home-baked, and if there's extra you may be able to take home a loaf. The tables here are set up on the open second floor of Moray's B&B. It's all very mellow, and definitely not to be missed.

Pizzeria El Cactus. On the road from the south end of Playa Negra to the highway. ☎ **506/755-0276.** Reservations not accepted. Pizza or spaghetti $3–$8.50. No credit cards. Tue–Sun 4–10pm. ITALIAN.

There are only a few tables at this small open-air restaurant, so be sure to arrive early if you have your heart set on pizza. Try the pizza Cahuita, which is made with tomatoes, mozzarella, salami, red peppers, olives, and oregano. There's also one made with hearts of palm. The pizzas are just the right size for one hungry person. Also on the menu are seven types of spaghetti, salads, and ice cream.

➒ Restaurant Edith. By the police station. ☎ **506/755-0248.** Reservations not accepted. Main courses $3.40–$11.50. No credit cards. Daily 7am–12pm and 6–10pm; also often open for lunch. SEAFOOD.

Miss Edith is a local lady who decided to start serving up home-cooked meals to all the hungry tourists hanging around. If you want a taste of the local cuisine, in a homey sit-down environment, this is the place. While Miss Edith's daughters take the orders, Mom cooks up a storm out back. The menu—when you can get ahold of it—is long, with lots of local seafood dishes and Créole combinations such as yuca in coconut milk with meat or vegetables. The sauces here have spice and zest, and are a welcome change from the typically bland fare served up throughout the rest of Costa Rica. After you've ordered, it is usually no more than 45 minutes until your meal arrives. It's usually crowded here, so don't be bashful about sitting down with total strangers at the big table. Miss Edith's place is at the opposite end of town from the park entrance, and is just around the corner from the main street.

4 Puerto Viejo

200 kilometers E of San José; 55 kilometers S of Limón

Though Puerto Viejo is even smaller than Cahuita, it has a slightly more lively atmosphere due to the many surfers who come here from around the country (and around the world) to ride the village's famous Salsa Brava wave. For nonsurfers, there are also some good swimming beaches, and if you head still farther south, you will come to the most beautiful beaches on this coast. The waters down in this region are some of the clearest anywhere in the country, and there is some good snorkeling among the coral reefs when the seas are calm.

You may notice, as you make your way into town from the highway, that there are cacao trees planted along the road. These trees are all suffering from a blight that has greatly reduced the cocoa-bean harvest in the area. However, you can still get delicious cocoa candies here in Puerto Viejo. Don't miss them.

ESSENTIALS

GETTING THERE & DEPARTING   By Bus   Express buses to Puerto Viejo leave San José daily at 10am and 3:30pm from Avenida 11 between Calle Central and Calle 1. The trip's duration is 5 hours; fare is $5. Buses leave from the same station for Sixaola at 6am and 1:30pm, and will leave you at the turnoff for Puerto Viejo about 5 kilometers outside of town.

Alternatively, you can catch a bus to Limón (see above for details), and then transfer to a Puerto Viejo–bound bus in Limón. These latter buses leave daily at 5, 8, and 10am, and 1, 4, and 6pm from Radio Casino, which is one block north of the municipal market. Buses from Limón to Manzanillo also stop in Puerto Viejo and leave daily at 6am and 2:30pm. Trip duration is 1 1/2 hours; fare is $1.10.

Express buses leave Puerto Viejo for San José daily at 6:30 and 9am, and 4pm. Buses for Limón leave daily at 6 and 8:40am, and 1, 4, and 5pm. Buses to Punta Uva and Manzanillo leave Puerto Viejo daily around 7am and 4pm. These buses return from Manzanillo at 8:15am and 5:15pm.

By Car   To reach Puerto Viejo, continue south from Cahuita for another 16 kilometers. Watch for a dirt road that forks to the left from the paved highway. This road will take you into the village after another 5 kilometers.

ORIENTATION   Arriving   The dirt road in from the highway runs parallel to Playa Negra just before entering the village of Puerto Viejo, which has all of about six dirt streets. The sea will be on your left and forested hills on your right as you come into town.

FAST FACTS   Public phones are located at Hotel Maritza, El Pizote Lodge, and the ATEC office, where you can also mail a postcard and obtain visitor information. The nearest **bank** is in Bribri, about 10 kilometers away. There is a Guardia Rural **police** post near the park on the beach. It's another 15 kilometers or so on a bad gravel road south to Manzanillo.

WHAT TO SEE & DO

Most people who show up in this remote village have only on thing on their mind— **surfing.** Just offshore from the village park is a shallow reef where powerful storm-generated waves sometimes reach 20 feet. These waves are the biggest and most powerful on the Atlantic coast. Even when the waves are small, this spot is recommended only for very experienced surfers because of the danger of the reef. There are also popular beach breaks south of town on Playa Cocles. For swimming, head out to Playa Negra, along the road into town, or to the beaches south of town around Punta Uva, where the surf is much more manageable.

If you aren't a surfer, the same activities that prevail in Cahuita are the norm here as well. Read a book, take a nap, or go for a walk on the beach. However, if you have more energy, you can rent a bicycle or a horse (watch for signs) and head down the beach toward Punta Uva, which is a little less than 8 kilometers down a potholed gravel road.

You should be sure to stop in at the **Association Talamanqueña de Ecoturismo y Conservacion (ATEC)** (☎ 506/798-4244) office across the street from the Soda Tamara. This local organization is concerned with preserving both the environment and the cultural heritage of this area and promoting ecologically sound development in the region. In addition to functioning as the local post office and information center, they have a little shop that sells t-shirts, maps, posters, and books. You can pick up Paula Palmer's oral history of the region *What Happen: A Folk-History of Costa Rica's Talamanca Coast* (Publications in English, 1993) here. They also publish and sell *Coastal Talamanca, A Cultural and Ecological Guide,* a small booklet packed with information about this area. They also offer quite a few different tours. There are half-day walks that focus on nature and either the local African-Caribbean culture or the indigenous Bribri culture. These walks pass through farms and forests, and along the way you'll learn about local history, customs, medicinal plants, and Indian mythology, as well as have an opportunity to see sloths, monkeys, iguanas, keel-billed toucans, and other wildlife. There are four different walks through the nearby Bribri Indians' **KeköLdi Reserve;** there are also more strenuous hikes through the primary rain forest. ATEC offers snorkeling trips to the nearby coral reefs, and snorkeling and fishing trips in dugout canoes. Bird walks and night walks will help you spot more of the area wildlife; there are even overnight treks. The local guides who lead these tours have a wealth of information and make a hike through the forest a truly educational experience. Don't miss an opportunity to do a tour with ATEC. Half-day walks (and night walks) are $11, and full-day walks are $17. A half day of snorkeling or fishing will cost around $20 per person. The ATEC office is open Monday through Saturday from 8am to 8pm, and Sunday from 8am to noon and 4pm to 8pm. If you're looking to stay here for an extended period of time and would like to contribute to the community, ask about volunteering here.

If you continue south on the coast road from Puerto Viejo, you will come to a couple of even smaller villages. Punta Uva is 8 kilometers away, and Manzanillo is about 15 kilometers away. It is possible to walk along the beach from Punta Cocles to Manzanillo, a distance of about 10 kilometers. Another enjoyable hike is from Monkey Point (Punta Mono) to Manzanillo (about 5½ kilometers). There is a reef offshore from Manzanillo that is good for snorkeling. Still farther south is the **Manzanillo-Gandoca Wildlife Refuge,** which extends all the way to the Panamanian border. Within the boundaries of the reserve live manatees, crocodiles, and more than 350 species of birds. The reserve also includes the coral reef offshore. On one 5½-mile-long beach within the reserve, four species of sea turtles nest between March and July.

Color Caribe, across the street from Cabinas Grant, sells hand-painted T-shirts and coconut-shell jewelry. There are also a couple of *pulperías* (general stores) in the village.

If you'd like to learn more about the culture of the local Bribri Indians, look for a copy of *Taking Care of Sibö's Gifts*, written by Paula Palmer, Juanita Sánchez, and Gloria Mayorga.

As mentioned in the section on Cahuita above, Puerto Viejo is showing some troubling effects of the combined tourism and drug trades. An increase in robberies and a few violent crimes have made headlines in recent years. Be careful here, especially after dark.

WHERE TO STAY
MODERATE

✪ **El Pizote.** Apdo. 230-2200, Coronado. ☎ **506/798-1938** or 506/229-1428. Fax 506/229-1428. 8 rms (none with bath), 6 bungalows. $50 double without bath, $82.50 double with bath; $66 triple without bath, $97 triple with bath; $76 quad without bath, $108 quad with bath. MC, V.

Although it originally billed itself as a surf resort, this comfortably rustic little lodge is ideal for anyone who simply wants to get away from it all. Located about 500 meters outside of town, El Pizote is set back across the road from a long black-sand beach. The rooms are in two beautiful, unpainted wooden buildings that are completely hidden from the road and even from the parking lot. You have to walk through a dense grove of dracaena plants, which you might recognize as a common houseplant. The rooms are cool—with polished wood walls, double beds, and absolutely beautiful bathrooms that have wood-slat floors in the showers and huge screen windows looking out on dense jungle. There are unusual burlap-and-bamboo window shades, as well as ceiling fans and reading lamps. For activity, there are hiking trails in the adjacent forest and a volleyball court; you can rent snorkeling equipment, as well as sea kayaks. There is also good birdwatching here. The restaurant serves only breakfast ($8) and dinner ($14.50), but drinks are available all day. There is a set menu each evening, which might be lobster with broccoli or an equally delectable fish plate. If arriving by bus, ask the bus driver to let you off at the entrance to the lodge. It's on the stretch of road that runs along the beach just before entering town.

INEXPENSIVE

⑤ **Cabinas Black Sands.** Puerto Viejo, Limón. ☎ **506/798-4244** (leave message). 3 rms (none with bath). $20 double; $50 for up to six people. No credit cards.

The owners of this rustic, beachside thatch house are refugees from chilly Wisconsin. They offer basic accommodations in a secluded spot near the end of the long black-sand beach. The three rooms are all in a single rustic, thatched-roof building, which has a communal kitchen and dining-room table. If you want, you can rent the entire house. If you don't have the whole place to yourself, remember that the folks next door can hear everything you say because the walls don't go all the way to the ceiling. It's wonderfully tranquil out here, and although it's a bit of a hike to the nearest restaurant, there is a general store nearby where you can buy groceries for doing your own cooking. If arriving by bus, be sure to get off at the Pulpería Violeta before the road reaches the beach. Otherwise it's a long walk back out from the bus stop in town.

✪ **Cabinas Chimuri.** Puerto Viejo, Limón. ☎ **506/798-4244** (leave message). 4 cabins (none with bath). $14–$20 double; $24.50 triple; $28.50 quad. No credit cards.

If you don't mind being a 15-minute walk from the beach and are an inveterate camper, I'm sure that you'll enjoy this rustic lodge. It's built in traditional Bribri Indian style with thatched-roof A-frame cabins in a forest setting. In fact, it's a short stroll up a trail from the parking lot to the lodge buildings, and there are other trails on the property as well. This lodge is definitely for nature lovers who are used to roughing it; accommodations are very basic, but there is a kitchen for guests to use. The lodge also runs several different hiking trips into the rain forest and the adjacent Bribri Indian Kekoldi Reserve. If arriving by bus, be sure to get off at the trail to Cabinas Chimuri before the road reaches the beach.

Cabinas Jacaranda. Puerto Viejo, Limón. No phone. 4 rms (3 with bath). $12.20 double without bath, $16.90 double with bath; $20.30 triple with bath. No credit cards.

This basic backpackers' special has a few nice touches that set it apart from the others. The floors are cement, but there are mats. Japanese paper lanterns cover the lights, and mosquito nets hang over the beds. The Guatemalan bedspreads add a dash of color and tropical flavor, as do the tables made from sliced tree trunks. If you are traveling in a group, you'll enjoy the space and atmosphere of the big room. If the hotel is full, the owners also rent a few nearby bungalows. The Garden Restaurant, adjacent to the rooms, serves the best food in town.

✪ **Casa Verde.** Puerto Viejo, Limón. ☎ **506/798-4244** (leave message). 12 rms (4 with private bath). $10–$15 double without bath; $30 double with bath. No credit cards.

This little hotel is located on a side street on the south side of town. The older rooms, with shared bath, are in an interesting building with a wide, covered breezeway between the rooms and the showers and toilets out back. The front and back porches of this building are hung with hammocks. A quiet sense of tropical tranquility pervades this place. The newer rooms are behind the house next door and are a bit larger than the older rooms. These new rooms have high ceilings, tile floors, and a verandah. Everything is well maintained, and even the shared bathrooms are kept immaculate.

Escape Caribeño. Puerto Viejo, (Apdo. 704-7300, Limón). ☎/fax **506/382-2572.** 12 rms (all with bath). $30 double; $40 triple; $50 quad. MC, V.

Located just outside of Puerto Viejo on the road to Punta Uva, Escape Caribeño consists of 12 little white cabins with brick pillars and tiled patios. Clerestory windows, vertical blinds, and rather fancy hardwood furniture give these cabins the aesthetic edge over many area places in this price range. There are reading lamps by the beds and small refrigerators in every room. The attractive gardens have been planted with bananas and palms. It's a 5 minute walk into town or out to a beautiful beach that has a small island just offshore.

NEARBY PLACES TO STAY
EXPENSIVE

Punta Cocles. Puerto Viejo, Limón (Apdo. 11020-1000, San José). ☎ **506/234-8055**, 506/234-8051, or 800/325-6927 in the U.S. Fax 506/234-8033. 60 rms. A/C TEL. $70 standard room, can accommodate up to four people; $90 with kitchenette, can accommodate up to six. AE, DC, MC, V.

Though this is the largest and most expensive hotel in the area, it is certainly not the best. The two biggest complaints I have are that no consideration was put into preserving the property's rain forest when the hotel was built, and it is a long, hot walk to the beach. Situated several hundred yards from the beach, the hotel is in a huge clearing in the jungle and offers virtually no shade and hardly any landscaping. Rooms do not get any sea breezes and consequently must be air-conditioned. Though the rooms are for the most part large and modern, they lack character.

Dining/Entertainment: There's a large open-air restaurant that serves overpriced meals, and a bar by the pool.

Services: Laundry service, sports-equipment rentals, tours.
Facilities: Swimming pool, children's pool, and small playground.

MODERATE

✪ **Playa Chiquita Lodge.** Avenida 2 between calles 17 and 19 (Apdo. 7043-1000), San José. ☎ **506/233-6613.** Fax 506/223-7479. 11 rms (all with bath). $49 double; $65 triple. No credit cards.

This place just oozes jungle atmosphere and is sure to please anyone searching for a steamy retreat on the beach. Set amid the shade of large old trees a few miles south of Puerto Viejo toward Punta Uva (watch for the sign), the lodge consists of unpainted wooden buildings set on stilts and connected by wooden walkways. There are wide verandahs with rocking chairs and seashell mobiles hanging everywhere. Rooms are dark and cool with wide-board floors and paintings by local Indian artists. The top of the bathroom wall is screened so you can gaze out into the jungle as you shower. There is a short trail that leads down to a private little swimming beach with beautiful turquoise water, as well as tide pools. Meals here cost from $5 to $13, and choices range from spaghetti to lobster; since the management is German you can expect a few German dishes as well. Throughout the day there are free bananas and coffee.

Las Palmas Resort. Edificio Cristal, Fifth floor, Avenida 1 between calles 1 and 3 (Apdo. 6942-1000), San José. ☎ **506/255-3939.** Fax 506/255-3737. 80 rms (all with bath). $40 double; $55 double with air-conditioning; $60 triple; $75 triple with air-conditioning. All rates include breakfast. AE, DC, MC, V.

Located 5 miles south of Puerto Viejo at Punta Uva, Las Palmas Resort is one of the only true beachfront hotels in the area. The only drawback is that on the weekends throngs of people flock to the beach right in front of the hotel, and the peace and quiet disappear. The beach here stretches for miles, and when the water is calm, snorkeling is good among the coral just offshore. Guest rooms are clean and comfortable, but not very attractive. Basically what you're paying for is the location, not the atmosphere or decor. The open-air restaurant serves moderately priced Tico and continental meals, with an emphasis on lobster and seafood. There is also a bar/snack bar near the entrance to the hotel. Additional amenities include a small octagonal swimming pool with a swim-up bar and two tennis courts; various tours and horseback rides can be arranged through the hotel. This hotel was enveloped in controversy, with charges that construction was conducted without proper permits and destroyed fragile mangroves.

Villas del Caribe. Puerto Viejo, Limón (Apdo. 8080-1000, San José). ☎ **506/233-2200.** Fax 506/221-2801. 12 apts. $69 double; $79 triple; $89 quad. AE, MC, V.

If you want to be right on the beach and have spacious comfortable accommodations, there is not a better choice in this area. Villas del Caribe, built in a sort of contemporary Mediterranean style and set on a 100-acre nature reserve, offers two-story townhouse apartments with full kitchens and a choice of one or two bedrooms. The living rooms have built-in sofa beds, and just outside there is a large terrace complete with barbecue grill. The kitchens are attractively designed with blue tile counters. Bathrooms are tropical fantasies with wooden-slat shower doors, potted plants on a platform by the window, louvered and screened walls that let in light and air, and more blue tile counters. Upstairs you'll find either a large single bedroom with a king bed, or two smaller bedrooms (one with bunk beds). Either way, there's a balcony, with hammock and ocean view. The water, which is usually fairly calm, is only steps away through the coconut palms, and there is some coral just offshore that makes for good snorkeling. The hotel can arrange horseback rides, fishing trips, snorkeling and diving—even oxcart rides. When I last visited, there was talk of opening a restaurant on the grounds.

INEXPENSIVE

☉ Cabinas Selvyn. Punta Uva, Limón. No phone. 10 rms (all with shared bath), 2 apts. $7.50–$10 double; $150–$200 per month for an apartment. No credit cards.

The atmosphere here is friendly and funky. Rooms are located in two old wooden buildings, behind the small open-aired restaurant. There are no fans here, so try to get one of the second-floor rooms, which receive a bit of the sea breezes. All the rooms come with mosquito nets, but beyond that, the accommodations are spartan. Nevertheless, the hotel is located 100 meters down a dirt lane from one of the most isolated and beautiful stretches of beach in Costa Rica, and owner Selvyn Brown is a great cook.

Miraflores Lodge. Playa Chiquita, Puerto Viejo, Limón. ☎/fax **506/233-2822.** 10 rms (6 with bath). $25 double without bath; $40–$50 double with bath. All rates include breakfast. No credit cards.

Located a few miles south of Puerto Viejo on the road to Punta Uva, Miraflores Lodge is a former private home and ornamental flower farm turned bed-and-breakfast. Because it was a private home, the decor is far more attractive than at other lodges in the area. The large second-floor porch, which is virtually an open-air living room, is decorated with wood carvings, masks, and Panamanian and Guatemalan textiles. Huge vases hold fresh flowers, and there is a free-form table made from a slice of tree trunk. Surrounding the lodge is the flower farm where heliconias, ginger, banana, anthurium, and orchids are grown. The guest rooms with private bath are very large, and can sleep up to six people in two sleeping areas. Walls and doors are faced with cane, and there are hardwood floors in the second-floor rooms. The hotel's restaurant now serves three meals a day, with an emphasis on fresh fruits, vegetables and fish.

WHERE TO DINE

To really sample the local cuisine, you need to look up a few local ladies. Ask around for Miss Dolly and see if she has anything cooking. Her specialties are bread (especially banana) and ginger biscuits, but she will also fix a special Caribbean meal for you if you ask a day in advance and she has time. Miss Daisy makes pan bon, ginger cakes, patties (meat-filled turnovers), and coconut oil (for tanning). Both Miss Sam and Miss Irma serve up sit-down meals in their modest little sodas. Just ask around for these women and someone will direct you to them. Be sure to try run-down soup, which is a spicy coconut-milk stew made with anything the cook can run down.

Cafe Pizzeria Coral. On the road to the soccer field. No phone. Reservations not accepted. Pizza $3.65–$6.80; pasta $4.05–$4.75. No credit cards. Tue–Sun 7–11am and 5:30–9pm. ITALIAN/PIZZA.

Although this place bills itself as a pizzeria, your best bets are the breakfasts, desserts, and fresh breads. While the pizza here is mediocre, the chocolate cake is a standout. You'll find the Cafe Pizzeria Coral about two blocks from the water in the center of the village. The open-air dining room is up a few steps from the street and has hardwood floors and wood railings. The whole place is walled in by flowering hibiscus that attract plenty of hummingbirds in the morning, which is why this is my favorite breakfast joint in town.

✪ **The Garden Restaurant.** Cabinas Jacaranda. No phone. Reservations not accepted. Main courses $4–$8. No credit cards. Thurs–Mon 5:30–9pm. Closed May–June and September. CARIBBEAN/ASIAN.

Just up the block form Cafe Coral, this restaurant serves the best food in Puerto Viejo, and some of the best in all of Costa Rica. The co-owner and chef is from Trinidad by way of Toronto and has created an eclectic menu that is guaranteed to please. You'll find such surprising offerings as chicken saté (a Thai dish), fresh garden salad with passion fruit dressing, Jamaican jerk chicken, calypso curry fish, and chicken Bangkok. There are also daily specials and lots of delicious, fresh juices. Many of the ambrosial desserts are made with local fruits, and there are also such delights as ginger spice cake and macadamia chocolate torte. Every dish is beautifully presented, usually with edible flowers for garnish.

⑤ **Soda Tamara.** On the main road through the village. No phone. Main courses $2.50–$5. No credit cards. Wed–Mon 7am–9pm. COSTA RICAN.

This little Tico-style restaurant has long been popular with budget-conscious travelers and has an attractive setting for such an economical place. There's a small patio dining area in addition to the main dining room, which is a bit dark. The painted picket fence in front gives the restaurant a very homey feel. At the counter inside, you'll find homemade cocoa candies and unsweetened cocoa biscuits. These are made by several ladies in town, and are definitely worth a try.

NEARBY PLACES TO DINE

El Duende Feliz. On the main road, Punta Uva. No phone. Reservations not accepted. Main courses $3.50–$10.50. No credit cards. Sat–Wed 11am–2pm and 6–9pm, Thurs–Fri 6–9pm. ITALIAN.

Isn't it reassuring to know that even in the middle of nowhere, you can get a decent plate of gnocchi? El Duende Feliz is on the outskirts of Punta Uva Village and serves a wide selection of authentic Italian dishes. Seafood shows up quite a bit, of course. Depending on the day's catch, you can get seafood spaghetti and pizza with clams, among other dishes. There are also steaks and plenty of pasta dishes. You can even finish off your meal with a scoop of gelati and an espresso.

Index

FROMMER'S COMPLETE TRAVEL GUIDES
(Comprehensive guides to destinations around the world, with selections in all price ranges—from deluxe to budget)

Acapulco/Ixtapa/Taxco
Alaska
Amsterdam
Arizona
Atlanta
Australia
Austria
Bahamas
Bangkok
Barcelona, Madrid & Seville
Belgium, Holland & Luxembourg
Berlin
Bermuda
Boston
Budapest & the Best of Hungary
California
Canada
Cancún, Cozumel & the Yucatán
Caribbean
Caribbean Cruises & Ports of Call
Caribbean Ports of Call
Carolinas & Georgia
Chicago
Colorado
Costa Rica
Denver, Boulder & Colorado Springs
Dublin
England
Florida
France
Germany
Greece
Hawaii
Hong Kong
Honolulu/Waikiki/Oahu
Ireland
Italy
Jamaica/Barbados
Japan
Las Vegas
London
Los Angeles
Maryland & Delaware
Maui

Mexico
Mexico City
Miami & the Keys
Montana & Wyoming
Montréal & Québec City
Munich & the Bavarian Alps
Nashville & Memphis
Nepal
New England
New Mexico
New Orleans
New York City
Northern New England
Nova Scotia, New Brunswick & Prince
  Edward Island
Paris
Philadelphia & the Amish Country
Portugal
Prague & the Best of the Czech Republic
Puerto Rico
Puerto Vallarta, Manzanillo & Guadalajara
Rome
San Antonio & Austin
San Diego
San Francisco
Santa Fe, Taos & Albuquerque
Scandinavia
Scotland
Seattle & Portland
South Pacific
Spain
Switzerland
Thailand
Tokyo
Toronto
U.S.A.
Utah
Vancouver & Victoria
Vienna
Virgin Islands
Virginia
Walt Disney World & Orlando
Washington, D.C.
Washington & Oregon

FROMMER'S FRUGAL TRAVELER'S GUIDES
(The grown-up guides to budget travel, offering dream vacations at down-to-earth prices)

Australia from $45 a Day

Berlin from $50 a Day

California from $60 a Day

Caribbean from $60 a Day

Costa Rica & Belize from $35 a Day

Eastern Europe from $30 a Day

England from $50 a Day

Europe from $50 a Day

Florida from $50 a Day

Greece from $45 a Day

Hawaii from $60 a Day

India from $40 a Day

Ireland from $45 a Day

Italy from $50 a Day

Israel from $45 a Day

London from $60 a Day

Mexico from $35 a Day

New York from $70 a Day

New Zealand from $45 a Day

Paris from $65 a Day

Washington, D.C. from $50 a Day

FROMMER'S PORTABLE GUIDES
(Pocket-size guides for travelers who want everything in a nutshell)

Charleston & Savannah

Las Vegas

New Orleans

San Francisco

FROMMER'S FAMILY GUIDES
(The complete guides for successful family vacations)

California with Kids

Los Angeles with Kids

New England with Kids

New York City with Kids

San Francisco with Kids

Washington, D.C. with Kids

FROMMER'S AMERICA ON WHEELS
(Everything you need for a successful road trip, including full-color road maps and ratings for every hotel)

California & Nevada

Florida

Mid-Atlantic

Midwest & the Great Lakes

New England & New York

Northwest & Great Plains

South Central & Texas

Southeast

Southwest

FROMMER'S WALKING TOURS
(Memorable neighborhood strolls through the world's great cities)

Berlin

Chicago

England's Favorite Cities

London

Montréal & Québec City

New York

Paris

San Francisco

Spain's Favorite Cities

Tokyo

Venice

Washington, D.C.

SPECIAL-INTEREST TITLES

Arthur Frommer's Branson!

Arthur Frommer's New World of Travel

The Civil War Trust's Official Guide to the
Civil War Discovery Trail

Frommer's America's 100 Best-Loved State
Parks

Frommer's Caribbean Hideaways

Frommer's Complete Hostel Vacation Guide
to England, Scotland & Wales

Frommer's Food Lover's Companion to
France

Frommer's Food Lover's Companion to Italy

Frommer's National Park Guide

Outside Magazine's Adventure Guide to
New England

Outside Magazine's Adventure Guide to
Northern California

Places Rated Almanac

Retirement Places Rated

USA Sports Traveler's and TV Viewer's
Golf Tournament Guide

USA Sports Minor League Baseball Book

USA Today Golf Atlas

Wonderful Weekends from NYC

FROMMER'S IRREVERENT GUIDES
(Wickedly honest guides for sophisticated travelers)

Amsterdam	Miami	Santa Fe
Chicago	New Orleans	U.S. Virgin Islands
London	Paris	Walt Disney World
Manhattan	San Francisco	Washington, D.C.

BAEDEKER
(With four-color photographs and a free pull-out map)

Amsterdam	Greece	San Francisco
Athens	Greek Islands	St. Petersburg
Austria	Hawaii	Scandinavia
Bali	Hong Kong	Scotland
Belgium	Israel	Singapore
Budapest	Italy	South Africa
California	Lisbon	Spain
Canada	London	Switzerland
Caribbean	Mexico	Venice
Copenhagen	New York	Vienna
Crete	Paris	Tokyo
Florence	Prague	Tuscany
Florida	Provence	
Germany	Rome	

FROMMER'S BY NIGHT GUIDES
(The series for those who know that life begins after dark)

Amsterdam	Los Angeles	New York
Chicago	Miami	Paris
Las Vegas	New Orleans	San Francisco
London		

FROMMER'S BEST BEACH VACATIONS
(The top places to sun, stroll, shop, stay, play, party, and swim, with ratings for each beach)

California

Carolinas & Georgia

Florida

Hawaii

Mid-Atlantic (from New York to Washington, D.C.)

New England

FROMMER'S BED & BREAKFAST GUIDES
(Selective guides with four-color photos and full descriptions of the best inns in each region)

California

Caribbean

Great American Cities

Hawaii

Mid-Atlantic

New England

Pacific Northwest

Rockies

Southeast

Southwest

FROMMER'S DRIVING TOURS
(Four-color photos and detailed maps outlining spectacular scenic driving routes)

Australia

Austria

Britain

Florida

France

Germany

Ireland

Italy

Scandinavia

Scotland

Spain

Switzerland

U.S.A.

FROMMER'S BORN TO SHOP
(The ultimate guides for travelers who love to shop)

France

Great Britain

Hong Kong

London

Mexico

New York

TRAVEL & LEISURE GUIDES
(Sophisticated pocket-size guides for discriminating travelers)

Amsterdam

Boston

Hong Kong

London

New York

Paris

San Francisco

Washington, D.C.

UNOFFICIAL GUIDES
(Get the unbiased truth from these candid, value-conscious guides)

Atlanta

Branson, Missouri

Chicago

Cruises

Disneyland

Euro Disneyland

The Great Smoky & Blue

    Ridge Mountains

Las Vegas

Miami & the Keys

Skiing in the West

Walt Disney World

Washington, D.C.